F

Other books by Jeanne Avery:

The Rising Sign, Your Astrological Mask
Astrological Aspects, Your Inner Dialogues

JEANNE AVERY

Chpt 11
pg 208
Past Life
Conditioning

Dyslexia 126 289

Astrology and Your Health

A FIRESIDE BOOK
Published by Simon & Schuster
New York London Toronto Sydney Tokyo Singapore

Fireside

Simon & Schuster Building
Rockefeller Center
1230 Avenue of the Americas
New York, New York 10020

Copyright © 1991 by Jeanne Avery

All rights reserved
including the right of reproduction
in whole or in part in any form.

FIRESIDE and colophon are registered trademarks
of Simon & Schuster Inc.

Designed by Chris Welch
Manufactured in the United States of America

10 9 8 7 6 5 4 3

Library of Congress Cataloging in Publication Data
Avery, Jeanne.
    Astrology and your health / Jeanne Avery.
      p.   cm.
    Includes index.
    1. Astrology and health.   2. Alternative medicine.   I. Title.
BF1729.H9A84   1991
133.5'861—dc20   90-24690
                                                           CIP

ISBN 0-671-64926-4

To four adorable people
who bring a special dimension of love
into my life. That love is the best healing
agent of all.

To my grandchildren,
Charles and Stephanie Andrews,
Lucas and Charlotte-Jane Henesy.

With deepest gratitude to the number of people who have helped me compile the material in this book, I'd like to offer special thanks to the invaluable editorial assistance of Barbara Gess and Nan Gatewood and to all of the unsung heroes at Simon & Schuster who have contributed their special expertise in making this book a reality.

I'd like to thank all the dedicated, open-minded physicians and health-care workers who believe in the ultimate goal of making life more healthful and beautiful along the way.

A physician cannot safely administer medicine if he is unacquainted with astrology.

—Hippocrates

Contents

Foreword

Classical mechanistic scientists view astrology with great skepticism if not derision. It could not be possible, they maintain, that inanimate solar bodies could transmit qualitative information across vast stretches of the empty vacuum of space to influence the character and fortunes of human beings.

Despite this classical scientific disclaimer, clinical and statistical evidence demonstrate that there is truth to astrology: the planetary bodies of the solar system can influence human character and behavior. In thirty years of psychiatric character analysis, I have found a remarkable correspondence between the ways in which patients think and behave and their astrological makeup. Personal experience with myself, spouse, children, and friends also indicate that we are, indeed, under the influence of the stars.

The apparent contradiction between classical science and our impressions about the validity of astrology can be resolved by recent findings of leading-edge scientists about the nature of the planetary bodies, space, and the human energy field.

There is now ample observational and experimental evidence to show that planetary bodies are not dead chunks of matter careening through an empty vacuum. The major planets have atmospheres, air glow, and auroras, all manifestations of life energy in its atmospheric expression. Like all life forms, each planet has a unique quality that radiates out through the planet's energy field, affecting all of space within its proximity.

Wilhelm Reich demonstrated experimentally that space is not an empty vacuum, but is filled with a primal, cosmic energy, "orgone energy." His work has been confirmed by recent discoveries about the so-called "zero point energy" of space: billions upon billions of minute oscillations created in the primal fabric of space by the collision and annihilation of subatomic particles, arising from some stratum deeper than the traditional framework of four-dimensional space-time. The power from the primal energy within the vacuum of the ordinary light bulb, if harnessed, could boil all the oceans of earth! Clearly such an energy could be the oft-sought "ether" that would serve as the medium for the transmission of all information through space, including the qualities inherent in the planets.

Reception of this information, which is below the threshold of ordinary perceptual faculties, such as sight and hearing, could take place in several ways. One way is via the human energy field, which, as both Reich and Yale University's Harold Saxton Burr demonstrated, is extremely sensitive and responsive to very fine and subtle energetic influences traveling through the thousands of miles of the earth's atmosphere and through space from the sun and moon.

People could also receive this planetary information by absorbing energy directly through the skin, which the biophysicist Fritz Poppe has demonstrated, takes place via coherent photons of light. A third method is through what Princeton University's Robert Jahn and Brenda Dunne have described in their man-machine interaction and precognitive studies as a quantum-mechanical process of resonance between the transmitting and receiving bodies through the primal energy of space.* As their experiments have shown, this mode of transmitting information is independent of the usual considerations of four-dimensional space-time.

Whatever the specific mechanism, whether through direct en-

---

* *Margins of Reality*, Robert Jahn and Brenda Dunne, published by Harcourt Brace Jovanovich, Inc., 1987.

ergetic influence on the material substance of the body or on the body's energy field or the creation of states of resonance, there is little doubt that transient, semipermanent, and permanent energetic states have a profound influence on the structure, organization, and physiology of the body. This has been well documented in experiments by Burr; and my experience practicing Reich's psychiatric orgone therapy shows that mobilizing life energy in the patient's field and body can influence even the most debilitating of physical disorders. The powerful effects of homeopathic preparations, which often contain less than a molecule of mass substance, is further evidence of how energetic excitation with specific resonance can alter corporeal mass. That astrological patterns can influence our structure and functioning, as Jeanne Avery so well documents, should come as no surprise.

Fortunately, traditional medical science is becoming aware of these energetic influences, albeit this acceptance is late and slow in coming. At least it is now recognized that the time of day at which medications are given plays an important role in the body's acceptance of them. I suspect, however, that it will be many more decades before the evidence of astrology, homeopathy, orgonomy, and many of the other therapeutic modalities described by Ms. Avery are accepted within the armamentarium of medicine.

Jeanne and I have been friends and mutual clients for many years. She is a world-class astrologer, who has a wonderful talent for making difficult, esoteric subjects like astrology comprehensible. One of the most adventurous people I know, Jeanne writes of first-hand experiences. We may be grateful to Jeanne, the author of several well-received books on astrology, for this, her latest offering.

—Richard A. Blasband, M.D.,
President,
American College of Orgonomy
Box 490
Princeton, NJ
08542

Introduction

My interest in health, and especially in alternative forms of medical treatment, began at a very early age of about three. Although I wasn't aware of it at the time, that interest was evidently stimulated by an incident in my mother's life. I remember seeing my mother faint and vividly recall my feeling of panic and helplessness. That memory resurfaced at later, unexpected times as nameless fears that swirled around my head like a dark cloud. I knew nothing about the cause of Mother's illness, but later on both my mother and my sister filled me in on some details. It seemed that my adored mother had developed an infection in her leg that wouldn't heal, and that kept her bedridden for some time. She consulted several highly respected doctors, but she was told that her condition was so serious it might be necessary to amputate her leg. (My nightmares as a child took the form of seeing people with amputated limbs, which was extremely horrifying to me throughout most of my young life. I didn't understand the true cause of those nightmares until my adulthood and my own regression session into past lives.)

When I was about eight years old, my mother told me her version of the incident. Evidently someone suggested that she investigate an alternative treatment before taking such an irrevocable step as amputation. They took her to see an old woman who lived in the hills some miles away from the small southern town where we lived. The woman, who lived like a hermit, allowed no one to enter her house except my mother. She told Mother how to get rid of the infection and also passed on a secret for removing warts, after making her promise not to tell that secret to anyone else while she lived. The old woman, obviously a natural healer, prescribed making a poultice of leaves from the plentiful Georgia peach trees and applying it to the infected area on the leg. My sister and I, along with several cousins, were recruited to pick the leaves from the trees, and my aunt was in charge of making the brew. My mother followed the instructions carefully and quickly recovered without the necessity of an operation.

The incident made a very deep impression on me, as I was a very sensitive child and very protective of my mother. Mother promised to pass the secret of wart removal on to me, but she died before I was old enough to claim that special information. I still wish I knew how to do it, although I come across very few warts in my life today. However I did receive another kind of secret information, along those lines, from a wonderful Hungarian woman who was a special friend. This gifted skin specialist psychically received and later developed a natural herbal formula that removes dead skin, along with scars and wrinkles, in a completely harmless way. My friend had used this formula throughout her long and successful life, benefitting people both here and in Europe. When she lived in Paris after World War II, she used her knowledge to remove the tattooed numbers from the arms of concentration-camp victims. So cycles repeat themselves, and although I don't know how to remove warts, I'm now able to do something even more important, bringing an additional healing to men and women alike through a rejuvenating and very healthful natural process. (The skin is the largest organ of respiration in the body, and with the sloughing away of dead skin, as well as with the increased circulation that occurs, the healthful and rejuvenating benefits are multifold.)

Perhaps as a result of those early impressions, I had a brief flirtation with the idea of attending medical school and becoming a doctor. However, I realized that with my very sensitive system, I could easily faint at the sight of blood, freeze at the thought of cutting up a cadaver, and become quite ill without a full night's sleep. I wouldn't have been able to get through the first semester of a premed course, much less an internship in a hospital. My respect for the doctors who made it through is boundless. I'm awed to think of the vast stores of knowledge and scientific data presented throughout the years of medical training, much less the accumulated wisdom stored in the minds of doctors who devote their lives to research and the healing of the sick. I pay homage to my father-in-law, Dr. Herbert H. Schoenfeld, who was a brilliant neurosurgeon and to one very special doctor in my extended family who has exhibited not only a profound medical capability, but also the deep compassion so essential to the administration of treatment and the eventual curing of disease.

My dream is that I will live to see the day when astrology, traditional medical care, and natural healing methods are acknowledged as partners to each other. In countries other than the United States, natural healing methods are honored and respected, released from skepticism and puritanical judgments because they have been tried and found to be effective over many centuries of use. The research, like astrological information, is based on empirical data, that of observing results and tracing history. In ancient times and in many modern cultures, astrologers were, and are, considered to be wise men and the students of cycles, not fortune-tellers. Fortunately, as the Aquarian Age comes closer and gaps in the effectiveness of more traditional methods of treatment are acknowledged, both natural health methods and astrology are being seen in a different light.

In presenting this book, I can only hint at the role astrology can play in the future of medical diagnosis and in prevention of serious illness through early awareness of the need for treatment; for it is very clear that without the intense research that precedes anything new, whether it be a treatment or a perspective, the ultimate value must be suspect. I fully acknowledge that we are far away from the kind of concrete data that is necessary to incorporate the analysis of an astrological chart with medical diagnosis, treatment, and the selection of the right time for operations or treatment. But I can only hope that any information I can reveal about the relationship of astrology and medicine might stimulate thought and pave the way for future consideration of the value of that relationship.

Astrology and Its Description of Health

What Is Health?

Traditionally, having good health is considered to be only a matter of physical well-being. The evidence of healthfulness is concrete and tangible, for if an individual is energetic and all body parts seem to be working moderately well, he is considered to be healthy. Actually, from an esoteric point of view (that is, the viewpoint of what lies behind what can be discerned by the physical senses alone), health means much more than that. True health means being in balance on many levels. In reality, according to all esoteric teachings (or those teachings that deal with hidden forces), the human constitution incorporates many layers of energy, most of them unseen by the human eye, or even a microscope. True health means keeping all these layers vibrant and in balance. If such a balance can be attained and maintained, an individual need never be ill, disabled, or unhappy as disease or infirmity is merely a manifestation or reflection of the fact that some part of the entire system is out of whack.

Today, doctors work to cure illness of the physical body. Psychiatrists and psychologists deal with the health of the mind, or the mental body, and ministers or religious counselors deal with the health of the spiritual part of man and are unconsciously working with the spiritual body. In former times, the country doctor fulfilled all of these roles at least some of the time. In this age of specialization, however, doctors rarely have time to do more than work in their particular area of expertise, attempting to get people back on their feet so they can function again.

Keeping the world healthy is an overwhelming task. Medical science wrestles with the daily business of curing symptoms. Research scientists work frantically to find cures for cancer and our current dread disease, AIDS, but it seems that as soon as some relief is found for one particular kind of illness, another one comes to light. Is it possible that a brand-new form of disease lurks in the shadows of the future to taunt already overworked physicians and research scientists?

In the last few centuries, mankind has been moderately free from the plague, and in the last few decades, the threats of tuberculosis and polio have been almost vanquished. Medicine has made great strides. Yet emphysema, for instance, is still a cause of health problems with no definitive cure in sight. No research has revealed a cure for nerve paralysis, muscular dystrophy, epilepsy, or retardation. Millions of people suffer pain or have physical impairment. Heart attacks, cancer, diabetes, osteoporosis, kidney failure, brain tumors, and accidents hit rich and poor, noble and vindictive, saints and sinners indiscriminately.

Why do people get sick? There seems to be no simple answer to that question. Illness is always a surface manifestation of some problem that exists somewhere in the overall system. In reality, illness may play a far more important role in life than is readily apparent. For instance, illness or debilitation may be the only way an individual can be forced to take stock of his spiritual life or his need for additional psychological and inner growth. Shocking situations are sometimes required to force a person to look at life from a new perspective.

One of the ways an individual can attempt to understand how his physical system functions and what his individual health factors may be is through his astrological chart. An in-depth look at a person's horoscope is an excellent and comprehensive way to determine when and how illness might strike, as well as why it should occur at all. As an example, an astrological chart can describe the differing kinds of energy a person has at his disposal at specific times in his life. It can also indicate how he might best utilize that energy. Astrology is a powerful tool to use in conjunction with medicine and healing. Hippocrates, the patron saint of medicine, advised all physicians to have a working knowledge of astrology. He said, "A physician cannot safely administer medicine if he is unacquainted with astrology."

AKASHIC RECORDS

All events in a person's daily existence, whether related to illness or not, are simply manifestations of the inner dialogues he consciously or unconsciously projects onto the mirror of his life. Every deed and every thought of each person is imprinted onto a magnetic field of energy, called the Akasha, much like words might be typed into a computer. Those messages, internal arguments as well as positive messages, translate into concrete daily events that can sometimes bring positive conditions and opportunities, or can act like a boomerang, coming home to shake a person to the core of his being. Some messages relate to a spiritual level of life. Others relate to mental levels or emotional levels, as well as to the physical state. Positive projected messages return as constructive and productive opportunities or events, but the negative or nonproductive messages produce external conflicts that force growth through a specific kind of challenge. The position of each planet around the wheel of the astrological chart, the specific sectors or houses in which they fall, and their aspects or relationships to each other describe the probability of the events a person is liable to project into his conscious experience of life as a result of what has been imprinted in the Akashic Records. The positions of the planets also describe the kind of physical, mental, emotional, and spiritual challenges a person might experience in his life. An individual astrological chart accurately describes events on the trip through life, just as a road map describes the conditions one might meet when taking a trip.

PHYSICAL PLANE

The material, or physical, plane is the level of existence we can touch, taste, see, feel, smell, and acknowledge through our physical senses. These physical experiences may actually camouflage more than what appears on the surface, however, for existence on earth, or on the material plane, is the lowest, most dense form of the manifestation of energy. Sometimes unknown, esoteric conditions are manifest into a more concrete form so that we can experience them in daily life through our five senses and therefore find resolution. Man is, in the final analysis, a problem-solving mechanism. Each individual is a cocreator and, with the aid of divine energy, can become quite adept at finding solutions for problems. In fact, his growth on all levels of consciousness depends on his exercising his ability to transmute nonproductive situations into productive ones. This change can only be made on the material plane and in a physical body. Many of the conditions that exist in each person's life on more subtle levels of consciousness, and the resultant emerging patterns on the physical plane, are clarified with the aid of astrological symbolism and their interpretation in an individual astrological chart.

As an example, Pluto is the planet that indicates the major struggles and major initiation processes in one's life. The ruler of Scorpio, Pluto, is found somewhere in the chart of each individual. The placement of Pluto in a chart, as well as the sector of the chart that is ruled by Scorpio, describes the area of life where transformation and transmutation, perhaps born of a spiritual crisis, can take place on the physical plane. For instance, when that planet is placed in or rules the first house, or ascendant, or is placed in or rules the sixth house in an individual chart, the greatest initiation (test) and spiritual transformation in the life of that individual may be in relation to his health and physical well-being. In her book *Archetypes of the Zodiac*, Kathleen Burt describes a process of resolution as it relates to that planet. She says, ''Many a Scorpio rising or Scorpio Sun sign undergoes his test of faith the day when his own willpower, or his bodily stamina, is not sufficient to con quer disease or depression. S/he feels powerless or out of control. If s/he responds to the crisis with faith in God and his physicians—spiritual, physical, or psychological—s/he helps with his healing. When, however, s/he reacts with pride or skepticism—when s/he refuses to allow God room in the healing process—the cure is likely to be slow, arduous, painful, and even unsuccessful. . . . Often as a result of his/her trauma, s/he goes through a conversion experience. Many are called to the transformation during a time of intense physical suffering or emotional crisis.''

THE PART ILLNESS PLAYS IN LIFE

There may be karmic reasons for illness in the present existence or life. Illness may be the only way to grab the attention of a person so that he will face what he might like to ignore. Since we set in motion the conditions that clearly reflect whatever we need for soul growth, even if that is illness, we might be able to learn how to make more productive choices—choices to foster the development of a higher quality of soul consciousness rather than ill health. It is important to realize that each individual has not only a different set of circumstances in his current life, but a different karmic preconditioning that creates a tendency toward weakness in some area of the body. The subtle atomic structure of each being varies according to what he or she has built into the individual consciousness throughout time. Therefore, treatment that might be effective for a condition that exists for one person may not be the solution for another individual with the same condition.

Some disturbing physical conditions may be too subtle for accurate diagnosis without a deeper look into the underlying energy structure. An individual may have a seemingly unexplainable reaction to substances such as chemicals or compounds in the earth, as an example. Another may have a built-in weakness in the lungs. Another may have an annoying sensitivity to changing atmospheric pressures that causes problems, but which goes largely unrecognized in the overall picture of his health. Such weaknesses as these lie on more subtle levels of the body system than we are usually cognizant of, and may not be easily detected by present-day scientific methods.

Ideally, the physical condition of each one of us reflects our inner state of being, but the average hard-working person under daily stress and pressure may find it difficult, if not impossible, to maintain the ideal state of mind and sublime conditions that produce the inner balance necessary for complete health. It takes strong motivation, concentration, and determination to operate on that level of consciousness all the time. But with awareness, often born from necessity, it is possible to correct and cure conditions on the etheric level before they take hold throughout the system and manifest in the physical vehicle. At the point where imbalance is entrenched in the physical body and is already obvious in the manifestation of some form of dis-ease, it may be far along in development and harder to resolve than if it is corrected early on. The trend toward preventive medicine is still in the early stages, but part of that prevention package may require the inclusion of past-life awareness.

At the conclusion of a regression session, my clients become aware of the continuity and thread of consciousness that exist from lifetime to lifetime, including the quality of health and the physical conditions that are brought forward from a former existence. Life-time to lifetime is just like yesterday to today. The conditions and events of yesterday are still in our framework of experience and, depending on how traumatic those conditions and events may or may not have been, are very much with us in our consciousness. Just as it is important to let go of upsetting emotional reactions before the time for sleep, so that the degenerating capacity of trauma, hurt, and sadness is released and a new day of joy can be fully experienced, it is equally important to let go of a lifetime of traumas before death so that a new life can begin with joy and the greatest possibility of fulfillment. Although in death we leave the physical vehicle behind, we carry with us emotional, mental, and spiritual burdens unless we first release them. These conditions can be manifest in the new life as physical disabilities even as early as birth.

One very beautiful and special young girl discovered the reason for her retardation in this lifetime during a regression session. She

saw herself in the womb as quite mentally alert and joyful, eager
for her new life and feeling like an actress ready to go onstage in
a new role. She saw herself as brilliant (and commented to me,
"Wouldn't THEY think it was funny if they could hear me say
that?"). Then she saw her birth and heard the doctor say, "Oh my
God, she's retarded." This lovely girl asked me, "Did you hear my
speech clear up when I was describing my prenatal state?" Indeed,
the hesitancy in her speech had disappeared from that point on
in her regression session. Going back farther, she saw her relationship to her mother in a past life. A former condition of enmity
caused her to come back as the woman's daughter in this life. The
condition of her retardation ensured that they would be tied tightly
together in this existence, and she is unmistakably dependent on
her mother. What she discovered from a new look at the relationship was a deep-seated need to forgive and forget the events
of the past life. Although that awareness may not completely reverse the retardation, a new perspective, especially her sense of
her inner brilliance, can help her infuse a positive energy into her
life that will make external conditions easier to bear.

So far, medical science cannot explain the cause of all birth
defects, or a predisposition to certain diseases or conditions. The
genetic code inherited from parents can clarify the cause of many
physical problems, but the unanswered question is why one person
in a family, and not another with the same genetic predisposition,
might be tapped by the fickle finger of fate and be forced to go
through life with an impairment? Why do accidents happen that
have nothing to do with genetic factors? Many inherent weaknesses in the physical system can date back to disabilities or accidents from previous lifetimes. This becomes apparent during
regression sessions into past lives, where a predisposition toward
particular health problems can often be clearly revealed. People
learn a lot about their physical makeup and can achieve a new
understanding of their health problems by recognizing conditions
from the past that lead to physical conditions in this lifetime. A
personalized astrological chart can indicate quite clearly what those
past life conditions may have been.

THE AURA AND THE SUBTLE
OR ELECTRIC BODY

Many of the problems we face in connection to healing stem from lack of information about health from a holistic point of view. Even though we have sophisticated procedures, drugs, and techniques, cures are not always effected. The constitution of man is far more complex than is commonly acknowledged, although scientists are now beginning to suspect the true nature of man's makeup. One factor that is unknown to the medical profession at large is the existence of a field of energy, or aura, that surrounds the body and clearly reflects the condition of health in the physical system. When a person is in good health, the colors of the aura are bright and clear. Changes of color in the aura, or muddiness of those colors, can indicate impending health problems. Many psychics and some sensitive people can see the aura. Almost everyone can develop an ability to see auras, if the desire is strong enough, through specific exercises. (See Chapter 16.)

In 1970, a book entitled *Psychic Discoveries Behind the Iron Curtain* reported, along with other amazing developments, the discovery of a process by which the aura could be photographed. Named after its inventor, Semyon Kirlian, this method of photography enabled practitioners to detect the flow of energy around people and, even more amazingly, around plants and vegetables. That ability to detect the life force around every living thing has so far eluded the attention of medical science. The medical profession utilizes and acknowledges the validity of the X ray and other methods of revealing internal organs, bones, and blood vessels, but photographing the aura is practically unheard of in medical circles in this country.

Until Russian scientists discovered Kirlian photography, it was left to psychics and people with extremely sensitive perception to describe what an aura might look like. Such descriptions were often discounted as products of a vivid imagination, since few of these sensitivities were associated with science. The aura was thought not to exist, yet an aura was always painted around heads of religious figures in ancient paintings. Someone, in bygone ages, must have known that auras existed.

In the 1960s Dr. Thelma Moss, a clinical psychologist, conducted extensive research into the use of Kirlian photography at UCLA's prestigious Neuropsychiatric Institute. After obtaining her PhD, Dr. Moss was offered a position in the institute, which houses the Brain Research Institute, the Medical School, the Eye Institute, the Institute for Nervous Diseases, and the School of Dentistry, all within one massive structure. After her appointment, it was made clear that the Department of Medical Psychology, which belonged to the Department of Psychiatry, and the Department of Psychiatry, which belonged to the Medical School, and the Medical School, which belonged to UCLA, and UCLA, which belonged to the state of California, which paid her salary, were all required to observe her work to decide whether or not she possessed the required skills for the job. Not only that, she was told that lab space would be made available only if she presented a satisfactory research proposal. Consequently, Dr. Moss engaged in a constant clash with the conservative scientific establishment at the institute over her chosen research program. The main area of dispute was whether parapsychology was a valid area of research for a clinical psychologist.

In her book *The Body Electric*, published by J. P. Tarcher in 1979, Dr. Moss describes her struggles with the bureaucracy of the institute and the opposite, exhilarating experience of traveling to Iron Curtain countries where she was stunned to discover the freedom with which the Russian scientists were able to conduct their research. "It was startling to hear the papers of those few Soviet scientists who did attend (the conference in Prague)," she writes, "for they were respected physicists and biochemists discussing openly and in scientific terms such ideas as levitation, dowsing, and PK (psychokinesis)." She describes in detail how she won her battles to continue the research and how she proved beyond a shadow of a doubt that the aura exists and can be photographed.

Dr. Moss's work revealed that the physical body is laced with an electrical system, manifestations of which produce the phenomena called an aura. Her scientifically conducted research confirms the existence of the subtle body, that esoteric body of energy that interpenetrates the physical system. Through her determination and courage, Dr. Moss has paved the way for further investigation of healing on the etheric level, and within the unseen electrical system. Dr. Moss made an invaluable contribution to the whole field of healing with this carefully conducted and documented research.

So the aura is the external manifestation and reflection of the conditions that exist in the subtle, or electrical, body. Fortunately, with the scientific proof that a subtle body exists, research into healing can move to a new level. Recognition of those subtle levels of energy is a first step toward effecting better physical conditions, since illness actually begins in the etheric body; that is, on that electric body level which underlies the entire physical system. The manifestation of weakness in the physical system may appear at unexpected moments, as it can take some time for dis-ease, or imbalance, to work its way through many layers of more subtle planes of existence into the physical body. (See Chapter 2.)

CHOICES DICTATED BY ILLNESS

John Addey, a much beloved and highly respected English astrologer, was crippled as a result of a fusion of his spine when he was in his early forties. John recovered to the point that he could continue his work on a part-time basis until his death in 1983. He was in his early sixties at that time. Each summer he taught an astrological course in Harmonics at Cambridge University. In fact, during the week-long astrological sessions, John, always the gracious English gentleman, delighted in serving coffee or tea to the ladies of the group, even though it meant walking slowly and probably painfully on canes. Self-pity was not part of John's makeup, and he never allowed anyone to feel sorry for him. He remarked that if he had not been forced to stay in bed for several years, he would have wasted his life. Before the onset of his illness, John loved going to the racetrack and playing golf, but with a debilitating condition, he had nothing to do but lie in bed and think. As a result of that enforced solitude, he devised a system for astrology called Harmonics. One of the most important developments in the astrological field, it might never have come to light if it were not for illness. John came to the realization that the infirmity was part of his personal growth.

Illness has a way of forcing an individual to slow down, take time to go within and take stock of his life. But it should be possible to avoid ill health altogether, bypassing such drastic measures of forced growth, by simply acknowledging what it is that the illness eventually accomplishes before sickness has a chance to strike. Could John Addey have avoided his illness by accepting earlier in his life what he was meant to contribute to humanity?

ALTERNATIVE METHODS
OF HEALING

The swing of the pendulum goes on. Lately, there is new interest in alternative methods of healing. These methods, out of fashion since the late 1800s, have been investigated and developed primarily by people outside of the scientific community. Since medicine is still in its infancy (even human development is still in its early stages), quick answers and logical explanations for disease are still somewhat out of reach. However, disgust with the high rate of failure of more traditional systems seems to have triggered a desperate search for new—or as the case may be, old—methods. There are many adventurous and courageous scientists and doctors who are beginning to investigate theories which were formerly considered to be unscientific, even old-fashioned. In the United States in particular, however, new discoveries must take a tortuous route of laborious scientific investigation before gaining acceptance on a broad scale. Many doctors in other countries have built extremely successful clinics that attract American patients in droves because they utilize both ancient and new techniques to improve the quality of life, health, and well-being. Some of these methods are simple, quick, and very effective. What could have happened to cause doctors to close their eyes to natural, fundamental, innovative, and sometimes age-old cures, especially since many of these simple cures may have existed in some form or another since the beginning of time?

ALLOPATHY AND HOMEOPATHY

For some time, a conflict of opinion has existed between two medical traditions: allopathy and homeopathy. In the 1800s, European and American society sanctioned both approaches to healing. Patients had a choice of using doctors, called allopaths, or natural healers, called empirics or homeopaths. These two groups waged a continual, bitter philosophical debate. The allopaths called their approach "heroic medicine." They believed the physician must aggressively drive disease from the body. They based their practice on what they considered to be scientific theory. The allopaths used three main techniques: they bled the body to drain off the bad humors, they gave huge doses of toxic minerals like mercury and lead to displace the original disease, and they also used surgery. At that time, few patients were willing to have surgery, as it was a brutal procedure without anesthesia. Satirists of the day remarked that with allopathic treatment, the patient died of the cure.

Competing with these doctors were the empiric healers. They believed in stimulating the body's own defenses to heal itself. Instead of administering potentially poisonous minerals and drugs, they used vegetable products and nontoxic substances in small quantities. They especially favored herbs learned about from Native Americans and old European traditions. The empirics said they based their remedies not only on theory, but on observation. The satirists of the day added that with empiric treatment, the patient died of the disease, not the cure. Unfortunately, some of the empiric healers began to sell their tonics at carnivals and medicine shows. Charlatans began tricking the gullible public by selling watered-down versions of herbal combinations that might have otherwise been quite effective. The association of herbal medicine with the carnival was one factor that gave the whole homeopathic medical system a bad name and was a prime reason for the deteriorating popularity of healing with herbal remedies. Since the whole naturopathic system of healing was tainted by unscrupulous practitioners, the allopathic method began to gain favor.

One of the empiric systems that has been relatively unused in the United States until fairly recently is that of homeopathic medicine. Dr. Samuel Hahnemann, a German doctor born in 1755, is given credit as the founder of the homeopathic system. He discovered the principle of "like cures like" almost accidentally. During research experiments for the treatment of malaria, he ingested Chinchona bark just to see what might happen. Chinchona bark was the most popular medicine used to treat malaria in that day. To his surprise, he ran a fever and exhibited the very symptoms of an actual case of malaria. He began further experimentation by treating different diseases with medicines that reproduced the symptoms of the illnesses. He took careful notes not only on his patients' physical reaction, but on their emotional and mental reactions as well.

In the course of his research, Dr. Hahnemann discovered several significant factors. First, he observed that the smaller the dosage, the greater its curative effect. Second, he discovered that medicine which had been subjected to vibration produced more rapid results. As a country doctor, he was forced to visit his patients at their homes, often arriving after bouncing over rutted dirt roads in a wagon or buggy. The medicines he carried with him were considerably jiggled and shaken during the journey. Patients living at greater distances from his home seemed to have more astounding cures than those who lived nearby or visited him in his office.

Inadvertently, Dr. Hahnemann founded a branch of medicine that is especially effective and is still extremely popular in Europe today. Homeopathic medicine can be bought over the counter and without a prescription in European countries. In the United States, however, most homeopathic practitioners are medical doctors. The fight by doctors to place homeopathic medicine in its rightful place in the medical community includes a desire on the part of these homeopathic doctors to restrict the prescribing of homeopathic remedies to none other than medically licensed physicians.

Dr. Edward Bach, a prominent English physician with a practice on London's Harley Street, founded a system of treatment with flower remedies after he had experiences that were similar to Samuel Hahnemann's. Dr. Bach discovered that after ingesting a particular flower or plant, he manifested symptoms in his own system that related to a specific condition. It began to follow, in the manner of "like cures like," that he could find a treatment for a specific emotional disturbance by isolating the flower that produced those very symptoms. Whereas homeopathic medicines seemed to work on a physical level, it was clear that the Bach flower remedies cured emotional disturbances. Bach flower remedies have been used consistently in Europe since their discovery, and today they are experiencing a new popularity in the United States.

In the early 1900s, Wilhelm Reich developed a method for measuring what he termed *orgone* energy, his word for the life force or etheric energy that interpenetrates all substances on earth. Reich's search for this unknown bioenergy ultimately led to his persecution and death. His claim that he could harness and utilize orgone energy for healing was particularly threatening to traditionalists. An injunctin was obtained by the FDA, and even though Reich protested that scientific matters could not be judged by a court, the injunction remained. When Reich was away on a trip, a colleague, Dr. Michael Silvert, transported an orgone accumulator across state lines, thus defying the injunction. Reich and Silvert were then arrested, prosecuted, found guilty, and sentenced. Reich died in prison, but not before the ultimate blow of having his books burned!

Wilhelm Reich was the originator of two types of therapy. His body work, called psychiatric orgone therapy, led to such spinoffs as Primal therapy and Loewens' work with bioenergetics. The bio-emotional method of treatment was capable of alleviating many long-standing problems by mobilizing the body's orgone energy through a combination of character analysis and relief of patterns of chronic muscular armoring. The second form of therapy was the experimental use of the orgone accumulator. On a strictly anecdotal level, there was evidence that this method could prevent colds and had an effect on rheumatism, hypertension, and tumor regression. (The history of the development of the accumulator, physical and biological effects related to orgone energy, and personal observations of the use of the accumulator for maintaining health are discussed in *The Orgone Energy Handbook* by Dr. James De Meo, published by Natural Energy Works, P.O. 864, El Cerrito, Calif. 94530.)

After Reich's death in 1957, Dr. Elsworth Baker, trained by Reich, organized a group of scientists and physicians who were devoted to Reich's work and who began research with practical uses of channeling orgone energy. In 1967, the first *Journal of Orgonomy* was published and the American College of Orgonomy was formed. (The *Journal of Orgonomy* is available through Orgonomic Publications, Inc., Box 490, Princeton, N.J. 08542.)

Dr. Richard Blasband, a board-certified psychiatrist, was a member of the original group and is now president of the American College of Orgonomy. Primarily interested in Reich's discoveries concerning the origin of life and the development of disease, Dr. Blasband incorporates Reich's bio-emotional therapy into his psychiatric practice. He also continues Reich's experimentation with manipulating energy—not only to heal the human mind and body but also to heal the earth. For example, Dr. Blasband has organized many excursions, as a public service, to create rain in drought areas. In 1950 Reich had been approached by farmers in Ellsworth, Maine to relieve the drought. Reich was able to create rainfall that saved their blueberry crop. Following that line of Reich's work, the American College of Orgonomy has been sponsoring weather control operations to fight drought for the last thirty years.

Moving faster than the earth, energy is present as an ocean in the atmosphere. According to Reich, this energy is the motor force that makes the earth spin. In this ocean, seen from space as the blue halo several miles deep surrounding the earth, weather spontaneously forms. Moisture, as an example, is attracted to a high concentration of orgone energy. By shifting the high concentration of orgone energy, moisture will move to those centers and clouds will form. So by using the cloud-buster device, the skilled orgone energy weather operator can draw and disperse pollution and amplify and create rain.

In 1986, a drought covered an area from southern California up through the Northwest and into eastern Montana. By mid-June it had extended into the northern plains of the Midwest and became the worst drought since the dustbowl of the thirties. Under the direction of Dr. Blasband, a weather-control operation was started early in July in Kansas, with the goal of decompressing the high-pressure system that had dominated the atmosphere for months. Within a few days, the high-pressure system collapsed, and it began to rain in Kansas, the Dakotas, and Iowa, as well as in the Ohio Valley and parts of the South. The displacement of the high-pressure system was accompanied by the reunification of the polar jet stream, which had been split and was now returned to its original path.

These orgonic operations into weather manipulation have never been acknowledged by the scientific establishment even though reports have been made to NOAA (National Oceanic Atmospheric Administration).

In the 1920s and 1930s there were many scientists and physicians who ventured into what proved to be treacherous waters. They dared to conduct research experiments outside the strictures of the medical establishment. In 1933, Royal R. Rife, a San Diego scientist, isolated a virus which he claimed was the primary cause of cancer. Using an advanced light microscope of his own design, which achieved magnification and resolution still unmatched by light microscopes today, Rife was able to see the *live* viruses which cause cancer, polio, herpes, and other diseases. (The electron microscope deals with dead microbes.)

After curing cancer in animals by painlessly ''blowing up'' the cancer virus with a specific radio frequency or electromagnetic wave form, Rife joined with Dr. Milbank Johnson of the University of Southern California to conduct a successful human cancer trial during the summer of 1934. Sixteen out of sixteen cancer patients diagnosed as terminal were healed with Rife's painless, three-minute treatment, administered every third day. Three subsequent trials from 1935 to 1938 verified the initial success. However, in 1939 the American Medical Association unleashed its considerable power to stop all research with Rife's energy instruments. Physicians using the Rife technology were threatened with the loss of their medical licenses and even jail unless they stopped the treatment. Rife was dragged through an abusive court trial which started him on a long road to alcoholism and bitterness. He died in 1971, the year Nixon's ''War on Cancer'' began.

Every six weeks, the number of cancer deaths surpasses the total number of Americans killed in Vietnam. From 1972 to 1988, the National Cancer Institute spent $15 billion on cancer research, yet Rife's method has never been fairly evaluated. It was only in the late 1980s and into the 1990s that a revived interest in Rife's work developed as a result of the book *The Cancer Cure that Worked*, by Barry Lynes, published by Marcus Books, Queensville, Ontario, Canada.

In the 1840s, John Hoxsey, an Illinois veterinarian, accidentally discovered an herbal cure for cancer when his prize stallion developed the disease. He had put the horse out to pasture and left it to die. Hoxsey observed the horse eating plants that were not part of its usual diet, and three weeks later the tumor had stabilized. Within a year the horse was well. John Hoxsey began experiments on other animals, adding popular home remedies to the herbs. He claimed success and passed the formulas down through the family.

Harry Hoxsey, the great-grandson of John Hoxsey, opened his first clinic in Illinois in 1924 and used the formulas in the treatment of tumors and cancer in people. He immediately incurred the wrath of the medical profession. Labeled the worst quack of the century, he was arrested more times than any other man in medical history—over one hundred times in a two-year period. In spite of great opposition, his clinic, which moved to Dallas, Texas in the 1950s, became the biggest privately owned cancer clinic in the world. Thousands of people were professing to be cured and were sending other cancer patients who had been declared terminally ill by their physicians. After watching patient after patient get well, an *Esquire* journalist wrote an article entitled "The Quack Who Cures Cancer." The article was never published.

One of the people declared terminally ill was Delea Mae Nelson, whose daughter was a nurse. Mildred Nelson did her best to dissuade her mother from going to the clinic and finally decided she should go with her mother so that she could protect her as best she could. Mildred had heard the wildest medical stories of her life about the Hoxsey clinic and the cancer cures, and was determined to get her mother away from the clutches of Harry Hoxsey. As soon as she arrived, Hoxsey offered Mildred a job. She decided the best way to expose him was to work for him and thus have access to his records, which she was sure were falsified. Before her eyes, her mother began to get well. Delea Mae Nelson is still alive today, and Mildred Nelson stayed on to run the clinic for Harry Hoxsey.

The most fantastic case of all may have helped earn Hoxsey a reputation for quackery. Mandice Johnson was considered to be almost dead. The top of his skull was rotting with cancer. After treating Johnson in his clinic, Hoxsey removed the tumor in front of a massive live audience, just like in a carnival show. Mandice Johnson lived another thirty years with no recurrence of the problem.

One of his most determined prosecutors was Mr. D. A. Templeton, who wanted to close down all the clinics. Hoxsey was arrested so many times by Templeton that he began carrying hundred dollar bills in his pockets so that he could bail himself out. Hoxsey could afford to engage in the unending legal battles because he had discovered an oil well. But sometimes he would stay in jail for a few days just to prove a point. On those occasions, patients who had been cured of cancer would come to the jail in droves, bringing him food and offering testimonials. Hoxsey would soon be released just to save his jailors embarrassment. When Mr. Templeton's brother developed cancer and was declared terminally ill by his doctors, he entered the Hoxsey clinic and was cured. D. A. Templeton, who had been Hoxsey's worst prosecutor, became his lawyer.

Even though two federal courts upheld claims of the therapeutic value of Hoxsey's treatment, by 1963 legal battles were so overwhelming that he moved his clinic to Tijuana, Mexico, where it exists to this day. Nurse Mildred Nelson has managed the clinic for forty years and claims that the biomedical center has an 80 percent rate of cure. She said, "I know I'm not supposed to say the word *cure*, but some of these people are still surviving after forty years. I can't prove my claim because of the lack of proper medical investigation. However, the medical ratio for cancer is that two out of five patients die within five years."

The method of treatment used by the clinic is both internal and psychological. The internal treatment combines the Hoxsey tonic—a number of herbs combined with potassium iodide, which both detoxifies the body and builds up the immune system—with proper diet, which plays an important role in the healing process. Since the attitude of the patient is considered essential to the effectiveness of the healing process, the psychological well-being of the patient is fostered by an atmosphere of positive reinforcement, optimism, and humor. Ms. Nelson said, "When a patient arrives saying, 'I'm here to accept whatever you can do for me,' I know they'll get well. When they come in the door saying, 'I'm here because someone told me it works, but I don't really have much hope for a cure,' nothing on earth can make that person well."

The Hoxsey clinic attracts mostly terminal patients or people referred by friends who have been diagnosed as terminally ill with cancer. If cures for cancer have existed since the early thirties, why have the medical profession and research scientists consistently looked the other way in the face of such evidence? How is it possible to ignore the testimonials of so many people who have had remission of their cancer or are completely cured? How is it possible to overlook the suffering of so many people who need treatment even though the methods that seem to work may be unorthodox? Are the methods too simplistic to be considered effective?

DEVELOPMENTS WITH ADVANCED BIOFEEDBACK

In 1980 Sigmund Bereday, a physicist, developed a sophisticated process that seems to have a profound healing effect on many debilitating conditions. Sigmund Bereday, believing his method to be a form of neuroimmunomodulation, uses the term *performance synchronization* to describe a process in which the body's electrical activity is monitored and the participants themselves are trained to put their body's various electrical systems back into better sync. He sees it as a kind of advanced and sophisticated biofeedback system.

As is the case with many inventions, Mr. Bereday discovered the real benefit of his new system almost by accident when his wife developed painful arthritis in her hands and in the lower portions of her body, in particular her hips and knees. True to the

allopathic system of healing, doctors suggested treating her condition with dosages of gold, the most final and drastic method
known to relieve the horrible pain associated with the disease. The
side effects of treatment with gold include possible damage to the
kidneys. Frustrated and wanting to help her, Bereday used an
instrument he had developed that would monitor the low currents
of electricity in her body. To his great surprise, not only were the
symptoms reversed, but the cause of the pain was eliminated. After
only three sessions ten years ago, she is still free from any pain or
tendency toward recurrence of arthritis.

In 1985, Mr. Bereday invited Dr. Herbert Spector of the National
Institutes of Health in Bethesda, Maryland, to arrange a clinical
trial to observe him and his son and evaluate the treatment. Dr.
Spector went to New York and observed patients ranging from five
to eighty-eight years old. The number of sessions ran from one to
ten, with the average session lasting about thirty minutes. Subsequently, he made a report to NIH on his findings, and said, "Some
of the reports are based upon what the patients told me, others
are based on what the relatives or Mr. Bereday told me, but most
of the [results], I observed myself."

One of the more touching reports is as follows, "On the 4th of
October, I saw a young girl, aged five, along with her mother, her
physician, and the Messrs. Bereday. I had a long discussion with
her mother, who told me in great detail the history of the child's
problem. At age two, while they were living in Poland, the child
was diagnosed as having cerebral palsy and she was given physical
therapy. This physical therapy was at first passive but later on, in
the United States, less passive physical therapy was used. At that
time no medication was given and she is not under medication at
the present time. When she came to the United States, two years
ago, the child could not sit up and was extremely spastic. She
could not raise her head and was quite weak.

"In desperation, upon the recommendation of a physician, the
mother brought the child to Mr. Bereday for a session. She says
the child is now much stronger, much better in every way. The
child can write, sits very nicely and walks fairly well. I saw the
child. She is a very happy, sprightly youngster. She sings songs,
she dances, she runs about. Her feet are now fairly straight although I was told that originally her feet were turned inwards and

it was extremely difficult for her to walk. Before the session, she cried all the time when she was massaged.

"Mr. Bereday reports that when he first saw this patient, she was five years old and had the appearance of a limp rag doll, with very little strength. She was unable to lift her head. After the first session with Mr. Bereday, she no longer cried and said that it didn't hurt when she was being massaged. So far, there have been a total of 9 sessions (between April 10, 1985 and September 20, 1985). During the course of this time, the mother claims that there was miraculous improvement."

One man, aged forty-four, had total paralysis of his vocal cords caused by the accidental mishandling of a tube during surgery. After two sessions, there was a complete return of his voice. A physician who had acute eczema needed only one session, as the eczema stopped itching and dried up during the session. A professor had a viral infection contracted in Africa. He was declared totally disabled by urologists at Yale. His symptoms were complete bladder failure, an intermittent 106-degree fever, pain, and sinusitis. Within ninety minutes following a three-hour session, he made a complete recovery with no recurrence of symptoms. A sixty-eight-year-old businessman had rheumatoid arthritis of fifty years' standing. He had chronic and intractable pain of the hands, wrists, back, and knees. After ten sessions, the patient was free of pain and had complete mobility. A thirty-six-year-old movie director had Bell's palsy. One eye would not close and his mouth was misshapen. After two sessions, he has made a complete recovery. Dr. Bereday's biofeedback method has also been effective in alleviating the debilitating side effects of chemotherapy.

One of Mr. Bereday's special cases concerned a woman who was bedridden with a severe case of osteoporosis. She had been to every specialist she could find only to be told by everyone that nothing could be done to help. The woman's appearance was tragic. She looked older than her years, her hair was quite gray, and her face was very wrinkled. As Mr. Bereday began to treat her, he noticed a side effect of the wrinkles disappearing. She began to look younger, and although the color of her hair remained the same, her youthful vigor returned. She soon began to walk thirty blocks a day. Her favorite pastime was visiting the doctors who told her there was no hope.

Sigmund Bereday has had amazing results in his work with people of all ages with learning disabilities. One young man, aged twenty-one, with acute dyslexia had vertigo as well. He had no sense of balance, and walked by weaving from side to side. Although he had 20/20 vision, he had no peripheral vision. After three sessions with Mr. Bereday, his peripheral vision was restored and his overall vision improved to 10/12. His dream was to become a fighter pilot, and indeed, with restored health, he was able to pass a six hour flight physical. He is now eligible to become a test pilot as well.

In addition to its intended use as a sophisticated method of biofeedback, this method stimulates the immune system and in 85 percent of the patients, substantial relief is evidenced following the first session. The level of relief increases with subsequent sessions. Bereday Biofeedback has been applied to several thousand patients over a ten-year period, exclusively on physicians' requests, for such conditions as lupus, multiple sclerosis, Parkinson's disease, LAS (Lou Gehrig's disease), Bell's palsy, stroke paralysis, osteo- and rheumatoid arthritis, chronic pain, allergic reactions, and acute viral infections. These conditions have been alleviated with no side effects. The patients referred to Mr. Bereday for sessions by various medical doctors, as well as osteopaths and chiropractors, were the "hopeless" cases.

REVERSAL OF LONG-TIME DISABILITY

I met with Sigmund Bereday while attending a scientific conference organized by Dr. Richard Blasband. After hearing his lecture, I arranged for a series of treatments with the father and son team. My own sessions with Mr. Bereday were extremely successful in relieving allergic reactions to many substances and restoring my formerly high energy level. During one treatment, I felt my right adrenal gland swell, as if from a raisin to a plump grape. I had never had that physical sensation before. I also saw vivid colors in the room. I then met, and subsequently interviewed a well-known actress and playwright who had experienced several sessions with Mr. Bereday. She told me an amazing story. Kelly had suffered from a painful, debilitating disease since her early teens. It was diagnosed as rheumatoid arthritis, although her doctors were never really sure of that diagnosis. Even though she had to consume thirty-six aspirin every day just to keep her pain at a tolerable level, Kelly had learned how to live a fairly normal life.

Kelly talked about her disease. "After the diagnosis of rheumatoid arthritis, I was given massive doses of cortisone and gold. By my second year of high school, my symptoms were so bad I had to drop out of school for one year. My joints were so swollen, I could hardly move. The cortisone caused depression, hallucinations, and nightmares. My metabolism was completely wrecked; puberty had been delayed and confused. Finally by the time I was a sophomore in college and adult enough, I decided I'd rather die than take the cortisone and gold anymore. My doctor dismissed me and said if I wasn't willing to go along with the treatment, he wouldn't see me anymore. At that time my health was so precarious that the doctors said things to me such as 'You probably won't live to be twenty-one.'

"In high school, I began to keep a diary of my dreams to see if my dream life would tell me what was going on. In college, after my own discontinuation of medication, I began to pay attention to my diet, and my health immediately began to improve. By the time I was a junior in college, my mobility had increased enough so that I could fool people into not knowing anything was wrong with me.

"That's when I became interested in theater. I could walk across a stage, even in high heels, because it was such a limited space. I began to study acting and voice. Then the course of my life was set. Each year, my health improved as I monitored my diet and learned how to increase the mobility. I didn't smoke, and I watched my alcohol intake very carefully. I'm an energetic person with basically good health, and my body began to repair itself. My hands and feet were deformed as a teenager and I still experienced some pain, but I reduced my intake of aspirin from thirty-six a day to between twelve and fourteen a day. Every now and then I might get depressed, but by and large, I worked as an actress and lived very normally other than operating on a pretty rigid, organized schedule.

"When my cousin, who has multiple sclerosis, told me he was having a session with Sigmund Bereday, I decided to have a trial session, and after that one session, I felt a sense of well-being that I hadn't had in a long time. I felt light-headed and euphoric. After the second session, there was a real noticeable cessation of pain, and as I walked down the street on concrete, which is very hard for me, I noticed that I could walk farther and more comfortably without thinking about it.

"I used to lift weights, but it was an agony. Now I have had to add on more weight because it is so easy. As a result, even though I am not Miss Amazonia, all my muscles are beginning to tighten up. I lost a lot of edema, too. After the sessions I noticed that the puffiness around my eyes had disappeared. People began asking me if I had lost weight or if I had been on a vacation. But I was working harder than ever."

Kelly has Saturn, Mercury, Venus, and Uranus right on the ascendant. Saturn rules the knees, and arthritis is a disease described by Saturn, so I asked Kelly if she had experienced particular discomfort in that area. She said her knees were always swollen and very sore. "Along with my hands and feet, that was the worst area to be affected." Mercury rules the hands, whereas Uranus rules the nervous system. "I'm obviously a very high-strung person. I was very hyper, temperamental, and given to fits of temper as a child. The biofeedback method has also obliterated my migraine headaches. I might feel the start of a headache but it gets short-circuited. No more pulling down the shades and going to bed in misery.

"I think it is important to emphasize that Bereday's treatment can help people who are basically healthy, but who may suffer from allergies or from migraines or fatigue or low energy. It is especially beneficial for people who are performers or people who must come up with enormous bursts of energy. Mr. Bereday's treatment really helps increase your breathing power and your overall vitality."

The success of Kelly's treatment was obvious from the results of blood tests she had after the seventh session with Mr. Bereday.

Her sedimentation rate, an indicator of inflammation in the body revealed by a standard blood test, had always been around thirty-eight, but after her last session, it measured sixteen. Her hemoglobin count was better, and for the first time, she was not anemic.

In his report to the National Institutes of Health, Dr. Spector said, "If only 20 percent of the claims made are valid, this represents a revolutionary new development in therapy for a host of neurological and other diseases."

When will someone take the time or have the courage to set up a series of controlled clinical tests to confirm the results of the Bereday treatment? Dr. Spector added in his report that a series of these trials, or at least one series of controlled clinical trials starting with one or more neurological disorders, should be conducted by expert physicians in some clinical setting, preferably at the NIH, where a large group of patients having a similar neurological disorder could be treated and the results carefully evaluated. So far those doctors who were invited to observe the Bereday treatment have not felt it to be of sufficient importance to make the trip to New York.

Conductor Erich Leinsdorff, now eighty-two years old, has been quoted as saying that an artist has a responsibility to continue to create until he reaches a point that only he knows about. He likened the artist to a crystal or a prism, which allows pure light to shine forth. He said that the artist must continue to perform until the crystal becomes cloudy. Then and only then, it's time to stop. Sigmund Bereday's treatment seems to disperse the cloud from the crystal. It keeps the system pure and clean.

It is my opinion that what Mr. Bereday is able to accomplish in his work is of vital importance to the future of medicine, because it works directly with the electrical system in the body. The electrical system is the conductor of currents that course through the meridians, the esoteric level of the nervous system. This esoteric nervous system, described by Uranus, is especially activated in people who are forerunners of the Aquarian Age. This group includes everyone interested in the development of higher levels of consciousness, healing, astrology, music, humanitarian concerns, and new-age technology. As we enter the time where all of mankind will begin to relate with a cosmic sense of oneness, healing techniques must also grow onto the higher levels of consciousness.

Uranus not only rules the nervous system in the body and the meridians of the esoteric, or etheric, body, it also rules the breath. Breath is a prime conveyor of energy throughout the system, as the breathing mechanism enables oxygen to pass into the cellular level of the physical body. But the breath also carries prana, the higher, etheric level of oxygen. As an individual progresses along the path of his higher consciousness, his system requires the fuel of that higher level of existence. In my experience, one of the side benefits of treatments with Sigmund Bereday is the clearing away of blocks so that the esoteric system can absorb higher fuel such as prana.

Prana is a magnetic fluid which radiates from the Sun. The etheric body receives prana through the breath, but also through a center that is located between the shoulder blades. That center relates to the diaphragmatic action in the body, essential for conveying oxygen and prana throughout the system. The breathing mechanism depends on the proper alignment of the diaphragm and its position inside the rib cage. Carl Stough, director of the Carl Stough Institute of Breathing Coordination, Inc., located in New York City, has devoted his life to helping his patients live more healthfully by teaching them how to breathe rhythmically and how to regenerate the diaphragmatic action (see chapter 5), thereby bringing more prana into the system.

SCIENTIFIC AND METAPHYSICAL APPROACH TO HEALING

There are many doctors who express profound regret and concern over the factors that prevent them from considering alternative methods of healing, especially if such methods might produce statistically higher rates of cure or remission. It seems to be left to myriad people in fringe areas of the healing arts to forge ahead in the discovery and utilization of new techniques. However, as Alice Bailey stresses in her book *Esoteric Healing*, a combination of trained physicians and scientists working along with healers is necessary for the greatest results. She writes, "The dynamic use of energy in one of its seven streams, added to the sane understanding and work of the modern physician, aided by the healer (who works as a catalyst), can produce miracles when destiny so ordains." In other words, it may take science *and* the metaphysical to create the balance that will bring about real results.

Almost everyone outside of the medical profession who has chosen to adopt, develop, and work with alternative cures has a special interest in healing due to some personal motivating factor. Usually the search for health begins in response to one's own illness, or as in the case of Mr. Bereday, the illness of a loved one. It is rare for the average healthy individual to be interested in how the healing process takes place unless he has had some personal experience to motivate him. It is altogether too common for a person with an extremely vital constitution to adopt a superior attitude toward illness by saying "It's all in the mind," as did Kelly's doctor. That is simply a way of avoiding the responsibility of proper investigation of the cause of illness; it is also a way to avoid admitting that the doctor or lay person may not know what is happening or how to effect a cure. Although the origin of disease may lie on the mental level, making the judgment true to some extent, it is too simplistic an approach. Finding the causes and cures that will be truly effective demands a deeper look.

In defense of all open-minded and forward-thinking doctors, there is a real problem concerning the development and acceptance of new cures or techniques. Scientists and doctors must work within some framework of approval, such as that imposed by the American Medical Association or the Food and Drug Administration. This rigid system of safety regulations is important for the safety of the public, but it can also severely hamper any venture into uncharted territory. Fear of malpractice suits and legal ramifications can thwart all but the most stouthearted physician who might want to experiment with alternative forms of medicine. Insurance costs are now so high that doctors must be very courageous to stray far away from the tried and traditional methods, even if these methods fall far short of ultimate success. Simple cures are sometimes considered too simple to be effective. With lack of time and support from medical institutions, the whole system of holistic or alternative medicine is largely ignored. But sometimes the baby is thrown out with the bathwater.

SEARCH FOR THE FOUNTAIN OF YOUTH

The two major health trends that exist today focus attention on preventive medicine and the search for eternal youth. Exercise classes, weight-reduction classes, running shoes, youth-guaranteeing vitamin pills, antiaging products, and self-help video and audio tapes are all in high demand. The subliminal message is that internal health will come about as a result of all these new fitness aids. It is my contention that this may be like putting the cart before the horse. An abundant and vital internal energy system is probably the best insurance against premature aging.

Myths about the fountain of youth have existed since earliest recorded history, and there are many stories about people who have been able to retain their youth despite their chronological age. One of the most amazing concerns Comte Claude Louis de St. Germain, a French philosopher who lived in the 1700s, at the time of the revolution. He succeeded to the war office in the court of Louis XVI after the death of the Comte de Muy. He was a brilliant and uncompromising soldier who instituted many reforms into the army by opening it to the rising middle classes. These reforms were resented by the ruling classes, who until that time had been the only men able to obtain a commission. Consequently, he was in office for a very short time. After his release from office, he returned to a comfortable life that included heavy involvement in the masonic lodges, which exist to this day. The masonic lodges were organizations, extremely popular among the nobility and the intellectual strata of Paris, that held liberal intellectual discourses at a time of great social ferment.

St. Germain is considered to be one of the masters who returned to earth for the purpose of helping mankind. Even in what were considered to be his middle years, he had a very youthful appearance. Rumor has it that he was actually about 90 or 100 years old during the time of the French Revolution, when he appeared to be in his mid-forties. He was in an important position to guide the monarchy during the troubled times before the revolution. If his advice had been followed, the course of history might have been changed. St. Germain left esoteric literature that is considered to be invaluable even now. His discourses on alchemy give rules for healthful existence which are still very relevant.

It might be an easy task for someone at that advanced stage of evolution to attain eternal youth and perfect health, but the rest of us can at least take note and emulate an example in our attempt to reverse the aging process. That process of reversal is not so important from the point of view of vanity, but from the perspective of gaining greater control over the quality of life and the tasks at hand. Perhaps even the process of dying could be an easier transition and more within the jurisdiction of our conscious will if we made a stronger commitment to life. As St. Germain demonstrated, helping the process of enlightenment of all our fellow men may be the most important task of each individual after all, and worthy of our efforts to stay healthy and in a vibrantly functioning mode.

PIONEERING EFFORTS OF RESEARCHERS AND DOCTORS

By examining the results of research and techniques developed by respected investigators, such as Dr. Moss, Mr. Bereday, Carl Stough, and Dr. Blasband, we can begin to paint a picture that will lead mankind to better awareness of health and eventual mastery of self-healing. The findings of all these researchers lend strong credence to the theory that an electrical system is part of the underlying structure of man's constitution. If a concerted research effort were pursued by the medical establishment and the scientific community, enormous strides in truly effective healing techniques could be made quite rapidly. The pioneering work has already been done.

Any healer who has developed an effective technique has discovered from his or her own point of view exactly what every other healer has found to be true about the underlying physical structure and constitution of man and the electrical component. The next step is for general practitioners to have an open mind and conduct their own type of research. If they, too, discover what healers, working on a more subtle level, have found to be true, a veritable gold mine of possibilities will open up. Great riches can unfold from increased national health. If we can do away with the high costs of medical care now draining our individual pockets and the national budget, what we save can be put to use in creating a better life for all concerned. Funds now spent on the maintenance of illness can certainly be redirected into support systems for the maintenance of dynamic well-being.

Medical practitioners will never become obsolete. Even with a redirection of the focus of healing, we need our doctors. It is not always wise or easy to diagnose our illnesses and prescribe our own treatment, and trial and error can not only waste a lot of time, but can be dangerous. However, it may be possible for each individual to ascertain what works best within his or her own particular system, and then to have the confirmation and expert exchange of healing energy from an accomplished doctor or practitioner. Ultimately, each individual will learn to heal himself to a greater degree. That may mean looking beneath surface manifestations and physical symptoms to determine the probable cause of an illness. It may require the asking and answering of many questions: Why did I need this sickness? What does it accomplish in my life? Is there a lesson to be learned? What will have to happen so that I can allow myself to get well? Did I need an excuse to get some rest? Do I have unshed tears? Am I holding in anger? Where does this illness originate in my overall system? Is it only on the physical level?

Many people get tired and just give up, not realizing that what is left undone or unresolved in this lifetime must still be addressed in a future one. As a person progresses ever closer to the end of his life, the ability to stay in a healthy, functioning mode begins to wane. The physical mechanism has an ever decreasing ability to heal itself. As we get tired and start to run down on a very subtle level, death occurs in many ways. Cells begin to die and slough off, hair follicles decline, eyesight becomes weaker, organs function with less efficiency. In the book *Stages of Life* by Joseph Campbell, he reports that Carl Jung expressed a belief that the entire last half of a lifetime is actually a preparation for death. Jung felt it important to prepare for and to program the last moments of life very carefully, since they predescribe conditions of the next life. It is possible to predescribe conditions of a new life by concentrated attention toward that end, just as one sets goals in the present one.

It is never too late to grow in awareness. Dr. Brian Weiss, chairman of the Department of Psychiatry at Mt. Sinai Hospital in Miami, Florida, wrote about his own spiritual awakening in his book *Many Lives, Many Masters*. After years of training and scientific indoctrination as a physician and psychiatrist, as well as the achievement of a serious level of credibility in his own practice, Dr. Weiss had a profound growth experience that came about in a most unexpected way. After a series of amazing sessions with a patient who spontaneously regressed to past lives under hypnosis, Dr. Weiss decided to write about his experiences and to share what he had witnessed and learned. In this sensitive and moving account of what happened in the sessions with his patient, Dr. Weiss takes a courageous stand as to the value of past-life regression in connection with standard therapeutic practices. He is now pioneering a whole new phase of psychiatry by training doctors to conduct regression sessions. (Dr. Weiss, a true shaman, is a Scorpio.) Because of Dr. Weiss's prestigious medical background and strong credentials in scientific fields, he is in a unique position to make a profound contribution to the marriage and integration of science and metaphysics. Perhaps physicians will take heed and follow his example, researching the methods and practices metaphysicians have maintained to be effective for many centuries. What a glorious world can unfold before our very eyes when this happens.

Constitution of Man

Vibrant health, more than anything else, seems to depend on a dynamic flow of energy throughout the system. When illness occurs as a result of the interruption of that flow, many modern-day practitioners only treat the symptoms; somewhat like putting a finger in the proverbial dike to stop the flow of a river. It is natural for practitioners or doctors to apply their own particular specialization to the situation at hand, but sometimes these individualized approaches can be at war with each other. If a medical doctor, therapist, or healer fails to consider other parts of the body that might be affected, or other treatments that are being administered, other complications may develop and a true healing may not take place.

To illustrate the point, if a person stands on the perimeter of a circle, he sees only one facet of an object placed in the center of that circle: the facet that faces him. If he were able to stand directly above that object, he could view it in its entirety. Only then could he really understand what the object looked like or its true composition. The same is true in viewing the human system. With the lack of an overview, overt physical symptoms may seem to disappear while the root or true cause of the illness remains to emerge later on, perhaps in some other manifestation and in some other part of the body.

Although the lack of a holistic approach may be due to lack of time, quite often it is due to lack of understanding of the true nature of man's constitution. It is essential to look at the human energy system from a more esoteric viewpoint. A microscopic, or limited, viewpoint quite naturally gives an altogether different picture than a macrocosmic, or wider, view. Since science deals with what can be measured, analyzed, and dissected, the scientific or medical approach to healing is necessarily a limited one. As a new age is dawning, we are discovering and rediscovering much in the world that is unseen to the naked eye. There are many factors emerging from new technology that cannot yet be measured, touched, or tasted. Many of those unseen factors can have tremendous influence on man's energy and physical vitality. A different look brings new factors into focus and indicates the necessity of their inclusion in areas of research. If science only considers what physical senses reveal, some new findings may be quite startling. Luckily, some of these new factors are coming to light almost on a daily basis and are being utilized in new kinds of treatment.

UNSEEN FACTORS THAT CAN AFFECT HEALTH

The existence of radon and its detrimental effect on the physical system was completely unheard of a few years ago. Yet it is now a fairly common practice to test homes for evidence of radon rays emerging from the ground. At a conference for physicists held in New York City in 1987, Dr. Andrijah Puharich presented some astounding facts about dangerous radiation levels that exist as a result of our sophisticated experiments with nuclear energy. He pointed out that in 1875, when Edison was experimenting with electricity, the only light that reached earth was from the sun, moon, and stars. Now we have electrical waves that come from many sources—radio and TV waves, for example. These are nonionizing rays thought to be harmless to the human system. However, evidence indicates that nonionizing radiation can be harmful to anatomy. If this is so, the future of mankind is already in some kind of jeopardy. These rays cannot be seen by the naked eye, but we know they exist.

The electrical system in the body cannot as yet be measured, but it exists. Those harmful nonionizing rays may not affect the physical system in a way that can be traced, but if human rays, nonionizing rays, and electrical rays are all mingling somewhere in the atmosphere, there may be more damage to health on the unseen level than we suspect. The world of medicine is beginning to recognize many new potentially dangerous substances, but only as a result of the clamor of victims or the environmentalists, who are now demanding more control over these invisible pollutants. Scientists have recognized that the constant use of a computer may have a detrimental effect on the human system, as computers emit Very Low Frequency and Extremely Low Frequency electromagnetic radiation and Magnetic Fields, all of which have been correlated with illness. There is the suspicion that a higher incidence of miscarriage may occur with women who are exposed to computer energy on a daily basis. Since computers utilize crystals as a main component, and crystals can be programmed with positive energy or can carry negative energy, it might be important to know what specific energy computers emit into the atmosphere. (See Chapter 22.)

There are many highly sensitive people working with computers, X-ray machines, and in ultraviolet light who react adversely to even that small an amount of radiation. Indeed, X-ray technicians wear protective lead covering or absent themselves from the room when X-raying patients. There are people who are especially sensitive to microwave ovens and have found, only after an investment in equipment, that they must give up a fast method of food preparation. In addition, many people are sensitive to atmospheric pressures such as electrical storms. One doctor friend of mine who lives in California can sense an earthquake coming from hundreds of miles away. He develops a dreadful pressure in his head several hours before an earthquake is sensed by seismographic equipment. A rain- or snowstorm can also produce symptoms that vary in intensity from mild fatigue and lack of energy to severe headaches.

Such reactions have not generally been taken seriously by medical researchers and practitioners in the past.

Understanding how and why some body systems react to unseen factors more than others may help us understand why disease occurs. It is reassuring to know that many enlightened investigators, using strictly controlled scientific research principles, are coming up with some new answers. We may not have definitive cures as yet, but it is not unreasonable to expect that we could be completely disease free at some point in the future. If scientific man is able to comprehend and solve complex problems in connection with space—the larger macrocosmic view—similar techniques and knowledge should be available for looking at the microcosmic, or mankind. It is time to give credence to the outstanding results of unorthodox treatments and not dismiss what is new, unfamiliar, and esoteric. An empiric view combined with scientific methods could bring dynamic results.

ORDER OF THE UNIVERSE

Understanding the order of the Universe and the constitution of man is somewhat like trying to understand Einstein's theory of relativity without having any knowledge of science. It is a bit easier to explain some facets of the way man and the Universe interact now that personal computers are in popular usage; computers are like the microcosmic view of the macrocosm. For instance, if a person attempted to grasp the concept of the Akashic Records (which store every thought, deed, and action of every person throughout his entire history) before the advent of computers, he might not accept that such storage could be possible. However, since we understand that microchips can store enormous amounts of data in very limited space, the idea becomes comprehensible.

And just as we pull up files onto the screen of the computer to read what we previously wrote, man pulls up his personal experiences on an unconscious level, to relive the experiences over and over again. When we look at a computer, we know that we can edit, rewrite, or completely erase the data on the screen. Most people have a hard time believing that we can rewrite our own life scripts simply by changing the way we look at things. Words and phrases such as *visualization* and *the power of positive thinking*, among others, attempt to convey that concept, but most people continue to live out what they wrote in their personal computers (or in the Akashic Records) many centuries ago.

And then there are the hidden files in a computer. How many hours are wasted trying to persuade a computer to do what you tell it to do when, all along, the hidden codes and files are telling the computer to do something altogether different? The karmic experiences of each person are similar to those hidden files. If a person has a deep-seated guilt about his relationship with another person from another lifetime, he may go through all kinds of torments trying to make a present-day relationship compatible, when, all along, his subconscious mind is telling him something completely different from what his senses convey.

When it comes to health and the present-day energy patterns, many factors come into play that we may not be aware of on a conscious level. Those factors must be taken into consideration before an individual can experience true sense of well-being.

There are a variety of planes of consciousness and related bodies, or vehicles, that make up the subatomic structure of the human system. All the information and esoteric teachings that have emerged from a variety of what might be called the wisdom schools seem to correspond in their interpretation of these varying planes, bodies, and structures of matter. Myths and legends that have survived throughout history depict in fantasy language much that the esoteric schools teach. Even the symbology of ancient religions reveals secrets of the order of the Universe for those who have eyes to see and a mind that can interpret the somewhat obscure language. During the so-called Dark Ages, the only way to preserve the thread of truth was through these tales and stories.

In her novel *Silk Road*, Jeanne Larsen uses the story of Nu Wa to describe the complexity of the Universe. She writes, " 'All under heaven' was Great Tang. But people knew that this was only the human realm. They lived in a multilevel cosmos that included paradises in the sky, palaces of divinities on faerie islands or beneath great lakes, and a fearful underworld. The people of the

Tang understood that all things known through the senses, the ten thousand things, manifest the endless alternation of two essential forces; darkness and light, inaction and action, yin and yang. As followers of the Buddha, they also recognized that the phenomenal world is the senses' trick. All the while they lived in an enchanting multiplex world where events on one plane of reality resonated with those of other realms."

She described creation as the result of Nu Wa's piquish personality. She said, "Before the beginning, blanker than an eggshell, blanker than the blankest scroll, blanker than all the hungry wordless pages in the hungry word-filled dynasties of what will someday be the future, is the uncarved block. And then there is Nu Wa. Who gets bored. She twitches her divine and snakey tail. She hums a tune, sweet and nasal as the flutings of reed pipes. Heaven and Earth, and the ten thousand things that litter them, have now been born from that watery womby uncarved block, but none of this is quite amusing enough for Nu Wa. 'That's it!' cries Nu Wa. 'I shall make a creature that will see one thing as two. It will look at moon as moon, and pearls as pearls, and it won't see that moon and pearl are the same thing. In fact . . . it will see only the ten thousand things and not the One.' "

It is that seeing of the ten thousand things, not the One, that has caused man to be out of balance with nature, life, and health. I think that was what Einstein was trying to say in the theory of relativity.

CHAKRAS

If it is part of life on earth to continue seeing the ten thousand things, perhaps we can simplify matters just a little by trying to describe only a few of these things that relate to the makeup of man and his consciousness. According to all information that has emerged from all the wisdom schools and other reliable sources, there are seven batteries, or chakras, in the body that are unseen and are, so far, undetectable by a microscope or an autopsy. These chakras, or batteries, transmit energy from the higher level of

cosmic consciousness, where all is one and the one is energy, into
the etheric body and then into the physical system. The chakras
connect the spiritual body to the dense physical body and govern
the flow of energy throughout the electrical network that permeates the entire physical vehicle. This system is much like the
electrical wiring that runs throughout buildings. That wiring allows
electrical current to be sent into every part of the house or structure,
so that it can be utilized as is needed. The body's electrical system,
called meridians, runs through the etheric system and corresponds
to the nervous system in the physical body. It has specific connecting points that are like circuit breakers in a house. Circuit
breakers allow for the restoration of current in case of a power
failure or some other malfunction. The connecting points in the
etheric physical system are the acupuncture points utilized in
Chinese and Oriental medical techniques. In our sophisticated
Western world, medical practice has ignored the function or even
the existence of that highly charged wiring system of the body,
which relates to and determines the condition of the nerves and
nervous system in the body. (See Chapter 19.)

Chakras are charged and recharged by means of automatic contact with the stream of cosmic energy in the atmosphere, just as
houses and buildings are connected to a power center in a city or
town. That cosmic energy, called prana, is unending and available
to everyone, unless there is some restriction in the atmosphere or
in the dense physical body that prevents its natural flow into the
system. If the wiring is sound, and no restrictive factors are in
evidence, the physical system can take in this high level of fuel,
and the batteries, or chakra system, continue their work of dis-
tributing high-level fuel and energy into the body, ensuring continual good health.

Now, each of these seven chakras relates to a specific organ of
the body and connects the physical body to the other six bodies,
or vehicles. The vitality of each chakra allows each body to operate
on a different level or sphere of existence, just as the placement
of seven different generators would produce electricity on each of
seven floors of a building. The chakras are located in the center
of the body (see diagram), one above the other. Each chakra relates
to an organ or function of the body, vibrates to a specific color,
and can be described by an astrological symbol. The level of energy

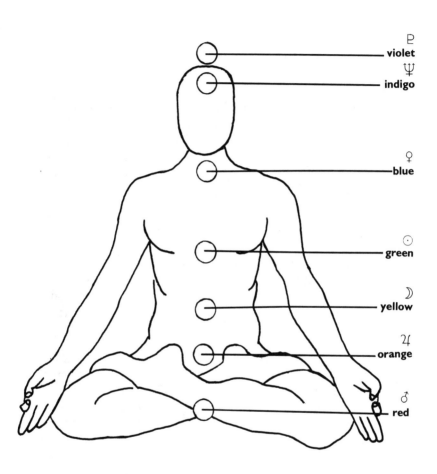

The Seven Chakras

and vibration in each chakra also relates to the level of consciousness of the seven bodies.

S E V E N   B O D I E S

The human being has seven bodies or vehicles that correspond to seven different planes of awareness and consciousness. Each vehicle is composed of a gradually lesser degree of density and substance, with the physical body the most dense of all. In order to comprehend this idea more fully, we can think of each body as a different automobile. Each automobile is made of a lighter substance than the preceding one, and each one traverses a road of gradually lighter material, existing on gradually higher gradations above the earth. For the most part, an average man is engaged in a struggle to learn how to operate only three automobiles or corresponding vehicles and to comprehend the three lowest planes on which they can exist. Those three lowest automobiles and their separate planes relate to the physical, mental, and emotional levels of existence.

B A L A N C I N G   O F
V E H I C L E S   O R   B O D I E S

An individual may have no physical problems, yet suffer on an emotional level. Another person may have no emotional or mental problems, yet the physical form can be weak. Many individuals who operate on a strong intellectual or mental level may not have well-developed physical form, and many athletic individuals with superb physical forms are not especially interested in heavy mental activity. (This example is, of course, very general.) Learning to balance and integrate these three qualities of life is like trying to learn how to drive three cars simultaneously. Just to complicate matters, these cars are not situated side by side, or one above the other, but actually built around each other. The central automobile is made of heavy metal. That would relate to the physical, or most dense, body. The automobile surrounding that original vehicle might be made of plastic (relating to the emotional body), and the third one could be constructed of heavy canvas such as was formerly used in the manufacture of gliders, let's say. That vehicle relates to the mental body. The framework of each vehicle, as well as its construction, is lighter than the former one.

Not only are the vehicles interpenetrating, but the heaviest vehicle (the physical) is the only one that has its wheels firmly on the ground. The plastic vehicle (the emotional body) is slightly off the ground, and slightly above the physical vehicle, riding on a current of air like a hydroplane rides above the water, and can be particularly volatile and hard to control, while the third and lightest of the vehicles (the mental body) is actually floating on strong air currents quite far above the ground. So they are not exactly automatically synchronized, even though they interpenetrate.

The chakras, located in the esoteric body of man, are the controls of each vehicle. Those controls are interconnected and are located in the central vehicle of heavy metal. Therefore, the operator of all these vehicles (the consciousness) can place himself in the driver's seat of the heavy metal vehicle and take control of all the vehicles that float above the ground. (The heavy metal vehicle is the body we unconsciously, or consciously, operate while we are on earth.)

To make it more complex, however, the substance of the machinery in the varying automobiles is also made of increasingly lighter material. The gear of the second car is also made of plastic, while the gear of the third car is also made of fabric. Each gear demands a lighter touch. They are connected, yet independent at the same time. If the driver shifts the vehicle of heavy metal (the physical), there is a corresponding shift in the other two vehicles (emotional and mental), but unless the driver's effort is very concentrated, each vehicle is capable of going off slightly in its own direction. Therefore, any shifting of gears of the heavy metal car must be carefully coordinated with the shifting of gears of each individual vehicle (mental and emotional).

Now, there is a set of panel instruments for each vehicle as well. These instrument panels in the physical body are the organs, whereas the instruments on the other levels are the endocrine glands that correspond to each organ in the physical system. Now these varying panels are sitting side by side, interconnected, but independent as well. However, the panel instruments of the heavy metal car (organs of the physical body) reflect the condition of the panel instruments of each of the other two. In fact, the condition of the heavy metal car (the physical body) is really reflective of the condition of the other two vehicles (the emotional and mental), for any dents in the fenders of the emotional body and mental body will show up on the fenders of the heavy metal vehicle. In other words, the condition of the physical body reflects what might be wrong or out of alignment on our emotional and mental levels. In a later chapter, I will describe how one can see the emotional traumas that are stored in the physical body from the earliest moments of childhood.

Are you confused enough? Is it any wonder that life on earth is so complicated, especially when we try to grow in our awareness? Now, with the attainment of greater awareness, many people are struggling to incorporate a fourth vehicle, and that is like driving four cars instead of three. Let's imagine that the fourth car (intuitional body) is made of a sturdy wool fabric that is softer than the fabric of the third vehicle but still has some weight. It also has an instrument panel and inner structure that are similar to the construction of the vehicle.

It takes constant attention, effort, determination, and intense desire to make contact with all those vehicles and to coordinate them to the point where one could embark on a trip. If that coordination is achieved, the driver can make astounding leaps and strides in an upward climb onto other levels of consciousness or onto other levels of existence. The path is not linear and bound to the earth, but goes in a spiral that climbs onto other spheres. If all levels of consciousness can be reached and coordinated, no ill health could possibly prevail, for then the ten thousand things become as one again and tremendous cosmic energy can flow through each vehicle, like a gas line tying each system together. One of the ways of balancing all of these interpenetrating vehicles is to achieve the proper vibratory rate of each chakra, which are like the batteries of each car. If the batteries are charging and discharging current on a constant rate of flow, the vehicles begin to stabilize. That is what can be achieved by meditation, but specific meditative work with each chakra can be enormously effective in regulating the engines of each vehicle.

Sometimes achieving balance is merely a matter of seating oneself firmly in the driver's seat of the car. The spiritual body is very light. It contains the consciousness of the part of the system that longs for home, that longs to float freely on the natural spiritual plane of existence. The body, or physical vehicle, can be restrictive and confining. The spirit frequently wants to take a little flight of fancy, to get a breath of fresher air, and so, periodically, the spiritual side of man leaves the body. In many instances, especially when Uranus rules or aspects the first house in an astrological chart, the spirit body remains poised for flight and is never quite firmly seated in the center of the physical vehicle. It is my impression that the description of being *centered*, a term that is commonly used in this day and age, is really a description of a fully seated spirit body with both "hands" on the steering wheel and both "feet" on the proper pedals of the vehicle, or physical body.

As I thought about this concept, it occurred to me that during the times in my life when I was accused of being "scattered" or "spacey," I wasn't sitting upright within myself. I was terribly offended when people applied those terms to me, but actually my image of the way I drive my vehicle is that I have the left arm partly out of the window, steering with my left hand, while the right hand is sticking out of the sun roof, waving in the breeze, inviting anyone to pull me out if they want to! With Uranus a facet of my personality (Cancer rising, and Moon conjunct Uranus in Aries), part of me longs for more air, freedom, space, and exhilaration. This aspect is what I call the suicidal complex. That term does not imply a maudlin urge to do something self-destructive, but merely a feeling of "Stop the world, I want to get off." With conscious awareness of that attitude, I can choose to seat myself more upright in the vehicle, place both hands on the steering wheel, make a stronger commitment to life. Therefore I will be able to drive my car more effectively. I have discovered that this situation is not uncommon and is especially related to Uranian indicators in the astrological chart; or to those people with the planet Uranus ruling the twelfth or first house, placed in those houses, or in hard aspect to a planet ruling or placed in the twelfth or first house. It can apply to any person with Uranus strongly stressed in an astrological chart. (See Chapter 4.) This planetary placement, if in difficult aspect to other planets in the chart, can also indicate physical problems connected to the breath and the breathing processes, as well as assimilation of oxygen into the system.

As a person is ready to attain another level of existence and another plane of consciousness, he finds the exact conditions he needs to urge him forward on the upward spiral toward higher consciousness. Sometimes, like Nu Wa, the urge to go onward may be due to frustration with present conditions. He may become bored. Perhaps he gets tired of juggling the ten thousand things and wants to experience the one again. It may be that patterns of ill health provide an opportunity necessary to force him onto other levels of consciousness and onto other planes of existence. Boredom may not exist on the conscious level, but may actually originate on one of the higher levels of awareness. Ill health rarely originates on a conscious level of choice. Few people in a rational frame of mind would choose debilitation as a means of forcing growth, for one could simply grow while retaining healthy physical vitality.

Now, there is actually a fifth, sixth, and seventh level of existence and consciousness, with corresponding vehicles and corresponding instruments. In order to have an overview of the patterns of health, it is imperative to consider that blocks could occur on any of those more subtle levels of experience or existence. Imbalance on any level always manifests as illness or debilitation in the physical body or vehicle.

The Beethovens, Shakespeares, Michelangelos, and the great teachers who have walked on earth may have succeeded in touching existence on higher planes of experience and inspiration. For those of us who have not yet touched even a momentary pinnacle of consciousness of the higher levels, much less made total contact, any attempt we make toward climbing higher on the spiral is better than remaining stuck or static on a lower plane of existence. As we get bored or begin to desire higher levels of experience, and we come closer to being in contact with other levels of consciousness, all the bodies, or vehicles, necessarily become clarified, more purified, and more translucent. It is part of the growth process, and a necessity, that all the bodies or vehicles become more sensitive and lighter so that we can reach the higher levels of existence. Ill health or disease cannot exist at the supreme level. It does exist along the way, however, as higher and higher realms of atmospheric change occur in the system and may relate to the process of changing consciousness, like a snake shedding an old skin.

The condition of the physical vehicle is somewhat of a reflection of progress on the individual path and may mirror the blocks we encounter on our journey toward resolving our karmic conditions and attaining complete balance. It is extremely important, however, not to be critical or to make judgments about the level of evolution our fellow men, or we ourselves, may have attained or where our consciousness may lie. Spiritual one-upmanship is a sure way to fall down the ladder again. Ill health may be a reflection of a momentary cleansing process as a person goes through stages of awareness. An individual may have chosen a limited physical condition, or other restrictive conditions, even before he entered the earth plane in any particular lifetime to force his consciousness onto other planes. Those beings who have succeeded in contacting other planes of experience may have different symptoms of maladjustment, or what we might think of as illness, than an individual operating on lower levels of consciousness.

In diagnosing where the root of illness may lie, determination of which vehicle is out of balance is half the battle. Therefore, a prime requisite in healing is the development and use of new insights and greater compassion for the individual struggle rather than any tendency to make judgments about it. It is most important to develop compassion toward our own struggle, for the pattern of growth is attained through struggle, and any struggle toward completion, any attainment or new step on the path, is to be congratulated. But this growth process may relate to what we term "divine discontent."

SEVEN PLANES
OF EXISTENCE

If we tried to draw a diagram of the seven planes of existence or seven bodies, we would see them as surrounding each other and interpenetrating, but it is difficult to use words to describe what lies on levels above the physical, for words are necessarily physical instruments. Just as long as we are on the earth plane, we automatically view things from a limited perspective. We therefore tend to describe each plane as separate and distinct. However, with even a little elevation and imagination, it is possible to learn the concurrent operation of several vehicles and levels of experience, and to bring in and utilize energy of ever higher planes of existence. Higher energy can then interpenetrate matter and the vehicles on the lower planes to bring about better health conditions. It is necessary, however, to have a conscious awareness of being properly seated in the physical body.

Meditation is the most important discipline for gaining more elevation of consciousness, and it enables the spiritual part of man to gain more of an empathetic connection with his physical body. Therefore he can become properly seated in his physical vehicle. Artificial means of elevation, such as drugs or psychedelic substances or alcohol, do not bring about the balance that is necessary for total integration. There are no shortcuts. The practice of meditation is essential in the effort to make contact with higher levels of awareness as it shifts attention to and lifts the lighter vehicles and allows the gravitational pull of the lower paths to be cleared, bringing about greater alignment with higher energy. When the higher energy courses throughout all the systems and vehicles of consciousness, it becomes easier to drive all those vehicles simultaneously and to see the One thing. (See Chapter 25.)

Physical Plane

The seven planes of existence have been given names to help identify them. The first level is called the physical plane. The study of anatomy is a method of learning about all of the components (blood vessels, organs, glands, etc.) and the true makeup of the physical body. The physical plane incorporates those parts that can be seen under a microscope, be analyzed, and be tested for health and balance by the use of physical equipment. Life lived solely on a physical plane of consciousness is like being an "evolutionary" newborn baby who comprehends hunger and discomfort, and is satisfied with experiences on that level alone. The emotional nature of such a baby might be very primitive, and his mental equipment might register very little. (I use a baby as an example because in former times it was thought that a baby only needed physical comforts attended to. Now we know that is not true, as babies are extremely aware on many levels and certainly need a lot of emotional security, as well as some information that will explain matters to them that they otherwise might find confusing. Many babies are extremely cognizant of life on many levels and may be very evolved souls.)

Astral Plane

The next step above the physical plane is the astral plane, also described as the lower emotional or psychic plane. This is the plane of consciousness that is ruled by the lower nature. Life lived primarily on this level is governed by emotions and gratification of selfish desires alone. If a person has a conscience, it is apt to be put aside if it interferes with pleasure. An individual functioning largely on the lower astral might have no sense of moral duty to mankind, as an example, or any concept of higher idealism. This could describe the level on which sociopaths operate, or those who seem to have no moral conscience.

Consumption of drugs and alcohol can propel a person into experiences that exist on the lower astral plane, for instance, depending on the sensitivity of his various systems. It is essential not to make judgments or label a person with an addictive personality as weak or bad. The tragedy is that even though a person may have achieved a higher level of soul growth and actually functions on a higher plane of consciousness, he may altogether lose his sense of duty or fitness if he comes in contact with or becomes addicted to those substances. Addiction to heroin or even cocaine, as an example, can cause a person to do almost anything to obtain money for his habit, including robbing or killing. In that moment, he loses his sense of humanity and becomes trapped on the level of the lower astral. There are many drug addicts who have a higher level of consciousness and overcome the addiction, but the effort needed to do so is enormous. The nature of the lower astral plane is that of entrapment.

In the beginning phase of existence on the lower astral plane, drugs and alcohol enable the individual to see only the pretty pictures of the astral plane, and to simulate a sense of higher idealistic existence. After a while, hallucinations take over, causing him to see the seamier side of the lower astral. The pictures of creatures and monsters, which actually exist on the dark side of the astral, become very real to an addict. Everyone around him believes he is imagining and hallucinating, but to him the visions are real.

The danger that exists on this level is actual possession. There are disembodied spirits who want to make contact with a physical form in order to have conscious experiences once again. These spirits are like sociopaths on a lower astral level. They have no conscience or sense of responsibility for the individual they want to possess. Drugs, alcohol, and hallucinogens open up channels that allow negative entities to enter the body. Playing with substances that are likely to cause open rents in the system, allowing for a takeover, is like leaving an automobile unattended with the keys in the ignition, the car idling in neutral, and the door wide open. It's an open invitation for someone to steal the car, especially if the car is left in a bad neighborhood where such thefts are known to occur.

The war on drugs must begin with instruction about what can happen to an individual on other levels of consciousness if even a mild flirtation with those substances is begun. An accomplished psychologist in Texas has had a high rate of success in treating and curing people who are addicted to drugs and alcohol because she can detect the degree of possession of the body of the addict by one or more invading negative spirits. If an individual has reached a point of addiction, he is also surely possessed by invading entities. The psychologist can effect cures by first ridding the person of these negative spirit influences. She utilizes her own levels of conscious-ness and energy to chase the invading spirit away.

It is as important to acknowledge the existence of earthbound spirits, who attack very sensitive people, as it is to warn children about taking candy from a stranger. When more therapists and healers acknowledge the possibility of possession or negative in-fluence from destructive forces, there can be easier cures for serious psychological problems. Possession may even be a partial cause of many physical problems. Hollywood has produced many scary, or funny, films that illustrate the existence of ghosts, possession, and other phenomena. Yet because of the exaggerations and the con-text in which these films are written, the reality of such phenomena seems as remote as science-fiction films might have seemed in the 1930s. These entities are very real, even if they are unseen by the naked eye. They exist on that level of consciousness in the spirit form because their own level of development may not have been very evolved. The earthbound spirits who exist on the lower astral plane cannot enter areas of light and purity. This gives even more credence to the practice of meditation and explains why, for the health and well-being of an individual, it is so important to stretch and grow onto the higher spheres of consciousness, especially if that individual has a very sensitive physical system.

When higher energies pour through the system, they purify and prevent any invasion of foreign influence. That includes developing an ability to shrug off Aunt Nellie's advice on the physical plane, too. A sensitive person can be vulnerable to domineering Aunt Nellie's influence and may forget to think for himself. It is impor-tant to note that possession and attunement to our spirit guides or protectors are very different. Meditation can enable a person to receive guidance from highly evolved spiritual beings, like seeking advice from a wise person or expert in a particular field on earth. Whenever a person allows the conscious mind to be unduly in-fluenced or to be put aside or out of control, possession on any level is possible. Living in a state of possession is like being in a relationship where one person completely controls and dominates the other. It is not a healthy state of existence on any level, as the control is usually taken by someone who does not have the in-dividual's best interests at heart.

In many cases of mental disorders such as paranoia and paranoid schizophrenia, possession may have occurred very early in childhood as a result of heavy trauma or abuse. The child leaves his body to avoid the pain of the experience and leaves it open for the existence of one or more invading personalities from the astral plane. In the case of multiple-personality disorders, the individual creates another personality to take over to handle the pain. Usually, the people who develop multiple personalities are mediumistic and may be evolved on a highly spiritual level. Therapists who have treated both schizophrenics and people with multiple-personality disorders have actually spoken to all the personalities at one time or another. The most dramatic story of possession was revealed in the book and film *The Three Faces of Eve*. The heroine of the story was actually possessed of several different personalities. She describes the hidden abuse that occurred in her childhood and which created fertile ground for the condition. Such a person's discomfort is almost always compounded by a fear of telling anyone what is going on. Up until now, if a child were to try to enlist help from his parents in the understanding of even positive associations with the spirit world, he would usually be told he had a vivid imagination. Child abusers do far more damage than merely inflicting physical or psychological pain. If we consider what can happen when the young child leaves his body to avoid a searing experience, it is clear that he can become polarized on a lower level of experience, even if possession does not occur. Blocks are built in his consciousness that affect his entire existence, for they prevent his natural choice of growth on that spiral of experience. In regression sessions, many women have uncovered incidents of sexual abuse that occurred in their childhood and which had been completely blocked from their conscious memory. In all cases physical symptoms, such as asthma, bronchitis or allergies that related to the experience were set in motion. In such instances, the physical pain is like a dam that must burst, releasing the poison behind it.

The second plane, or the astral plane, has a positive side as well as a negative one, for this level also encompasses the upper astral. Feelings of a higher emotional state such as romantic love can exist in this sphere. However, polarization—life lived on this level alone—may cause a person to be totally controlled and governed by his passions. Negative feelings such as anger, hate, fear, and jealousy can control the being instead of the higher emotion of love. When a person wants to possess the person he loves, he becomes polarized on this level. If the prime concern of life is to create a particular image in the eyes of the world, or to attract other people to do his bidding through superficial persuasion of the personality, this is the level that is in operation. People who live life on this level are usually physically neat, clean, and well groomed, for that is part of the level of consciousness of this plane. (This should not be interpreted to mean that everyone who dresses well and is carefully groomed is living life solely on this plane. The upper astral describes the stratum where the only concern in life is about these matters.)

Mental Plane

The third plane is called the mental plane. Illness can sometimes occur when a transition is in progress from polarization on the emotional level to operation on a mental plane. However, polarization can occur simultaneously on many levels. This factor complicates the possibility of simple diagnosis of the origin of health problems. When the shifts of energy relate to the mental plane, the momentary disorientation that accompanies this kind of change of consciousness may produce symptoms that appear to indicate mental illness. This is especially true if an individual has chosen to tackle many issues all at the same time in his life experience. Operation exclusively on the mental plane produces what might be termed a "concrete mind." On this level of existence, all experiences are processed through left-brain functions. A person may be skeptical or simply dependent on what can be seen, analyzed, and measured. He has an addiction to facts, just as life on the lower astral produces an addiction to the pictures of phenomena. Vision, dreams, and concepts hold little interest for one whose security comes from dependence only on things that can be touched or seen. This exclusive dependence on concrete facts can produce blocks to the flow of energy affecting all the lower vehicles. A static condition may manifest in illness, especially to organs that need the beneficial flow of higher forms of energy. As an example, higher love energy keeps the heart chakra open and vitalized. Heart attacks might become a thing of the past if gentle love energy is used as a therapy for the prevention of constriction in that area. A person operating on the level of the concrete mind may be an atheist or nonbeliever. However, life lived on the mental plane can be a prelude to the next step, which is the bridge to higher consciousness.

Intuitional Plane

The fourth plane is the first of the planes that relates to higher consciousness; that is, the consciousness of higher energies that cannot be measured, touched, felt, or seen. This plane is called the intuitional or higher mental plane. It is the level where abstract thought processes begin to function. Life on this level produces individuals who are visionaries, idealists, and great thinkers. For a person who is operating in this sphere or plane, evidence is not enough. The individual who dwells on this level of comprehension is much more interested in what he cannot see or hear, for he needs to look beyond and behind thoughts and actions to discover motivations and hidden patterns of existence. His creations exist first on the level of concepts. This includes people who are mystics and visionaries as well as artists, musicians, and highly creative people. The fourth plane describes anyone who utilizes concepts as his everyday tools. He becomes adept at the manifestation of his dreams and visions. This is different than the desire nature; desire originates on an emotional level, whereas visions originate on a level of higher mind.

Spiritual Plane

The fifth plane is the spiritual plane. This state is sometimes achieved unexpectedly at moments of true spiritual ecstasy. Experiences that relate to an attunement to the divine spark of energy or that occur during religious experiences can bring about contact with this level of existence. This is the plane where the spiritual will begins to emerge, eventually replacing willpower or the lower will, which says "I want what I want when I want it." Conscious development on this level eventually enables a person to merge his consciousness with the sixth plane of abstraction, or the upper spiritual plane.

The Monadic Plane

The sixth plane is called the monadic plane. Existence on this level does not necessarily incorporate the need for a physical body. In fact, the physical vehicle can be a handicap, as physical needs for things such as food and drink are only distracting. There have been some avatars, saints, and sages who have reached existence on this plane while still in the physical body, but relatively few. Consumption of food is almost unnecessary at this stage of consciousness, as food merely pollutes the delicacy of the system. Speech, too, is unnecessary. Pilgrims who have taken a vow of silence and are working toward the achievement of this level of consciousness can more easily attain their goal. At that point, information and teachings are transmitted telepathically.

As an example, high-level spiritual teachings as contained in the Alice Bailey books were transmitted to her by a being who calls himself the Tibetan. In an extract from a statement published in 1934, he says, "I live in a physical body like other men, on the borders of Tibet, and at times preside over a large group of Tibetan lamas when my other duties permit. I am a brother of yours, who has travelled a little longer upon the Path than has the average student, and has therefore incurred greater responsibilities. I am one who has wrestled and fought his way into a greater measure of light than has the aspirant who will read this article, and I must therefore act as a transmitter of the light, no matter what the cost." The information given to Alice Bailey by the Tibetan was transmitted telepathically. There have been few known to man in this life who have reached this high level of enlightenment while existing in a physical, mortal life. Exaltation of this type transcends all that is earthly. The monadic stage represents life lived totally in tune with the will of the divine. It is the transcendency to which Yogis strive and some attain.

The Divine

The final plane is that of the divine. It is sometimes called the atmic and is the level of the spirit. It is undifferentiated, cosmic, and merged monadic consciousness. It is impossible to say very much about this stage of existence unless one has reached this level of oneness. At that point, however, words would be totally foreign and nonexistent, for all is blended and merged and oneness at this point of consciousness.

ATTAINMENT
OF BALANCE

Clearly, many highly evolved people operate concurrently on many levels. Life is a constant struggle to integrate and balance expression on many planes of existence. While we live in the physical world, the prime concern is the attainment of balance on the first four planes. If man can find the balance between his life on the physical level and his reach for the higher concepts of his true spiritual nature, the light of the soul penetrates and heals conditions that might otherwise prove debilitating and burdensome. Meditation is the ultimate way to energize each level of consciousness and to bridge the gaps along the way.

SHIFTS OF
CONSCIOUSNESS

Each time a major transition of consciousness occurs, the whole atomic structure of a person's bodies or vehicles begins to shift. Physical manifestations of ill health or debilitation that can occur at these times should be recognized as part of an initiation process. An individual evolves onto each plane with an initiation that is similar to the process of birth, for in actuality, birth is really the initiation into the physical realm. When a person enters the earth plane, he polarizes his consciousness into a dense form that in itself is a jolting change of consciousness. In between lives is a resting place and a place of reevaluation. In that state, one sees the One thing. As the spirit enters the dense form of the physical, he brings into the consciousness of that persona whatever level of existence he has already reached on his evolutionary path. That level may not exist in the conscious mind of the newly born, however, but is built in on some level of awareness in the new life form. Transition onto earth, or birth, or the exit from the earth, or death, can be easy or difficult depending on the level of awareness of what is occurring. Birth and death can be facilitated through careful preparation and conscious choice on the part of the individual undergoing the shift of consciousness. Birth is a shift of consciousness on a downward spiral, or into more density, whereas death is a shift of consciousness on an upward spiral, or into more light. People who have had near-death experiences always describe a bright light that summons them onward with a joyous force that is difficult to resist. Those who have returned to life to describe the experience say they want to go forward to be embraced by that dynamic energy. They only return because of a sense of unfinished business, or because the love of someone left behind pulls them back. In regression sessions that I have conducted, many people describe the sense of oneness that exists in the in-between state. They indicate that there is a joyousness of belonging that defies the impulse for individualization. One young lady described seeing herself as a squiggly, existing blissfully along with all the other squigglies. However, she was aware of the lack of individualization on that level.

THERAPY AND CONSCIOUSNESS

In his book *Many Lives, Many Masters*, Dr. Brian Weiss writes of his growth onto new levels of consciousness as a result of sessions with a patient who regressed to past lives under hypnosis. One of the most profoundly moving parts of his true story was the account of the information that came forth from his patient when she was in the state of existence between lives. When she reached that phase of her experiences, the lady became a medium for the masters. They told Dr. Weiss that the patient had come to him not for help, but to teach him about levels of consciousness and what exists in the unseen world. The account is particularly important because the whole experience of his patient regressing to a past life was quite unexpected. Dr. Weiss was steeped in traditional scientific methodology. Before the experience with this patient, Dr. Weiss did not accept the theory of reincarnation and neither did the patient! The teachings that came through her have not only changed his life, they have paved the way for the birth of a whole new therapeutic process.

ASTROLOGY AND CONSCIOUSNESS

Since astrology indicates conditions and acts like a road map or guide, the natural progression of the planets may help to describe the stages of development of other levels of consciousness. Planets are placed in a certain order because of the speed of movement around the zodiac. The exception is the placement of the Sun and the Moon, called the lights. The Sun is always considered first in the lineup, and the Moon follows in second place. Then Mercury, the fastest-moving planet, comes in third, with Venus following in the fourth spot. Mars falls into fifth place with Jupiter coming in sixth. Saturn is the seventh planet, Uranus the eighth, and Neptune the ninth. Pluto falls into the tenth position in the lineup.

There are two planets that need interpretation other than what is usually applied. One is the Sun and the other is Saturn. In the usual interpretation, the Sun relates to ego, self-esteem, leadership qualities, and executive ability. But in another way of looking at things, the Sun describes the quality of soul consciousness. It relates to the soul in this sense. When we are just the One, with no differentiation, there are also no individual experiences. When a portion of spirit breaks off from the whole and chooses to incarnate, it does so for the purpose of individualization. The vehicle that is built for the protection of that fragile spirit is the soul body. As the soul enters the physical body, it has a chance for self-expression and the gathering of individual experiences. The Sun describes a bright light, and the quality of the soul is naturally brilliant and light. So if we consider the Sun as descriptive of the light of the soul, it is easy to see that the expansion of consciousness is a goal. The process of gathering as many positive and productive experiences as possible takes away the onus of the usual interpretation of ego, since those experiences are to be taken back to the One, or the whole, to enrich the quality of the One. Everyone's positive experiences accumulated in the experience of the thousand things enlarges the consciousness of the One.

Although Saturn relates to structure, and especially the bony structure of the physical body, it also describes the earth's plane and its gravitational pull. Let's consider Saturn as the line of differentiation between the physical forms and conditions and the higher spiritual levels of experience. Every planet in the lineup before Saturn describes earth experiences, levels of consciousness, and existence. Whereas everything that comes after Saturn relates to more spiritual levels of consciousness. These later planets are called the higher octave or transpersonal planets. They are Uranus, Neptune, and Pluto.

The Moon is the light that relates to the emotional plane, with Mercury related to the mental level of existence. Venus, Mars, and Jupiter describe conditions of experience and attitude.

So the Sun also represents vitality and ego, and the Moon, emotion and sensitivity. A person who is operating on a purely egocentric level, the limited quality indicated by the Sun, is completely overshadowed by an individual with compassion, the highest attribute connected to the Moon. But the person who deals only on an emotional plane (the lower attitude described by the Moon) is instantly leveled by someone who is rational and thinking, energy described by Mercury. Clear observation of facts and events (Mercury) is a natural antidote for overreaction (Moon). Love (Venus) modifies analysis (Mercury). Love can conquer and mitigate argument. Action (Mars) takes care of any tendency to inertia (a less productive quality attributed to Venus) and is more productive than passivity (Venus). Enthusiasm (Jupiter) is far more enriching than blind frustration, undirected ambition, or anger (Mars). Practicality (Saturn) can accomplish what a Pollyanna attitude (Jupiter) cannot. Blind faith (Jupiter) can keep one wandering on an endless search, but structure (Saturn) produces results. Spontaneity and openness to new ideas (Uranus) are like letting go of the tree trunk's security (Saturn) to walk out on the edge of a limb. For it is in working through the scare and taking risks (Uranus) that exciting new conditions exist. Yet vision (Neptune) is important to prevent a total scattering of energy (Uranus). Finally, the power of attunement to the universal, divine plan (Pluto) reaches out to the ultimate, cosmic level and describes the greatest degree of effectiveness. Obviously the trick is to utilize the positive quality of energy associated with each planet in the most productive manner possible in order to hasten the upward spiral of consciousness.

It seems a bit unfair that no one is given a road map or a specific set of instructions as to what to expect or what to do when we enter the earth plane. Perhaps none of us would come into this sphere of existence if we knew what was ahead of us. The constant necessity to adjust and readjust to our circumstances is somewhat like walking up the wrong road in the dark, getting sidetracked onto a narrow, rocky path, and having to backtrack and search for the lighted way. The struggle, which seems to be part of the plan, eventually causes mankind to find his own special and individually lighted path. Unfortunately, ill health may be a necessary part of that struggle. The result of strenuous effort to find balance and to learn what it is that we need to learn forces each individual to grow onto a different plane of soul consciousness and a different level of existence. Hopefully, an individual astrological chart can be invaluable in giving some guidance and comprehension of conditions that exist on each step along the pathway to greater enlightenment.

Astrology as a Diagnostic Tool

*H*ippocrates, the father of the medical profession, said, "A physician cannot safely administer medicine if he is unacquainted with astrology." For the past few centuries, the medical profession has chosen to overlook that advice completely. Every physician takes the Hippocratic oath before he begins his medical practice, yet he ignores a mandate made by his patron saint. Since the time Hippocrates delved into the field of astrology, medical practices have become more complex, just as life has become more complex and stressful. Astrology has kept pace and is also a more intricate study. What might have been a simple diagnostic tool in the days of Hippocrates has become like a lotus bud, unfolding tens of thousands of petals.

For the same reasons that medical practitioners may avoid thorough investigation of alternative healing methods, many scientists and doctors avoid the idea of utilizing an astrological chart as a reference point. It is left to psychiatrists and psychologists to appreciate the value of using astrology as an aid to the therapeutic process, and fortunately, many therapists are now utilizing a patient's horoscope to help them comprehend the underlying structure and conditions in his life.

FULL MOON

It may be quite some time before physicians routinely use astrology as a diagnostic tool. There is one small chink in the medical armor, however. It has been duly reported in newspapers that many surgeons have observed a greater tendency for excessive bleeding at the time of the full Moon, and some surgeons are now exercising caution in scheduling operations at that time.

I remember an incident many years ago when a famous actor and very close friend of mine was scheduled to undergo surgery. Naturally I checked the scheduled time of the operation to see what the aspects might be in relation to my friend's chart and was horrified to realize that the operation was to commence at the very worst time possible, just before the full Moon. There was real danger of my friend bleeding to death. I decided to appeal to his family for some help in convincing the doctor to postpone the operation for even a few hours, as the adverse Moon aspects would then have passed. The family didn't quite laugh at me, but they really didn't take me seriously. I was better known as an actress at the time, and although I was also working as a professional astrologer, my credibility was simply not strong enough. I was reminded of the exalted reputation of the surgeon, and I got the message that I was to stay out of it.

I didn't want to alarm my friend, who was already nervous about the operation, and since I found myself in an untenable situation, the best I could do was go to the hospital and wait with the family in case there was an opportunity to express my concern. After several hours of nervous waiting, someone emerged from the operating room to inform the family that the doctors were waiting for a supply of blood to be sent from another hospital before beginning the operation. After my friend had been prepped and was already under anesthesia, they discovered that the hospital had no back-up supply of his blood type. The operation had to be postponed until an adequate supply could be found. My friend would indeed have bled to death if this error had not been discovered. The adverse aspect indicated the probability of the situation, but could not describe the way in which the scenario would manifest itself or the fortunate outcome.

Unconscious self-determination, will, fate, and positive energy manifested around an individual by others can transmute what might have been a dreadful outcome into a positive result. It is important to take many factors into account in order to fully describe any situation, and in astrological interpretation this is especially true. The astrological aspects surrounding my friend's operation did clearly indicate a need for concern about that specific moment in time. If I had done a sixth or eighth harmonic of his chart, for instance (that is, a deeper structural viewpoint), which would give a more comprehensive picture of the health aspects of my friend, or had I looked more deeply into the aspects directly after that scheduled moment, I might have been able to describe more precisely all of the circumstances concerning his operation.

M O O N   V O I D   O F   C O U R S E

Another general aspect to avoid when planning an operation, or anything for that matter, is a Moon void of course. That term, *void of course,* means that the Moon, or any planet, is at such a late degree, such as twenty-seven or twenty-eight degrees of any sign, that it will not make an aspect to another planet before it changes signs. In the case of the Moon, this can occur for a few hours every other day and, depending on what degrees other planets are traversing, even when it is at an earlier degree of any sign. It would be difficult for an average person to know just when this might occur. However, a personal experience taught me not to ignore such an aspect. Fortunately, I have a computer program that shows the position of the planets in the heavens at any given moment of any day. I can pop the program onto the screen, even while I am writing, to see what the aspects might be at that specific time. This enables me to conduct a kind of research that makes interpretation of charts even more precise.

One morning in late March I decided to run an errand before I began the day's writing. Although I noted that the Moon was void of course, I ignored the warning and got into my car. The weather was mild and, as I needed only a light sweater, it didn't occur to me that the lovely, hilly road I was taking might be slippery. But there had been a heavy morning dew and the dirt road had frozen. As I hit a patch of frozen mud, my brakes locked, and the car careened wildly down the wooded, winding road like I was on a toboggan course. I had no choice but to remove my foot from the brake and attempt to steer the speeding car. I prayed I could stay on the road and not hit a tree. Finally the car bounced off an embankment on the side of the hill and slowed down. Although I was quite scared, I wasn't hurt. The barely damaged car body concealed the fact that the frame was bent and eventually the repairs were extensive and costly. If the void of course Moon aspect had occurred simultaneously with another drastic aspect in my own chart, I might easily have gone over the side of the hill and been seriously injured. Extensive research on the time that accidents occur might reveal some astounding facts, including that of a void of course Moon. That particular aspect is certainly worth checking out before planning an operation, as an example. I can assure you, I'm more careful about planning activities during the time when the Moon is void of course. The void of course Moon is a time for internal spiritual work, not a time for running errands or for an operation.

DIAGNOSTIC FACTORS TO CONSIDER

There are many factors and aspects to consider when looking at an astrological chart, especially if something critical pertaining to health is to be diagnosed. It is too simplistic to look at the Moon's phases, or the planet that rules a specific part of the body, or the planet that rules the house of health, for instance, to give a sophisticated diagnosis about particular health hazards that might exist. But a logical place to begin is with the ancient rulerships of the astrological signs that are associated with body parts and the planets that describe body functions, as well as the position and transits of Chiron, the Virgo asteroid that relates to health and healing. (See p. 293.)

HEALTH INDICATORS

Two of the major indicators of health in an astrological chart are the ascendant and the sixth house of health. The ascendant, determined by the time of birth, describes the birth process, the quality of the moment of the first intake of breath, and the life script of the individual. It describes the physical constitution, the appearance, and basic survival issues, whereas the sixth house of health indicates the quality of health and the specific characteristics of the genetic makeup of an individual. Aspects in a chart can give us further information. Aspects are the mathematical relationships between the various planets in an individual's chart. These relationships, or angles, describe many psychological predispositions in a person's life and can indicate how they might be reflected in the physical constitution. Elements in a horoscope are particularly significant as a diagnostic tool, for they describe whether an individual makeup is more earthy (physically strong), fiery (excitable and dynamic), airy (intellectual), or watery (emotional). A look at the sixth harmonics* of a person's system paints a picture of the health of the subtle body.

There are almost as many systems of astrology as there are astrologers, but there are some fundamentals upon which all astrologers agree. After some basics have been learned, every astrologer begins to devise his or her own system. Each astrologer's interpretation of any one chart will vary slightly, depending on individual experiences. Competent astrologers say the same things, but in different ways and with different words. The analysis of an

---

* Harmonics is a system devised by English astrologer John Addey that "folds" a chart over on itself a certain number of times to reveal deeper information. Each number represents an age in the life of an individual, one of the twelve houses, or a philosophical question. Adolf Hitler's chart gives a perfect example of the information that can be revealed through harmonics. On the surface, his chart is all Venus, with the Sun in Taurus and Libra rising. That explains his love of music and art, but would also tend to indicate a strong social consciousness. When examining his seventh harmonic, the number representing the spiritual or soul motivation, aspects are revealed that confirm and underscore the horror of his warped actions in his concept of social reform.

astrological chart is only as inspired as the experiences of the astrologer himself.

Astrology is a prime example of how empirical data works. The astrologer observes conditions, personalities, and events, and works backward to find patterns that occurred in the past that will give him clues to the conditions of the present. He considers many factors, such as the placement of planets and the mathematical relationships between one planet and another, as well as how the current movement of planets modifies and describes inherent tendencies. He correlates all of his research and develops a system for interpretation. He considers the overall diagrammatic structure to determine focal points or stress points, much as an architect would study the blueprint of a building to locate any structural faults. He may utilize several astrological systems to gain more insight about conditions in the life of an individual at a particular moment in time, like a lab technician looks at blood or tissue samples through a microscope to get a picture of current conditions in the human body.

There are many planetary indicators that can explain to an astrologer why a particular event or situation should occur. But for medical astrology to gain acceptance and have validity, it is necessary to start at the very beginning. In order to correctly synthesize the many factors involved in diagnostic astrology, serious research programs must be conducted to obtain valid statistical data. If such programs were conducted, it would be easy to use an astrological chart for diagnosis, as the underlying health factors could easily be detected. Much time could be saved and many errors in treatment of disease could be avoided. Since such major research programs are not widespread, it is necessary and possible for each person to learn some very basic astrological facts so that he could detect the possibility of weakness in his own system. So informed, an individual would be able to take precautions that could prevent major problems.

During a lecture at a health conference, I described the effect that difficult aspects to Uranus might have on the body. I related that planet to breath and to a need for a great deal of space, among other things. A participant volunteered confirmation of what I was saying by telling of an experience that had occurred that very morning. A friend of hers had also expected to attend my lecture, but when she discovered that the room was located at the top of the building, she was unable to participate. With Saturn conjunct Uranus in her chart, she suffered from severe claustrophobia and was unable to breathe in elevators. Although the aspect confirmed her symptoms, that knowledge could not help the lady in question at that late date. If her mother had known of a tendency toward that condition when she was an infant, she might have been able to head off the more severe ramifications that hardened and set in with time. There are ways to correct conditions such as shortage of breath, as an example. One of the most important techniques for the restoration of proper breathing is taught and demonstrated by Carl Stough. Carl Stough Institute has helped to restore the health of even bedridden emphysemics in veterans hospitals by instructing them in rhythmic breathing procedures which help restore the condition of the diaphragm. (See Chapter 5 and Chapter 7, Gemini ruling the sixth house.)

The value of using astrology as a diagnostic tool is that it offers the ability to locate and observe the tendency toward weakness in a particular part of the body and apply antidotes to the conditions before they can manifest as a serious illness. Preventive medicine can be applied more effectively if a person has some clue as to where to focus attention, as well as some understanding of why and when an illness might strike.

As an example, infant mortality and illness could be avoided to a greater degree if doctors were equipped to read the natal horoscope. What might otherwise be overlooked at the time of birth could be noticed and corrected immediately, and positive steps could be taken before the intervening passage of time allowed for an illness or malady to take firm hold in the infant's system. Psychological conditions that result in physical illness could also be prevented if greater knowledge about astrology existed. When a child is born with Capricorn rising, for instance, or with Saturn strongly placed on the ascendant, or in the first house, the psychological indicators describe the soul's resistance to entering the earth plane at all. Parents would be on alert to give this child an extra special welcome and extra reassurance about the love, help, and support he or she will be given. Sometimes, some sense of rejection causes the child to develop an illness, if only to say, "I'm here! Pay attention to me!" This child needs extra reassurance that he or she won't have to be perfect to live up to the expectations of those around him or her, and that he or she won't have to do it all alone. When this aspect is in evidence, a predisposition to tension causes blocks of energy throughout the whole system. A therapeutic technique that helps such an infant involves gently massaging the spine and top of the shoulders, with large amounts of love poured through the fingers. This helps the child relax.

Many doctors resent a patient's interpretation of his own health patterns, but sometimes an individual has a better sense of his own predilection to a weakness in a part of his body than a physician and can sense where illness may manifest itself. An astrological chart gives marvelous confirmation of what one suspects about his own patterns, whether those are health patterns or psychological ones that might turn into health problems.

Astrology is even valuable in selecting and determining the health of a pet. As I shifted my life-style to live in the country, I wanted a puppy to care for and love. But since my work requires concentration and attention to my clients (sometimes with no interruption), my prime requisite was to have a quiet, affable dog. So I set about looking at breeds known to be placid. I found an adorable bunch of newborn long-haired dogs of a specific breed and inquired about the specific time of their whelping. When I set up the charts for the puppies, Saturn was located in the sixth house of health. That was too much of a warning signal to ignore, so I declined taking one of those adorable dogs. I later learned that the particular breed has a natural tendency toward brain disorders, and the illness is very painful and the following death difficult. I later spent time consoling a close friend whose dog of that breed had just died. It was a painful and disabling death, more agonizing for my friend because of the suffering of the animal.

I then looked for a breed that does not shed. I found a wire-haired fox terrier puppy ready to be adopted and set up her chart. This adorable imp has her Sun in Aries, Moon in Leo, and Gemini rising. With no thought to my former guidelines of a gentle and quiet personality, I was snowed under by the enthusiastic greeting from my little angel, Samantha. She kissed, squealed, and squirmed in ecstasy and said, in no uncertain terms, "I've found you again, and this time I won't let you get away." She was only six or seven months and still a small puppy when cold weather started to settle in. Samantha developed a cough as she was exposed to chill air. Gemini rising rules the pairs in the body (lungs, arms, legs, ears, eyes, etc.) and in her case, the lungs were her weak area. It was never a major problem, however, as I took great precautions to cover her chest with a warm sweater and not to allow her to breathe in very cold air for extended periods of time. She also began to run a slight fever when her ears were exposed to the cold. (Aries rules the head and Mars describes fevers.) I can cure Samantha's fever by using some of the healing techniques described later on. Her ears return to a healthy pale pink from a threatening red, and her nose becomes frosty cold again. If I were not aware of her health tendencies, I'm sure I would already have spent a lot of time at the veterinarian's office with many shots to pull down her fevers and cure her coughs.

If nothing else, an astrological chart acts as a road map, describing the potential troubled areas in life. An astrological chart can pinpoint the area where a malady begins. It can support and confirm what a person senses or observes about his own physical system. Since it is human nature to project fault onto someone else, it is all too frequent an occurrence to call a person a hypochondriac, when one may not know what to do about a situation. It has been my observation that this projection is common among many medical practitioners when they are not on safe ground in diagnosis or treatment of a stubborn symptom.

But with the emergence of a trend toward holistic medicine, it may not be long before we see the incorporation of astrology into more traditional methods of diagnosis of the physical system.

• • •
•   •

PART 2

Relationship of Astrology to Body Energy

Planetary and Sign Associations

*E*ach sign of the zodiac (Aries, Taurus, Gemini, etc.) has a ruling planet. Aries is ruled by Mars, Taurus is ruled by Venus, Gemini is ruled by Mercury, and on down the line. Each sign of the zodiac rules a part of the body and also relates to a physical function that is associated with that part of the body. Each planet rules a bodily function. Let's first take a look at the signs and their planetary rulerships.

ARIES—MARS	LIBRA—VENUS
TAURUS—VENUS	SCORPIO—PLUTO
GEMINI—MERCURY	SAGITTARIUS—JUPITER
CANCER—MOON	CAPRICORN—SATURN
LEO—SUN	AQUARIUS—URANUS
VIRGO—MERCURY	PISCES—NEPTUNE

For a preliminary diagnosis of health factors, look at your individual astrological chart to determine the sign that rules the ascendant, the sign that appears on the cusp of the sixth house, and the ruler of that house. (See table in Appendix to determine the ascendant or rising sign.) The ascendant describes physical appearance, as well as body types. It also describes health factors that might be associated with the birth process or with childhood. The sixth house indicates genetic health factors that are part of your physical makeup. After that, look at the placement of planets in your individual chart to determine which planets reside in either the first or sixth house.

Next, look at the table of astrological signs and the parts of the body they rule. Then check the planets that lie in the first and sixth houses of your chart to see what bodily functions they relate to. (If you do not have a copy of your astrological chart, see Appendix for information on ordering one.) And finally, it is important to correlate the planets in the first and sixth houses to the signs in which they are located in the individual chart. The sign placement of each planet indicates an additional color or facet that brings forth more comprehension of health factors.

SIGNS THAT RULE PARTS OF THE BODY

ARIES—	THE HEAD	LIBRA—	PANCREAS, SPLEEN
TAURUS—	LOWER JAW, THROAT, THYROID GLAND	SCORPIO—	REPRODUCTIVE ORGANS
GEMINI—	ARMS, LUNGS, BODY'S PAIRS	SAGITTARIUS—	HIPS, KIDNEYS, LIVER, SCIATIC NERVE, UPPER LEGS
CANCER—	ABDOMINAL CAVITY, STOMACH	CAPRICORN—	SKELETAL STRUCTURE, BONES, KNEES
LEO—	HEART	AQUARIUS—	NERVOUS SYSTEM, LOWER LEGS
VIRGO—	INTESTINES, GALL BLADDER	PISCES—	FEET, LYMPH GLANDS, IMMUNE SYSTEM

PLANETS THAT GOVERN BODILY FUNCTIONS

SUN—   CIRCULATION, FLOW OF VITAL ENERGY THROUGHOUT SYSTEM, INDICATOR OF GENERAL VITALITY AND ABILITY TO RECUPERATE

MOON—   DIGESTIVE PROCESSES, FLUIDS IN SYSTEM (TEARS, SECRETIONS), RETENTION OF WATER IN CELLS

MERCURY—TWO HALVES OF BRAIN, AUTONOMIC FUNCTIONS OF BODY (INCLUDING LUNG FUNCTION), INTESTINAL ACTIVITY

VENUS— SECRETION OF INSULIN, ASSIMILATION OF SUGAR OR CARBOHYDRATES, DIGESTIVE PROCESS RELATED TO SALIVA, MECHANISM OF SWALLOWING, TASTE, TOUCH, SMELL

MARS— BLOOD (RED BLOOD CELLS IN PARTICULAR), PRODUCTION OF ADRENALINE, SEXUAL ACTIVITY

JUPITER— GROWTH, KIDNEY AND LIVER FUNCTION, ASSIMILATION OF FATS, PROCESS OF DETOXIFICATION, ELIMINATION OF POISONS

SATURN— BONY STRUCTURE AND STRENGTH OF BONES, ASSIMILATION OF CALCIUM AND MINERALS, TEETH

URANUS— NERVOUS SYSTEM, DIAPHRAGMATIC FUNCTION, ASSIMILATION OF OXYGEN, ALLERGIC REACTIONS, ASTHMA, BRONCHITIS

NEPTUNE— LYMPHATIC SYSTEM, DUCTLESS GLANDS, PROBLEMS WITH FEET

PLUTO— REGENERATION, ENDOCRINE ACTIVITY, REPRODUCTIVE SYSTEM

Now that you have looked at your own individual horoscope to determine the sign placement of the specific planets that relate to health, it is necessary to look at the aspects those planets make to other planets in your individual chart. Since a symbiotic connection is made with planets that are in aspect to each other, it is important to look at all those other planets and their location in a particular sign to determine the related areas of stress in the body.

To illustrate that point, suppose Mars is positioned in the first house of your chart, and it is placed in its own sign of Aries, which rules your ascendant. Since Mars is the ruling planet of Aries, and Mars describes conditions that might exist in the head, a badly aspected Mars in an individual chart can indicate a predisposition to headaches and sinus problems. This will be especially true if you do not get enough exercise or have a great degree of frustration and delays in your life.

To further complicate matters, however, remember that each planet also describes another bodily function, or organic function. Mars rules the blood, for instance. Now, Mars may be square to

Uranus in your chart. If that is the case, since Uranus rules the nervous system, you might have a predisposition to accidents, especially as a result of nerves and impulsive action. Injuries that occur might be to the head and could produce severe bleeding, as an example, or in an extreme case, accidental blows to the head could produce neurological damage. In such a case, it would be very important to avoid taking risks that could lead to accidents.

As you go through each chapter of this book, you can begin to correlate the variety of health factors that are indicated in your astrological chart and areas that might be problematic in your life, and find ways to provide an antidote or a therapy which could resolve the problem that appears as a possibility.

Opposite signs reflect each other. Just as opposites attract in relationships (each person finding qualities in another person that express an opposite viewpoint), opposite signs of the zodiac reflect each other in connection with health matters. Opposite qualities in human relationships are always just the two sides of the same coin (male and female, for example), but each person can learn from the other so that those opposite qualities can be brought into balance, working in harmony with each other. So it is with health matters. The factor expressed in the opposite sign may be the very characteristic necessary to bring health into better balance within oneself.

For instance, Mars, ruler of Aries, relates to blood in the body and describes production of adrenaline. Venus, ruler of Libra (the sign opposite Aries), governs the pancreas, which produces insulin necessary to regulate the sugar levels in the blood. (Venus also relates to sugar.) If the blood sugar is out of balance, there is a lack of balance in energy levels. Hypoglycemia can be one manifestation of sugar imbalance and is related to malfunction of the adrenal gland. So these two signs and their ruling planets work together to describe the regulation of energy in the physical system. If Mars is in difficult aspect in the individual chart, it is necessary to look at the aspects to the opposite quality, Venus, to determine if sugar could cause a physical problem. Aries relates to matters connected to the head and to soul and spiritual levels of consciousness. Libra relates to matters connected to the part of the body below the diaphragm and to the physical level of consciousness. Aries describes action and Libra is the sign of moderation.

Taurus-Scorpio polarities relate to regulation and reproduction. Taurus rules the thyroid gland, which regulates the metabolism, and Scorpio rules the ovaries or gonads, which enable us to reproduce. If the production of thyroid is out of balance, it is difficult for pregnancy to take place. The throat allows sustenance to pass into the individual system, keeping the *present* life sustained, and the ovaries or gonads provide the materials necessary to bring about a *new* life. Taurus relates to matters in the head (lower jaw) and spiritual level of consciousness. Scorpio relates to organs located below the diaphragm and to physical level of consciousness (reproduction).

The Gemini-Sagittarius polarities relate to the two arms (Gemini) and two hips and upper legs (Sagittarius). The interaction of both arms and legs stimulates energy to the brain. (See Mercury, p. 106.) Gemini rules the lungs, which release waste (carbon dioxide) through the external openings of the nose and the mouth. Sagittarius rules the kidneys, which release waste through lower openings. Gemini rules organs located in the upper body, describing consciousness on a soul or spiritual level, and Sagittarius rules organs located in the lower body, describing risk taking or physical activity.

Cancer is paired with Capricorn. Cancer relates to the stomach and to the mothering parts of the body—breasts and womb—and to body cavities, whereas Capricorn relates to the bony structures or skeleton, and the fathering function of protection. The gall bladder is placed and functions in close relationship to the stomach (Cancer). One major acupuncture point of the gall bladder meridian is located in the knees (Capricorn). Cancer relates to organs of the body below the diaphragm, or risk taking, and Capricorn relates to the legs, also the practical, physical level of existence.

Leo-Aquarius polarities relate to the heart and nervous system. The heart pumps blood, sending oxygen and energy throughout the body, and the nervous system allows electrical currents to flow throughout the body, keeping the body energized on the spiritual level (Aquarius). (See Part IV—Relationship of Astrology to Spiritual Health.) The flow of blood throughout the body and the flow of energy impulses through the nervous system are two of the most necessary functions for life. The heart is the central organ of the upper body and is related to soul consciousness (Leo). The nervous system relates to spiritual consciousness. Both rule upper body functions.

The Virgo-Pisces pair of opposites describes elimination. Virgo rules the intestinal tract and Pisces rules the glandular and lymph system in general. Pisces also rules the immune system. The immune system is dependent on wastes being eliminated from the body. Virgo rules organs located below the diaphragm and which are physical in nature. Although Pisces rules the feet, and the feet contain acupuncture points that relate to every single part of the body, Pisces is connected to the spiritual level.

To determine whether you are more inclined toward development of soul consciousness or more inclined toward development of the physical level of consciousness and risk taking, count the number of planets in your own astrological chart that fall into each category.

ABOVE-THE-BELT ACTIVITY
(SOUL LEVEL OF CONSCIOUSNESS)

Aries
Taurus
Gemini
Leo
Aquarius
Pisces

BELOW-THE-BELT ACTIVITY
(RISK-TAKING FACTORS)

Libra
Scorpio
Sagittarius
Cancer
Capricorn
Virgo

Planets That Rule Bodily Functions

THE SUN

The sun is the planet that rules the sign of Leo. Since Leo rules the heart, the prime bodily function connected to the Sun relates to the pumping of the heart and concerns the distribution of the life force, or vitality and energy, throughout the system. Since the qualities of energy associated with the sign of Leo are strength, dominance, leadership, and regality, the placement of the Sun in an individual chart describes the specific area in the life of an individual that will bring him the greatest sense of pride and related vitality; or with difficult aspects to the Sun, the areas where the ego may be wounded and the energetic life force depleted as a result of tension in the area around the heart.

The Lion is the symbol of Leo, and the characteristics that are associated with that animal also describe characteristics of that sign. For instance, a group of lions is called a pride. A male lion is known to defend his mate and cubs against all predators and to maintain a dominant position where his territory is concerned. He is called the king of the beasts. People born under the sign of Leo have a tremendous sense of pride and will defend their family to the bitter end. They exhibit strong leadership and executive abilities.

The heart is the central organ of the body. Located in the cavity above the diaphragm, it is the central organ relating to the qualities of soul consciousness. (See Chapter 25—Meditation.) When the natural Leo position of authority is denied or repressed, and when there is a lack of acknowledgment, either of his contribution or of his natural generosity, the Leo suffers a blow to his pride. His heart constricts and the vibrant flow of abundant vigor and vitality throughout his system is blocked. It is essential for someone of this sign to have abundance of recognition, ego strokes, and positive reinforcement. Illness can come about as a result of a lack of acknowledgment in his life. He must be valued in order to feel the full force of a potential that leads to great accomplishment. If the Sun is not well aspected, instead of assuming a natural role of authority, he may look for permission from other people to do things and perform tasks that normally would come easily to him. The flow of energy through the heart relates to the flow of acknowledgment (energy) from others. The generosity of his nature may not be obvious on the surface, but if he feels valued, his heart swells and he responds graciously and magnanimously. More importantly, he remains healthy and in balance. If he does not feel valued or if he is not given the acknowledgment he feels he deserves, his heart constricts.

The Sun in the heavens is the body around which everything celestial revolves. If we think of the human system as a microcosm of the heavenly macrocosm, the heart is the organ around which all bodily functions must revolve. The proper functioning of the heart muscle is the single most important factor in the health of an individual, for life ceases when the heart stops pumping blood through the body.

The Sun, wherever it might be placed in the individual's chart, describes the inner self as related to soul energy. In the spiritual sense, mankind is part of the whole. We are all one on the highest conceptual level. In a cosmic sense, there is no ego and no division, but a blending. When man enters the earth plane, however, he must necessarily create a division between himself and all other spiritual forms. He begins to focus attention on the self and on the development of everything that signifies self-expression. It is only through the process of individualization that he can find the specific qualities of his energy system that must be balanced and harmonized. He finds experiences and survival strategies that will flame his fire and augment the quality of his heart. After his inner flame burns so brightly that nothing could diminish its intensity and vibrancy flows throughout his individualized energy system, he then begins the process of the transmutation of ego. He develops a stronger sense of self, never losing his own identification, but relating to the oneness of all on a higher level. At that point, his task is to gather experiences that will enrich the cosmic whole when his life's journey is over.

The development of a dynamic sense of self-worth can frequently be misunderstood and falsely labeled as ego. Yet deliberate steps to develop greater comprehension of one's inner nature are positive steps toward unification and enrichment. Ultimately the process leads to a soul connection. All constructive activities related to "above-the-belt" situations in life imply transformation. Above-the-belt experiences include development of such qualities as love, compassion, and thoughtfulness. Experiences related to developing the true quality of love of self, the self that is part of the whole and therefore of all mankind, requires an opening of the heart. That is clearly an above-the-belt activity and is the first step in stabilization of health.

When individual man identifies only with his mistakes, developing guilt and shrinking in his value of himself, he does irreparable harm to his physical energy and his soul development. Rather than expanding and bestowing vital energy like the Sun, which hastens his return to the cosmic level of existence, he continues to trap himself on the wheel of karma. Devaluation of self is like an anchor that holds the soul fast on the foreign shores of life. The gravitational pull and continued incarnation cause him to lose contact with his soul, shutting himself off from true vitality. He then wanders in darkness until he so yearns for what he has lost that he necessarily begins the painful uphill journey home again. In a practical sense, the most important asset he can develop on the road to transformation is the sense of his own worth. The heart, the seat of his vitality, must pump vibrantly again, giving him the energy to pursue the path of return. Ultimately, love is the quality of energy streaming forth from the heart center, leading him to a connection with all other souls and forms of life and eventual cosmic joy. With the heart fully open and receptive to love energy, he finds himself and the path home. The closing off of love feelings closes the connection to his greatest source of vitality.

In times of emergency, the heart pumps blood faster than usual, sending out increased energy and strength through the blood-stream to the entire system. An open and relaxed heart muscle functions efficiently and is best equipped to handle the tasks at hand. In times of pain and stress, however, the heart center is often the area that constricts as a person hangs on in the effort to remain strong. During regression sessions, when a traumatic or painful moment is revealed, I suggest that the person look inside his body to see where the memory of that pain might be stored. Many people become conscious of a predisposition to place stress on the heart. This often begins very early in life. With repeated blows to the ego and sense of pride, and bruises that may come with lack of recognition, a person begins a lifelong process of clamping down the heart center. When beauty and love are obstructed in life, the heart forgets how to swell with joy. The individual may set in motion a weakness of the heart muscle or an actual heart attack that can manifest at some future point in his life.

Since the heart muscle is much too fragile to bear the brunt of that kind of stress, it is wise to become aware of any tendency to constrict that part of the body. There are muscles of greater size and strength that can bear the brunt of traumatic moments more efficiently. Therefore, for everyone, the heart is the first organ to check when searching for the unconscious focus of stress in life. That means becoming aware of where tension might develop in the body when in a stressful situation. This will be particularly true for individuals with the Sun ruling the ascendant or placed in the first house, as well as ruling or placed in the sixth house of health. That indicates a susceptibility to block energy in the heart center under pressure. Since pride goeth before a fall, the placement of the Sun in an astrological chart can describe specific areas of life where wounded pride may cause constriction of energy and vitality, especially when a blow to the ego is delivered.

THE MOON

The Moon rules the sign of Cancer. Cancer is the sign that governs the stomach, and the bodily function associated with the Moon is that of digestion and assimilation of food. The Moon also describes the flow of liquids in the body, all liquid secretions, and fluid wastes. (Cancer is one of the four water signs.) On a psychological level, the Moon indicates emotional reactions, both productive and nonproductive. The Moon relates indirectly to the endocrine system, but especially to the hypothalamus. That gland, part of the endocrine system, is the seat of emotions in the brain. The thyroid, another gland of the endocrine system, governs proper metabolism and assimilation of food. It is obvious that excess intake of food is closely related to emotional stress. If one can stimulate the endocrine system, it is possible to avoid overreaction or emotional compulsions that are food related.

When an individual is hurt and reacts emotionally, he frequently allows that reaction to reside squarely in the stomach area. The stomach is connected to solar plexus activity. The solar plexus is the center that connects the emotional body to the physical vehicle. Since many people are working on integrating these two bodies, many people experience stomach problems. When stomach disorders occur, it is important to check on the emotional stress level of the moment, especially to see if feelings of abandonment are in evidence. Stress directed into the area of the stomach causes discomforts that escalate from mere indigestion or gas to more serious stomach problems. Although the stomach may not be as critically sensitive as the heart, stomach problems can cause more discomfort over long periods of time and eventually bring about disease that may spread to other parts of the body. As the heart is the central organ in the upper torso, the stomach is the central one in the lower torso.

Activities connected to situations "below-the-belt" are those that imply risk. Emotional risks are the ones most likely to backfire and cause a blow to the solar plexus. Emotional reactions are not logical. A person may not be able to anticipate the kind of blows he may receive on a gut level, but if he becomes aware of the possibility that a risk exists, he may be able to transfer the control of his reactions onto a mental level. Energy transferred into the head, away from the lower body, no longer relates to a risk situation. So the mind is the antidote for the emotions.

If a person shuts down and blocks emotional response, he closes off the solar plexus area. Then he shuts down the general flow of etheric vitality coming through that chakra. Working only on a level of logic can polarize an individual on the mental level and into above-the-belt activity. However, a purely emotional reaction polarizes the person onto the astral level, working only with below-the-belt activity. For the perfect flow of energy throughout the system, a balance needs to be maintained between mind and feeling. Mood disorders benefit from mental activity and the conscious development of objectivity, whereas too much analysis can benefit from development of a greater degree of compassion. Writing about things that are upsetting can bring them into focus, using both mind and feeling. In that way one can conquer any overreaction.

The German composer Robert Schumann was afflicted with severe mood swings, exhibiting manic-depressive behavior. When his mood swings were black, he was suicidal and was unable to compose. Since the Moon describes the mothering qualities inherent within a person (his own quality of compassion), as well as how he was nurtured, a look at Schumann's mother gives some insight into his particular situation, for she was afflicted with severe depression. He was probably very disillusioned with his mother. She may have been a disillusioned lady herself. Some scientists believe that severe mood swings have a biological or chemical link to the mother herself. The Moon placement in Schumann's chart is in the sign of Virgo and automatically describes an objective quality to his emotional reaction, but it is in difficult aspect to his Neptune (manic) and Saturn (depressed). The conjunction of Neptune and Saturn in a chart describe a "What's the use?" outlook. Tied into the Moon, it describes the highs and lows of a manic-depressive emotional nature quite accurately. Schumann was a Gemini Sun sign and Virgo Moon sign. An abundance of mental energy, described by his Sun and Moon signs, probably helped pull him through the manic crises, but the depressive side of his mood swings were not helped by shutting down emotionally. As long as he was writing music, his moods were in check, and his music was brilliant.

It has been discovered through statistical research that the Moon is strong in the astrological charts of writers. When someone with extreme sensitivity can write about his feelings, he begins to resolve them. He discovers that he may not be alone in the experience of specific painful events. As an example, a sense of abandonment or of having been orphaned is strong in the Cancerian makeup. When the person with Cancer or the Moon in strong placement in the chart recognizes other people with similar experiences, he begins to develop compassion, a higher form of emotion. He stops rescuing people and begins to encourage them on their path. His own experiences may be valuable to others, but only if he has found solutions for his suffering through objective self-examination.

Quite often it is very constructive for a sensitive, vulnerable person to participate in activity where he can attempt to heal the sufferings of others. He may be able to feed people by preparing food for them or by dealing with food. He may choose to nurture them in a different way. Cancer is a feminine sign, but now that we are more enlightened, both men and women are encouraged to express vulnerability and emotion. In former times, a greater preponderance of men who had Cancer strong in their astrological charts may have suffered from stomach disorders and ulcers because they were told it wasn't manly to show feelings and emotions.

The stomach is located in close proximity to the spleen. Esoterically, the spleen is the organ connecting spiritual and etheric energy to the physical system. When emotional reactions are out of control, positive energetic links to spiritual vitality are broken. Depression, suicide, and emotionally compulsive behavior cannot exist in the serene and vibrant light of spiritual energy. Ideally, the emotional level must be as calm as a sparkling lake in order to reflect the beauty of life and nature. Anything that separates man from his fellow man is a true sin (also the Spanish word for without), but it is the separation of man from his spiritual nature that causes the most pain. Compassion for ourselves ultimately leads to compassion for our fellow man. Once this is achieved we can operate on the higher level of soul consciousness.

MERCURY

Since there are twelve signs of the zodiac and at this point in time only ten planets to consider (excepting Earth and including the lights, Sun and Moon), Mercury and Venus are each assigned rulership of two signs. Mercury is the ruler of both Gemini and Virgo. Gemini is a dual sign and therefore describes the pairs in the body, such as the two arms, the two halves of the body, the pair of lungs, the two sides of the brain, two eyes, and two ears. Mercury rules the functions of the body that relate to thinking processes. Therefore, it describes communications, decisions, writing, speech, thought, and all matters concerning the mind.

Gemini is an air sign and Virgo an earth sign. The quality of Mercury's expression is very different in these two associations. Mercury is always descriptive of left-brain energy and thought processes, but Virgo, the earth sign, rules the intestinal tract. It may seem farfetched and very diverse for Mercury to describe energy associated with parts of the body having such different functions, but a more careful look brings some logic to the association.

Movement of the pairs of limbs stimulates brainwave development early in life. It is imperative for a baby to go through his crawling stage before beginning to walk. With this important co-ordination of arm and leg movement, he not only develops the muscles of his limbs, but exercises and develops his brain waves. It has been discovered that if a baby skips the crawling stage, he is more likely to have learning disabilities. Grown-ups can also stimulate mental alertness by simulating the cross crawl, moving alternate arms and legs simultaneously. (See Chapter 17 on Exercise.) If an office staff were encouraged to take a cross crawl break instead of a coffee break every morning and afternoon, productivity and efficiency would speed up dramatically. The energy directed into the brain combats fatigue that comes with long hours of concentration on a job. (See Part V—Types of Therapies.)

If the parts of the body ruled by Mercury are afflicted, it might be important to take a closer look at what is going on with the mind. National Institutes of Health scientists have recently conducted some experiments with compulsive-disorder behavior patterns. They have discovered that this kind of behavior may be indicative of irregular brain wave function rather than psychological disturbance. Their findings seem to indicate scrambled brain waves in some cases, a condition described as having a kind of hiccup in the brain. In other cases, there may be a chemical imbalance, such as a superfluous amount of seratonin in the brain. A person with a disorder in the brain could manifest abnormality in the behavior of his hands, ruled by Mercury, as an example. There have been many cases of individuals who wash their hands compulsively or constantly wring their hands. Conversely, a disorder in the hands may clearly indicate some lack of proper function of the brain waves. My former tendency to switch letters and words in my manuscripts indicated some disruption of proper messages going from my brain to my fingers. I found a type of exercise that would immediately correct that error. It involved crossing one hand over the other, using one leg and one knee, and then putting fingertips together for a few moments! After doing this exercise for about two minutes, my brain sent the proper signals and I could proceed to type with speed and accuracy. (See Chapter 17.) With some research into the effectiveness of this exercise on dyslexic children, this simple method could easily solve many learning problems in schoolrooms.

I asked a friend with Gemini rising if he ever had problems with weakness or fatigue in his arms. He replied that his arms are extremely strong, and he can win an arm wrestling contest with anyone. However, he experienced great weakness of the arms in his dreams. If he dreamed that someone was attacking him, he wouldn't be able to lift his arms. If an attack figures in his dreams, there is a strong indication that he may have some worry or pressure which does not surface in his waking state. Weakness of his arms in the dream state is as meaningful as if they were weak in the waking state.

It is fascinating to observe how the left brain, described by Mercury, speaks through the arms or hands which are ruled by Mercury. The arms play a major role in the technique of muscle testing called kinesiology. Applied kinesiology is based on the fact that there is a direct relationship between specific organs and muscles in the body. (See Chapter 18.) In this process the muscle strength of the arm clearly indicates areas of the body that are out of balance, but it can also indicate whether a substance or object strengthens or weakens the entire system. There is also a method of questioning oneself and getting a response through the thumbs. Kinesiology gives confirmation that an individual has all knowledge within himself, especially as to how his own body relates to emotions, people, and substances. Muscle testing amplifies inner messages so that the individual can hear himself.

The Virgoan quality of mental energy is quite different from the Gemini type. It is no less rapid and interesting, but the thought processes are more organized, sedate, analytical, precise, and critical. Mercury's association with the intestinal tract can be more clearly understood when we realize that toxins collected in that area of the body can be a prime cause of mental fatigue. When constipation occurs, one of the first symptoms is a dull headache. Mental sluggishness is clearly related to intestinal sluggishness. Undigested food particles can easily collect in the pockets of the intestines if one is not conscious about diet, exercise, and internal cleansing. As time goes on, this residue can become crusted and hard, blocking the essential absorption of nutrients into the bloodstream. Laxatives cannot solve the problem and may cause damage to the natural functioning of the intestines.

The Essenes, an ancient Jewish sect, are credited with writing the Dead Sea Scrolls. They were motivated by spiritual principles and purity of body, mind, and soul. They are said to have instigated the practice of colonics, or the cleansing of the intestinal tract by internal washing. Logically, there is no other way to dispense with the collection of poisons that accumulate. It is probable that if an individual were totally conscious of the exact ratio of roughage needed to cleanse this circuitous part of the system, he might never need a colonic, but with many years of eating an impoper diet, the entire system becomes clogged and begins to break down. For example, mental functions can deteriorate noticeably as one grows older. Mental energy is always higher after a series of colonics, and sometimes after even just one. (See Chapter 20.)

Problems with colon activity may be an underlying cause of boredom, incorrect processing of data, inability to make decisions, and lack of facility in expressing oneself. Conversely, awareness of nonproductive mental functioning can be an important clue to the need for intestinal irrigation. But there are other ways of exercising the colon, too. One yoga exercise involves a conscious rippling of the muscles of the stomach covering the intestines, so that the passage of food is facilitated and the collection of debris is minimized. Whatever method one chooses, it is as essential to exercise that part of the body as it is to keep the spine limber.

VENUS

The planet of love, Venus, also rules two signs, Taurus and Libra. As with Mercury, the qualities of the earthy Taurean Venus are different than the qualities of the intellectual and airy Libran Venus. Taurus, an earth sign, rules the lower jaw and throat, and the Taurean Venus describes the bodily function of speech (and song). The Libran Venus rules the sensory organs and relates to the experiences of pleasure. It describes the desire for nature, beauty, and anything artistic and sociable. The Libran Venus also relates to the functions of the body that keep everything in balance. On a psychological level, creation of balance in life requires both duty and beauty. (Venus is the antidote for Saturn, which describes duty.) Venus is also associated with socially just causes, legal matters, and diplomacy.

In considering the Taurean Venus, which rules the throat, it is necessary to consider the surrounding territory of the lower jaw, the larynx, tonsils, mouth, and tongue. On a very simplistic level the Taurus quality is easygoing, but only up to a point. Stubbornness can set in almost arbitrarily, just in case someone thinks the Taurean bull is a pushover. A set jaw is one way to describe stubbornness. Venus also rules the thyroid gland, located at the base of the throat. The throat chakra is the power center. When a condition of hyperthyroidism or hypothyroidism (overactive or underactive productivity of thyroid) exists, power issues may be a major source of concern in life. The balance of power may be distorted. Once again, an interconnection between all the endocrine glands—the pituitary, hypothalamus, thyroid, adrenals, and ovaries or gonads—makes it necessary to consider all the planets that relate to these glands as clues to the source of a specific problem. Without fail, a person with Taurus on the ascendant has a beautiful voice, even if the person is unaware that such a talent exists. The quality of the voice depends not only on voice production, but on the structure of the pharynx (throat area) and the larynx (the voice box). Whether one uses the voice for singing or for speaking, words carried on the breath of the Taurus voice are powerful. With a small amount of training, a glorious voice can emerge and a joyful talent can be developed to bring pleasure to many or, if one so desires, to oneself. A well-trained and mellifluous speaking voice carries more power than one that grates on the ear.

Taurus is the second sign of the zodiac. The second house around the wheel of the horoscope is the house of finance. It is interesting to observe that when a sore throat develops, there is usually some concern about money. There may be obvious reasons why an individual has developed a sore throat, but behind the fact that he or she forgot to wear a scarf may lie another more subtle reason for the ailment. When funds are in short supply, an imbalance in life exists. Chronic worry about money may lead to more serious throat ailments. If worry about cash flow or bills causes the throat to constrict, the energy flowing naturally through that part of the body is cut off. Lack of money usually means giving up little luxuries or pleasure in life. The balance of work and play is distorted.

The Libran Venus has different constitutional strengths and weaknesses. Libra is an air sign. Venus rules the balance of sweetness in the body (sweetness being associated with pleasure). One organ ruled by the Libran Venus is the pancreas. The function of the pancreas is to produce insulin. If that organ is working properly, insulin production is accurate and the blood sugar levels are kept in balance. Venus rules sugar and describes substances that are sweet or that are considered to be delicacies. Sweetbreads (the pancreas organ) are a very special delicacy for anyone with a gourmet palate.

When Venus is strong in key areas of an astrological chart and is in difficult aspect to other planets, a tendency toward hypoglycemia (low blood sugar) or diabetes (faulty insulin production) is indicated. Almost all people who are psychic, or who work in areas where psychic energy is an essential commodity, have a predisposition to hypoglycemia or diabetes. This is particularly true of clairvoyants, mediums, and astrologers. Such problems are also common in people who work as therapists and healers. People in these fields seem to have a particularly heavy draw of energy from the solar plexus area, which includes the pancreas. This is the center ruling the emotional body. If the balance of love and pleasure is disrupted or destroyed, that area of the body may be afflicted. It is very important for healers to allow pleasure and love to be a major part of their lives. These dedicated people give a great deal of their universal love energy and frequently have a lack of that energy on a personal level. With this kind of imbalance, energy is also drained from surrounding organs such as the kidneys, spleen, and gall bladder. It is necessary to consider all of the related planets when a diagnosis is made.

Since Venus describes a need for love, beauty, and pleasure, imbalance also occurs when an individual is self-indulgent. Self-indulgence may manifest in many areas of life, even on a subtle level. When it concerns food it is quite obvious. Craving for rich foods, whether of the gourmet variety or those foods heavy in sugar content, may indicate self-indulgence as a way of compensating for the lack of love in life. The results are much the same. Indulgence in alcohol falls into this category because of its high sugar content. Overindulgence can weaken an already sensitive sugar-producing area. The catch-22 of this particular form of imbalance comes with an insatiable craving for sweet things or alcohol, and an allergic or excessive reaction to the precise foods one craves. To compound the situation, the imbalance of energy throughout the afflicted area causes retarded ability to process rich foods or drink. To add more insult to injury, the Venusian quality of energy is passive, not active. Theoretically, the sugar intake could be burned off in fuel for the body if enough physical activity could be generated. But a Venusian individual is more inclined to sit and look at the view than to take a walk through the woods.

Elizabeth Taylor has talked about this very self-indulgence when discussing her days in Washington, D.C. as the wife of politician John Warner. After his campaign for the Senate was won, Elizabeth's active part of the partnership was over. John was tied to Capitol Hill, with long hours at his desk and the pressure of his responsibilities. His time with Elizabeth was limited. Elizabeth has Venus conjunct Uranus placed in her seventh house of marriage and coruling her Libran ascendant. That indicates the very strong influence of Venus in her chart. Coupled with the Libran Venus's need for companionship is a Uranian restlessness and rebellious trait. Elizabeth felt a distinct lack of companionship and perhaps a lack of love and pleasure in her life, as well as the excitement. Rebelliously, she ate anything that came to mind, by her own admission. She became quite obese, hiding her beauty behind layers of fat. The delicate balance of her physical body was clearly upset.

When Elizabeth's family gathered around her hospital bed to tell her how much they loved her, they were able to convince her to enter the Betty Ford Clinic. After a program of detoxification and therapy, Elizabeth went on a diet and found her way back to a positive source of pleasure in life. Although she has not found another marriage partner to date, resuming her work in a pleasurable and artistic field makes up for the lack of debilitating sugar in her diet. The key for Elizabeth was in taking the active step rather than remaining passive. That step was encouraged and brought about through the essential Venusian quality: love.

M A R S

Mars is the god of war. This symbolism serves to describe Mars's energy as aggressive, innovative, daring, and courageous. Mars describes bodily functions connected to the blood, and particularly to red blood cells. Mars is the planetary ruler of Aries, and Aries rules the cranial cavity or the upper head. Aries is the sign of action and is particularly descriptive of headstrong kinds of action.

This association with action is apt, for Mars rules the adrenal glands, which regulate energy in the system. When an emergency occurs, these glands instantly secrete extra adrenaline into the system, supplying the consequent burst of vitality that helps a person deal with the emergency. Individuals have been known to perform superhuman feats in life-threatening situations; a few years ago, the story of a mother lifting a car off her son, trapped beneath the wheels, made news headlines. It was undoubtedly adrenaline combined with will that enabled her to do so.

Mars energy relates to competitive situations that stimulate adrenal activity and the pumping of the blood through the body. A person must have a great deal of high energy to participate in occupations that require the continual battling down of obstacles. It takes courage, fight, drive, and high adrenaline output to engage in athletic competitions, for instance. The results of such challenges are never entirely logical. Determination to win is often the factor that makes or breaks a champion athlete. If he falls, he must pick himself up, dust himself off, and try again and again. High energy is also a necessary commodity for actors, singers, and entertainers. One of the occupational hazards of such professions is constant rejection. Unless a person can summon the courage to fight back, he will not be able to make a dent in the entertainment business. He must also possess the kind of resiliency that enables him to go on stage and do his job, sick or well. Few actors would think of staying in bed if ill, especially when in the middle of a film or play. The show must go on. Personal tragedies are rarely used as an excuse for missing a performance. This kind of indomitable persistence is instinctual. But the energy for such action must be there to be called on. When there is a strong placement of Mars in the chart, vitality is an innate quality.

The reverse side of the coin of bold action and high energy is frustration. When a person with strong Mars energy is deprived of an opportunity to express himself, he may develop problems with blood, adrenals, or any of the vessels connected to the pumping of blood through the body. Fevers are often a physical manifestation of inner frustration. The blood is figuratively boiling inside. Exercise is a perfect antidote for frustrations and aggravations. Recovered heart attack patients, who are encouraged to exercise to strengthen the heart muscle and to keep blood flowing throughout the system, may unwittingly benefit from the redirection of frustrated energies that comes with vigorous physical activity.

Mars also rules sexuality and sexual functions. The planet Pluto describes the reproductive process, but Mars, as the first planet of the zodiac, is the initiator of that process or of the sexual act itself.

The ancient rulership of Scorpio was Mars, and some systems of astrology still consider it to be so. Scorpio energy is transformational. The sexual energy can be an important tool for the transmutation of physical energy into higher consciousness. Kundalini Yoga is a discipline specifically designed to raise the level of consciousness through arousing the serpent fire, coiled at the base of the spine. These techniques can be dangerous if the arousal of this energy is premature and the centers are not conditioned to hold and carry the level of fire energy that burns through the esoteric vehicle. The energy usually released in orgasm is related to the Kundalini energy. In the Indian discipline of Tantra Yoga, that energy is utilized and transmuted into energy that releases in the top chakra instead of the lower chakra. After experiencing sexual activity in this manner, there is never a desire for orgasm in what is thought of as a traditional way. The method of Tantric Yoga teaches the prolongation of orgasm. In order to reach spiritual heights through this practice, careful preparation and dedication is necessary on the part of both people involved. There is a purity associated with sexual energy at that stage that unites not only the physical bodies of two people, but their spiritual bodies as well.

People with strong sexual desires are said to have "hot blood." Since Mars rules the head, symptoms such as headaches may have a direct relationship to frustrated sexual energy. Migraine headaches, in particular, have been known to occur when regular sexual activity suddenly ceases. Migraine headaches sometimes occur on a periodic basis, indicating an association with a woman's menstrual cycle. Severe headaches can occur if the monthly rhythm is disturbed. The function of the ovaries is connected to the adrenal glands. Menstruation can suddenly terminate when extreme stress occurs in life. The balance between all glands of the endocrine system is delicate, and if one of the glands is malfunctioning, symptoms connected to the other glands can occur.

The written symbol for Mars is also used to identify the male sex and can describe male sexual organs in particular. Venus may more aptly describe feminine sexual organs, but male or female, sexuality can be described by the individual's aspects to Mars. Difficult aspects can relate to and describe sexual malfunction. If sexual activity is missing in the life of an individual with a strong Mars placement in his chart, or with difficult aspects to Mars, he is well advised to find activity that will challenge and direct that all-important energy into a healthy outlet. The important thing is to avoid repressing his drives, ambition, and need for action. Such repression may invite blood disorders, maladies connected to the head, and problems with the basic flow of energy throughout the body. Physical exercise keeps the blood flowing freely, bringing oxygen and health along with it.

One of the most obvious physical manifestations of a person's frustrated energy is a tendency to cut or burn himself. Fevers, headaches, annoyance, eruption of temper, and accidents involving blood are all related to Mars functions. Health conditions related to blood disorders, sexual dysfunction, and head injuries are the body's way of pointing out what is really out of balance with the system. The first step of the antidote is to replace the negative expression of an energy with a positive one.

J U P I T E R

Jupiter is the planet that rules Sagittarius. Sagittarius rules the hips, sciatic nerve, kidneys, and liver. The bodily function of Jupiter is related to purification and elimination of waste. The symbol of Jupiter is the centaur, half-horse and half-man. The lower part of the centaur is strong and earthbound, whereas the upper man is an archer, shooting toward the skies. In relation to health, Jupiterian energy translates into strong hips and upper legs, combined with tremendous optimism about goals in life. The classic Jupiterian enthusiasm seems to go hand in hand with abundant vitality.

If problems occur with hips, upper legs, or the sciatic nerve, this is an indication of a need for detoxification, with the basic problems probably stemming from liver or kidney disorders. When disappointments weigh on a person with a Jupiterian nature, an unhealthy cycle is created. When events conspire to bring about a series of psychological letdowns, enthusiasm wanes, and a compulsion to overindulge in food and drink can set in. With intake of excess food and alcohol, the liver can be overtaxed. At that point energy begins to flag, health begins to deteriorate, and the person with formerly high vitality eats more in order to bring about more energy.

The prime function of the liver is to regulate and control the body chemistry and to purify the bloodstream. It produces enzymes that convert any poisons entering the system into harmless substances that can be easily eliminated through the kidneys. Purification of the system depends on proper elimination. It is essential for the body to rid itself of whatever is not needed for growth and the maintenance of health, especially substances that could be poisonous to the system. This is also true of situations in life that have become poisonous. Ill health occurs with the accumulation of toxins in the system, whether they are physical or psychological. With his eyes always on the horizon, the Jupiterian person may neglect to look behind at the old debris that can clutter up his life, body, or aura.

Jupiter is also associated with expansion and growth, both figuratively and physically. With challenge the key to Jupiterian energy, and disappointment the reverse side of the coin, too much disappointment may result in a predisposition to growths or tumors in the body. Jupiterian energy must always be directed outwardly. Inner frustrations clog the system and may even create a predisposition to or a susceptibility to cancer. Growth of cancer cells can be related to worry on a psychological level, but disappointment may better describe the psychological predisposition to that illness.

In all of the successful unorthodox treatments of cancer, detoxification of the body is the first step. Colonic irrigation is one important way to speed the process of detoxification. (See Chapter 20.) It stands to reason that if the body cannot eliminate poisons, its defense mechanism—the immune system—builds a wall of tissue to prevent the whole body from being contaminated. If the cancerous growth continues, it cannot be contained. The growth then begins to encroach on the healthy cells of the body. When the body is detoxified and the poisons eliminated, there is a better chance of reducing the rate of growth of the cancer cells.

Encouragement and optimism about the chances of recovery seem to be equally necessary in the treatment of cancer. One new patient entering the Hoxsey clinic in Mexico for the treatment of his cancer recalled the sound of laughter pervading the atmosphere. He said, "I couldn't believe I was coming into a place where people had terminal cancer and were threatened with death." Surrounding the patient with a strong support system and lots of encouragement seems to be one of the unmeasurable factors in the Hoxsey clinic's high success rate. Hoxsey himself was known for his ebullient spirit and unquestioning faith in his own cure. He gave all the patients tremendous emotional support and kept them believing they would regain their health.

There are probably many toxins we take into our bodies unwittingly, but even the ones we know about we don't always avoid. In spite of all the medical reports on the debilitating effects of smoking, for instance, many people persist in this dangerous habit. With childlike rebellion, people continue to inhale poisonous fumes that they know are deleterious to delicate lung tissue. Alcohol is produced by fermentation. Yet the same person who enjoys drinking liquor or wine would not dream of consuming food that has spoiled in his refrigerator. And ingesting sugar is the same thing as taking a daily dose of poison.

Nature has an extremely clever way of getting rid of the poisons that human beings deliberately stuff into their systems. The detoxification network in the body, including liver and kidney functions, is a sophisticated mechanism given free of charge at birth. More valuable than a treasure chest filled with gold (Jupiter rules wealth, and gold in particular), this gift is usually taken for granted. It is so important not to overtax the organs related to the elimination process. A deliberate attempt to challenge the efficiency of the elimination system by presenting an overload of toxic substances seems sadistic at the least. If there is so much poison in the system that these organs cannot function efficiently, a breakdown ensues. A visit to a hospital where patients have kidney dysfunction and are on dialysis machines can paint a picture of the value of the purification network.

Since Jupiter describes growth, the opposite side of the Jupiterian coin includes a tendency to become overweight. Sagittarius rules the hips and Jupiter rules fat. One of the first places fat begins to accumulate is on the hips. People with a strong Jupiter or Sagittarian emphasis in their chart may tend to be "hippy" in body type. Major disappointments in life may cause an individual to eat foods that are high in calories or fat, which he might resist during happier times. Overeating, a Jupiterian trait, only inclines one to put on weight. Jupiterian aspects can describe a tendency to eat when happy and excited, as well as a tendency to eat when disappointed.

The liver produces enzymes which regulate the chemical balance of food. Nutritionists are now considering that proper maintenance of weight may to some extent depend on the proper combining of foods to maintain that balance. When the chemical balance is upset, the liver works harder, the kidneys are less able to function efficiently, poisons are not eliminated properly, fat accumulates, and the whole network is further upset. The system becomes sluggish, a person gets tired. When he is tired he eats for energy, usually choosing the wrong foods for his system. It is a vicious cycle that leads to decreased energy and increased fat.

Although most people understand the function of the kidneys, knowledge about the adrenal glands, which sit on top of the kidneys, is less common. The function of the adrenals is to manufacture cortisol and adrenaline. Both cortisol and adrenaline help maintain the proper sugar balance in the blood, but adrenaline kicks in instantly when it is needed. In a crisis situation, the surge of energy is from the adrenals into the body is like pumping gas into an automobile when speed is necessary. The swift reaction of adrenal glands relates to Mars energy, but the abundant production of the adrenaline is related to Jupiter. Jupiter follows Mars in the planetary lineup, and the Mars-ruled adrenal glands sit on top of the Jupiter-ruled kidneys. All bodily functions interact, and all planetary patterns interact. Nothing stops and starts on a dime. When using astrology as a diagnostic tool, it is important to take this fact into account.

SATURN

The planet Saturn marks the last of the earthbound planets and heralds the beginning of the spiritually-oriented, or outer-plane, planets. Saturn is the ruler of Capricorn. Capricorn rules the skeletal structure, the bones in the body, teeth, and fingernails. Saturn rules the parathyroid glands, which regulate the metabolism of minerals necessary for strong bones. Saturn describes all functions of the bones and bone marrow. From a higher perspective, the most important function described by Saturn is that of providing form, structure, and limits. When man enters the earth plane, he must build a vehicle to protect the fragile soul and spirit. The skeleton is the vehicle for the inborn spirit of man.

Saturn also rules the knees. The intricate hinge mechanism of the knees provides support for the spine, as it allows for the shifting of balance of the whole physical structure. Therefore, when the knees are afflicted, there is an indication that part of the problem may be connected with the balance of the skeletal structure. In an emergency, or if health is suddenly impaired, people often feel weak in the knees, unable to support themselves. (See Chapter 18—Kinesiology.) Chronic weakness in the knees may indicate a problem related to the gall bladder, since in the system of acupuncture, an important gall bladder point is located at the knees. (See Chapter 19.) The gall bladder produces bile, which is necessary for digestion. The relationship between the pair of opposites is obvious here. Cancer, the sign opposite Capricorn, rules the digestive system. When the gall bladder is afflicted, gall stones can develop. Saturn rules those stones. Arthritis is another disease described by Saturn. Arthritis becomes especially painful when calcium deposits accumulate in the joints or between the bony parts of the body. Saturn rules any area that absorbs calcium in the body. A person with difficult Saturn aspects in his chart may also have a calcium deficiency, which is easily recognized by brittleness of those body parts.

The Saturn guardianship of the system focuses on two extremely important areas of protection: the ribs and the spinal column. Ribs protect the lungs, which expand to allow for breathing. Breath carries oxygen to purify the bloodstream, but more than that, the breath of life carries spiritual energy throughout the system. The spinal column protects the nervous system, which carries messages from the brain to the body. Uranus is the planet that rules the nervous system and describes spiritual essence. It falls to Saturn to protect the spiritual energy, enclosing it in the physical structure. The all-important line of demarcation between Saturn, the earthbound planet, and Uranus, the first of the spiritual octave, can be seen in the interaction of rib cage, diaphragm (Saturn) and lungs

(Uranus), as well as the relationship between the spinal column (Saturn) and nervous system (Uranus).

The reverse side of the wonderful guardianship of Saturn is a predisposition to rigidity. When Saturn describes conditions of health, maintenance of flexibility is key to well-being. Saturn describes a tendency to shut down when too much physical or emotional pressure is brought to bear. Rigidity restricts the flow of energy throughout the body. Just as the knees must bend and give so that a person can walk over rough ground, the whole system must remain flexible to deal with the rough terrain of the earth plane and its tests. Stretching exercises are important for prevention of rigidity in the body. (See Chapter 17.)

The rib cage is extremely flexible due to the brilliant design of bone and muscle, which allows for expansion of the lungs with the intake of air. The dividing line in the body between the upper torso and the lower torso is the diaphragm, also ruled by Uranus. The diaphragm provides the boundary at the bottom of the lungs, separating them from the abdominal cavity. It is connected to the spine at only one strategic point, which coincides with the lung meridian in the back. The rest of the diaphragm is connected to the rib cage by fibrous tissue. Lack of understanding about the function of the diaphragm has resulted in the common conception that lung disorders such as emphysema render the victim totally helpless. And it's true that to date, medical science has no remedy for this malady except rest and inhalation of oxygen.

Fortunately, a dedicated healer named Carl Stough, nicknamed "Dr. Breath" by the Yale University track team, has made incredible strides with desperately ill victims of emphysema. Carl was engaged to work with patients in the advanced stages of emphysema at the West Haven Veterans Hospital in West Haven, Connecticut, and was successful in getting many bedridden patients out of the hospital and back into the mainstream of life. He was subsequently hired by the United States Olympic Committee as a respiratory consultant, and then went on to work with the Yale University track team. At the Carl Stough Institute, Carl works with many private patients who exhibit a variety of respiratory problems, including those that result from breathing toxic New York City air. First comes an examination of the patient to determine the irregularities in the breathing mechanism and then begins the process of correcting those faults through instruction in co-ordinated breathing. When breathing is coordinated, the dia-phragm rises into the lung cavity, massaging the heart and other organs along the way.

Most people begin to hold their breath unconsciously at a very early age, even infancy, disturbing the natural breathing pattern. Irregular breathing begins to push the diaphragm and the bony structure of the rib cage out of place, compounding the problem by shoving the surrounding organs out of their natural positions. Carl has observed that when breathing disorders are severe, the rib cage protrudes unnaturally. Conversely, proper breathing al-lows the rib cage to fall into its natural position, allowing the breath to pass in and out of the lungs. When Carl's patients master his coordinated breathing techniques, many body aches and pains disappear, as do maladies associated with surrounding organs. His patients immediately feel a burst of new energy when extra oxygen enters the system and reaches the brain, often for the first time in their adult experience. The improvement of general health is a surprise bonus when the movement of the rib cage is freed. Carl has written a book entitled *Dr. Breath: The Story of Breathing Co-ordination*, and is in the process of writing a second volume to educate people about the taken-for-granted process of breathing.

In 1987, I went to Carl Stough for the required five sessions. It takes exactly that many visits to learn the system of proper breath-ing; sessions beyond the first five are for the purpose of reinforce-ment. I have been a student of voice since I was sixteen years old, and one of my unrealized ambitions has been to be an opera singer. Even though I was offered my first opera role as Susanna in *The Marriage of Figaro* in the early seventies, I refused, fearing I lacked sufficient breath control and support. I went to Carl in the hope that I could finally increase the amount of oxygen I can take into my system for singing, as I still study voice whenever I have time. My reaction to the sensation of extra oxygen reaching my brain for the first time in my life was truly a heady one. The color in my face changed to a rosy glow as a result of the new energy in my head, and the "high" from my own oxygenated breath was indescribable. A side benefit was proper voice production. Every-one has a natural singing voice. The problem in producing it comes when the column of breath cannot reach the larynx in order to project the sound into the natural resonating chambers in the head. After that first session with Carl, my comment was, "How is it that I have spent thousands of hours and thousands of dollars on voice lessons, and after one session with you, my voice is in the perfect place with no effort?"

Early traumas, causing a person to shut off the breathing mechanism, describe one way ill health begins on a psychological level and then manifests in the body. Saturn describes the rigidity apparent when an individual holds on to some part of the body psychologically or physically. Since this process usually begins very early in life, the person may be unaware of clamping down. The placement of Saturn in the astrological chart, and the aspects it makes to other planets, indicate any blocks in the flow of energy when there is severe restriction of any of the bony parts of the body. One obvious kind of clamping down is when an individual clenches or grinds his teeth. This can distort the hinges of the jaw. If the clenching is extreme and the bite is disturbed, the hinges of the jaw begin to wear down and the result is a malady called T.M.J. (temporomandibular joint dysfunction). One of the symptoms of T.M.J. is a clicking sound of the jaw when chewing. This syndrome is extremely painful and can cause related problems within the joint itself, such as fractures, arthritis, tumors, bone spurs, and arkylosis (bony fusions). Outside of the joint, T.M.J. may cause or promote dental pain, sinusitis, muscle spasms, and inflammation of blood vessels and muscles. The less obvious side effects may concern organs in the body that have shifted position as a result of the shift of balance in the skeleton. This shifting can put stress on organs and tissues that are too delicate to withstand unneeded pressure.

T.M.J. and its range of related symptoms are often caused by poor dentistry. Saturn gives the clue that these maladies may occur, especially if dentistry is undertaken at a time when Saturn is in difficult aspect to other planets in the chart, or if Saturn is crossing the ascendant, as an example.

The importance of Saturn's placement in the chart, as well as the way it relates to other planets, cannot be underestimated. Saturn indicates most of the conditions, physical or otherwise, that one can experience during a sojourn on the earth plane, because it describes gravity. The true importance of Saturn's interpretation relates to its relationship and placement next to Uranus, which describes the beginning of an awakening process onto higher spheres of consciousness. That in turn leads to more freedom in relation to the restriction of existence on earth, but Saturn's weight helps keep the feet on the ground.

URANUS

Uranus is the ruler of Aquarius, and Aquarius rules the nervous system in the body. The primary bodily function associated with Uranus is breathing. Uranus also describes the meridians (the unseen electrical currents that run throughout the system). These meridians are related to the etheric body, also called the electric body, and operate on the spiritual level of activity. Meridians are analogous to the nervous system in the physical body. Uranus is the first of the higher octave planets and has an esoteric function as well as a bodily one. Both levels of functioning relate to energizing the body.

The breath carries oxygen throughout the bloodstream, and it also carries prana, or spiritual energy, which is the esoteric correlation to oxygen. Prana energizes the physical body through a network of meridians—the fine channels that are components of the silver cord or the thread of life—by sending energy through the etheric or spiritual network. The force currents along these lines are linked with each other, and with the nervous system of man. They enter the body through the spleen. (See Chapter 2—The Constitution of Man.)

Proper breathing may be the body's second most critical function next to proper functioning of the heart. Oxygen is brought into the body with the breath and is pumped throughout the bloodstream by the heart to invigorate all the cells of the body. Oxygen purifies the blood, and prana, the higher octave of breath, purifies the nervous system. Sunshine carries prana, which enters the body through the esoteric or etheric organs, primarily the spleen, and energizes the entire underlying physical system. Since disease originates in the etheric body, it is essential to good health to keep the etheric body pure. The energizing agent of the etheric system is *thought,* however, not breath. It is thought, on the most elevated level, that enables man to tap the spiritual level of existence. This explains, in part, how disease or ill health can have psychological roots.

In considering the pairs of opposite astrological signs and their rulership of body parts, it is interesting to note that Aquarius and Leo are opposite signs, with Uranus and the Sun the respective ruling planets. (For the sake of simplicity, we will call the Sun a planet.) The Sun rules the heart and describes the quality of the soul, whereas Uranus rules the breath and describes the quality of the spiritual or etheric body. In considering the threefold nature of man, the physical body is the vehicle for the soul, whereas the soul is the vehicle for the spirit. Man cannot be separated from his soul and spirit. Abundant health depends on keeping all these vehicles pure.

Also acting as interconnecting links between the etheric body and the physical vehicle are the seven spiritual centers, or chakras. They are the batteries of the etheric system. Health depends on keeping those batteries charged. This is accomplished through meditation (higher thought), which has the very practical function of keeping the seven spiritual centers active so that the physical body can be properly energized. There are other ways of maintaining purity of the etheric body. (See Part V—Types of Therapies.) The future of medicine lies in understanding exactly how these unseen electrical currents relate to illnesses of the physical body, as most diseases have their origin in the etheric body. The medical establishment's knowledge about that system is woefully slight at this time.

There are, however, scientists and physicians who are experimenting with this invisible network of energy and making incredible inroads into uncharted territory. Dr. Richard Gerber, a physician in Michigan, presents a scientifically documented review of his research into alternative methods of diagnosis and healing in his book *Vibrational Medicine.* For twelve years, Dr. Gerber investigated many approaches, including the use of Kirlian photography for cancer detection. Preliminary results suggest that a Kirlian "gun" is highly accurate in pinpointing the presence and specific location of tumors within the body.

The work of Sigmund Bereday is an example of how the energizing of the body's electrical system can stimulate the body to heal itself. (See Chapter 1) Amazing research conducted by Dr. Bernard Grad at McGill University in Montreal, Canada, indicates the possibility that electrical stimulation may promote the regrowing of limbs that have been amputated or injured. Tadpoles and salamanders naturally grow back body parts, but so far, more complex forms of life have demonstrated no natural ability for regrowth of extremities. Using electricity as a stimulant, Dr. Grad has been able to regrow the legs of frogs after they were surgically removed. The most amazing stride in this field of research came when a human infant was able to regrow the first joint of a finger with the aid of electrical energy. These experiments give strong evidence of an electrical network in the body.

The etheric body is the archetype upon which the physical body is molded. It is an exact replica of the physical body and has its own nervous system, the meridians, which correspond to the nervous system in the physical mechanism. The etheric body conditions the physical body, which responds automatically. One phenomenon that has gone unexplained in scientific circles is phantom limb pain, or the lingering sensation of a limb that has been amputated. It is common for victims of amputation to experience tremendous discomfort or pain in the parts of the body that are no longer there. No doubt they feel the injury and nervous sensations of the etheric body, which still exists.

There is an axiom, "As above, so below," which can help explain the relationship of the etheric system to the physical mechanism. Man is a part of the vibrant whole. He connects with all levels of life and energy through his etheric body. The etheric body stores radiatory light (prana), transmitting it to the body through the spleen and then circulating it through the meridians and into the nervous system. When the spiritual fuel is properly assimilated in the body, the furnace burns brightly. The condition of the nervous system, ruled by Uranus in the astrological chart, is an indication of the quantity and the quality of prana, or spiritual fuel, and how easily it is being assimilated into the body. The section of the body that relates to Uranus is the lower legs and ankles. If there are problems with ankles or lower legs, the source may lie with the assimilation of prana into the system, and the condition of the spleen connection. The chakra system, acting as connecting batteries between the physical and the etheric systems, may need recharging. Sunshine, meditation, electrical stimulation, and music (See Chapter 21—Color and Sound) are alternative methods of healing that affect the etheric body and can help resolve problems related to a lack of energy permeating the etheric system. If a person suffers from nervous energy, he may be severely lacking in prana.

Dyslexia is the physical manifestation of reversed meridians. In a dyslexic person, the force lines that carry pranic energy into the system are flowing backward in a reversed fashion and the brain cannot process information in a normal manner. Stimulation of the meridians can keep energy flowing properly throughout the nervous system, energizing the brain and helping all autonomic nerve function to operate more smoothly. Children with dyslexia have often been miscast as having lowered intelligence. Quite the reverse is true. It is quite likely that dyslexia is possibly connected to genius potential. Strong Uranus aspects in specific sectors of a chart can indicate a higher and greater degree of electrical energy in the system. With more pranic, spiritual energy infusing and stimulating the brain, a person has greater access to the network of universal thought. Dyslexia and nervous disorders often indicate a stronger attunement to the esoteric network than to the physical. There may be more etheric energy coming into the spiritual network than can be easily assimilated into the nervous system. If that is the case, it can jam the network and simulate a blown fuse somewhere in the physical body. This may result in neurological disabilities such as multiple sclerosis or epilepsy, which have so far defied attempts to find a complete cure. Uranus rules the function of hearing. Clairaudience is a distinct likelihood with Uranus strong in the chart, as Uranus relates to all extrasensory abilities, and the higher octave of mentality. The inspirational levels lead to more advanced thought processes.

Since Uranus relates to strong spiritual energy, the natural habitat for a person with this planet very pronounced in his chart is on the spiritual plane. The supportive Saturnian bony structure of the body keeps the spirit confined and operating on the physical level, but basically, the spirit longs to escape and go home. If the physical structure is out of balance, a loss of vitality may be due to the spirit prematurely trying to take leave of the body. In this instance, the spiritual body may be stronger than the physical body.

If the experience of temporarily leaving the body, sometimes called astral traveling, is consciously prepared and carefully surrounded with protection, it can be a revitalizing and a mystical experience. Otherwise, it is like springing a leak in the physical automobile and losing valuable fuel.

Many spiritually evolved people can leave their bodies at will, but for the average man, the maintenance of balance within the physical structure grounds the spiritual essence in a positive way. Since man operates on the physical level, the properly charged physical vehicle cannot fully serve its purpose if the spiritual body is not carefully placed in its package. Coordinated breathing patterns, as taught by Carl Stough, help to center the etheric body in its proper place. Chiropractic adjustments too are important for maintenance of structural balance. (See Part V—Types of Therapies.) With proper structural balance, coordinated breathing (which means proper alignment of the diaphragm in the rib cage), enough etheric stimulation entering the esoteric systems, and periodic external techniques which will stimulate self-healing, health factors should remain stable, allowing a person to live on the highest level of inspiration possible. What a wonderful world of idealism might be in evidence then.

NEPTUNE

Neptune is the ruler of Pisces, which in turn rules the feet, the lymph glands, and the immune system. Neptune is also associated with right-brain activity and eyesight. The lymph system is concerned with the activity of white blood cells, which are part of the body's immune system. White blood cells discriminate between substances that are safe for the bloodstream to absorb and those that are poisonous. Ideally, the white blood cells rise to the defense of the body by absorbing poisonous elements into the lymphatic system in the body. To keep the immune system operating at peak efficiency, it is important to stimulate lymphatic activity with specific exercises. (See Chapter 17.)

But the lymphatic system can be strengthened by the ingestion of bee propolis. Bee propolis is the resin or sap from twigs and trees that bees gather and line the hive with so that hundreds of bees can live in the hive without infection. It is thought to kill every virus and every bacteria that exists. In his book *Propolis, Nature's Energizer*, Carlson Wade, noted writer, researcher, and author of over fifty books and articles on health and nutrition writes "Scientists recognize the importance of having a strong thymus gland. Found at the root of the neck, it consists largely of developed lymphocytes, the white blood cells needed to provide immunization." Mr. Wade quotes Dr. John Diamond on the subject of the powerful, natural substance propolis. Dr. Diamond, President of the International Academy of Preventive Medicine and a foremost authority on the function of the thymus, says, " 'Of all the natural supplements I have tested, the one that seems to be the most strengthening to the thymus, and therefore to the life energy, is bee resin or bee propolis, the resin secreted by trees then metabolized by the bees, and brought back to the hive to line the interior. This substance is the subject of considerable clinical research in several European countries. For many years [propolis] has proven to be effective against bacteria, virus and fungi. We now know that the reason for this is that it activates the thymus gland and therefore gives resistance to infection.' "

I have discovered that I can prevent an onset of flu by taking bee propolis immediately upon feeling the symptoms. This preventive measure can prove to be very important to elderly people, as an example, whose very life may be jeopardized by a severe bout of influenza or infection.

Neptune rules all activities that are associated with the right hemisphere of the brain. Right-brain activity describes idealism and a sense of the overview. The right hemisphere of the brain relates to conceptual ability, whereas the left hemisphere relates to concrete analysis. The proper functioning of both sides of the brain allows an individual to conceptualize and bring visions and dreams onto a concrete, practical level. Right-brain functions enable a person to see ahead of the stumbling blocks in front of his nose that could limit his vision and keep him stuck in the mundane tasks of daily life. It is essential to achieve a balance between the activity of both hemispheres of the brain. Stimulation of the chakra located between the brows helps to maintain a dynamic equilibrium between reality and conceptual awareness. (See Chapter 10, Dr. Chrene.)

Neptune is the second of the higher octave planets. It also has two levels of function. Eyesight is physical seeing, but visualization is etheric seeing. The eyes, ruled by Neptune, are like cameras. A person photographs each second of his experience and stores those visual images in the file cabinet of his memory. If he sees and experiences too many painful and destructive situations, especially early in life, he sets in motion patterns that continue to repeat, and thus he manifests more painful experiences. Right-brain, Neptunian functions enable the individual to replace those painful photographs with mental images of loftier, happier circumstances.

The power of positive thinking is very real. Brian Boitano, winner of the Olympic gold medal for figure skating, has said that when he was practicing as a ten-year-old, he saw the exact moment of his victory in his mind's eye. He added that the way he stood, the way the medal was presented to him, and the response of the crowds was exactly as he had visualized it. Obviously Brian was impressing his subconscious and patterning the ethers with a very precise picture. It took nine years to manifest, but that's the stuff champions are made of. Without the power to look beyond the momentary circumstances, man is trapped in the "glamour" and illusion—or pain and disillusionment—of the earth plane.

Science is slowly discovering what metaphysicians have long known to be true about the aura and colors that surround the human form. (See Chapter 21.) The auric emanation has been depicted in religious pictures as a halo, but everyone has an aura of some kind. Kirlian photography can photograph the aura of a human being (or even a vegetable), but only in black and white. The aura emanating from the body describes its physical health and well-being. This emanation is ruled by Neptune. There are other ethers that permeate the atmosphere like a cosmic fluid. Think of a cloud of fluffy foam. It is possible to take a finger and draw designs and patterns in that foam. Man actually predescribes his own life by consciously or unconsciously making patterns in the ethers that surround him. He projects onto life's mirror his own particular script. What he sees with his etheric eyes is what manifests on the physical level. Neptune describes the ability to see beyond the density of what appears to be real on the earth plane.

The ability to see health in the body can be transforming. Visualization techniques have been important in the success of Dr. Gerald Jampolsky, of Washington, D.C., who works with children with cancer. Dr. Jampolsky encourages the children to draw pictures of their cancer and to gradually make the monsters less menacing. In many instances, the tumors shrink as the drawings become more benign.

Neptune rules mysticism. Mystics don't live in what the rest of us call the "real" world. They live on a plane that is akin to utopia. True mystics have little need, beyond the bare minimum, of earthly substances such as food and drink. Their realm of idealistic existence seems strange beyond comprehension to those of us unprepared to experience cosmic joy and the extraordinary bliss of universal consciousness.

Uranus, the first of the higher octave planets, is vitalizing, whereas Neptune is devotional and inspirational. If a person has a problem with eyesight or with the immune system, it is important to look at his devotional, inspirational activities. It is really true that man cannot live by food alone. He must have finer food to give sustenance to the etheric system. Idealism, fantasies, and dreams are the food that charge the immune system and enable the individual to live on the high side of life rather than the low side. Free will and choice also enter into the picture, because it is man's ultimate choice to imprint that foamy medium surrounding him in any creative way he wishes. In his book *Intermediate Alchemy*, St. Germain describes visualization exercises involving the white, foamy cloud surrounding the body. (See Chapter 25.) The realization that life has a high side keeps the Neptunian visionary looking for the bright colors in the rainbow. (See Chapter 21.)

Neptune has a dark side as well, for it is this planet that rules drugs and alcohol. If an idealistic individual is disillusioned for a period of time, he may turn to drugs or alcohol to lift him above the gloom and onto an artificial high. The problem is that the high is artificial, and a crash is inevitable. Drugs and alcohol project an individual onto the astral plane, not the higher intuitional level. They can open the inner eyes to the sight of entities and creatures who are trapped on the lower astral. Neptune's true place is on the fourth plane or the intuitional. (See Chapter 2.)

There is no way of proving that problems with the immune or lymphatic system relate to disillusionment, but it is important to keep the etheric immune system working properly by finding fresh inspiration to help combat the poisonously difficult or painful everyday experiences that are indigenous to life on the earth plane. Neptunian vision is like a photograph of a beautiful rainbow. If the camera is in focus, the colors are sharp and clear, but some dead twigs might be part of the foreground. If the choice of the photographer is to blur the focus, hoping to obscure the dead twigs, the colors of the rainbow will not be sharply defined. If he chooses to focus the camera, he may decide to crop out the dead twigs from the picture later on, or he may acknowledge their existence. Sometimes the contrast makes the rainbow even more beautiful.

Neptune also rules the feet. If there are problems with the feet, there may be corresponding problems with eyesight. When Neptune has a strong placement in an astrological chart, it can describe a tendency toward myopic vision or a resistence to confrontation. That tendency is akin to choosing to blur the focus of the camera to see only the rainbow. A person with sore feet might be well advised to look for a situation, perhaps right in front of his nose that he would prefer not to acknowledge or confront. In some cases, the immune system or the lymph glands may take the brunt of denying the right brain an opportunity to step in and participate in solving the problem.

The pair of opposites, Pisces and Virgo, work in a most interesting way. Even though the feet (Pisces) are on the bottom, and the brain (Virgo and Pisces) is on the top, they are closely interrelated. The brain governs the voluntary and involuntary bodily functions, but the feet have acupuncture points that relate to and stimulate every organ and every system in the physical body. (See Chapter 19—Reflexology.)

P L U T O

Pluto is the ruler of Scorpio. Scorpio governs the reproductive organs—in the male the gonads, and in the female the ovaries. Therefore, Pluto relates to the bodily function of secretions relating to the creation of new life. In the female, Pluto describes ovarian production of eggs, and in the male it describes the production and secretion of sperm. Pluto is the last of the higher octave planets and also has its esoteric function. On the higher level, it describes the state of cosmic consciousness. To review, these are the three higher octave planets: Uranus, which indicates the vitalization of the physical system from the etheric level of spirit; Neptune, which describes inspiration that energizes from the intuitional level; Pluto, which describes the conscious transmutation of will to the higher will, giving birth to the higher consciousness of the soul.

Just as the body has a glandular system which regulates existence in the physical mechanism, the etheric body has a corresponding system that allows for simultaneous existence on a level of soul consciousness. That system includes the seven spiritual centers, or the chakras, which act as batteries between the etheric body and the physical body. The chakras can be vitalized individually, which results in revitalization of the entire system. (See Chapter 25.)

The Kundalini fire, ruled by Pluto, lies at the base of the spine. With the right preparation and commitment, it can rise throughout the seven centers, but only if the batteries are fully charged and operating on their specific frequencies. This should be attempted very cautiously, with total devotion and only through meditation. Until such time as the individual is consciously dedicated to the vitalization of that spiritual energy, that serpent fire lies coiled at the base of the spine, polarizing man in his physical body and on the physical plane. The activities connected with the base chakras are those that relate to the creation of new life, or sexual activity. When this powerful energy is able to rise through properly constructed channels connecting the chakras to each other, it reaches the crown chakra located at the top of the head. This sends the energy onto the highest level of existence, preparing for life on the seventh or divine plane. On this plane man makes conscious soul contact and lives by the laws of the soul, not by the laws of the physical.

The Plutonian energy is the most powerful of all. When it operates on a purely physical level, it is potent, dynamic, and very effective. Imagine the potency of the union of the egg and sperm. Operating alone each substance is ineffectual. Yet that quiet but incredibly dynamic connection instantly produces new life. And the growth that takes place is rapid and more powerful than any force on earth.

The connection that is made between the physical mechanism and the soul is just as dynamic on a cosmic level. The life that is made within the individual, as a result of this coming together, is as miraculous as fertilization of an egg to produce new life. The level of ecstasy in this union cannot be imagined through limited physical senses. Sexual union, coming under the overall jurisdiction of Scorpio, can produce beautiful, exciting sensations, or just the opposite. Devastating lack of fulfillment can run the gamut from disappointment to disgust. The union of the physical man with his soul produces only the most joyful sensations, compounded to a level of ultimate ecstasy. It is said that the sexual urge, with its resultant letdown after orgasm, is really a microscopic counterpart to the macrocosmic urge for union with the soul.

The key function of transmuation from the lower levels of existence to the higher is through the will. It must be man's conscious choice to find his way to his own ultimate union. As long as he enjoys the fruits of the earth plane, he lives by the laws of the earth, including karma and retribution. These basic laws are an eye for an eye, and a tooth for a tooth. Many of the conditions each person finds in his environment reflect the karmic payoff from past lives. Illness can kick a man into the realization that he is saturated with the pleasures of earth and that his system has become cloudy and clogged. He is no longer a beautiful prism of light, easily able to reflect into his outer life the conditions that he chooses. The prelude to the search for the ecstasy of union with the soul is the disillusionment, described by Neptune, with the illusions of life. So man begins his attempt to transmute pain into pleasure. This union must be accomplished and realized while he is still on the earth plane. On the spiritual levels, and in existence between lives—what we call death—man can only reflect. He cannot make the connection. That is life's secret and its ultimate purpose; the birth of soul consciousness.

The little will must give way to the higher will of the soul. When man says, "Thy will be done," he is really attuning himself to his oversoul and turning over the choices to the part of him that is infinitely wise and powerful. The transmutation, which is joyful and dynamic, can only be accomplished through moment-to-moment dedication to that end and through meditation. He builds an atom in his consciousness that bridges the gap leading to the levels of the cosmos. When the individual is preparing to make a soul connection, he begins to live his life in a state of meditation. But as this transition is in the beginning stages, when the higher self is ready to give a little gentle push to the lower consciousness, some imbalance or illness can occur in the system, as the shift of the focus of consciousness occurs.

Since Scorpio rules the sexual energy and the endocrine system in general, the esoteric counterpart is rulership of the top chakra, the pineal gland, located at the top of the head. Motivation for the good of all concerned, and the consciousness of any action that might hurt another human being is the beginning of the deliberate attempt to reach the soul level of operation. This demands moment-to-moment monitoring of motivation. The realization that mankind is truly one means that anything harmful to another human being really only hurts oneself. No one can evolve beyond where his brothers are. He may be on a slightly higher rung of the ladder and have a greater degree of light energy within his system, but he must give a helping hand to his brother for his own sake.

The Masters who have evolved beyond the confines of the physical world do not sit on the clouds playing harps. Their total dedication and activity is for the uplifting of man, stuck on earth. They necessarily look for a person who can be an instrument on the earth plane, bringing about the right conditions for humanity. When an individual has progressed on his own evolutionary path, he may have enough of the pure light energy to be a strong beacon for others.

Awakening onto this higher level of consciousness always comes with trauma or with an earth-shaking event. That may be an illness, or a betrayal, or failure to achieve one's goals. The event is not as important as what the individual chooses to do about it, and how he chooses to handle it. With a revengeful attitude, he traps himself more fully on the level of the perpetrator of the injustice. He may even ground himself more fully into a trapped existence with an illness that makes him think about the true meaning of life. He sets in motion a boomerang effect. Illnesses that occur in connection with sexual functions, such as syphilis, herpes, and AIDS, may be the clue that a transmutation of sexual energy is necessary. With any such illness, the person needs to look at his motivations. In that way, he gains insights into his own condition. He can begin to transmute his life onto a higher level of fulfillment, by utilizing all of the higher octave planets to bring in the light of the spiritual existence. This is by no means a dull, boring experience. For the Universe has infinitely more exciting things in mind for us than we could possibly conceive for ourselves. The cosmos is the playground for the innocent, childlike spirit that is tired of being a grown-up in the harsher existence of the limited view of life.

Ascendant and Body Language

*A*n astrological chart is divided into twelve sections called houses. These houses describe different areas of the life of an individual. They are separated from each other by dividing lines called cusps. When considering health matters, there are two sections or houses that are particularly important to examine: the first and sixth. There is a major difference in the way these two houses describe the health of an individual. The first house describes the structure of the physical body and body language. It indicates where energy is most likely to be stimulated or restricted in the body. It indicates the quality of energy, or the blocks to the flow of energy, that condition external or physical behavior. It describes the way the physical body reacts to external stress. The sixth house indicates the innate quality of health, and the kinds of inherited genetic conditions that may affect an individual.

The ascendant, or the sign on the cusp of the first house (see Appendix to find your own ascendant), describes the physical body structure and appearance of the individual, as well as many other physiological and psychological factors. It tells the story of a person's entry into the world and everything connected with the beginning of his life. While the physical characteristics—the size and shape of a person's body—are genetically preconditioned, the entering soul and spirit infuse the physical vehicle with a specific patterning that makes him different from everyone else in the world. His physical makeup is more than just the color of his skin, hair, and eyes. He may also bring back physical conditions, both strengths and weaknesses, that were part of his past lives.

The ascendant is also known as the rising sign (so called because it is the astrological sign that is rising on the horizon at the time of birth). The characteristics ascribed to the planet that rules the ascendant of an individual's chart indicate many things about that individual. Among other things, they indicate probable choices a person makes at birth about the way he will survive. They indicate what happens to his body when he is faced with stress or shock, whether emotional, mental, or physical in origin. The ascendant also describes a person's specific birth experience. That all-important first change in life describes the way he will make changes and adjust to new conditions in the future. The first intake of breath sets in motion the patterns that indicate psychological predispositions and the probable choices the individual will make in his life. In other words, the way the twig is bent is the way the tree grows.

The earth plane, generally described by Saturn because of its gravity, is a foreign land for the soul. So the soul must have a vehicle that can survive the conditions of that unfamiliar territory. The physical body, generally described by Saturn, is merely the protective shell to house the inner self. It shields the fragile soul and spirit from any real or imagined dangers on the earth plane. Imagine driving alone in a car in a foreign land. The first choice about the trip is what kind of an automobile will be best suited for the journey. You could choose a Rolls-Royce, a Mercedes, or a Ferrari. You may decide to drive a Honda or a Toyota.

Man in his physical vehicle reacts in as many ways to problems, new conditions, or stress as the driver of the automobile might. Picture yourself on a rocky, steep coastal road. Raging below the narrow road is a torrent of water. The light of the Moon is obscured by a storm, and the road is slippery and dangerous. Suddenly, around the bend, lights signal an approaching car. The presence of another vehicle is slightly reassuring, but as the road is narrow, there is a new element of danger. As the driver of the car, what do you decide to do? You have several choices. You can pull over to the side away from the dangerous cliff to let the other car pass, but if the passengers are unfriendly, you may endanger yourself by stopping. You can drive faster to get to a wider place in the road, but with increased speed your car may slip on the wet roads. You may expend a lot of your energy in self-admonishment for placing yourself in such danger. You may be so trusting or so desperate that you decide to ask the other driver about the road conditions ahead. Or you may decide there is safety in numbers and ask to get in the other car to turn back, no matter who the driver might be.

The ascendant describes the car you, as the driver, have chosen to drive, as well as the kinds of decisions you are apt to make as you wend your way along mountainous roads and super highways alike. In dealing with the daily conditions of the earth plane, man adopts behavior characteristics that he presumes will keep him safe. These characteristics become fused with his personality and describe what happens to his body when he encounters anything new or unfamiliar in his environment. He tends to hide behind the mask of the physical body when dealing with unknown quantities or new experiences, often putting stress on some particular part of his physical system. This stress can cause wear and tear, which in turn creates a new form of stress itself.

The first unfamiliar circumstances of life are associated with the birth process or the entry into the physical world. The specific experiences of the birth process seem to precondition the way the individual will make important changes all his life. The way he views his particular environment, especially in childhood, is a contributing factor to all the decisions he will make about how he is going to live his life.

Adjusting to life on the physical plane can be a shock, a surprise, or a pleasant experience. The way a person reacts to the stress of birth and early life is an indication of the quality of his health later on. When he comes face-to-face with difficulties, he may begin to clamp down in some area of his body as a protection against foreign elements that invade his safe environment. This can happen even before birth.

During a regression session, I ask the person to describe his birth process in as much detail as possible. The individual observes himself during his own birth process and can see quite clearly what happens to his system when faced with ejection from the comfort of the womb. He observes the particular kind of constriction or contortion he undergoes to maneuver his body through the birth canal and how much he resists making that transition. He discovers the ease or difficulty of his first abrupt change and sees the kind of welcome accorded him when he arrives. He becomes aware of how the doctors and nurses treat him and whether they are rough or gentle. He knows if he is cold, angry, or scared at any time during his entry. He knows whether or not his mother holds him and comforts him. He sees exactly when he begins to tense up or barricade himself against external conditions and what part of his body might be involved.

I always suggest that the individual review the stages of his birth in order to devise a formula that describes each step of the process of change. I ask him to then review those steps in relation to changes that occur in his present experience. His reaction to change in the present, whether that change is with a job, a relationship, or an environmental situation, correlates to the way he reacted to the major change that took place at the time of his birth. I ask him to go over his own formula to see how he could have made the birth process easier for himself, and I ask him if that would make present-day changes easier as well. In almost every situation, the individual becomes aware of how he made the birth process more difficult for himself by resisting, tightening, or tensing some part of his body.

The tightening and resistance of body parts sets in motion physical patterns that are restimulated over and over again. The tendency to tighten up a particular area of the body acts like water continually dripping on a stone. Eventually, a hole is worn into the stone. Some part of the body begins to degenerate because the natural flow of energy is diverted around the constricted area. During regression sessions, I suggest a variety of ways to send special energy to the affected part of the body. (See Part V—Types of Therapies.) It is up to the individual to continue healing himself by focusing attention on injured parts until the natural flow of energy is restored to that area. The body needs to be tuned every day, like a fine violin. The most important part of restoring health is to find a way to reverse the tendency to place stress in a particular area of the body. Since like attracts like, it is essential to break the chain of a negative trend.

PROJECTIONS THAT MANIFEST AS DESTINY

When I interpret a horoscope, I describe the chart as a reflection of specific energies a person projects onto the mirror of life. Man unconsciously projects those images, which bounce back in the form of outer circumstances, in order to resolve conflicts that have prevented full realization of soul consciousness. An individual brings in a predescribed set of circumstances to be resolved, but he may only be able to see their reflection in the form of outer events. Sometimes they represent circumstances that are less than ideal. But each individual projects onto the mirror of his life exactly what it is that he needs to reconcile. Those projections may return like a boomerang to smack the individual in the nose. That way his attention is grabbed. When he finally begins to understand that the external conditions in life are of his own making, he can begin to break those negative patterns.

Inner conflicts create action and activity. The planet that rules the ascendant and the planets that are positioned in the first house describe the quality of energy a person utilizes in productive or nonproductive external activity. Sometimes those energies back up and cause the system to become clogged. The late astrologer Neil Michelson said that man is like a giant garbage disposal. The disposal functions perfectly until someone drops a fork into the unit. The fork gets bent and the unit stops until the bent fork is pulled out and the reset button is pushed. The human system operates in a similar way. Each person has his own particular bent fork. For one it may be sugar that clogs the system, for another it may be mental stress, and for someone else it may be an emotional reaction.

There are many qualities that can color and describe the ascendant. If a planet is in difficult aspect (see Chapter 8) to the planet that rules the rising sign or to one that is placed in the first house, it also colors the personality by reflection and should be considered in the overall health of the person. On occasion, many or even all of the planets in the zodiac relate to the ascendant by reflection. When this is the case, the individual is very complex in his physical and emotional makeup, and his personality is usually multifaceted. He may constantly switch gears between one survival decision and the next and the next.

All of the types of energy a person has at his disposal must be constructively released into the department of life in which each of the respective planets (energies) resides. It is then possible to have a clear, open, and truly balanced system. Only at that point can he be a prism through which the brilliant light of the soul can shine.

ARIES RULING THE ASCENDANT

When Aries is on the ascendant, Mars is the ruling planet. Since Aries rules the head, the person may be characterized as head-strong. Body language may depict him walking with his head thrust forward, as if to take the brunt of life with that area of his body. Vitality, zest, impulse, and rapid motion are part of his manner since Mars is the planet that describes action, activity, and vitality. Stress can lodge in the head and manifest as headaches, sinus problems, or anything connected to brain activity or the eyes, ears, or nose. Mars rules the blood, red blood cells in particular. But Mars also rules adrenal function and sexuality. People with Mars on the ascendant are not only vital, daring, and ambitious, but sexual and romantic. They have an especially high level of adrenal output, enabling them to mobilize energy for competitive activities, as an example.

The aspects to Mars give a strong clue about the birth process itself. They also describe whether a person will be able to take action, deal with stressful situations, and show initiative in life, or whether he will allow frustrations to immobilize him. The aspects and placement of Mars also describe the conditions of his birth, as well as the birth process itself. If the aspects to Mars are positive and easy, the birth process was probably rapid, smooth, and easy. The individual can direct his energy productively and can deal with competitive situations. In fact, competitive activities are necessary to burn off the high level of energy his system naturally produces.

Difficult aspects to Mars from other planets in the chart indicate the areas of frustration in life, probably stemming from the birth process itself. In regression sessions, people with this ascendant have been aware of their hurry to be born. They seemed very anxious to get on with life. But some feared that their own hurried, impetuous, and headstrong activity might hurt their mother during the birth process, and those persons began to hold back. That produced anxiety and pressure, even indecision, that may dog them the rest of their life. In most instances, as the frustration over the delay in getting born becomes stronger, the individual eventually and rashly plunges ahead, deciding it is better to get the birth over with. Mother will be hurt anyway. But he feels guilty if he thinks his mother has suffered because of him. Or he may get stuck in the birth canal, causing tremendous pressures around the head.

In life, the same patterns seem to exist. The person tends to pull his punches, stop himself in the middle of action, and hold back when someone else might get hurt. Frustration exists over what might be the proper action to take, and the resultant stoppage creates blocks in the area of the head. He sometimes unconsciously chooses to deal with delays and his own frustration rather than going forward in competitive situations and hurting someone else. He wonders why he suffers from constant headaches.

Exercise is essential for someone with this ascendant, especially when aggravating and frustrating conditions exist. It stimulates mental energy since exercise releases endorphins into the brain. That release acts like a natural high, facilitating clear thinking. If the individual can take action during stressful situations, all is well and good. If the person feels powerless, he may internalize his anger, creating stress in Mars-ruled parts of the body. The alternate probability is that an excess of adrenaline coursing through the bloodstream manifests outwardly in inappropriate and extreme outbursts of temper. The individual either feels charged with anger he cannot control or may feel totally incapacitated.

Mike Tyson, former world heavyweight boxing champion, obviously has strong Mars energy in his chart. In his battles with Robyn Givens, his ex-wife, and in myriad other situations, frustrations have caused Mike's headstrong temper to erupt with apparent consequent damage to whatever object lies close at hand. Head injuries, headaches, cuts, and burns are indicators that Mars energy is inner directed, not outer directed. (The sign placement of Mars in a natal chart can also indicate which part of the body may be afflicted.) Too much stress can put a strain on the adrenals, constrict the flow of blood through the body, and cause accidents to happen. If the blood flows evenly throughout the system, injury is less likely to occur.

TAURUS RULING
THE ASCENDANT

When Taurus is on the ascendant, the throat and jaw may bear the brunt of stress. The person may have a strong jawline or walk with his jaw jutted out or teeth clenched. His body language is fluid until he decides he may be too easygoing, and then he can plant his feet and become quite stubborn. Since Taurus rules the areas of the throat, he may be plagued with consequent sore throats, voice strain, and have a thyroid imbalance if he is under stress. Financial worries in particular cause stress in that area of the body. The throat center relates to the expression of power, so any issues connected to self-expression or lack of opportunity to be powerful can trigger physical reactions.

The Taurean ascendant describes a person with an extremely sensual nature. Pleasure and affection in life are important for the health and well-being of everyone, but they are essential for a person with Taurus on the ascendant. Lack of pleasure, love, or satisfaction of his sensuality may prompt him to find substitutes that are injurious to his health. Since Venus rules the liver and kidneys, those parts of the body can be affected; especially common is overindulgence in food or drink. Since Taurus rising predisposes an individual to delight in gourmet treats, he may consume foods that are too rich and sweet for easy assimilation into his system. He may momentarily feel better when he pours soothing liquids, especially those that taste good such as fine wine or liquors, into the throat area. In the long run, however, overindulgence will undoubtedly cause him more pain than pleasure. Singing is a positive throat exercise that provides pleasure and produces no detrimental side effects.

GEMINI RULING THE ASCENDANT

The Gemini ascendant describes a person with a need for mental stimulation and excitement. His body language is also vital and energetic, and he can be talkative and inquisitive. He is usually tall and lean. If life is worrisome, boring, or less than stimulating, stress can turn energy inward and cause problems in areas of the lungs. Stress can manifest as weakness in the arms or in any of the pairs of the body. Weakness in the eyes, limbs, or paired organs can give the person with Gemini rising a clue that he needs to introduce more external stimulation into his life. He may need to distance himself from a situation in order to develop a more objective viewpoint. Eye strain, for instance, may be related to mental pressures and fatigue that really have nothing to do with eyesight. Boredom, mental fatigue, or overt deprivation of mental stimulation can result in a debilitating lack of energy to combat illnesses such as asthma, bronchitis, or chest colds. Worries must be brought to the foreground and replaced with exciting and mentally challenging solutions.

CANCER RULING
THE ASCENDANT

When Cancer is on the ascendant, manifestation of a stressful birth process or early trauma is found in the solar plexus or stomach. This person may have felt orphaned or abandoned at the time of his birth, perhaps in connection with his mother or food, and develops a sensitivity and emotional quality that can be quite painful for him to endure. His body language shows a tendency to walk with a swinging gait, reflective of the way the crab walks sideways. He is not usually able to deal with life in a straight-on, forward thrust, but must come at situations almost sideways. When I was studying musical-theater techniques with the exceptionally fine coach David Craig, he told me my walk was too *wet*. What better way to describe a Cancer (water sign) rising.

During times of stress, or with feelings of abandonment, the person with this ascendant may feel like he has been punched in the middle of his stomach, or he may simply develop a dull aching pain in that area. Ulcers, gastritis, indigestion, nausea, and vomiting are clearly acknowledged as reactions to stress and emotional upset. The sensation of hunger and the overall tendency to feel reactions in the solar plexus may cause the person to eat rapidly and to consume too much food. Overeating only compounds the tension already created in that area of the body, and weight gain is the outcome.

The opposite can also be true. Bulimia, an obsession with food, is a malady that has only recently been openly discussed. Many bulimics consciously vomit to eject food they were unable to resist in the first place. Sometimes this occurs as an attempt to control weight, but whatever the motivation, bulimia is undoubtedly linked to emotional disturbance, just as is a tendency to overeat.

A person with Cancer ascendant tends to gain weight because of water retention, but he may also have unknown food allergies that cause the tissues of his body to swell. It is not uncommon for one with Cancer on the ascendant to have an allergic reaction to milk and dairy products. Since Jupiter rules the sixth house of health with this ascendant, the kidneys are also affected when emotional stress is at hand. The basic fears of people with Cancer rising are abandonment and hunger. It is important for the individual with this sensitive rising sign to fuel himself with activities and endeavors that produce a true nurturing feeling within and that can also elicit a sensitive response from other people.

LEO RULING
THE ASCENDANT

When Leo is on the rise, external pressure causes the individual to clamp down in the area of the chest. Stress may settle and reside in the heart muscle itself. Yet the heart chakra may be the most dangerous place for pressure to settle, as the heart is the central governing organ in the body. The restriction of the flow of energy throughout that important center can give rise to later heart problems or heart attacks. In order to be happy and stress free, a person with Leo rising needs to feel loved or, at the very least, appreciated.

Pride is a strong characteristic of a person with Leo rising. His manner insinuates great dignity and strength of character, and an innate sense of theater is reflected in his bearing. When his pride is hurt or his efforts go unacknowledged, the blow can lodge in the area of his heart. The best antidote for lack of recognition from external sources is the development of self-love and the expression of generosity of spirit toward others. The person with Leo rising can learn to give himself ego strokes and to consciously energize his heart chakra. One of the most important Tibetan meditations focuses on energizing the heart center by sending out love from that vibrant area to all of humanity. (See Chapter 25.) When love energy streams forth and is released from the heart, the heart swells and pumps vibrantly. The law of the Universe is that love sent out on a universal level must come back on a personal level.

VIRGO RULING
THE ASCENDANT

The individual with Virgo rising usually possesses a fine mind with excellent potential for objectivity, a left-brain activity. He is not slow, but he is prone to observe the situation around him before taking action. His bearing and body language reflect that quality of deliberation. He walks purposefully when he has observed and made his choice of action. The need for time to deliberate may be well masked behind a barrage of questions that act as his unconscious stalling device.

His ability to analyze is excellent, but with stress or lack of safety in his environment, he tends to hide behind his mind, even becoming quite critical. He is polarized on an intellectual level, and therefore stressful events or worry may cause tension or blocks of energy into the brain, creating mental toxins that poison his body as easily as material toxins. Another area of the body that can be affected by stress when Virgo rules the ascendant is the intestinal tract. Colitis, constipation, and intestinal cramps are indications of internal stress that could become chronic or severe. Regular colonics, or cleansing of the colon, prevent the buildup of poisons. Exercises can also help keep the muscle tone vibrant in that area of the body. (See Chapter 17.)

One young lady with Virgo rising had severe abdominal cramps when she was a teenager. The area just below her stomach would constrict when stress occurred in her life, but she never complained about her abdominal pain. When she had an emergency appendectomy at age twenty-one, it was discovered that her appendix had wrapped itself around part of her colon, cutting off a natural flow in the intestinal tract. Finally, the accumulated blockage reached a critical stage, creating a need for an operation. Worry and stress occur with many children and young people long before the pressures of life seem apparent, beginning the lifelong habit of restriction in some part of the body. One with Virgo rising can do a great deal to heal himself through his own thoughts and attitudes. The ability to transmute negative mental energy, or worry, into productive analysis and decisions brings about solutions to problems and can prevent constriction in parts of the body that have little or nothing to do with the stress of the moment.

LIBRA RULING
THE ASCENDANT

With Libra rising, the pancreas and spleen are areas of the body that can be affected by external pressures. The physical manifestations of birth trauma or difficulties in early childhood can settle in all of the organs that relate to assimilation, regulation, elimination, and balance in the system. The individual with Libra rising may have a sweet tooth and tend to eat foods high in sugar content. When external conditions are less than pleasant, or stressful situations are apparent, the individual may indulge his sweet tooth, causing his pancreas to work overtime and disturbing that balance so essential for health and well-being. He is left feeling tired and low in energy, which only stimulates the urge to consume more sugar or carbohydrates to produce a quick burst of energy.

One of the major personality traits for a person with this ascendant is a driving need to be nice; the emotional equivalent of the desire for sweets. He hopes that if he is very nice, gracious, and polite, problems may be resolved without his having to disturb the equilibrium. In fact, he may feel that his very survival depends on his being nice. A sense of being in limbo, with a tendency toward a placid temperament, may tempt him to ingest substances that will upgrade his vitality and give him more energy. Sometimes these substances are extremely detrimental to the inner vitality, producing a false high. Cocaine can be especially appealing, and extremely detrimental, as its level of social acceptance is high. A person with Libra rising is, above all, a sociable, gracious creature.

Since Saturn is an antidote for Venus, structure and a sense of purpose in life can help stabilize a tendency to inertia and bring about greater balance to the physical system. The best antidote for the paralysis of always being nice is to take action and develop a sense of purpose while creating an atmosphere of peace, harmony, and beauty. Fair play is very important for one with this rising sign. It can be essential for him to realize that qualities of tact and diplomacy can be active rather than passive.

SCORPIO RULING THE ASCENDANT

A person with Scorpio on the ascendant is imbued with a very dynamic, powerful personality. Tremendous personal magnetism gives an individual with this rising sign a potent ability to be effective in all of his endeavors. But stressful events in his life, especially if he feels he is being manipulated or betrayed, may cause him to exhibit very compulsive behavior and set in motion an urge to get even. If he resorts to the negative, revengeful side of his nature, he can cause severe problems for the people who are around his field of energy. However, the individual with this ascendant frequently turns energy inward, creating an internal time bomb. His physical reaction to stress or trauma may cause disabilities with the reproductive system and in the area of the root chakra, as well as with the whole endocrine system.

Eventually, the person with this dynamic rising sign must recognize the external tests that seem to come his way for what they really are. These tests may unconsciously be self-created and self-designed to prepare the individual for an initiation into higher levels of consciousness. Whatever areas of the natal horoscope are ruled by Scorpion or Plutonion energy indicate the areas of life where the major tests or initiation processes will occur. For the person with Scorpio rising, the greatest tests come in connection with his personal life and opportunities or avenues for self-expression. If he is willing to engage in a struggle with the dark part of his personality and the dark night of his soul, he wrestles with his inner angel on his own conception of the mountaintop. He eventually wins by releasing himself and his talent into the universe for resolution on a higher level. In effect, he turns himself over to his higher self. He successfully transmutes the willfulness of the compulsive childlike part of himself onto a level of higher will; that is, the will that works for the higher, greater good of all mankind. He finds himself more effective than ever, having turned a bad situation into something that is beneficial for everyone concerned. The most important thing for a person with this ascendant to recognize is the degree of damage he can do if he resorts to the negative side of his personality, for he is either the priest or the playboy; she, the priestess or the courtesan.

The painful struggles associated with this rising sign are often rooted in childhood deprivation. A natural, free childhood where fun and play stimulated natural imagination is an unknown commodity. Above all, he is a true child of the universe and can only play freely among the higher spheres of consciousness. This is the plane on which he actually lives. He can produce conditions and situations that are of great benefit to mankind. That, ultimately, provides the greatest sense of enjoyment for him. He learns to transmute forcefulness into effectiveness.

SAGITTARIUS RULING THE ASCENDANT

Optimism and a need for challenge are characteristics that describe a person with Sagittarius rising. Therefore, any kind of disappointment can affect his physical well-being. If he is severely let down by life and people, or overshoots the mark by overestimating his own potential, it is hard for him to restore his natural sense of humor. He can become paralyzed by inactivity, unable to set new goals or react to new challenges for fear of another disappointment.

The organs of the body that take the brunt of this particular kind of reaction are the kidneys, liver, and sciatic nerve. Problems or traumatic situations in his life can produce a poisonous or toxic condition and may manifest in weakness of the upper legs or with disabilities connected to kidneys and liver or to the hips. An obvious remedy for someone with this psychological makeup is to set new goals and create new challenges. He can avoid the possibility of new disappointment, and the consequent sense of paralysis, by investigating many new avenues of expression.

Since an individual with this kind of natural exuberance can express a quality of enthusiasm that is very contagious, stimulating himself to new heights as well as challenging others to do their utmost in life, an optimistic approach to life is essential to his very survival. Humor is the prime ingredient to ensure his overall good health. Challenging situations stimulate the entire physical mechanism, especially those organs connected with the processing of nourishment and the elimination of poisons from the system. The very description of what happens to food in the digestive system can describe what must happen in the life of a person with this ascendant: some people and opportunities will be nourishing and productive, stimulating new growth, and some must be quickly discarded and discharged before they have a chance to spread poison throughout the whole sphere of experience.

CAPRICORN RULING THE ASCENDANT

With Capricorn on the ascendant, the bony structure of the body bears the brunt of pressure from stress or trauma. One of the hardest hit spots in the body can be the point at the top of the shoulders. Capricorn rising describes an individual who is born with an Atlas complex; Atlas carried the weight of the world on his shoulders. An individual born with this serious, capable sign on the ascendant feels the weight of responsibility strongly. He may unconsciously tense his whole body to bear the brunt of life. This tendency can actually begin in the womb before birth.

Since the knees are the fulcrum of the skeletal structure, weakness in this area is a clue to an overstressful situation in life. The first thing that helps release some of the burden is a realistic appraisal of what he can actually accomplish and what he cannot. If this person observes a tendency to clench or grind his teeth, it can be a clue that burdensome situations are accumulating in his life and he may have to say no to some things.

Stretching exercises may be the most important therapy to include in the daily routine. It is important to keep the spine limber and to facilitate energy traveling freely along the spinal column. In this way energy is spread throughout the nervous system and from there to all other parts of the body. Yoga exercises in particular stimulate internal organs that otherwise may not receive the necessary attention for healthy and efficient functioning. It is also essential to adopt a daily routine for the care of teeth and gums, as these areas of the body may also suffer when a person with Capricorn rising is under stress.

AQUARIUS RULING THE ASCENDANT

The sign of Aquarius is ruled by Uranus, the first of the higher octave planets. Whereas Saturn describes gravity, responsibility, and regimentation, Uranus relates to freedom, spontaneity, and inventiveness. The person with Aquarius rising may have a unique and unusual appearance. His body language and mannerisms may include nervous habits, high-strung behavior, and an impulsive restlessness. At the worst, he may have physical disorders such as nervous tics, body jerks, and itches. Aquarius rules the nervous system. It appears that the person with this ascendant may have an extra degree of high-voltage electrical current that is not easily assimilated into his nervous system.

An individual with Aquarius rising may look as though he comes from another planet. He may have an overly large head or unusual eyes, for example. He also may not feel at home on the planet earth. He could actually be allergic to almost everything that relates to earth, including dust, pollen, animals, and certain foods. His dietary preferences are unusual, and he can almost live on air, as the need for oxygen is like the need for food.

Along with his desperate need for freedom, he may have a great longing to go home without knowing where home might be. He may not even understand what kind of freedom he is longing for, but his restlessness clearly indicates a soul searching for something other than what he can touch, taste, and see around him. He may be quite kinesthetic, or sensitive to what he feels, and what he feels may be indescribable even to himself. He may have a conscious or unconscious suicidal complex. He is not maudlin, but at times he wishes the world would stop so that he could get off.

Pressures and traumas can cause weakness in the calves or ankles, as Aquarius rules the lower legs. As an example, his legs may shake during times of stress. Uranus rules the breath, as well as the nervous system. When this person is under stress, he may experience shortness of breath or other breathing disorders such as asthma and emphysema. His lungs are not necessarily weak, but with trauma and pressure, he holds his breath and inhibits the flow of oxygen into his nervous system. He needs oxygen, or prana (the higher octave of oxygen that comes from sunlight) to bathe his nervous system. He also needs to learn how to seat his spiritual self in his physical body in a way that is more in tune with the earth plane. Being firmly centered in his skeletal structure relieves some of the anxiety about coping with real, earth-plane situations. (See Chapters 25 and 17.)

Since an Aquarian type of person is ill at ease with earth, his natural attunement is to the spiritual planes. He may have a strong sense of his spiritual helpers or guides and can exhibit genius potential in some field or another. He naturally relates to, and can be healed by, music or anything that is born of a high frequency. Some of his difficulties may stem from the pressure of time by earth-plane standards, as time has no function on the upper levels of existence. Structuring of time is helpful to an individual with this rising sign, as it can help to ground him. The combination of some structure in his life and the necessary excitement and freedom he craves in his daily activities can work wonders with his overall health and nervous system. He benefits by utilizing any higher octave healing technique such as meditation, visualization, color, sound, herbal remedies, and crystals. (See Part V—Types of Therapies.)

PISCES RULING
THE ASCENDANT

When Pisces is on the ascendant, the individual is naturally idealistic. He is a dreamer and views life as if he were wearing rose-
colored glasses. He may have a dreamy look about him, as though
he were living in a world of his own. He photographs beautifully,
as though he had a halo around his head, and he can either be a
true visionary or be very naïve.

Sometimes these personality traits act as a camouflage. When
life presents situations that are unpleasant, the individual with this
ascendant adopts somewhat of an ostrich quality, hiding his head
in the sand. It may be very difficult for him to face what others
think of as reality, as his reality may be quite different. He can
simply tune out what he doesn't want to face.

Confronting stressful conditions before they become too devastating is important for this individual. As long as he has an outlet
for his idealism and vision he functions well, but with disillusionment his dreams crash. Nameless fears can come into the consciousness if the individual is under stressful conditions. He may
need to consciously develop a greater sense of perspective and
analysis in order to counterbalance a natural tendency to idealize
people and put them on a pedestal.

When he experiences situations in his life that are traumatic,
both feet and eyesight may suffer, for Neptune rules those extreme
areas of the body. He may develop myopia or nearsightedness,
both physically and mentally, and must restore idealism by creating
new visions of how he wants his life to unfold. Since Neptune
rules the feet, and many acupuncture points are located in the
feet, massaging the soles of the feet can help increase vitality and
health. Foot reflexology is a very effective technique to stimulate
the inner organs and the flow of energy throughout the system.

Pisces also relates to the lymph system. Therefore, colds, infections, and flu can become common ailments if the individual allows
stress to get the best of him. The lymph glands are an important
part of the cleansing process in the body, since they involve the
immune system. But the lymph glands have no outlet in the body
to discharge any accumulated poisons. If the person with this as-

cendant has trouble with infections or colds, his immune system may be weak as a result of disillusion, as that reaction produces a type of poison within his system. When the rose-colored glasses finally come off, the glare of truth can be hard to take. The best exercise to keep the lymph system stimulated is to bounce on a rebounder. (See Chapter 17.)

CHAPTER 7

Sixth House and Quality of Health

The sixth house of a person's astrological chart describes some major issues in his life: the quality of his health, the kind of work he chooses for himself, and how well he performs in that job. The combination of these issues is not without logic, for the health of an individual determines his ability to work and may also predetermine the specific kind of a job he chooses. If he is low in vitality, he may naturally gravitate toward sedentary occupations, but if he is a dynamically vital human being, he may require a very physically challenging job that will utilize excess energy. As well as describing the kind of work a person needs for optimum health, the sixth house also indicates the kind of work environment and relationship with coworkers that will contribute to his overall sense of well-being.

In an equal house system of astrology (the only kind we can consider for a general analysis of the horoscope), the astrological sign ruling the sixth house of health is the fifth astrological sign after the ruler of the ascendant. For instance, if Aries rules the ascendant, the sixth sign is Virgo. If Taurus rules the ascendant, the sixth sign is Libra. The chart below lists relative first and sixth house sign pairings and includes the areas of the body ruled by the different signs.

Ascendant	*Sixth House*
Aries—adrenals, blood	Virgo—intestines
Taurus—throat, larynx	Libra—pancreas
Gemini—lungs, pairs of body	Scorpio—reproduction, chakras
Cancer—stomach	Sagittarius—kidneys, liver
Leo—heart	Capricorn—bony structure
Virgo—intestines	Aquarius—nervous system, legs
Libra—pancreas	Pisces—feet, lymph system, eyes
Scorpio—chakras, reproduction	Aries—adrenals, blood
Sagittarius—kidneys, liver	Taurus—throat, larynx
Capricorn—knees, bony structure	Gemini—lungs, pairs of body
Aquarius—legs, nervous system	Cancer—stomach
Pisces—feet, lymph glands, eyes	Leo—heart

Whereas the first house, or ascendant, describes the way the individual uses his body as a defense mechanism against stress, the sixth house indicates the basic predisposition to health and can describe inherited genetic patterns. Along with the ascendant, it can describe health patterns built into the system from past-life physical conditions. The combination of the energies described by these two houses gives a comprehensive picture of the relationship between genetic inheritance and environmental conditioning as it pertains to physical well-being in the present existence. The interval or mathematical relationship of the first house to the sixth house is similar to the inconjunct aspect. (See Chapter 8.) This aspect describes the greatest growth opportunities in an individual's life due to the effort required to integrate two very different qualities. According to astrologers Bruno and Luisa Huber, the inconjunct (two planets positioned 150° apart) describes a "stretch-growth" situation, like having to stretch to hit a tennis ball that is slightly out of reach. When the effort is made, perhaps with a great deal of focus and concentration, contact is made and the ball goes over the net. Anything, whether a planet or house position, placed 150 degrees apart qualifies to describe that growth effort. So the first- and sixth-house relationship basically describes the need to make an effort to integrate inherited genetic qualities with those imposed by the environment.

A rundown of the planetary rulerships associated with each sign that appears on the cusp of the sixth house, and the parts of the body they rule, will give some information about the inherited health of an individual. Then a deeper explanation of the total energy picture comes with comprehension of the stretch-growth aspect that is described by the two health houses. (An explanation of rulerships is found under "Planets That Rule Parts of the Body." See page 94.)

Another factor to be considered is whether the planetary rulers of the first and sixth houses are in good aspect to each other and to other planets in the chart. If those planets are in difficult relationship, there is an indication that poor health patterns exist. (See Chapter 8.) It is also necessary to consider planets that are placed in the sixth house, as well as the sixth-house rulerships and their relationships to each other and to other planets. It is essential to conduct a thorough analysis of the astrological picture to accurately diagnose the overall health and well being of an individual.

ARIES RULING
THE SIXTH HOUSE

When Aries rules the sixth house (that would occur when Scorpio rules the ascendant) or Mars is positioned therein, the supply of energy is high, and the natural state of health is vibrant. If Mars is well aspected, there is a strong indication that an abundance of rich blood flows throughout the vascular system, carrying plenty of oxygen to prevent illness from taking hold in the body. If Mars is not well aspected, health problems may relate to poor circulation. Since Mars rules adrenal function and conditions in the head such as sinus, headaches, head injuries, and brain function, aspects to Mars indicate whether or not there could be problems with those areas of the body.

Physical exercise is an essential activity for someone with this placement. Without enough physical activity, the person may be predisposed to headaches, cuts, burns, accidents or injury. Sports and competitive situations keep spirits high and blood pumping vibrantly through his system. Exercise not only enables the system to absorb greater amounts of oxygen, which feeds the vascular system as well as the nervous system, but it stimulates the release of endorphins into the bloodstream and eventually into the brain. Endorphins act as a natural high or vitamin to stimulate important brain activity.

In the selection of the type of everyday work, an individual with Aries ruling the sixth house may naturally gravitate toward the kind of activity that will utilize a high level of energy. Athletics, dance, or any competitive situation are natural outlets for someone with a strong Martian quality in the area of health and work. Since sluggishness is the antithesis of a Mars quality of energy, if a job situation is too sedentary, easy, or static, the person with this rapid, headstrong kind of vitality has unspent energy that can become detrimental to his physical well-being. Ambitions are stimulated partly because he possesses such a high level of adrenaline output. High-level activity challenges him to the utmost physical limits and stimulates blood flow throughout the system, thereby keeping him healthy. Since Mars is the god of war, he must find some way to indulge in aggressive activity and turn it into a constructive situation.

The best kind of occupation for someone with Aries ruling the sixth house of health is in an arena where he can initiate activities or plans. He is energized if he acts as a pioneer or icebreaker for others. He needs a good challenge or fight to be truly healthy. Since Mars rules metals, any activity involving the use of metals keys into Mars energy. Whether lifting weights, creating jewelry, or pounding on a typewriter, the effort and consequent resistance from the object strengthens his vitality.

TAURUS RULING
THE SIXTH HOUSE

When Taurus rules the sixth house (that would occur when Sagittarius rules the ascendant) or Venus is placed in that sector of the chart, Venus describes health and work patterns. Since pleasurable activities stimulate a sense of well-being in the person with this house placement, any activity connected to art or beauty, social functions or social consciousness keeps him healthy, vital, and on an even keel. The individual with this cusp placement must have harmony and beauty in his work environment in order to do his best. He must enjoy a sense of camaraderie with his coworkers and have an easy working relationship.

When Taurus rules this house, Sagittarius rules the ascendant. Sagittarius describes a person who can inspire others. He is a natural teacher. The outstanding personality trait of an individual with Sagittarius rising is optimism and enthusiasm. Since Taurus rules the throat and larynx, if he can use his voice to express his contagious exuberance and goodwill, he stimulates his entire body with that sound vibration and is likely to remain healthy and happy. The happiness, pleasure, and joy that return to him as a result of his efforts continue to stimulate an even greater sense of well-being.

Self-indulgence resulting from disappointment is the negative trait that may tempt this individual to consume foods and drinks that are too rich for easy assimilation. If Venus, the ruler of Taurus, is not well aspected in the horoscope (indicating a tendency toward self-indulgence), the pancreas, kidneys, liver, and throat can be affected. Liver or kidney problems, in particular, can increase with improper diet, as these organs help to regulate digestion and elimination. Rich foods high in sugar or fat content may seem to soothe the system and provide momentary pleasure, but the price can be extravagantly high.

If the individual can relate to the stretch-growth situation implied by this house position, he may discover that through the use of his voice he can provide for himself a more lasting pleasure than he can by consuming good-tasting foods. He might then notice a substantial improvement in his health and energy levels.

Public speaking, singing, and salesmanship provide productive professional outlets for the person with Taurus ruling the sixth house.

GEMINI RULING
THE SIXTH HOUSE

people

When Gemini rules the sixth house, Capricorn rules the ascendant. Gemini energy relates to the pairs in the body, especially the arms, lungs, eyes, ears, and the two halves of the brain. Mercury, the ruler of Gemini, relates more to left-brain activity, but Gemini, a dual sign, describes the ability to swing back and forth between the left and right hemisphere (between facts and concepts), to find the balance within that facility. The use of the mind is extremely important for an individual with this house placement. He must have an occupation that is mentally challenging or the boredom manifests in physical malfunction related to the mind or the pairs of the body. Work that relates to the process of analyzing situations, and that results in decision making, is beneficial to the overall sense of well-being. Any occupational situation that incorporates a necessity to examine both sides of the coin keeps this individual mentally challenged. Born with an inquisitive mind and a facility for thought, the person may benefit from doing two jobs at once, or by having two facets of a job to resolve. The preservation of his good health may also depend on his being able to introduce new and exciting avenues of thought and ideas into his work. Since Saturn rules the ascendant when Gemini is on the cusp of the sixth house, occupations that are less physically demanding and more intellectually stimulating are more suitable to the overall system.

Oxygen is required for feeding the nervous system and thus the brain, preventing mental stagnation. Since the lungs are one of the body pairs that might suffer with neglect, it is interesting to note that when Capricorn is on the ascendant, the bony structure of the body may be somewhat rigid, inhibiting the lungs and consequently preventing enough oxygen from entering the body. If this is the case, indicated by adverse aspects to Saturn, the individual may tire easily. He may suffer from depression or worry. Diseases associated with the lungs or weakness of the arms may be symptomatic of mental stagnation. But that mental stagnation may be due to lack of fuel, or oxygen, coming into the brain and the rigidity of the body may be due to lack of proper breathing.

If the diaphragm is the source of breathing problems, exercise (other than yoga) is not the solution. When the diaphragm is prevented from traveling its natural path through the lung cavity and instead hits the rib cage (Saturn), exercise may only exacerbate the situation. The diaphragm, in its proper position, acts like a bellows, rising to a point within the bony cavity of the rib cage with the exhalation of breath, thereby massaging the internal organs—the heart in particular—as it moves upward. However, most people restrict the natural breathing early in life by holding the breath. If this kind of shallow breathing becomes chronic, the diaphragm begins to weaken and begins to get caught on some part of the rib cage instead of rising to a high point inside the chest. At that point, shallow breathing is intensified because the diaphragm cannot rise in its proper position. The original holding of the breath becomes compounded into everything from respiratory disorders to lower back pain and even scoliosis (curvature of the spine).

As a result of ten years of research, a new branch of science called respiratory science was born. Carl Stough, director of the Stough Institute in New York City, has documented that there is an absolute way that air goes in and out of the body, and has named this process "breathing coordination." After working with emphysema patients in veterans hospitals, and with anyone suffering from shortness of breath, asthma, or related breathing problems, Carl discovered that it is possible to develop, or redevelop, the diaphragm to its ultimate potential even though the diaphragm is an involuntary muscle-organ. As a result of his discovery, it is possible to correct respiratory faults.

Carl commented that when the rib cage is out of alignment, it also affects the spine because the ribs are attached to the spine. People can get lower back pain or even scoliosis as a result of improper breathing, but by the time a person with scoliosis is documented as having a breathing problem, the damage is already done. For it is the lack of coordinated breathing that causes the scoliosis, not the other way around. So Carl's work begins with manual manipulation to put the diaphragm back into its proper position. When Carl is able to begin to maneuver the diaphragm so that it sits higher inside the rib cage, he then teaches the individual a way to strengthen the diaphragm so that it will stay in the proper position. Then the proper positioning of the diaphragm allows for the massage of the internal organs, especially the lungs and heart, and vibrant health as well as renewed mental activity is stimulated. That internal stimulation keeps all the related organs in healthy working order. Correct breathing is important for everyone, but it is especially indicated when Saturn relates to either the ascendant or the sixth house. (See Chapter 4 on Uranus and Chapter 5—Planets that Rule Bodily Functions, as well as Chapter 17—Alignment of Body Structure.)

CANCER RULING
THE SIXTH HOUSE

When Cancer rules the sixth house of health (and Aquarius rules the ascendant), or the Moon is placed in that sector of the chart, the Moon relates to conditions of health. Cancer rules the stomach, whereas Aquarius rules the nervous system. When these two sensitive signs rule the houses of health, the stability of the emotional nature and the nervous system predescribe the conditions of health. The Moon, planetary ruler of Cancer, relates to emotions, feelings, sensitivities, and vulnerabilities. Illness can manifest in the stomach and solar plexus area as a result of hurt feelings, overreaction to external conditions, and special sensitivity, but it may also be due to nervous disorders. The sign placement of the Moon in an individual chart reveals additional information about health characteristics and describes other parts of the body that may be affected. When the emotional balance is disturbed, this sensitive and vulnerable individual may react by overeating. He allows his emotional reactions to color common sense and tends to take everything personally.

The Moon describes feelings of having been orphaned or abandoned. Yet the Moon is the strongest planet in the charts of writers, as an example. When a person with this house placement can work through his own emotional reactions and pain, he discovers that other people have experienced similar conditions in their lives. He then develops a quality of compassion which enables him to express a nurturing concern for their welfare. At this point, he is able to identify with the needs of others. If he can use this higher quality of sensitivity in his work, he remains healthy and fulfilled.

The nervous system is energized by the breath. With proper intake of oxygen, the emotional nature is calmed and there is less likelihood that the stomach will be upset by the consumption of food. Proper functioning of the stomach and the digestive processes depends on the kind of food that is consumed and the way in which it is eaten. Emotional upsets may cause a person to eat too rapidly, as an example. On the other hand, if a person is unable to eat due to nervousness, gastric juices can create a burning sensation or even cause ulcers. When Cancer, or the Moon, relates to one of the health sectors of the chart, there is a strong possibility of food allergies, especially to milk or milk products. Muscle testing can be invaluable in determining which foods strengthen the system and which ones are detrimental or weakening. (See Chapter 18 on Kinesiology.)

A special kind of work or occupation is essential for the natural well-being of the individual with this house placement. Sensitivity to the needs of others and a quality of vulnerability can bring enormous response from the public and from women in particular. The opposite side of the coin, however, is that a gut connection or symbiosis with people can cause a tremendous drain on the emotional system unless the individual knows how to protect himself. Sometimes the demands of his job are more than his nervous system can handle. This person's health can be stabilized by working at something that puts him above the demands of negative people. He must be able to set his own pace and work in his own time. If this individual is forced to work where his nurturing qualities are unappreciated, or where he is too regimented, or where coworkers are insensitive, his health can suffer. The sign placement of the Moon and its position in the chart will further describe the areas of the body where trouble is liable to manifest. If the Moon is in Aries, for instance, he might have headaches; if the Moon is in Capricorn, his knees or the bony structure of the body might be weak.

Dealing with food or food products, or any activity that feeds mankind on a spiritual or emotional level, can provide an outlet for this person. With this house placement, the ability to sense the needs of the public and respond to them through his work augments the emotional satisfaction he needs to keep him healthy. Any work where he can act as a caretaker or express compassion brings him satisfaction. He may be a natural writer as well. Public response to his work can give him a special sense of well-being, and when he combines his inner, gut reaction about the needs of the public with his attunement to a higher level of inspiration, he is able to rise to the heights of his potential and express natural inventiveness and genius.

LEO RULING
THE SIXTH HOUSE

When Leo rules the sixth house of health (and Pisces rules the ascendant) or the Sun is located in the sixth house, the Sun relates to health matters. The heart is the most vulnerable area of the body, and a person with this house placement may inherit some genetic weakness in that part of his body or begin to constrict and tighten the muscles around the heart at a very young age. Lack of acknowledgment, either from the self or others, can be deleterious to health, and the consequent disillusionment is likely to create the poison that will undermine the quality of his health. Use of color as a meditative technique is invaluable in relaxing the heart muscle and energizing the area around the heart chakra. (See Chapter 21.)

Pisces is found on the ascendant with this house placement, and it rules the lymphatic system and the feet. Neptune, the planetary ruler of Pisces, relates to vision and therefore to the eyes, and describes right-brain activity. In some cases the individual may be myopic or nearsighted. Problems occur when events threaten to bring disillusionment to the idealistic Pisces personality. If he develops a psychological predisposition to hide his head in the sand rather than look at the reality of a situation, he is like a camera out of focus. He blurs the situation and impairs not only his ability to see things clearly, but his ability to create what he chooses on the mirror of life through his innate and magical power of visualization. With lack of confrontation, eyesight can become distorted. There are, however, yogic exercises that are extremely successful in strengthening the eye muscles and improving the quality of the individual's vision. (See Chapter 25 on Meditation.) The prevention, in this case, is to confront the situation immediately to avoid slipping into naïve behavior.

When this individual is able to take control of situations around him, he has many choices and can make constructive decisions. He also needs a job situation or a type of work that will bring him some degree of honor and recognition. With a strong executive ability, indicated by Leo ruling the sixth house, the individual with this house placement must have some degree of authority on his job or work in an area where his name can become known. Neptune rules film, as an example, and Leo describes a natural acting ability. If this individual is involved with film or the world of theater, he has a natural outlet for his energy.

Pisces rising describes a prophetic or poetic quality. This individual can have great vision, conceptual ability, and an idealistic quality, but naïveté can be a hazardous trait. Drug and alcohol addiction are dangers, since the individual may look for a way of being high on life. Pisces rules the feet, and massaging the soles of the feet has a profound regenerating effect on his energy system, since all of the organs in the body are represented in reflexology points on the feet. As Neptune rules vision, it is interesting to note that there is a technique for determining illness in the body by looking in the eyes. This diagnostic technique is called iridology.

With this house position comes a profound ability to love and to be loved. This person needs self-love above all, for when he values himself and works only in areas that are his own choices, he feels in charge and in control of his own destiny. The pitfall for him is waiting for permission from others to do what he really wants to do and only involving himself in activities that will bring ego recognition. As a young child, he can begin to learn how to visualize and conceptualize the conditions he wants around him, so that he feels he is the captain of his own destiny. Then his heart pumps vigorously and sends abundant healthful energy throughout his system. He has a magical and natural ability to create his own reality and can live within an aura that will prove to be fertile ground for his imagination. He can manifest ideal conditions in his life with such inner authority.

VIRGO RULING
THE SIXTH HOUSE

When Virgo is the sign that falls on the cusp of the sixth house (Aries rules the ascendant) then Mercury is placed in the sixth house and relates to health matters. The combination of an Aries ascendant and a Virgo sixth house rulership describes a very interesting set of energies. Impulsiveness and a tendency to be headstrong, indicated by an Aries ascendant, are qualities that are the antitheses of a need to work carefully and analytically, described by Virgo's ruling the sixth house. Rash, irrational behavior alternates with objectivity and the ability to analyze a situation and can be the cause of physical problems.

Mercury, the ruler of Virgo, relates to the intestinal tract; Mars, the ruler of Aries, describes, among other things, the function of the adrenal glands. Since both of these body parts lie below the midline of the body in the lower torso, they relate to risk-taking activities. But the planetary rulers of both Aries and Virgo relate to matters connected with the head and brain. So balance depends on getting the mind and gut to work together. Mars relates to impulse, adventure, courage, daring innovation, and headstrong activity; while Mercury, describing left-brain functioning, relates to coolness, analysis, and calculation. The attempt to integrate these qualities can bring about a great deal of growth, but it can also put stress on the physical system. The health of the individual is dependent on activities that must be carefully planned and thought out. But, when the left brain is in disproportionate control of a situation and too much pressure is exerted from the cautious analytical mind, impatience (related to Mars) may stir up additional adrenaline. This can cause an individual to throw caution to the wind, thereby creating risky situations that threaten the logical mental process even more. Or the opposite can happen. The individual may find himself in a kind of paralysis until his mind and body get together.

For example, when the adrenals whip into action under stress, the energy they generate can be blocked in the intestinal tract, unless that part of the body is in good working order. The intestinal tract must be kept clean and pure if health is to be maintained. Proper diet, colonic irrigation, and specific exercises strengthen the intestinal walls and prevent a major buildup of toxins in that area. Headaches or debilitating lack of energy are strong clues that the intestinal tract is collecting poisons that will block mental energy.

Developing physical skill in dance or athletics offers a chance to coordinate the need for activity and the need for logic and analysis. Exercise, or practice, is only part of the rigorous daily training necessary to become a good dancer or athlete. Mental concentration and methodical analysis are essential in developing a technique which will ensure the ability to re-create a high performance each and every time. When coordinated energy surges through the body, stimulating the flow of blood, poisons are eliminated from the system. If the person with this interesting set of conflicts can also find occupations that enable him to pave the way for others, using his analytical mind to find solutions to problems, he preserves good health and the natural vitality that goes with this house placement.

LIBRA RULING
THE SIXTH HOUSE

The Libra-Taurus combination is another especially challenging set of energies. When Libra rules the sixth house of health, Taurus rules the ascendant. Taurus rules the throat, larynx, neck, and jaw; Libra rules the pancreas. Venus is the ruler of both Taurus and Libra. The positive qualities of Venus are an elevated social consciousness and an ability to deal graciously in a social milieu. Venus also describes beauty, art, theater, diplomacy, or any activity that relates to the creation of balance and fair play. Beyond anything else, Venus describes pleasure. With the combination of Taurus and Libra in a stretch-growth relationship, the individual must find pleasure in his daily activities and in his work environment. Growth comes when he finds a way to bring pleasure to himself through work that relates to diplomacy or the creation of harmony and beauty. Stagnation comes with excessive indulgence, for when he becomes self-indulgent, he disturbs the balance so essential to his well-being.

Since Taurus rules the throat, pleasure comes from activity associated with that area of the body and through activity related to the throat chakra or the power center. A young restaurateur with this house placement described the sensual pleasure he received from feeling liquids pass through his throat. He said, "When I was a child, I would gulp a milkshake because I loved not only the taste, but the feeling of it going down my throat."

A person with Taurus rising almost invariably expresses an artistry in the preparation of food. Unfortunately, gourmet foods are often rich in ingredients not easily assimilated into the system. Gourmet desserts are rarely low in sugar or fat content, for instance. When the pancreas is overstimulated, due to the ingesting of too much sugar, excess insulin is circulated throughout the system. The blood-sugar level drops, causing reactions ranging from a feeling of light headedness or dizziness to a loss of consciousness. A quick dose of sugar or a glass of wine or alcohol may temporarily restore the feeling of well-being. This can initiate a vicious cycle, however. When the pancreas secretes too much insulin for too long a period of time, it threatens to lie down on the job and produce no more. The resulting illness is diabetes.

The condition that precludes diabetes is hypoglycemia, still misunderstood and sometimes totally invalidated by many physicians. This illness has been responsible for many undiagnosed disabilities. One woman was practically bedridden and almost totally incapacitated, but traditional tests revealed nothing that could be diagnosed. Her family presumed she was either a hypochondriac or was bordering on mental illness. A former voice teacher (with Taurus rising; Venus ruling the throat), she was so depressed that she could not find the strength to work or enjoy life. She knew nothing about the effect of diet on her condition and continued eating foods that aggravated her symptoms. Finally a friend suggested that she undergo a seven-hour glucose-tolerance test to determine the curve of her blood-sugar level. (This test is not administered as a matter of course, even in thorough physical examinations. It is generally only administered when there is reason to suspect blood-sugar problems. Therefore, this disease is not easily detected even though it can be the cause of many problems, including severe depression.) When the results of the test revealed a severe case of hypoglycemia, and she found a physician familiar with the illness, she began to eat properly and was completely cured of all symptoms. Her life began anew.

When a hypoglycemic's blood sugar hits its lowest point, the individual may display fits of dreadful temper and possible violence or extremely emotional reactions, bordering on hysteria. (A dreadful temper is also a negative attribute that is associated with Taurus rising.) If the level of sugar imbalance is not extreme, less extreme reactions may be present, such as slight depression or low energy. Because this malady is only accurately diagnosed when a blood test is taken, many people are unaware they have it and need to monitor not only their sugar intake, but their intake of any carbohydrates. Given the varying degree of imbalance of pancreatic function, and the resulting varying degree of symptoms, it might be important for a person with this house placement to observe the effects on his emotional stability when there is an excess of sugar or carbohydrate in his diet.

Occupations that are conducive to the health of a person with this house placement relate to the use of the voice and power issues in particular. An innate diplomat, he can find outlet in many professions, but involvement in social causes can be especially fulfilling. The creation of beauty and pleasure in the lives of others brings great satisfaction to this individual when he discovers that what he says will be of value to people in the solution of their problems and in bringing harmony into their lives.

S C O R P I O   R U L I N G
T H E   S I X T H   H O U S E

When Scorpio rules the sixth house of health (and Gemini rules the ascendant) or Pluto is located in the sixth house, the level of energy can be atomic and dynamic, as it relates to powerful Pluto. The dynamic energy described by this sign underlines the necessity for the individual with this house placement to work in an area where he can touch masses of people, or where his special, high level of effectiveness is required to produce big events.

Gemini rules the ascendant when Scorpio appears on the sixth-house cusp. Occupations must be exciting enough to grab the interest, for the person with Gemini rising simply cannot tolerate boredom. He needs mental challenge and external stimulation to keep his Mercurial personality fed and invigorated. Therefore, when he works in areas that allow him to utilize his quick mind, he is able to be particularly effective. The satisfaction and mental stimulation he derives from his work can bring more stimulation than any activity he might conjure up based on a purely restless need.

A Plutonian outlook describes a cosmic viewpoint. The aspects and placement of Pluto in an astrological chart can describe major initiations or tests that will come in the life of an individual. The position of Pluto in the natal horoscope, as well as the position of Scorpio on the wheel, designate the areas of life from which those tests will arise. When Pluto rules the sixth house, health factors may bring about the greatest growth in life. That growth may come about as a result of difficulties with work or may even come about through ill health or disability. This individual may have to come face-to-face with decisions about the level on which he chooses to be effective. He will have a clear choice as to whether he will work on the lower, or manipulative, level or, with the highest motivation for the welfare of all concerned, become involved with situations where he can effect far-reaching changes in whatever field into which he chooses to put his energy.

Pluto rules the ovaries and gonads. These are the areas of the body that come under stress when the dynamic energy described by Pluto is not channeled into areas that will eventually make a difference to mankind. The nonproductive Plutonian pattern is particularly harmful when it relates to work. The individual pushes himself beyond what is reasonable to expect and may wear out the batteries that connect him to his highest self. The connection to the higher self seemed to manifest in a surprisingly different way in the case of one young man with this house position. He worked in a noisy, frantically paced gambling casino. The ambience was also conducive to some nefarious schemes that were quietly cooked up. But this young man, who had a very sensitive system, found it difficult to work in such an atmosphere. He planned to find another occupation, but the income he derived from working in the casino was hard to give up, so he kept putting off making a change. Then this young man was involved in an accident, unrelated to work, and suffered disabilities to his arms that prevented him from continuing to work. It would seem that his higher self found a way to prevent him from continuing to work in an environment that was poisonous to his overall well-being.

If the person with this house placement becomes aware of an ability to work on a higher level of consciousness, he begins to let go of manipulative (underworked-connected, as in the case of the young man in the casino) or stagnating work situations, and begins to focus on areas where he can be truly potent. The transmutation usually occurs when he has forced and pushed, plotted and planned to get what he wants, and he eventually creates his own tar baby situation (he gets stuck and has no one to blame but himself). When a backfire occurs, or he feels the rug being pulled out from under him, he learns to let go of nonproductive situations and people. If he can use the difficult learning experience to consciously effect a transmutation of motivation and lets go of efforts to simply get his own way, he begins to work on a higher level of consciousness under the guidance of the higher will. Different motivation focuses energy toward activity that will benefit all mankind. At that point, his life begins to manifest subtle benefits that come about quite naturally as a result of higher motivation.

Dr. Ilan Bohm, a New York City chiropractor with this house placement, is a true new-age doctor. His knowledge of the human body extends to an awareness of the esoteric body, its functions, and the interconnecting links to the physical body through the spleen and chakras. Dr. Bohm uses many methods to diagnose weakness or illness, including reflexology, iridology, pulse spots on the temples, and the Chinese system of taking the pulse. He has a set of crystals in his office that have been calibrated to a particular vibrational level for the purpose of healing specific organs of the body.

Dr. Bohm is aware of his healing potential and utilizes more than the sophisticated devices he has in his office. With a very quick, bright mind, he is able to make a swift diagnosis and is then able to recharge the systems of his patients on many levels simultaneously, using his own energy. He is up-to-date on the newest techniques and is able to research their efficacy by means of a psychic technique that gives him confirmation of what will work for each individual. It is interesting to note that Dr. Bohm overcame many of his own health problems before he was able to heal others.

The stretch-growth needed in this particular combination of rising sign and sixth house is the refusal to compromise principles and the decision not to work for the purpose of surface gratification. Dr. Bohm could easily use his facile mind to bring about relief of symptoms on a physical level alone, but his higher sense of ethics and responsibility helps him reach people on an even deeper level.

SAGITTARIUS RULING THE SIXTH HOUSE

When Sagittarius rules the sixth house of healing and Cancer is on the ascendant, Jupiter describes the conditions of health. Cancer is a water sign, whereas Sagittarius is a fire sign. The growth-stretch aspect that relates to this sign combination is as difficult as combining fire and water. For when the emotionalism described by a Cancer ascendant is undirected or out of control, it can put out the fiery enthusiasm connected to work, described by Sagittarius ruling the sixth house.

Cancer rules the stomach area. That includes all organs involved in the digestive system. Sagittarius rules the kidneys, liver, and all organs that relate to the elimination system. Proper digestion of food and elimination of wastes are especially important for the health and well-being of a person with this house combination. Both systems described by these signs are ruled by organs that are located in the part of the body relating to risk taking in life. If this individual has lost his zest and has been disappointed, he becomes even more vulnerable to situations that might be hurtful. He allows conditions to overwhelm him and a feeling of paralysis creeps in, causing him to resist taking new risks. With a lack of goals and objectives, he has a tendency to hold on to negative conditions in his life. His whole system becomes flooded with the poisonous waters of emotionalism, and he begins to eat foods that, while they might soothe his stomach, might also be the very ones that will create toxins in his system. A person with this placement can consume vast quantities of food, as the act of putting something into his stomach gives him a momentary sense of satisfaction.

Cancer rising indicates a predisposition for water retention. He tends to collect fluids in his tissues just as he collects pain and hurts. The kidneys cannot function properly if the liver is over-stressed and is lazy in the production of the enzymes that are necessary for good digestion. With sluggish digestion, the kidneys do not eliminate liquids properly, and the individual's tissues begin to swell. Food allergies (a Cancerian trait) increase a predisposition to swelling tissues. If the person is upset over his burgeoning silhouette and eats more to soothe the disappointment, a self-sustaining cycle begins, causing weight gain, sluggish elimination of fluids, and more emotional upset. With a small amount of dietary planning, he can consume enough food to satisfy his hunger without excessive caloric intake. It is important for him to know that the poisons of hurt, pain, and disappointment can be as disastrous to his health as consuming small amounts of cyanide.

With Jupiter ruling the area of work as well as health, the person needs a challenge with his job, for unless he has a goal or goals, he is apt to be less than productive. When he can accomplish a task too easily, it is no longer stimulating and risky. He loses enthusiasm and feels disappointed. He begins to hang on to outmoded conditions, and his physical system becomes stagnant. Humor, joy, and challenge bring rewards that are cause for celebration and essential ingredients for his good health. The stretch-growth aspect, relating to this house placement, demands that the individual replace physical hunger needs with a more productive stoking of the emotional furnace. With new goals in sight, the individual is challenged to reach out for new conditions in his life. The conditions that cater to the needs of mankind, and especially womankind, are particularly fulfilling.

Jean Neiditch, the founder of Weight Watchers, started an exciting adventure by encouraging her overweight friends to follow her diet plans. (Jean was born with Cancer rising.) She combined a caring, nurturing quality with her own contagious enthusiasm and began her trek on the road that led to an income of millions. Jupiter rules encouragement, enthusiasm, and sales. With enough enthusiasm and enough belief in the product, the person with Cancer rising can relate to mankind's needs and keep himself challenged beyond his own need for momentary stomach-oriented satisfactions. The ultimate key to good health and physical well-being for persons with this house placement is to avoid the overconsumption of rich foods that put a strain on the digestive system.

CAPRICORN RULING
THE SIXTH HOUSE

mike

When Capricorn rules the sixth house (and Leo is on the ascendant) or Saturn is placed in the sixth house, Saturn describes health patterns. Saturn, the ruler of Capricorn, rules the skeletal structure, the knees, and calcium in the system. Leo rules the heart. Most often, external pressures cause the individual to clamp down on some part of the body. If the heart is the focus of attention, as it is with this ascendant, pressures can cause restriction of flow through that central organ.

Saturn, in its negative sense, is associated with judgment. In a positive sense, Saturn is associated with responsibility and discipline. The individual can easily live with a Spartan routine which satisfies the need for structure, both in his life and work, and is reflected in areas of health. Regimentation of the intake of food can be healthful, as the digestive system is never overloaded. But the tendency of this person to go to the extremes, denying himself proper sustenance, must be avoided. He needs to develop a healthful regimen of diet, exercise, vitamins, and sleep to give him the kind of energy he needs for his work.

Acknowledgment from others is as much of a requirement for a person with Leo rising as is food and water. The development of self-esteem and self-love can go a long way toward mitigating the need for ego strokes from others. In fact, when the flow of energy through the heart chakra is blocked, it may be due to lack of self-love or of expression of love toward others. Self-love is different from excessive ego gratification. The kind of ego that is associated with grandiosity is really a reflection of a lack of self-esteem. Self-permission, doing what one chooses to do because of a need for self-expression, is a positive step toward developing true self-love.

AQUARIUS RULING
THE SIXTH HOUSE

When Aquarius rules the sixth house of health (and Virgo appears on the ascendant) or Uranus is placed in that sector, Uranus relates to health in the chart. Both of these signs relate to mental energy. Virgo describes left-brain activity and the power of analysis, whereas Aquarius describes a higher level of mental energy, that of inspiration. When these two qualities of mental energy are in harmony, the result can be pure genius. The growth-stretch involved in the harmonizing of inspiration and analysis depends primarily on the purity of the two systems that fuel the mind.

Aquarius rules the nervous system, but it also rules the breath. That includes the quality of the breathing process, as well as the quality of oxygen carried by the breath and absorbed into the bloodstream. Proper intake of breath is essential to the nervous system, since oxygen is fuel for the nerves. Oxygen first passes, via the breath, into the bloodstream and keeps that system pure. It reaches the brain to help distribute the messages, sent by the brain along the nervous system, to their proper destination. Oxygen acts like a bath for the higher-octave sensitive nervous system, just as certain foods act like a cleansing agent for the digestive system.

Virgo rules the intestinal tract. Since the prime function of that system is the elimination of poisons, it is essential to keep the intestines free from toxins that can collect in the pockets. Colonics are especially important for a person with Virgo ruling one of the houses of health. Keeping the lungs healthy and pure so that they can fully perform their purification of the bloodstream is as essential as keeping the intestinal tract clean. Exhalation of breath eliminates carbon dioxide from the body; carbon dioxide is the residual toxin left in the lungs when oxygen has been assimilated into the bloodstream. Proper oxygen intake and exhalation, and proper diet and elimination, keep the nervous system and the digestive system invigorated.

Improper function of the brain can manifest in learning disorders, depression, or impaired concentration. They may all stem from lack of oxygen in the system. Blocked intestinal activity also impairs the function of the brain. Poisons collected in that part of the body can manifest as headaches, lack of clear thinking, or dullness of mental activity. Worry and anxiety may be a clue that some type of toxin is blocking the system, either in the intestinal tract or as a result of a lack of intake of oxygen and discharge of carbon dioxide.

Uranus, ruler of Aquarius, describes an even more important function of the human system, however, which is so far unrecognized by medical science. It describes the influx of energy from esoteric levels that determine the quality of the electrical system of the body. The nervous system is the important link between the esoteric bodies and the dense physical body. Therefore, when Uranus rules the sixth house, subtle remedies that carry special vibrational frequencies are the best agents of healing. An individual with this delicate, high-strung, sensitive nervous system responds to treatments that work directly on the esoteric body. Those treatments include acupuncture, healing with color and music, flower remedies, crystals, breathing, and meditational techniques. Learning proper breathing techniques is especially important for the health and well-being of an individual with this house placement. Consumption of drugs and medicine put more toxins into a system that might already be overloaded.

Mentally stimulating work also helps keep the individual healthy. The type of work that best suits a person with this house placement is that which allows him to express his own unique level of inspiration. Activities that relate to music, new-age technology, recordings, healing, astrology, and the utilization of electronic devices can be outlets for this kind of high-vibration energy, since they operate on a higher frequency than other activities. With a release of energy onto a level where inspiration is the key to the successful completion of tasks, the person with this placement discharges any excess of electrical energy from his system and keeps the channels open.

PISCES RULING
THE SIXTH HOUSE

When Pisces rules the house of health (and Libra is on the ascendant) or Neptune is placed in the sixth house, Neptune describes health patterns. The bodily systems described by these signs are the lymph system (Pisces) and pancreatic function (Libra). The stretch-growth relationship between the two signs is subtle, as both of these planets describe energies that are sensitive, gentle, and delicate, not rough, tough, and earthy. The planetary ruler of Pisces, Neptune, relates to the thymus gland, which produces the lymphocytes that help fight infection, and to the immune system itself. Venus, planetary ruler of the Libran ascendant, relates to the sugar levels in the body.

The pancreas secretes insulin that regulates blood-sugar levels in the body and therefore relates to the balance of energy levels. The cells in the lymph glands produce antibodies that fight infection in the body. When a consistent balance of energy is maintained, with no swings between extreme highs or extreme lows, an individual is less likely to succumb to infections, even the flu or a simple cold.

Problems with energy and health occur when the individual is unable to maintain a balance and begins to work on the less productive side of energy described by these two planets. The negative manifestation can be fatigue or passivity and may be due to overproduction of insulin, which then floods the system. The overproduction occurs when an excess of unrefined carbohydrates, sugar, or alcohol is consumed. Drugs also stimulate insulin production. Neptune describes drugs and addictions. Those addictions usually relate to substances that produce a feeling of euphoria. Drugs do just that in the beginning phase of use. As the body loses its delicate balance, the immune system ceases to work effectively. Drug intake is particularly disastrous to an individual with this sensitive health system, as it stimulates a vicious cycle of highs and lows. Eventually the lows induce vague fears and phobias that lead to ever increasing use of substances in hopes of dispelling those negative feelings.

Venus describes not only sugar, but also love. The quality of love relates to the heart chakra. There is a subtle link between the heart chakra and the thymus gland, which is, in turn, linked to the immune system. In order to maintain the necessary balance in all areas of his life, the person with this house position needs love and pleasure. It is also important to eliminate anything toxic in his life, whether the toxins are related to food, substances, conditions, or people.

The individual with this house placement experiences a physical sense of well-being when he can work with idealistic projects or where he can create on a fantasy level. Neptunian work activities include therapy, film, and association with the so-called glamour world. With a Libra ascendant, artistic projects or activities connected to diplomacy, social matters, and social consciousness enable the individual to act as a balance wheel for others. Since Neptune is the second of the higher octave planets and describes the higher mind or right brain, the individual has a particular potential to create ideal conditions in his work through his power of visualization. Dreams and fantasies play an important part in his life, as his health is vital when he can function on a higher level of mind and concept.

Neptune describes the eyesight. That includes the quality of vision as well as the ability to see. One of the side effects of sugar imbalance and overproduction of insulin is impaired vision. The range of disability can vary from slightly foggy vision and minor pain to more serious maladies such as diabetic retinopathy. (Eyesight can be improved through specific exercises. See Chapter 25 on Meditation.)

An individual with this house placement must have balance, pleasure, and easy environmental conditions in order to survive and feel vibrant and healthy. Pressures, worry, negativity, and strife are especially detrimental for the health and well-being of such an individual. Since Neptune rules the feet, and all of the organs and parts of the body are represented in acupuncture points on the feet, increased health, vitality, and the restoration of hope, dreams and visions can be stimulated by foot massage. (See Chapter 19 on Reflexology.) The quality of the lymph system, subtly strengthened by pleasurable experiences and love, can be increased by rebounding, or bouncing, on a trampoline. Physical stimulation of the thymus gland can also be attained by gentle pounding on the chest just above the heart chakra. These exercises are particularly important for an individual with this house placement in order to maintain a healthy and harmonious physical system.

Aspects

When astrology is used in the diagnosis and determination of health patterns, subtle and underlying factors must be considered. Simple statements about planetary rulerships in relation to health cannot paint a complete picture of health conditions. The relationship of one planet to another in an individual astrological chart modifies and qualifies the overall situation very specifically. These relationships are called aspects. So the third thing to consider, after looking at the planets that rule the two health sectors of the chart, is the mathematical relationships between the planets that rule those houses (the first and the sixth) or are placed therein, and any other planet they may touch.

Aspects can describe many psychological predispositions, including the tensions and conflicts a person brings into his life as part of his individual grand plan for growth. Aspects can also describe the easy situations and conditions in life. When they describe problem areas, they also indicate how those problems can be solved. (In each question lies the answer, and in each problem lies the solution.) In my book *Astrological Aspects, Your Inner Dialogues*, I discuss only the hard aspects, which describe difficult conditions in life. The hard aspects are, in the long run, positive and beneficial in many ways, as conflicts and difficulties produce change and growth. The soft aspects describe conditions that need no resolution and are easy to express. There is no growth connected to soft aspects.

For the purpose of health, it is most essential to look at any planets in hard aspect to the ruling planets of both the first and sixth houses. Those aspects describe the probable physical stress factors which, unresolved, can lead to ill health or disease. They also describe psychological predispositions that may lead to particular susceptibilities or kinds of illness, since the body often translates frustration and inner arguments into physical manifestations.

Aspects can be analyzed on several different levels; they can describe the physical health of a person, as well as the mental and spiritual qualities of well-being. If one planet describes a quality of energy, we can call it a voice. Two planets interacting would then describe a conversation. The conversation can be harmonious or it can be an argument. That argument may take place on a mental level, or it may show conflict on the emotional plane. Arguments can also take place on a spiritual or soul level.

In relation to health, particular arguments between planets describe the specific *areas* where illness is liable to manifest as a result of these arguments, or it may describe the *type* of illness or imbalance. With the eight planets plus the Sun and Moon describing all the inner voices of a person's health patterns, it is like a committee meeting in which everyone must have his say. If too many voices are raised in disagreement, a person may have a riot going on inside. He may not be aware of all of the specific conflicts within him, he just knows he doesn't feel very well or that he is in pain. It may be hard to pinpoint the differing qualities of warring energy in his system, much less the true source of that conflict and stress. As an example, if Saturn is making a difficult aspect to a particular planet, it is important to consider all of the difficult aspects Saturn makes in a chart to see what additional voices are being raised, and the additional areas of the body that might be under stress.

Sometimes the kaleidoscopic shifting of planetary aspects from day to day, month to month, or year to year can describe new and temporary situations within the system that need to be resolved. Temporary screams of the energy system manifest in symptoms that may be the devices needed to grab the attention of the individual. Ultimately, he awakens to the urgency of the situation around him and finds a resolution. Carl Jung said that any unrealized energy or potential will manifest or exteriorize as fate or destiny. Sometimes these manifestations are only annoying physical symptoms; sometimes they are serious health problems. And sometimes they are not directly related to physical health at all, but indicate imbalance or dis-ease on the other levels of existence.

The hard aspects that need to be considered in the astrological chart are the square (two planets 90 degrees apart), the opposition (180 degrees), semisquare (45 degrees), and sesquisquare (135 degrees). The growth-stretch aspect is the inconjunct (150 degrees). A conjunction, which is neither a hard nor soft aspect, adds an additional color or quality of energy that modifies the pure essence of energy described by a single planet positioned alone. Conjunctions describe two or more planets that sit right next to each other, occupying the same longitudinal degree position. Oppositions are the easiest of the hard aspects to resolve, as they describe a pull between two diametrically opposing situations or qualities of energy. This pull can be balanced by utilizing the positive qualities of the two energies together. The most difficult aspects to resolve are the square and the sesquisquare, as they describe seemingly irreconcilable qualities of energy. The inconjunct is the most important of all the aspects to resolve. This aspect describes the greatest growth opportunities in an individual's life.

If Mars rules the ascendant, for instance, and is square to Uranus, the adrenals (Mars) and the nervous system (Uranus) are hooked into a negative responsive cycle. Too much electrical energy may course into the nervous system. This rush of energy can cause the person to feel restless, impetuous, and can cause accidents, cuts, burns, or the unpredictable disposition of adrenaline throughout the body. Abscesses can occur as a result of impurities in the bloodstream, and there may be problems with allergies or asthma. The natural antidote for such a condition can be extra exercise and extra intake of oxygen to facilitate the assimilation of the undue amounts of electrical currents available to the individual. Activities that relate to inspiration and spiritual levels of existence use up the extra high-level energy. It is important to cleanse the blood and propel excess energy onto higher levels of consciousness.

If Jupiter rules the sixth house of health, for example, and is square to Venus, the pancreas (Venus) may secrete an excess amount of insulin (Jupiter is the planet of abundance and excess), causing a predisposition to hypoglycemia or diabetes.

When Saturn is in hard aspect or relationship to other planets, illness may be easier to diagnose. Saturn describes a blockage of energy to some part of the body or some bodily function. Certain Saturn aspects can indicate rigid self-denial. Arthritis, conditions with the bones, or teeth and gum problems can be indicated when Saturn rules or is placed near the ascendant or in relation to the sixth house. If Saturn is in hard aspect to the Sun, a predisposition to cut off energy to the heart and heart chakra exists. When Saturn is in hard aspect to the Moon, the emotions are affected and depression is strongly indicated. The consequent blockage of energy may result in constriction of the stomach, which in turn causes maladies ranging from indigestion or ulcers to more serious stomach disorders. This aspect can describe abstemiousness with food. (I, with Saturn square the Moon, ate almost nothing as a child except carrots, apples, oranges, and some other fruits. I refused to drink milk or eat cheese and would only eat the yolks of eggs if all the white was removed. Red meat was completely out of the question, and I would only eat the white meat of chicken. Everything else made me very squeamish and sick to my stomach. In early childhood, my affinity for certain foods was an accurate guideline as to the proper foods for my system. Even today, my nutritionist, Dr. Elizabeth Dane cautions me against the consumption of red meat and dairy products, for example.)

When Saturn is in hard aspect to Mercury, worry can produce intestinal problems, lung disorders, or weakness in the arms and in the pairs of the body. Saturn-Venus hard aspects indicate a predisposition to illnesses related to the pancreas, throat, neck, larynx, or tonsils. The symptoms may be as simple as a cough, for instance, or as detrimental and painful as a strep throat. Saturn-Mars hard aspects relate to lowered adrenal function, sluggish production of red blood cells, blood disorders, and may indicate a predisposition to head injuries. Saturn-Jupiter hard aspects describe blocks to the kidneys and liver, problems with the production of enzymes, and hip disorders. Saturn-Uranus hard aspects may indicate rigidity of the rib cage and related breathing problems, including asthma and bronchitis. The tendency to hold the breath during times of crisis or stress leads to decreased oxygen intake. This aspect can also describe problems with the legs and nervous system.

Saturn-Neptune hard aspects describe restricted flow of energy into the lymph system, difficulties with eyesight, and trouble with the feet. Neptune can also describe anxieties, morbid fears, or phobias. Since Saturn relates to stress and pressures, those fears and phobias may manifest as a result of too much restriction or pressure. (See Chapter 11 on Past-Life Conditioning.) Saturn-Pluto hard aspects indicate blocked energy throughout the chakra system, the hormonal system, and restriction of energy into areas related to ovaries and gonads. The results may manifest in menstrual or prostate problems.

Astrological research concerning aspects alone falls short of concrete diagnosis. The mathematical relationships of one planet to another can only point toward the afflicted areas of the body. When related to the first and sixth houses in an individual chart, hard aspects are indicative of the parts of the body that may be affected by stress and pressures. Psychological relationships to illness can be determined by a deeper look at the meanings of each planet involved. (See Chapter 10 on mental energy.)

Elements, Cardinality, Fixity, and Mutability

There are several ways of breaking down an astrological chart in order to gain a deeper insight into the makeup of an individual. The signs of the zodiac can be grouped in two basic ways. They can be divided into three groups, with each incorporating four signs; or they can be divided into four groups according to ruling element.

The three groups of signs are called cardinal, fixed, and mutable. Cardinal signs include Aries, Cancer, Libra, and Capricorn; fixed signs include Taurus, Leo, Scorpio, and Aquarius; mutable signs are Gemini, Virgo, Sagittarius, and Pisces. The cardinal, fixed, and mutable groupings describe a subtle psychological predisposition. The cardinal signs are vulnerable, sensitive, active, and purposeful. Fixed signs are determined, rooted in their realities, intense, and reserved. Mutable signs are adaptable, flexible, and intelligent.

CARDINALITY

If a person has a greater number of planets in cardinal signs, he may be more easily impressed by his environment and specific conditions around him than someone with a greater number of fixed planets. If someone volunteers information or advice to the person with this sensitive disposition, he may go along with that advice whether or not it is to his ultimate benefit. He has a difficult time saying no and often must learn to take care of himself the hard way. He may discover through painful experiences that he is the target of projection (people project onto him what they are really telling themselves). He is more of a sensitive and overtly responsive mirror for others than are people with a majority of Fixed or mutable signs. His greatest challenge is to learn discrimination.

FIXITY

If a person has a preponderance of fixed signs in his chart, his character is one of determination and single-minded purposefulness. Very little can sway him from his chosen life path. He is not easily influenced by his environment or people around him. He knows where he is going and is determined to get there. His particular challenge is to become more open, with discrimination, and more adaptable, without being swayed from what he knows is best for his own life.

MUTABILITY

With a preponderance of mutable planets, an individual can be extremely adaptable, giving up his own desires or needs to adapt to the desires or needs of others. This is the kind of person who might give up his own life interests to care for an elderly parent, for example. With an extreme amount of mutability in the natal horoscope, the quality of adaptability may work to his detriment. Unless his sacrifice, or adaptability, is for a noble cause, he may find he has simply been swayed by whatever breeze has blown in his direction. The challenge in this instance is to become more focused on his own needs and more determined to follow the path that is productive for him, while he retains a degree of flexibility. Developing a healthy sense of purpose brings balance into his life. A preponderance of mutable planets in the natal chart does not denote being suggestible, as is one with an emphasis on cardinal planets, but it describes an innate desire for change. He may give into his own whims too often for his own good, as an example.

E L E M E N T S

The second way of analyzing the astrological chart is to divide the signs into four groups, which would then incorporate three signs in each group. These groupings are named after the elements and relate to the underlying makeup of man in relation to nature and his environment. Everything in nature is composed of either earth, air, fire, or water. These elements are also part of man's constitution. The earth signs are Capricorn, Taurus, Virgo; the air signs are Aquarius, Gemini, and Libra; the fire signs include Aries, Leo, and Sagittarius; the water signs include Pisces, Cancer, and Scorpio.

Analysis of the elements adds information about the physical makeup of the individual as well as his psychological predispositions. Each element describes the most natural response of an individual to the earth plane and the elemental conditions that will most stimulate energy within him. The ideal combination is to have all the twelve important indicators in your chart divided equally among the four elements. The important indicators are the ten planets plus the ascendant and the midheaven. Having three indicators in each element would describe a perfect balance between all the elements, each of which has a specific function in life.

Fire

With an emphasis on fire in the chart, enthusiasm and vitality describe the disposition and psychological makeup of an individual. If such fiery enthusiasm and energy is excessive, the person can be extravagant and wildly uncontrolled. He may exaggerate everything, not only to others but to himself. He can exhaust everyone around him and deplete his own source of energy by his excessive behavior. He operates either in top gear or is completely bereft of fuel. The manifest traits may appear to be self-exaltation, vanity, and love of pomp and grandeur, but what appears to be excessive ego may simply be an imbalance of fire in his nature. Excess fire in the horoscope predisposes an individual to a manic state. With too little fire in the chart, the individual may lack enthusiasm and may settle for an existence that maintains the status quo. The fear of disappointment or of overestimating his own potential may prevent him from developing ambitious goals.

Many planets in fire signs in the horoscope endows the individual with tremendous physical vitality. His outgoing energy predisposes him to overcoming physical limitations. He can be unconcerned with handicaps and unhampered by disabilities that might be devastating to someone else. A healthy amount of fire in the chart enables healing to take place quite easily. Heat, sun, and light are vital healing tools for the regeneration of the physical constitution. However, too much fire in the system can cause excess production of adrenaline and result in burnout. With this level of vitality, the individual may engage in high-risk activities, but he is prone to push himself beyond practical, healthful limits.

Earth

A healthy amount of earth in the chart enables an individual to deal with practical, earthy matters. He is concerned with activities and routines that stabilize his life and give him a sense of security. The prime ingredients for that feeling of safety are money, food, and property. He enjoys things that grow in the earth and he can gravitate toward matters that preserve life in others. (Taurus rising, for instance, is invariably able to express his pleasure-loving nature in the preparation of food. It is indeed an art form, but most of all, he enjoys feeding his friends and gravitates toward activities that provide them with a sense of security.) With an excess of earth in the chart, a person may tend toward stodginess, lustfulness, and sensuality, overlooking the balancing qualities of sensitivity and compassion. In extreme instances he may be greedy, fussy, or overly meticulous. With a lack of earth in the horoscope, the individual may not like to deal with earthly matters such as developing financial acumen, balancing his checkbook, or living a practical life-style. His discomfort with earthy matters may go as far as a dislike of housework or gardening because he might get dirt underneath his fingernails. He may dislike dealing with practical or organizational tasks. He may even be somewhat unsteady on his feet and may not easily walk a straight line.

Air

The air element relates to intellect. The air-dominant individual loves to collect data, observe behavior in others, and become aware of isolated facts so that he can find a relationship between them. He works on the mental plane and may focus on education in particular, whether it is formal or simply the result of his own observations. He may be curious about universal laws and the relationship between cause and effect. With too much air in the horoscope, the person may live in an ivory tower, be polarized in his brain, and neglect his feelings. He relates to everything on an intellectual level and may appear to be cold, unconcerned, and unfeeling. On a physical level, the tendency to be polarized in his head can prevent the natural flow of vitality throughout his system. Consequently, he may suffer from a lack of normal physical sensations, inured to pain or temperature, as an example. With too little air in the chart, the individual may not value his own level of intelligence. He may be uninterested in furthering his own education or in working where he must use his mind. Lack of air does not connote lack of intelligence, it simply implies that the individual's focus of attention goes toward other activities in his existence on earth.

Water

The water element relates to emotion. Water describes compassion and sensitivity, especially when it relates to the pain or welfare of others. Water can penetrate many substances, and an individual with a great deal of water in his chart may go into symbiosis with people around him. He is reflective, nurturing, and supportive. When an individual has an overabundance of water in his chart, he is extremely empathic. He may be so vulnerable that he cannot get past his own pain. He may appear unconcerned about others simply because he cannot stand the overload of feelings that occurs when he allows himself to be overly compassionate. He may become a rescuer, feeling things so deeply that he lacks objectivity. He may try to escape his overwhelming capacity to feel and personalize issues by drinking to drown his sorrows. He may be so maudlin in nature that no one is inclined to feel compassion for his sufferings. With a lack of water in the horoscope, just the opposite is true. The person may need to consciously develop more compassion and caring about the sufferings of mankind.

When an individual has a preponderance of water in his chart he may have a tendency to retain liquids, collecting excess water in his cell tissue, or to gain weight. He may experience problems with organs that relate to elimination of toxins and waste from his body. The psychological link to water retention is the emotional tendency to hold on. That holding on may include both people and possessions; he may discover that an effort to rid his life of clutter, as well as of people who are not supportive, helps him to regain better function of the organs of elimination.

SINGULARITY OR LACK OF AN ELEMENT

Special attention is warranted when an individual has only *one* planet in a particular element, or no planets at all in an element. With a singleton, or one planet, in any specific position in the horoscope, the emphasis is greater than with many planets positioned there. A singleton denotes a "finger of God" situation, or a mandate that this is an area where much attention must go. The inner dialogue or consideration is, "I want to, but I feel guilty about it," or "I don't want to, but I know I have to." The implied mandate is, "Stop arguing with yourself and just get on with it."

When there are *no* planets in a particular sector of the chart, it seems to indicate an area of life that has been completely resolved and presents no problem. The only danger in such a situation is that the person may be so unconsciously endowed with a particular attribute that he is intolerant of those without this attribute. When there is no earth in the chart, for example, the individual is far from being impractical. In fact, he is so automatically practical that he never has to worry about his ability to take care of mundane, day-to-day matters. He can allow himself to take more risks when he becomes aware of an automatic governing device in his makeup that keeps him from going too far, too fast. When there is no air in a chart, the individual may not realize he is exceptionally intelligent. (He may be very intolerant of stupidity or slow intellectual response in others, however.) Learning, the process of analysis, and the collection of data present no problem to this person. The individual may not dwell on his intelligence. He simply uses his mental faculties naturally and easily.

When there is no fire in the natal horoscope, the person has a natural exuberance that enables him to set goals, live up to challenges, and always land on his feet. He has innate vitality that prevents illness from taking hold in his system. When there is no water in a chart, the person possesses a natural quality of compassion without being overly sentimental or maudlin. This person would be unable to comprehend that someone else could be unfeeling or uncaring.

BALANCING AND HARMONIZING ELEMENTS

There are visual exercises that can help balance out the qualities described by the elements in the chart, enabling the individual to compensate for whatever natural lack may exist. Heat and warmth are vital commodities for an excess, or lack, of fire in the chart. Visualization and mental stimulation of adrenals can build energy, as an example. When there is a lack of earth in a chart, activities that connect a person to the earth (such as gardening, walking among trees and hugging them, etc.) can bring about a better ability to deal with practical matters. Proper breathing and conscious assimilation of oxygen into the system is essential to balance a lack or overabundance of air in the system. Proper breathing stimulates the brain by sending oxygen into that area, whereas shallow breathing deprives the brain of its most important fuel. Frequent bathing, showering, and drinking of water is essential for rebalancing when the water element is either limited or overly abundant. (See Part V on therapies, Chapter 21 on Color in particular.)

- - - - - -

Relationship of Astrology to Mental Energy

Part Mental Energy Plays in Health

A link clearly exists between the physical plane and the mental, but it is important to understand how that link works. Each individual creates the exact conditions that will manifest in his life through his thought processes. Every thought, as well as every action, is indelibly etched onto the Akashic Records, sort of like feeding information into a computer. (The Akashic Records are the storehouse of a person's experiences throughout all lifetimes. See p. 57.) These thoughts are either conscious or unconscious, but they weave part of the intricate tapestry of each individual's life, because those thoughts, actions, and inner dialogues manifest as events in the life of the individual. So it is essential to the overall well-being to put into perspective the part the mind plays in relation to physical health. However, it is too simplistic to presume that all physical disabilities or imbalances originate in the mind and that a cure can be effected merely by changing the way a person thinks. That might be true if an individual were always able to operate on the highest plane of consciousness and had the ability to maintain an alignment of all the systems that are part of his makeup. Then he might never be ill or disabled. He could consistently bring forth pure energy into his mind as well as into his physical makeup, and thereby influence activities in his daily life.

Most people living on the earth plane are working through a great deal of accumulated baggage, however, and that baggage precludes easy solutions to physical disabilities. There are factors in the environment and in the atmosphere of the earth plane, both known and unknown, that also affect an individual's health. The forces of energy in the environment, those that surround a person on a daily basis, also play a large part in the ability to maintain the alignment necessary for dynamic physical well-being.

The mind is the link between the soul and the body. Health disturbances arise on the etheric, or most subtle, level and the mind acts like a radio receiving station, transmitting and pouring soul energy into the physical system. This inpouring of energy includes both the negative imprints from past lives and disturbances in the present that might exist due to environmental conditions. For instance, life in a teeming, bustling city produces different kinds of stress than life lived in a pastoral setting. But also included are positive energies from the environment, as well as pure soul energy in the form of prana. If the nervous system is unable to assimilate both positive and negative energy and becomes overloaded, this inpouring of energy may cause problems in the physical nervous system. So, if for some reason the nervous system cannot properly perform as a conduit for positive energy, that energy may not be fully integrated into the body systems. Since the nervous system also acts as an instrument for transmutation of negative input, the quality of the inpouring energy, as well as the daily incurred stress factors, continually condition the nervous system. Therefore, it is the transmitted energy that is the prime cause of trouble, not the mental processes themselves.

Alice Bailey states that physical disabilities are not the result of wrong thought, but are far more likely to be the result of no thought at all, or the development of wrong attitudes toward individual conditions in life. The wrong attitudes to which she refers are more emotional than mental, however. Such reactions as worry, bitterness, disgust, hatred, and frustration do more to produce toxic conditions and consequent poisoning of the system than other causes that might seem more obvious. So ill health is really caused by a failure to bring higher energies into manifestation. This failure may be due to the mind's inability to transmit higher energies into the physical system, but is often the result of stress factors that prevent the right use of spiritual will to bring balance back into life. Ultimately, it is the function of the mind to make a choice about the specific level of consciousness on which to live, as the mind is the builder. The biggest decision in life is whether or not to work toward the elevation of consciousness and to live on the higher levels of existence.

Saturn describes the quality of gravitational pull in an individual's earthly experiences, and Uranus relates to the spiritual qualities, as well as the nervous system and the breath. Uranus also describes a person's ability to absorb prana into the physical body through the nervous system. Mercury and Neptune describe the two hemispheres of the brain.

The individual chart, and the aspects of these four planets to each other, indicate the way a person is predisposed to think and what assumptions or thought patterns he may need to change in order to achieve his goals. It also clearly indicates the conditions that have been brought into this life from past experiences, and what extra baggage a person incurs through his environmental conditioning. Those past-life experiences are generally described by planets situated in, and aspected to, the twelfth house. (See Chapter 11.) Finally, the horoscope gives a person clues as to how he can solve the problems he has brought in from birth and has chosen to resolve in his present life.

Since Saturn describes gravity and the way the physical body might handle stress, it is important to understand more thoroughly how stress affects the body and the mental processes. Dr. Virgil Chrane, an alphabiotic researcher with a private practice in Dallas, Texas, confirmed that stress factors play a major role in mind function, and consequently in the lack of balance which precedes ill health. He explained the sequence of events that results in degenerative disease and clarified the role the mind plays in physical health. "I've come to the conclusion that ill health and degenerative disease are really caused by a misdirection of energy, as a result of an improper stress response. With high stress we appropriately lateralize into one hemisphere of the brain or the other. That produces weakness on one side of the body, with resulting physical imbalance. If this persists over a long period of time, ultimately a serious degenerative disease process becomes apparent in the physical system."

Trained as a chiropractor, Dr. Chrane developed alphabiotics, a new approach to the concept of brain/mind balance. He said, "The major health problems in the world today, as I see it, are stress related. Anthropologists tell us that human beings have not changed, physically, in the last 10,000 years. We are NOT well designed, biologically, to deal with the pervasive, ongoing, day-to-day, physical, chemical, and emotional stresses of our time. It is very difficult for human beings to adjust to persistent low-level stress. Such things as job pressures, time pressures, money problems, congested expressways, noise, chemical, and electromagnetic pollution can and do, over a period of time, cause tremendous problems. Mankind is massively overwhelmed by an incredible amount of negative sensory input that affects the brain and nervous system. Since we are almost constantly affected by an ongoing, low level of stress, man reacts as if he were on emergency standby when there is no emergency. This throws him into a roller-coaster state of adrenal highs and lows."

Dr. Chrane went on to reveal the result of his research in this area. He states, "Ninety percent of nervous-system activity has to do with the sensory input into the brain. Only 10 percent of the nervous system has to do with motor function; that is, thinking, feeling, metabolism, and relating to the body in its gravitational field. Recent studies show that 90 percent of motor function is spent relating man to gravity. That motor function acts like a guidance system in a missile which keeps it on target. The physical body uses an enormous amount of physical energy just relating us to gravity, so much so that gravity is our almost unconquerable opponent. The way a person copes with gravity has everything to do with how long and how well he can function within the physical body. Gravity is constantly pulling a person down, so that he must lie down at regular intervals to minimize its effects. If the hemispheres of the brain are in balance, a person uses less energy to adjust to that constant downward pull.

"Ideally, everyone should be whole-brain functional, and mankind should be able to easily access both hemispheres of the brain when needed. According to Julian Jaynes in his book *The Bicameral Mind*, human beings were essentially whole-brain functioning until fairly recently in history. When we experience pain, trauma, or something with high emotional content, we appropriately lateralize into one hemisphere or the other. If the wisdom of the body perceives a type of danger that demands quick action, such as jumping out of the way of a speeding automobile, where conflicting ideas from each hemisphere are inappropriate, we tightly lateralize hemispherically. Each brain hemisphere is like a separate personality. When we need to act quickly, we should be locked into one or the other hemisphere in order to make a quick decision.

"The prime directive of the brain and nervous system is to regulate and coordinate the physiological functions of the body and to maintain structural and metabolic homeostasis. Since the brain and nervous system work in a priority way, danger is a higher priority than maintaining structural and metabolic balance, as danger can mean life or death. So a huge amount of energy must come from somewhere to cope with the problem. This energy must be focused outward to be ready for fight or flight. That extra energy can come from either hemisphere of the brain. The person tends to lock into one hemisphere—usually their dominant hemisphere—and that half of the brain becomes inappropriately more active.

"Each hemisphere of the brain controls half of the body. If a person shifts into left hemisphere, the analytical, critical, judgmental, rational, and linear side of the brain is more active, but if he shifts into right hemisphere, the creative, feeling, emotional, sensitive, nonlinear side is overly activated. If a person is locked into the left hemisphere and becomes aware that something is missing in his life, that he has lost an old feeling of wholeness that he once had, he tries to get more information. If that doesn't work, he tries to get different information, or better information, until finally, in a left-brain way, he knows a lot of stuff but his life is still chaotic. Information collecting is an ego trap for left-brain polarized people. The right-brain person feels that same void, but he usually gets lost in diversion, thinking that if he does busywork, the confusion will go away. He may become a workaholic, alcoholic, a drug addict, or overly involved in sports or TV. If he is spiritually inclined, he often gets lost in phenomena, thinking that if he can do phenomenal things, like being a good psychomotorist or being able to see auras, he will be a better person. This is the ego trap of the right-brain dominant person. When a person integrates the two hemispheres, he taps into a higher level of consciousness, the true inner self, the higher self of inner wisdom. Truly, the whole is greater than the sum of its parts.''

The position of Mercury and Neptune in an astrological chart, plus their aspects to each other, indicate whether an individual is more liable to polarize into the left or right hemisphere. If Neptune and Mercury are in harmonious aspect to each other, the individual has a higher probability of integrating the two halves and tapping higher consciousness, indicated by Pluto and its aspects in the natal chart.

Each hemisphere of the brain controls half of the body. If a person shifts into left hemisphere, the right side of the brain focuses energy for fight or flight, and the left side of the body literally goes weak, and vice versa. This can be demonstrated through standard kinesiological testing. (See Chapter 18.) Since we are polar beings, if the muscles go weak on one side of the body, the muscles on the other side go into contraction.

Dr. Chrane continued, ''Muscle tone is one of the prime factors of health. If two muscles are pulling equally against something in the middle, balance is maintained. If one muscle becomes flaccid and weak, the other muscle, even if it is normal, will go into contraction since it's lost its partner. There are 244 muscles attached to the spine like guidewires. When a muscle on one side goes weak, the muscle on the other side contracts and pulls a spinal vertebra out of position. This dramatically alters the structure and balance of the body.

''So the sequence is this: first comes danger, then the shift into one hemisphere or another, then one side of the body goes weak, the other goes into contraction, and a big chunk of energy shifts and focuses outwardly to be ready for battle. That is appropriate when there is high stress or real danger. It is not appropriate when the brain lateralizes and stays in that dichotomy. That shifting and polarizing onto one side or the other is beginning to happen at earlier and earlier ages, and stays that way for the rest of our lives. The average twenty-five-year-old has more stress in one year than his parents, at twenty-five, had in ten years. It is important to note that it is a more stressful world for right-brain people. A right-brain person would rather be a free spirit, out on a mountaintop, than deal with the pressures of our time."

Saturn describes not only gravity, but the physical bony structure of the body, the skeleton. The degree of success in life can be seen by the position and aspects to Saturn in the natal chart. For instance, if Saturn is placed in either one of the houses describing health (the first or the sixth), the physical system may tend to hold on to more tension when the individual is under pressure. Saturn ruling, or placed in, the first house indicates that pressures and stress start early in life and can affect the structural balance from the very beginning of life.

Dr. Chrane went on to describe his method of directly accessing the brain instead of the bodily imbalance. He said, "The medical profession addresses the symptoms, whether they do this with natural methods or with medication. The osteopaths and chiropractors proved that if there was a functional problem, there must also be a structural imbalance that preceded it. It's basic in science that structure and function are related. About fifty years ago, muscle therapists began to work with the muscular structure, because muscles move bones. Rolfers, for example, work on relaxing the muscles, because if there is no muscular tension, no bones will be out of place. Then Dr. George Goodheart, in 1964, proved that weakness precedes tension, so people doing energy work began trying to get power back into weak muscles, using electromagnetic techniques to strengthen the weakened areas. This sequence—weakness, tension, imbalance, and the ultimate disease—is all the result of inappropriate stress response. My position is that they are all symptomatic of inappropriate brain lateralization. I communicate with the brain in a powerful, nonthreatening, physical way so that the brain can integrate itself and refocus energy, which has been wrongly focused outside ready for fight or flight. This energy can then be refocused back into the body so that the wisdom within can do the things it knows to do and wants to do."

Disease has an indirect relationship to thought, as disease is the misuse, or lack of use, of the forces of the etheric, astral, and physical planes. Mental activity only *registers* plans and ideas onto the mirror of an individual's life, it doesn't *cause* disease. Mental activity in relationship to disease is like a telephone which only transmits a conversation. Problems can arise when frustrated idealism (Neptune), or lack of a balance between the right and left hemispheres of the brain (conceptual and rational thought) produces emotional reactions (the Moon). Thwarted ambition and the failure to manifest concepts and plans into physical reality, as an example, can cause a person to become embittered. When impatience (Mars) or worry (Saturn) supersedes rational thought processes (Mercury), the physical body manifests disease wherever the physical system might be weak (Saturn).

Since no two individuals are alike in physical makeup (just as no two snowflakes are alike), a combination of many factors predetermines the quality of the physical vehicle. The accumulation of energy patterns from many lifetimes is undoubtedly one factor. Stress patterns, worry, and fear can be carried over from many lifetimes. The degree of this type of stress can be indicated by Saturn placed in the sixth house, for example. The etheric body carries not only the imprint of the physical appearance, but the quality of the physical structure and inner workings. If some part of the physical body has been injured in a past life, the patterns are carried over into this one. It is possible, however, for an individual to lessen the impact that such weaknesses may have in his life by developing the right attitude about his disability or condition. If he can understand why he has to bear a particular burden, his acceptance of the situation can help heal the condition for a future existence, if not for the present one.

Positive mental attitudes can help a person overcome difficulties by enabling him to view his life circumstances as though they were a glass half full rather than half empty. Dr. Chrane reported that in 1936, Alexis Corell, a two-time Nobel prize winner, discovered that 95 percent of our self-talk is negative. And, unfortunately, like attracts like, so with negative inner dialogue, more negative conditions manifest in life. Now we know that when a person is not whole-brain functioning (that is, working in frontal lobe area), he shifts into those areas of the brain that store all the negatives— the dos, don'ts, and can'ts, of early childhood. Unfortunately, most people are inappropriately lateralized into one hemisphere or the other, according to Dr. Chrane, and live their lives repeating those negative messages. The frontal lobes, the areas of the brain that are utilized when mental balance is attained, relate to the pituitary and are described by Pluto in the astrological chart. This area is only fully stimulated when both halves of the brain are activated.

Dr. Chrane continued, "It is very difficult for a hemispherically unbalanced person to maintain positive thinking. However, a person can move in a balanced way into those frontal areas of the brain, the storehouse of present-time consciousness, through meditation, intent, and the focus of mental attention. Activity in the frontal areas enhances the ability to look at things in a detached, rational way. [Pluto describes a cosmic view of life.] But since the body and the mind are a unit, you can't have muscle tension without having emotional tensions. You can't affect the body without affecting the mind and vice versa. Wilhelm Reich proved that we armour ourselves in a psychophysical way. Whenever we put a highly charged issue on the back burner, either by denial or suppression, it gets locked in the brain and in the muscle tissue of the body. We can, by intent, move into a frontal area, but our physical body is so distorted that as soon as we stop focusing on the intent, we pull right back into that negative garbage."

Focusing on a spot in the middle of the forehead (see Chapter 2) stimulates the pituitary, which is the prime feeder of most of the glands of the endocrine system. According to Dr. Chrane, there are over fifty thousand direct nerve circuits from the hypothalamus (the seat of the emotions) into the pituitary. So the brain controls the pituitary and is very closely connected to the function of the higher brain.

"With a new perspective about the true function of mind in connection with health, a person can begin to upgrade the quality of decisions and value judgments about himself, projecting whole brain function. With alignment and balance of the left and right brain, the wisdom of the body not only heals, but adjusts the physical body as well. This eventually upgrades the overall quality of life. A rational, inner-actualized approach to life is the most important mental attitude an individual can adopt. Acceptance of unavoidable conditions is not a passive kind of energy but a dynamic ability. When thought processes remain clear, the brain becomes a directing agent of the life force. Learning how to work with light energy, for instance, forces mental activity upward and onto a more conscious level and brings a more pure, inpouring of healing energy. That process is conducted on the mental level through the power of focused attention and visualization. In this way, the mind becomes a powerful agent for healing."

When I interpret an astrological chart, I explain that each person projects many messages and dialogues onto the mirror of his life. Those messages, some of them conflicting, relate to many levels of existence and weave an intricate part of the tapestry of life. An individual projects physical, mental, emotional, and spiritual conflicts, which rebound like a boomerang to create the exact same external conditions in his life. It is as if each person were constantly making a film of his own life, acting like a screenwriter who must make minute-to-minute choices about how he wishes his characters to behave. This is an apt analogy for a person with strong right-brain tendencies indicated by Neptune in the chart. He may decide to visualize his characters in happy conditions or in difficult circumstances. The problem with any individual's minute-to-minute decisions lies in his *believing* the script he has created and getting stuck in it. If a writer felt each word were indelibly etched onto the paper, he might never write another word. Luckily, he has a chance to make corrections and revisions. Each person can do the same with his own life. A different perspective naturally creates a different script.

If a person is more left-brain oriented, indicated by strong Mercury aspects in the chart, it is like working with a computer. Everything that has been entered into a program is recorded in that computer, but luckily, the text can be edited or completely rewritten by typing in new information.

Usually a person begins to reexamine his life when enough painful experiences or disappointments occur. He may begin therapy, ask for an interpretation of his astrological chart, or find some discipline such as meditation that enables him to adopt a different attitude. When he changes his question about life from "Why is life doing this to me?" to "What am I to learn from this?" it is only a matter of time before new conditions begin to emerge around him. It is important for a person to learn how to ask himself the right questions, for all answers lie within, and are inherent in, the question asked. During a regression session, the most important thing I can do is help a person learn how to dialogue with his own subconscious mind. When he understands how to talk to himself, he can locate the blocks that prevent the fullest self-expression and immediately create new positive situations as a result of like attracting like.

The ultimate creative self-expression is to manifest a life script that is exactly as we wish it to be. If an individual can visualize or manifest what he chooses in the reality of his daily existence and in his relationships with people, he can also visualize complete health and physical well-being. He can continue to exercise that creative potential until he gets it right. The mind becomes a healing agent when the individual develops an ability to be observant, objective, and without judgment.

Imbalance Due to Past-Life Conditioning

*L*ife on earth is merely a continuation of the existence of the spirit. If we view the soul's journey as a thread of consciousness, winding and weaving through many spheres of experience, it is easier to understand how that thread can become entangled on the craggy rocks of the myriad earth-plane shoals that crop up to ensnare the unwary. Edgar Cayce described the missing link, and man's original descent into life on earth, with a tale of just such an entanglement. He said that in the earliest times, spirits started hovering near the earth plane, fascinated by the lure of animal activity, especially sexual engagement. Spirits began to enter the bodies of the animals so that those pleasurable sensations could be experienced firsthand. At first, it was easy to come and go at will. But after more prolonged periods of dwelling in animal bodies, the spirits became trapped and could not leave. A more appropriate form had to be created for the soul's journey throughout the lower levels of experience. The design of the brain and the body, very sophisticated mechanisms, allows man to exist on earth and, eventually, to evolve back into the pure spirit essence.

Since that original entrapment on the wheel of karma, man has had a difficult time freeing himself from his physical body. Earth-plane experiences can tempt man into karmic debts, such as desires that must be satisfied at any cost, inhumanity to fellow man, and greed. These debts must be reconciled and repaid before the spirit is once again free from obligation. The spirit longs to go home, but it can emerge pure and unfettered only when the individual has balanced the scales and paid his debts. As long as the glamour of the earth plane attracts the individual, he must still work through the physical vehicle, driving his car through all kinds of road conditions.

Along the way, the automobile can become battered and bruised. Those dents in the physical structure are carried from lifetime to lifetime. Many physical disabilities, phobias, and weaknesses in the system are a result of injuries in past lives. They can be corrected only by going back to the source of the injury to determine the proper method of healing. There is a thread of consciousness that weaves throughout the existence of each human being from the time he first leaves the oneness of the highest planes until such time as he returns home again. This is sometimes called "the silver cord." The etheric body (see Chapter 2) is a network of fine channels called meridians that interpenetrate the entire physical system and are the component parts of this interlacing cord. One part of this cord magnetically links man to his physical and astral body. At the time of death, this cord is severed and the etheric body withdraws from the dense, lifeless physical form to return to the etheric plane. The thread of consciousness returns, with its collected impressions, to that plane as well.

Man's existence is merely a continuation of consciousness. Each productive thought, deed, and action is a pearl along that thread of consciousness. There are also knots that are tied on the same thread. All thoughts, deeds, and actions, both productive and non-productive, are magnetically preserved in the Akashic Records, much like photographing the entire thread of consciousness of each individual onto microfilm. There are no secrets in the Universe, as every single action and thought is preserved for eternity.*

* The Akasha is a cosmic substance of primordial ethers. It is the vitalized matter of the solar system that nourishes all. Akasha currents relate to the highest place of existence where energy is undifferentiated. Pranic currents of electrical energy are carried on the etheric level and then into the physical.

When the etheric body once again enters the physical form at birth, the pearls along that thread reemerge and create positive conditions. The knots stimulate blocks. Since energy travels along that thread through the network of the etheric body, running from there into the physical form, it is easy to see how past-life conditions can affect a person on all levels of existence. The person brings in the talents, abilities, and specific conditions of health as well as the liabilities he has accumulated. Vitality is directly related to the information strung on that thread of consciousness, as the physical body is energized by and reflective of the spiritual body. The mind is the link between spiritual and physical levels, and therefore "as a man thinketh, so is he."

Just as sleep is a blessed relief from the pressure of each day, death blots out the overt sting of a lifetime of trying events. Just as an individual becomes tired after a full day's activity, he is also tired after a lifetime of lessons on the earth plane. Mercifully, when death occurs, the difficult experiences are absorbed onto the etheric level of mind, along with the positive ones, like storing files into the hard disk of a computer before turning off the power. Otherwise the overload in the new life might be too much to handle. Just as the files of a computer are out of sight when the machine is turned on again, painful memories may not exist on a conscious level of awareness. However, some people seem to have easier access to their files, or individual Akashic Records, than others. For instance, many children talk about their "other" mother and father as well as their "other" home and experiences. These records usually dim in detail as the child grows older and gathers new experiences, but even in adulthood, if it is important or necessary to recall past-life experiences, the process of accessing those hidden files is fairly easy through the experience of a regression sessic.1.

In my opinion, it is important for a person to learn how to dialogue with his own higher mind. Therefore, I do not use hypnosis in regression sessions, for it is quite possible for an individual to consciously access his own records by learning how to ask himself the right questions. By utilizing a simple formula, he can obtain information about his past lives and what he really came in to resolve in the present. Since every person has all of the answers to all of his questions within himself, it is incredibly important to gain access to those answers. Nothing is ever lost or forgotten in the universal consciousness.

Problems in this lifetime occur when past-life memories are so painful that the individual is unwilling to confront them. Since almost everyone has made some mistakes in the past, almost everyone has made a commitment to return to the earth plane for the purpose of working off his karmic debt. The debt may be to a specific person, society in general, or to himself.

The feeling of dread at what lies ahead in life may be one major factor that causes stress and creates less than robust health. This is particularly true when Saturn relates to the first house in the chart, as may be indicated by the placement of Saturn in the first house or the rulership of Capricorn. Saturn also relates to the first house when it's found in aspect to the ruler of the ascendant or a planet placed in the first house.

Psychological burdens in this lifetime are often connected to a deep-seated guilt. That guilt may relate to a sense of sin by commission or omission from a past existence. Karmic memories are sometimes hard to face; it is difficult to accept the responsibility that damage must be repaired and debts must be paid. It is far worse, however, to carry around a black cloud of anxieties due to unfocused painful memories than it is to face facts and make restitution.

Since the planet Saturn is the indicator of the knots in the thread of consciousness and thus the blocks that an individual brings into this lifetime from the past, analysis of Saturn in the chart is most important. Guilt, fear, worry, anxiety, dread, resentment, and negative judgments, all Saturnian qualities, tie the knots most tightly. The placement of Saturn in an individual horoscope plays a very important role in describing health conditions, for it describes the quality of the specific vehicle an individual needs in order to work out the particular situations of his life on the earth plane. That may include body type and genetic factors that connect him to his family. In the lineup of planets, Saturn is the last of the lower octave, or earthbound, planets. It relates to gravity and to karmic conditions that keep a person pinned down or restricted. Saturn in an individual astrological chart indicates the particular situation that causes a person to come into the earth plane in the first place.

Saturn describes the physical body and the bony structure that protects the soul and spirit dwelling therein from any destructive forces of nature or the environment. The body type and structure is determined by genetic factors, but like a tree growing on a windy hillside and molded by the force of the air currents swirling around its trunk, the physical form is also conditioned by environmental factors on the earth plane. These factors force a person to dig into and deal with life on the physical plane, just as a tree grows deep roots into the soil to prevent being uprooted. They can be positive as well as negative. With enough buffeting, however, the physical body may become bent and twisted according to the type of stress it encounters.

When Saturn's placement in the chart is viewed in relationship to health, it describes blocks to the free movement of energy, especially the higher-octave or soul-motivated energy that flows throughout the physical system. Ideally, with no major birth problems or karmic traumas to contend with, pranic energy moves freely throughout the various bodies, the chakras, meridians, and nervous system, stimulating all the organs and mechanisms of the human body. With stress, traumas, and the general wearing down that comes with age, energy begins to slow down. The atomic structure of the body is no longer fed with the full nourishment of the life force and the vehicle begins to deteriorate. This can happen at any time during the sojourn on earth, even very early in life. Saturn's transits through the sixth house of health or across the ascendant and into the first house of the horoscope can indicate specific times when health problems are likely to occur.

The twelfth house in an astrological chart describes all conditions that are brought in from the past. Planets that are positioned in that sector of the horoscope further describe those conditions. Any planet that may be in adverse aspect to a planet positioned in the twelfth sector of the chart will describe the subconscious psychological matters that require attention in the present existence. It is important to analyze energy represented by any planet that adversely aspects the planetary ruler of the twelfth house as well.

The first house, indicating difficult health conditions that have been brought in from the past, more specifically describes how the individual will deal with those past-life conditions on a physical level. It indicates the kind of tension, or block to energy, he may inadvertently create in a specific part of his body. The ascendant describes the mask, facade, or psychological barrier a person erects to separate himself from external conditions that appear unsafe, because it describes survival decisions made at the moment of birth, when the unspoken question is posed, "How am I going to deal with life?" These decisions translate into characteristics and specific qualities of physical energy. They are set in motion simply because mental processes stimulate physical blocks if the individual tenses part of his physical mechanism in order to survive.

The twelfth house indicates the overall quality of past lives. It describes the kind of psychological burden an individual may carry throughout many lifetimes due to subconscious memories of pain or trauma. When Saturn rules or is placed in that sector of the chart, or is in difficult aspect to any planet related to the twelfth house, the subconscious memories are particularly burdensome. In my experience, this indicates a karmic racial guilt. The guilt may be connected to a past-life sense of responsibility for a group or family situation that was ignored or unfulfilled. Sometimes an individual may have done the best he could under the circumstances, but still carries with him the memory of catastrophic events that happened to people around him. Even if he was not directly responsible, he may feel guilt at what he might have done to prevent tragedy from occurring. If that devastating event caused his own death, imprisonment, punishment, or illness, the physical body reflects those conditions in the present lifetime.

A client of mine whom I shall call Anna (all names in Chapter 11 have been changed to protect privacy) remembered dying of pneumonia in a past life. She had been accused of witchcraft in New England, and although her punishment was slight in comparison to what others suffered when they were burned at the stake, she was deeply hurt and wounded on a psychological level. During a regression session, she saw the two men who had betrayed her in that life and recognized them in her present life. One man was her husband in that former lifetime. Although he played no part in the accusations, he didn't defend her against the women who brought charges against her. The judge who tried her also knew that she was innocent. In order to placate the mob, but especially the group of women who envied her ability to heal and soothe people, he meted out what he considered to be an appropriate punishment. She was sentenced to being dunked in a pool of water for an entire day.

After being tied to a chair, Anna was immersed in the water and raised again, only to be dunked again, over and over. She was extremely frightened as she didn't know how long her punishment would continue or if it included her being drowned at some point during the day. Shortly after she was finally released, she contracted pneumonia and died. In an extreme state of despair over the weakness of two men she thought she could trust, she simply didn't want to live anymore; it was the betrayal that killed her, not the punishment. In the present lifetime, Anna has had weakness in her lungs, with consequent breathing difficulties. She also has problems with retention of water in her tissues. Anna has the Moon conjunct Uranus ruling her ascendant. Since these planets are in the sign of Aries, she has a great deal of unexpressed anger that is still disguised as despair. Her resentment has stayed with her on a subconscious level. The Moon indicates feelings of abandonment, and Uranus can describe scares. Uranus also describes a wish to run away and a flirtation with thoughts of suicide. Anna recognized a survival plan that came with her birth. If she could just hold her breath, she thought, she could leave the earth plane and go back to her spiritual home again. Anna has a psychological predisposition to extreme vulnerability and helplessness that goes hand in hand with rebellion, defiance, and a great need for freedom. Her fear of getting close to anyone, especially on an emotional level, is directly related to the sense of betrayal in the lifetime she recalled. Anna never married in this lifetime, although she had many opportunities to do so. One of those opportunities was to the man who was the judge in that long-ago trial.

Justine recalled living in the court of Louis XVI at the time of the French Revolution. She told of being guillotined because of her wealth and connection to the aristocracy. She has suffered from migraine headaches, sore throats, and excess mucus accumulating on her vocal cords since early childhood. The constant clearing of her throat appeared to be a nervous habit, but was actually her attempt to clear away some of the damage left over from the trauma of her death. She studied voice for many years and realized it was her way of healing the trauma to her etheric body with sound vibrations. She majored in speech therapy in college.

Justine has Scorpio on the ascendant, which is square Venus in her chart. On a psychological level this aspect relates to a power-and-pleasure syndrome. In Justine's case, the combination of the two factors in the past life she described caused extreme pain. In this lifetime, she is extremely hesitant to indulge in either power or pleasure. With Pluto ruling the pituitary and Venus ruling the throat, physical problems occur with blocked energy in the throat (the power center), the endocrine system in general, and the spleen (or splenic center), which is the physical connector to the spiritual network. Justine has been fearful of too much pleasure in this life in case it might deter her spiritual growth. On the other hand, the recollection of the opulence of her former life-style, described by Pluto ruling her ascendant, has presented a constant temptation to indulgence. She is now learning how to integrate pleasure in life with a sense of cosmic joy. That includes having some fun on the earth plane. She is also gradually allowing herself a greater degree of self-expression, which might place her in a power position once again. Some of her ideas about speech therapy have been recognized as important. She has not yet completely resolved her fears about achieving a greater degree of affluence, which might bring back the temptations of her former life-style.

William recalled being chained to a wall in another time and place. He was a champion of religious reform in Germany during the lifetime of Martin Luther. In his present existence, he suffers from arthritis in his hands and stiffening in his wrists. William has Saturn conjunct Mercury and Mars. Those planets are positioned in the twelfth house in his chart, describing imprisonment and restriction of activity. William's anger over the lack of a chance to defend himself at the time of his capture, and an inability to continue his work, carries over into this lifetime with a blocked ability to speak his mind, express some of his more innovative ideas, or defend himself when it is necessary.

UNIVERSAL PLANETARY
PATTERNS

Periodically, there are heavy energy patterns in the skies due to difficult interaction between planets; these patterns can describe major world crises. They can occur, for instance, when Saturn is in difficult aspect to a very slow moving planet. People born at those times share general characteristics and patterns that relate to and can be conditioned by external historical events. Sometimes these patterns can indicate very heavy conditions to be worked through in the present life, yet it seems that masses of people choose to incarnate at such times because the external environmental situation will contribute the exact conditions that will foster the reconciliation of karmic patterns, including physical ones.

One such pattern was at the time of the 1929 stock market crash and subsequent depression into the early 1930s. Saturn was square Uranus and opposing Pluto, describing a sense of stagnation and restriction which was reflected in the psychological and physical conditioning of many people. There was a lack of a sense of freedom and fun in the air, and there was a real lack of food. It is no wonder that masses of people gave a spiritual gulp and metaphorically held their breath when faced with coming into life on earth during those trying times. The physical patterns that were set in motion related to restriction of breath.

Another difficult time was during and just after World War II, when Saturn was conjunct Uranus. The external events once again created a serious feeling of the need for responsible reorganization. These were the attitudes that permeated the atmosphere. Continuation of freedom was assured, but at great cost to everyone, especially the families that had been separated or shattered during the war years. Restructure and serious reevaluations were necessary at that time. Homecoming soldiers had to contend with feelings of joy at having survived the war and sadness over things they had seen and experienced.

Nancy was particularly affected by her father's experiences during the war. During her regression session, she was aware of a dreadful feeling of aloneness throughout her childhood. She felt like a visitor in a household of strangers. The feeling of being born into a family of strangers is not uncommon, though her sense of isolation was particularly severe due to a close relationship between her mother and older sister. It seemed that they left her out of things, particularly shutting her out of their conversations and activities. She could have found ways to participate in their activities, as she had no feeling of being disliked by the female members of her family, but she didn't have a sense of belonging with them. It was clear to Nancy that she was born to be with her father, not her mother and sister. That awareness seemed strange to Nancy because she felt no particular emotional connection to him. She liked him, responded to him, but their relationship was not intense either in terms of love or hate.

The prominent issues that emerged during her childhood recollections were not related to herself, but to her father. He had been in the British navy during World War II, entering the service just after his marriage to her mother. Her mother's pregnancy with Nancy's older sister followed quickly, and the baby was born while her father was overseas. After a short time in service, his ship was torpedoed and he was one of the few survivors. He was blasted out into the water, alone, with no life jacket, boat, or piece of wood to hang on to. He was fortunately able to tread water for several days before he was finally rescued. During her childhood, Nancy often heard the story of his survival and how he had been sandwiched in a middle bunk, with a man above him and a man below him. Both of those men had been killed in the explosion.

Her father was discharged from the navy before the war was over. He suffered a great deal of trauma because of his agonizing efforts to survive the experience in the water, and even after his discharge he continued to be affected by the experience. The difficulties were compounded because it was somewhat of a disgrace to return home before the war was over, and he was especially suspect because of his seemingly broken spirit. He had a hard time adjusting to a wife and new baby, and it was difficult for Nancy's mother to adjust to a new husband who was unable to give her very much moral support. She quite naturally developed a close relationship to her child. When Nancy was born shortly thereafter, it was clear that she was already locked out of any family unit, in a sense, and would not receive the early nurturing that is so essential for the development of a sense of security in life.

When she reviewed her birth process, Nancy observed the way her body reacted to the stress of her birth. She had a great deal of difficulty breathing from the very moment she entered life; the predominant physical problem Nancy has encountered in this lifetime has been with respiratory illnesses, such as asthma, pneumonia, bronchitis, and chest colds. When Nancy reviewed a past life, she saw herself as a man in the uniform of an English soldier. She (he) left a loving wife and child behind when she (he) went off to war. While being transported by sea to a battlefield, Nancy realized that she (he) had been killed when a torpedo hit the ship she was traveling in. She suddenly knew that she was the soldier in the bottom bunk of the ship whereas her father, in this life, was the man in the middle bunk. Since she (he) was killed by her (his) lungs filling with water, the weakness in that part of her body persisted very strongly in this life. Nancy has a new perspective about her family, and her own physical problems. Although she may always have a predisposition to respiratory ailments, her new understanding about her life counterbalances the former sense of isolation.

In reviewing an astrological chart to determine how past-life characteristics can predetermine physical health, there are several factors to consider. First, the ascendant, or rising sign, describes the physical characteristics that are associated with survival issues in this life, but the twelfth house describes what came before to set up the particular circumstances that exist in the present. The opportunity exists to bring forward, into the light of the personality, characteristics that are described by the twelfth house or past-life conditions. It is easy to express characteristics described by the first house, but less easy to express what lies hidden in the twelfth.

Basic characteristics of each planet can be combined like a formula or a mathematical computation to give clues as to past-life experiences that may condition the health and well-being in the present. As an example, when Aries or Mars relates to either the twelfth or first house, and is in difficult aspect to another planet, there is a likelihood that violence may have been part of the experience in a past life. War, revolution, or fighting may have caused bloodshed. Physical symptoms in the present may relate to adrenal malfunction or problems with blood, blood pressure, brain, or afflictions connected to the head. The psychological connection to that aspect is frustration or anger.

Taurus or Venus in that part of the chart, and in difficult aspect, describes past-life conditions connected to society, social conditions, charm, graciousness, and pleasure. Since Taurus relates to the throat, difficulties may lie with that part of the body and may be a power issue. George, with a Taurus ascendant, recalled a lifetime in England where his relationship to his sister ensured his position in the life of the court. His gracious manner and courtliness were attributes that were highly admired and respected in that society. He had money, power, and position as long as he could play the diplomatic game, staying on the right side of the changing political climate. It was a pleasurable existence. When his sister was suddenly out of favor, the young man found himself on the wrong side of the power structure and was imprisoned and sentenced to death, along with his sister. No amount of charm or courtly, diplomatic behavior could turn the tide of events around again.

In this lifetime, George was born with Saturn conjunct Venus, the ruler of his ascendant. George has a fear of becoming embroiled in social situations and of developing closeness to anyone who is extremely demonstrative. He abhors being in situations where he is valued for his charming manner rather than his inner worth, yet he is quite good at showing the charming part of his personality. In personal relationships, he has developed a habit of showing a tough side of himself. He works extremely hard in this life, and being hard on himself, expects everyone else to do the same. Although his professional position encourages expression of the diplomatic, gracious quality that is a natural part of his personality, he consciously puts up a bit of a wall, remaining somewhat aloof. This young man has had problems in the area of the throat, describing the trauma to that part of his body at the time of his death.

For analysis of the physical knots that have been tied on the thread of your consciousness, determine the planet or planets that relate to and rule the ascendant, and then the planet or planets that relate to the twelfth house. Ascertain whether or not these planets are in hard aspect to any other planets, then go back to Chapters 4 and 5. An awareness of physical blocks can enable each person to send healing energy into that part of the body, as well as into the areas of life that relate to those restrictions or blocks. Increased purposeful energy sent into specific areas of life through the mental process of visualization, as well as through specific therapies, enables healing to occur. Forgiveness is one of the most important healing commodities. When forgiveness is meted out and a person becomes aware of the contribution necessary in this life to balance the scales, new energy can enter the body from the etheric into the physical without being blocked by the power and judgment of the mind.

Nicole ♑ asc ♅♆ 12th ♄ 11 □ ♃
Laurie ♑ on 12th ♄ ♐ 10th ☌ ♀
Lori ♑ on 12th ♄ in ♐ 10th ☌ ♀

Audrey ♓ in 12, ♈ on 12th
♄ ☌ ♀ ♂ 10th ☌ ☉

Dale ♄ ♐ 3rd □ ♀ ♃ ♌ on 12th ☉ 5th

Steve ♑ in 1st ♄ ♏ 11th □ ♂
☌ ☉ ☽ ♀

Delanie ♑ on 4th ♄ ♒ 5 cusp
♍ on 12 ♀ ♈ 7th

Megan ♈ on 12th ♂ in 1st ☍ ♆ ♄

Mike ♋ on 12th ☽ ♉ 9th ☌ MC
♓ in 12, ♒ 7th

Katie ♊ on 12th ☿ ♐ 5th ☌ ☽ ♄
♋ ASC ☽ ♐ 5th

Olivia ♎ on 12, ♀ ♈ 5 ☌ ☉
♏ ASC ♀ in 1st
☽ in 12th ♎ ☍ ♀

Imbalance Due to Prenatal Conditioning

*edical science is now beginning to rec-
ognize that there is sentience in the womb.
In his 1981 book *The Secret Life of the Unborn Child*, published by
Delta Press, Dr. Thomas Verny presented fascinating data to confirm his theory that the unborn child is extremely aware of what
is going on in the immediate outside environment. Part of this
theory seems to confirm that the fetus is able to learn quite a lot
during his or her prenatal state. Modern trends encourage future
parents to play music, read nursery rhymes, and even teach math-
ematics to their unborn child. But what may be most important
of all for the fetus is the psychological preparation. It can be essential for his or her future well-being to have data about his place
in the family unit.

During regression sessions it becomes clear to many people that
future problems in life are set in motion because the unborn child
is left to figure things out for himself. The unborn child may be
very aware of some external conditions, but without communication and precise information from his parents, he can jump to
the wrong conclusions. Many people seem to know exactly what
kind of life situation is ahead and how their parents feel about

their impending arrival. If the fetus senses that the parents are unprepared for a baby and the pregnancy is a shock or a surprise, however, he may develop feelings of rejection even before birth. Awareness by the unborn child of the particular family circumstances evidently conditions the person to adopt a particular range of behavior that will help him survive life situations. Sometimes an individual becomes aware of which of his current thoughts, feelings, and reactions are merely extensions of attitudes formed during the critical preparatory stage of life. But most of these behavior modes are nonproductive in the long run, since they are based on assumptions rather than facts. In my experience with regression work, few people have described similarities of experiences in prenatal conditions. Each person has a very individual experience, yet one common shared feeling is that of resistance to being born.

The common denominator in the astrological chart that indicates a predisposition to a resistance to birth is again connected to a Saturnian caste to the ascendant or to the twelfth house. (See Chapter 11 on Past-Life Conditioning.) When Saturn rules the ascendant or the twelfth house (or is placed in the first or twelfth house, or is in hard aspect to a planet ruling or placed in those sectors), it indicates some degree of foreboding about what life holds. There may be a fear of being trapped by gravity and having to live by the rules of the earth plane. That dread of what life may hold seems to precondition an individual to adopt a stoic quality, with a consequent propensity for physical and psychological rigidity. As we have noted, the tightening of muscles or internal organs early in life (even during the prenatal stage) can cause later physical problems and indicate a predisposition to illness or disability in a particular area of the body.

One of the most important parts of a regression session is the review of prenatal experiences from the time of conception to the actual entry into the physical plane. A pattern seems to emerge that can describe the way each individual will handle major changes throughout his life. The individual becomes aware of a formula based on his reactions to his experiences in the womb, and to the birth process itself, that predetermines the way he will deal with any future new situation. That formula is not evolved on a conscious level and may remain unclear to the individual until he reviews the way he reacted to the first major change in life. The cloning of that original reaction is almost automatic.

As an example, let us say a person knows that he is due to be born. He hears his parents discuss their feelings about his arrival and reacts accordingly. If they are happy, he can be content and relaxed in the womb. But if he hears that his birth will cause a problem, he may be very hesitant to be born. Let us say that the parents are unwed. When the mother discovers that she is pregnant, she can make several choices. She may decide to bear the child and bring him up alone. She may decide to have the child, but give him up for adoption right away. She may tell the father about the pregnancy and hope that he will share the responsibility and marry her. The father may also react in several ways. He may be happy, in which case there will be no problem. He may be happy, but be fearful of announcing the situation to his family. He may have to quit school to get a job. The parents may decide to marry in secrecy and predate the nuptials for the sake of propriety. In any case, the unborn child reacts inside the womb accordingly. Usually his reactions are very strong.

Al was acutely aware of his parents' reactions to his mother's pregnancy. His mother and father were very much in love. They couldn't wait to make a life together on their own, both because of their feelings for each other and because both had a difficult situation at home. The news of the pregnancy delighted them, since it gave them a reason to be married at an early age. Al's mother was only sixteen and his father was twenty. If they had simply eloped, their problems would have been very different, and Al's life would have taken an entirely different course.

Al's mother's family was very poor—it was during the depression years—and when she told her family that she was pregnant, her domineering mother consulted a lawyer about getting money from the young father's family for the support of the child. The two families took control of the situation and decided the fate of the unborn child, precluding any discussion of marriage between the two young people. Al's maternal grandmother threatened his father with jail, using as a weapon the fact that their daughter was a minor. The young father panicked and left town, leaving the young woman he loved to bear the child on her own. Later, the maternal grandmother decided that her grandchild would be a perfect substitute for a young son she herself had recently lost.

In the review of his birth formula, Al saw himself as very content to be born to his parents. (Venus rules the twelfth house in Al's chart, indicating a prenatal sense of pleasure and contentment.) He saw that even though his mother was afraid of her mother, her future seemed bright since his father loved her very much. He saw himself as being relaxed and feeling secure. The next stage came when the grandmothers took over. Al observed with some horror that events were not going the way he wanted them to go, and he became aware of the reaction in his body. (Saturn is in opposition to Venus, ruler of the twelfth house, and describes a block and shadow over the original feeling of pleasure.) His heart hurt and his chest felt very heavy. He was extremely upset for his young parents. His mother was very sad and cried a great deal. Al felt helpless, angry, and frustrated over his inability to do anything about the situation. (Mars is placed in the twelfth house squaring the Sun, describing the frustration and blockage to the heart chakra.) At that point in his prenatal development, the die was cast and tension took hold inside his body. The disappointment and resignation settled in around his heart chakra and in his throat. He couldn't scream or tell anyone how he felt. He was helpless to do anything about the situation. Mars is also in opposition to Uranus and squaring Pluto. This can describe the paralyzing rage that is usually internalized. Such rage rarely shows on the surface, as the feeling is that of having one's hands tied—Al's prenatal inability to do anything about the situation. Uranus rules the fourth house in Al's chart and describes his mother's scare. Saturn placed in that sector of the chart indicates his mother's feelings of resignation and being stuck.

When it was time for his birth, he first heard people talking and then began to feel pressure around his body. He suddenly realized what was about to occur and, figuratively, planted his feet. He refused to turn around so that he would be born in the usual way, with his head down into the birth canal. Therefore the birth was extremely difficult. (Saturn in difficult aspect to the ruler of the twelfth house indicates the resistance on Al's part.) Al's mother was put to sleep with medication that also drugged Al's system. Neptune is in a semisquare, a hard aspect, to Al's ascendant, describing a feeling of being drugged. It also indicates the development of an Ostrich complex, or an unwillingness to look at the reality of a situation for fear of disillusionment.

Al became aware of his part in the long, slow birth process. He neither held back nor pushed forward. He felt completely passive (the Neptunian caste) about the whole thing, powerless to make things right (Mars square Pluto, relating to both twelfth, prenatal, and first houses, birth process), and frustrated (the Mars caste) over the thwarted desires for his life. (Saturn describes the resignation and feelings of rejection.)

In noting the stages of psychological development for analysis of later patterns, it became clear to Al that first comes joy over a proposed change of conditions. Stage two in his individual formula comes with a feeling of horror when he sees that he has no control over the changes that are occurring. Stage three comes when he is aware of great sadness from someone connected to his new situation. During his birth process, Al realized that he knew his maternal grandmother intended to take him away from his mother and raise him as her own child. Stage four comes with Al's passive resistance and refusal to play by the rules (his refusal to turn around the right way at the time of his birth), and, finally, a feeling of helplessness over the impending change in his environment.

After his review of the way he automatically adapted toward change in his life, Al took a look at a particular job change that had recently occurred. In the first stage, Al was content and happy over the prospect of the new situation. He seemed to be much admired by the people in power in the new company and felt quite comfortable with the contractual arrangements. Then, shortly after he started in his new job, the people who were specifically interested in his talents and abilities were ousted by new management. The situation changed quite drastically, and Al was no longer quite so secure about his future. He was now to work closely with someone of an entirely different personality. The executive who lost control of the organization was very sad over the turn of events, and Al felt a strong sympathetic connection with him. He dealt with the disappointment in a stoic manner, but noticed that his chest was very tight and his heart hurt with the disappointment. In retrospect, Al realized that his reactions to and participation in the changeover were exactly the same as at the time of his birth. He felt stultified, "drugged," and observed himself on a course of passive resistance. There was not much he could do about the whole situation except to go along with what was decided by others. Al's astrological chart clearly reflects the way he felt in the womb, as well as the way he handles present-life situations.

If an individual can review prenatal conditions and observe the emerging parallel patterns in his life, he can create better conditions. When the observant but nonjudgmental mind is in charge in a positive way, the person can rewrite his own script. Thoughts neither cause nor cure the situation, but a new perspective can enable an individual to create new conditions. Like a traffic cop, the employment of productive, positive, creative thought directs energy into areas that need healing, whether those areas are physical or psychological. For instance, Al realized that his greatest problem stemmed from his reaction to his mother's disappointment and sadness. (Uranus ruling the fourth house, with Saturn positioned therein.) His own life was not so badly affected, because his grandparents loved him and wanted him. (Al also has two grand trines in his chart, which indicates tremendous protection in his life.) He may even have fared better being brought up under their loving care—since he was particularly close to his grandfather—than by a nervous, inexperienced sixteen-year-old mother. Al's lesson in life seemed to be to avoid developing a symbiotic reaction to his mother, or the ousted executive, and to develop instead a compassionate vitality rather than allowing stagnation to take hold. The Moon in Al's chart is squared Saturn, indicating his mother's depression and his symbiotic depression in relationship to her. The Moon is also squared Neptune, describing a feeling of abandonment on his part and the inability to confront the situation that occurred at birth and later on with his job situation. In the past, disappointment, feelings of helplessness, and passive resistance kept Al tied to many nonproductive activities. He elected to remain tied to ineffectual people, even at times when greater opportunity presented itself. Al's major task in life is therefore to follow his own path in a free, joyous, deliberate, and effective manner.

Since Al already possesses an abundance of compassion in his makeup, he will never be cold or uncaring, but he can find balance by developing more objectivity. The transmutation of debilitating emotional reactions and symbiotic relationships onto a level of compassion for all of mankind is essential. In that way, Al can use his special quality of compassion more productively, and as a result, his own health and energy can be improved. When Al works on a broader level (that is, doing something for the betterment of humanity), a great deal of his own frustrated energy is productively channeled. Some people need to develop more of their feeling nature, but others, like Al, benefit by developing more objectivity.

The individual astrological chart is the road map that leads to greater awareness of how to balance given conditions in life. Planets that lie in the twelfth house, close to the ascendant, describe the prenatal decisions that precondition an individual's behavior at the time of his birth. The ascendant gives clues as to the exact decisions that are made at the very moment of birth as a result of those prenatal decisions. It is always important to consider all the planets that might give supplementary descriptions of the birth process, such as planets that aspect those that rule or reside in the twelfth house. The additional reflections by other planets in aspect characterize the variety of thoughts that produce birth survival decisions. Any planet that is in hard aspect to a planet ruling or placed near the ascendant indicates additional colors of the personality and additional decisions about how the individual will survive.

The purpose of this kind of analysis is to observe natural and unconscious reactions to situations—good and bad alike—encountered in daily life. Without conscious awareness of those reactions and with lack of deliberate new decisions, the reactions remain the same as at the time of birth. The unborn child's reactions are based on lack of experience in dealing with life problems. Any decisions that are less than conscious keep him in a traumatized-child state of being. Most reactions to stress are born from an unclear state of mind rather than from any clear observation or objective analysis of situations at hand. Such reactions condition both physical and psychological responses that set each stage of life on a specific course, keeping an individual trapped in his own birth script. It is possible to change, bringing in more energy to areas that might have been blocked at the time of birth. Each person seems to have a traumatized child within that needs to be nurtured, and each individual knows the specific quality of love and security his own inner child needs. No one can give that specific facet of love, attention, or information except he, himself. A new quality of self-nurturing releases the inner child to a more dynamic quality of life. (See Part II—Relationship of Astrology to Body Energy.)

Parental Messages

$\mathcal{T}$o determine inherited health patterns, it is necessary to look at the sixth house in the astrological chart. The planets that rule and are positioned in that sector of the individual chart describe genetic factors, such as the DNA molecular structure and the weaknesses in the body that have nothing to do with the stress of the birth process itself. (See Chapter 7.) However, there is an equally important factor to be considered in the overall look at health, and that is the subtle influences from other people. The exchange of energy between people in any relationship has a particular bearing on a person's health and vitality, but this is particularly important in parent-child dynamics. The psychological programming from one's parents begins even before birth and not only influences the quality of life from the beginning, but sets patterns in motion for all future relationships. Those early messages predescribe the psychological health patterns of an individual, which indirectly condition physical and mental well-being.

We live in a world of diverse and sometimes confusing energies. Emanations swirl in and around the physical form of each human being and of any living organism. Some energies and emanations are constructive, such as air and prana, but some are destructive, such as radioactive ions. Even more subtle are those thought-form vibrations emanating from our associations. The quality of the exchanged energy may be obvious, such as anger, jealousy, or hatred, or it may exist on a more subtle level. However, even the most subtle form of vibration can greatly affect individual stamina and vitality. The physical body may not register the resulting tension, but there can be a defensive reaction in the more subtle vehicles that is not immediately apparent. As a person becomes more spiritually sensitized, he becomes more attuned to his own particular degree of reaction to the environment, but he can also exercise more conscious control over his environment. He must, by necessity, begin to be selective about the influences he allows into his sphere of existence.

There have been extensive controlled studies conducted with plants that definitively showed the plants' responses to their immediate environment. Electrodes, connected to a meter, were attached to their leaves. A variety of substances were automatically introduced into the immediate environment of the plants, without any human element that might influence the studies. The sensitive needle on that meter registered positive or negative reactions from the plants. As an example, the plants reacted positively to music, whereas the introduction of an insect into the room brought forth a definite reaction of fear. If plants reacted so sensitively, it is clear that a human being must react equally, if not more sensitively, to influences in his environment. Recent studies conducted with people have shown that different kinds of music actually have a distinct influence on brain waves.

As an individual learns what he can handle and what he cannot, he makes healthier decisions about the people he chooses as associates and about his environment. Many people cannot live in crowded cities, for example, because the energy level is too much to assimilate. A person with a very sensitive physical makeup may not be able to go to crowded stores to shop, or to bars, restaurants, and discotheques, where the vibrational level is dense. If throngs of people, cigarette smoke, small particles of asbestos, and unseen radon rays have a noticeable effect on the physical system, the vibrations of unsuspected malice, anger, hate, or jealousy from others have an even greater detrimental influence.

When a baby is born, the connection to his parents naturally determines a great deal about the future quality of his life. It preconditions the way he will view the world. It is not only the words the parents speak, but their thoughts and their individual accumulated experiences that precondition the infant to his own views. Sometimes the influences condition the child to walk in his parents' footsteps, but even if the child rebels against his early programming, he works against specific qualities. But even more subtle programming exists in the womb. The exchange of the energy fields from parent to child have much to do with whether or not the child remains open and trusting in relation to his environment. If the energy fields are hostile, the unborn infant begins to defend his own system against invasion of poisons, sometimes successfully and sometimes not so successfully. In regression sessions, the individual becomes very aware of obvious poisons such as cigarettes, if the mother smokes, and drugs that might have been administered at the time of his birth. But he or she also becomes aware of whether or not the parents are familiar or are strangers to him. He discerns quite clearly whether or not the familiarity is welcome or whether it is dreaded. If the parents are strangers, he can feel apprehension about his future or excitement about the new connection. In any case, the subtle exchange of energy preconditions his own quality of health.

The planets and houses that describe parent-child relationships in the chart indicate those subtle messages that are conveyed. The tenth house in the chart of a female describes the relationship with her mother, the kind of messages conveyed by the mother, and the energy exchange between them. The fourth house describes the relationship with the father. In the chart of a male, the opposite is true. The tenth house describes the relationship with the father, whereas the fourth house indicates the relationship with the mother. The planets that rule those houses and are positioned in those houses, as well as their aspects to other planets, describe the quality of energy that is exchanged between parent and child. They describe the specific quality of the parents' personalities that the child photographs (or registers in his subconscious), and relates to, as well as the overt, and covert, parental mandates. The planets ruling and positioned in those sectors also indicate the overall personality factors and quality of life experiences of those parents.

In the life of a female child, the mother is the role model, therefore her career potential and proclivities (tenth house) are conditioned by the personality of the mother. The relationship with the father and the consequent photographs of him represent the quality of life-style and conditions of the home life (fourth house). For a male, the career choices are clearly set in motion by the qualities he photographs in relationship to his father. Mother represents the quality of life-style and the conditions of the home life. If there are many planets positioned in those sectors of the chart, the individual photographs many facets of the personalities of the parents. All of those facets must be considered in evaluating the way one is conditioned by the parents.

The fourth house also describes the conditions of life in the third portion of existence on the earth plane. That third portion may begin anywhere from an individual's mid-forties to his mid-fifties. It is logical to assume that as a person enters his later years, his attitude toward many things can change. Matters that were of critical importance early on may no longer hold much value. A look at the relationship with the parent of the opposite sex can indicate the kind of life-style and attitude that may take over as the person matures into the final phase of existence on earth. He may regain his youthful zest, find new avenues for exploration, or decide to rest on his accomplishments. He may begin to fulfill the unfulfilled potential of the parent of the opposite sex. Health matters can take on a different glow as a result of a new perspective. If he is unaware of the possibilities that exist for him and decides to settle for a lower degree of energy in his system, he can deteriorate dramatically in his health. However, with the awareness of all the possibilities that exist for healthful living and productive clarity of mind, the individual can allow new streams of consciousness and energy to enter the physical system.

THE SUN RULING
THE FOURTH OR
TENTH HOUSE

When the Sun rules the sector of the chart that describes one of the parents, the individual photographs that parent as possessing great strength, dominance, and leadership qualities. The individual may be very proud of that parent. However, the quality and degree of pride is in direct proportion to the level of self-worth exhibited by the parent. If the parent possesses a healthy sense of self-worth, he or she is able to give strong ego strokes to the child and instill in him a sense of his own self-worth. The child develops a healthy sense of ego and can give himself permission to express strength of character and leadership qualities. Since the Sun relates to the heart chakra, if the parent has a low self-esteem and is unable to reinforce the child on an ego level, the heart chakra is affected in an adverse manner. The individual might constantly look for ego strokes from that parent and may always need permission from others to feel confident about his ability to express himself or to strive for accomplishment.

THE MOON RULING
THE FOURTH OR
TENTH HOUSE

If the Moon rules or is placed in one of these two sectors of the chart, the relationship with that parent is based on emotion and compassion. Strong symbiotic ties develop between parent and child that may be nurturing or smothering early in life. Those ties can be hard to break later on as the child begins to establish his own identity. The parent may have been orphaned or abandoned and may be unable to convey the compassion and nurturing needed by the child. The result is that the child may feel abandoned by that parent, simply because the parent is unusually sensitive, vulnerable, and self-protective. That parent may be more inclined to protect his or her own feelings than those of the child. The parent may tend to take things personally, creating an uneasy emotional rapport with the child. The individual may feel that he must tiptoe around the feelings of that parent for fear that what he might do or say will hurt or affect the parent in an adverse way. Alternatively, a need for his own individualization may prompt the child to rebel and deliberately push all of the vulnerable buttons of that parent. It may be difficult to have a logical, un-emotional conversation with that parent. It can be difficult for the child to establish the dividing line between the parent's thoughts and feelings and his own, which makes it difficult to develop his individual interests.

When the quality of compassion and symbiosis developed in the parent-child relationship is strong and positive, the individual is naturally attuned to people. He can identify with the needs of many people, and he can sense public needs and trends, just as he sensed what the parent needed. The primary quality that the parent fosters in the child through their relationship, whether that is for good or for ill, is one of compassion. The area of the body that is stimulated in dealing with the parent, when the Moon rules or is positioned in that sector of the chart, is the solar plexus.

MERCURY RULING *Walt* THE FOURTH OR *Dale-Steve* TENTH HOUSE

When Mercury is the ruler of the fourth or tenth sector of the chart, the quality of the relationship with the parent so described is on a mental level. The relationship with that parent either stim-ulates the individual toward the development of clear analytical thought processes or, in an adverse way, toward an overly ana-lytical or critical outlook. The aspects to Mercury in the chart indicate how the person thinks, speaks, and expresses himself. The placement of Mercury in the chart indicates what the individual thinks about. When Mercury describes one of the parents, the individual thinks about that parent. He may be acutely aware, and sensitive to, criticism from the parent. He may tend to base his own decisions on expected approbation from that parent. He may agree with the ideas expressed by that parent or disagree with anything the parent says. The quality of communication with that parent may vary from sarcasm to a stimulating exchange of information. Since Mercury describes left-brain activity, if Mercury is well aspected, he would have a healthy objectivity toward that parent and intellectual respect. He would look to him or her for sound advice.

VENUS RULING THE FOURTH OR TENTH HOUSE

— Lorie, Laurie, Katie
— Nicole, Mike

When Venus rules the tenth or fourth house in the chart, love is the predominant quality of the exchange of energy between the parent and child. With positive aspects to Venus in the individual chart, the person photographs his or her parent as having a charming personality and gracious manner. He loves that parent and appreciates his or her quality of sociability. The parent, in turn, may have an artistic temperament and be very talented in the field of the arts. If Venus is not well aspected, the individual may feel that the parent took the easy way out in life or neglected to properly defend him in his early years. The individual may feel a lack of expression of affection from that parent. The positive exchange of energy predisposes the individual to expression of diplomacy or artistry, while the negative exchange may indicate a tendency to opt for the status quo in all public dealings. The individual may develop a laissez-faire attitude in public or social situations, or actually be quite lazy in connection with career potential.

Venus rules the pancreas, which governs and regulates sugar in the body. That part of the system may be genetically conditioned by the bloodline from that part of the family. If the relationship is a loving one, sweet things are not an important dietary factor, but if Venus is not well aspected, a craving for missed love may tempt the individual to indulge desires for sweets, carbohydrates, alcohol, or foods that metabolize as sugar.

MARS RULING THE FOURTH OR TENTH HOUSE

Nicole

Katie

When Mars rules the tenth or fourth house in an individual chart, the parent may be ambitious, courageous, inventive, and resourceful. If the aspects to Mars are mostly productive and positive in the horoscope, the person is able to relate to that parent in a healthy, competitive manner. This can translate into an ability to direct positive energy into ambitious projects later in his life. The opposite may be true, in which case the parent may be frustrated, feisty, and angry in connection with his own life. The child may experience tremendous aggravations and frustrations in his relationship to that parent and a competitive situation may develop between parent and child.

When Mars describes mother-son or father-daughter interaction in an individual chart, it describes the classic Oedipus or Electra complex. With positive aspects to Mars, the individual is given permission, by that parent, to deal with sexuality in a healthy way. The messages may be overt or subtle, but because the parent is able to acknowledge and utilize his or her own sexuality in a positive manner, the child is encouraged to express his romantic inclinations and sexuality in a positive manner in his own life. That particular quality of high energy can be experienced as courage, daring, and resourcefulness that may be directed into areas of public life.

When Mars is not well aspected, there may be a strong undertone of sexuality in the relationship with that parent. This may remain unexpressed and unacknowledged, or it may indicate an incestuous relationship on some level. However it's expressed, this in itself creates frustration, impatience, and anger. The overt manifestation in dealing with that parent is contention. It is easier to fight than to deal with highly charged sexual feelings.

Aspects to Mars in the individual chart also indicate whether or not the child is able to fight openly with that parent or engage in healthy competition with him or her. As an example, if the person were pitted against his parent in a fight, he might automatically pull back his punches to avoid injuring that parent, but his own frustrated feelings over giving up the fight could damage their relationship. Hidden resentments could surface later and lead to a predisposition to avoid competitive situations. He pulls his punches in career situations. He may seem to lack ambition, as an example, or be unwilling to engage in competition at all. He may encounter tremendous frustrations and delays within the realm of his own public activity. This aspect may also describe frustrations in connection to his life-style, if Mars rules or is placed in the fourth house.

The area of the body that is stimulated by the quality of the relationship to that parent is the adrenals. With positive affirmation about ambition and courageous action, the adrenals are active in producing a high enough energy level to deal with competitive situations. If the parental messages deactivate the person, the adrenals tend to be lacking in production of adrenaline as well. Sexual predispositions can also be influenced when Mars is posited, or rules, these sectors of the chart.

JUPITER RULING THE FOURTH OR TENTH HOUSE

Dale

When Jupiter describes one of the houses that indicates a parent-child relationship, the energy exchange is one of humor and joy. Jupiter describes luck, optimism, and a philosophical attitude. Those qualities are fostered in the individual, by that parent, either through verbal encouragement or by the naturally humorous, philosophical, and enthusiastic personality of that parent. The child is brought up in a positive atmosphere of religion or one where a sense of universality and philosophy is taught. The parent encourages the individual to seek goals and strive for bigger and better things in life. He, himself, may love a challenge and expects his child to expect good fortune and follow in his path of success.

If Jupiter is not well aspected in the horoscope, the parent may have been disappointed in his own life. This may lead the individual to avoid goals and challenges, for when disappointment is transmitted from parent to child, the tendency to hang on to outmoded conditions, for fear of loss, is very strong. The placement of Jupiter describes the basic attitude about elimination. The area of the body stimulated by the exchange of energy is the kidneys. In order to seek new goals, poisons and outmoded conditions must be eliminated from life—and then they are easily eliminated from the body as well.

With a well-aspected Jupiter, humor and a philosophical outlook on the part of the parent encourages the individual to go after what he wants and to let go of those elements of his life that are nonproductive.

SATURN RULING THE FOURTH OR TENTH HOUSE

Delanie

When Saturn rules one of the houses that describes either mother or father, a strong karmic relationship exists between parent and child. The child may feel responsible for the welfare of that parent, as that parent may have had an extra load of responsibility placed upon him. The parent may have had a hard life and may, consequently, be a strong disciplinarian, exhibiting a stoic, serious, responsible nature. The qualities taught by that conservative parent have to do with attention to rules and regulations, and the development of values. If Saturn is not well aspected, there may be aloofness, actual coldness, or even physical absence on the part of the parent.

Since the child feels somehow responsible for the conditions of the parent's life, if he feels unable to solve the problems, he may eventually put some distance between himself and the parent. Or if the parent is too controlling and the relationship between parent and child is too rigid, the individual develops a rigidity in his attitude toward life and in his physical bearing. He automatically tenses his physical and psychological defense system to deal with serious life situations.

The part of the body that is stimulated by the unconscious messages and subtle relationship with this parent is the skeletal structure. If he is barricaded and tensed to deal with serious life situations, the production of calcium in the body may also be affected. Since Saturns also rules the teeth, the person may grind his teeth and clench his jaw to deal with the tension of life. He may develop T.M.J. syndrome, which eventually affects the whole balance of structure of the skeletal frame.

If Saturn is well aspected, the programming from that parent places emphasis on the development of a more responsible attitude toward life. The individual may feel as though he has inherited an important mission in life from that strong, serious, and dedicated parent.

URANUS RULING THE FOURTH OR TENTH HOUSE

olivia
and Megan

When Uranus describes one of the parents, a quality of spontaneity and freedom is fostered by that parent. The parent may be inventive, rebellious, enlightened, and ahead of the time. If Uranus is well aspected in the individual chart, by his own example the parent encourages a sense of adventure and freedom in the child. The individual may achieve something special in his life that will propel him into the limelight simply because he was willing to take the risks necessary for success.

If Uranus is not well aspected in the chart, the parent may not be aware of special qualities within himself and may resist his inner urge toward freedom and spontaneity of self-expression. The negative manifestations in the life of that parent may be fear or an underlying hysteria. The parent may be high-strung and easily frightened, or have alcoholic tendencies. The part of the body that seems to take the brunt of the relationship with this parent is the nervous system. If negative qualities are projected, the individual may habitually run away from achievement just as things are about to take off in his life. His sense of timing can be off, due to impulsive behavior and nervous reactions that are imbued into his psyche by his relationship with his parent. The positive qualities that are stimulated are inventiveness and a special degree of intuition, as well as a strong sense of humanitarianism.

NEPTUNE RULING THE FOURTH OR TENTH HOUSE

If Neptune describes the relationship between parent and child, hero worship may be in effect. The child may photograph the parent as an idealist and a visionary or, if Neptune is badly aspected, as very naïve and unrealistic. There is a probability that the idolized parent will fall from his pedestal at some point in the life of the child, because the tendency is to project unrealistic characteristics onto that parent.

Neptunian qualities are considered to be gentleness and fragility, yet Neptune describes the iron fist inside the velvet glove. The parent with Neptunian attributes may be charming and appear to be very sweet, but underneath he may be a bit tyrannical. His tendency is to project onto other people, in this case the child, expectations that are unrealistic. The expectations of the parent may be quite different from the actual abilities or characteristics the child can express. If the child is unable to meet the parental expectations, the end result is a feeling of "You let me down!" on the part of the parent, and frustration or disillusionment on the part of the child. This principle can operate in reverse, as we have noted, in that a child may see his parent as being quite different from who he really is. The idealized interchange of energy may make confrontation impossible, leaving the child disillusioned and the parent confused about his relationship with his child. The part of the body that is affected is the immune system. The person may be susceptible to flu or viruses when he is disillusioned or let down. It is very important for the individual to confront the relationship with the Neptunian parent on a very concrete level to avoid setting up disillusioning conditions later in life.

PLUTO RULING *mike* THE FOURTH OR TENTH HOUSE *Lori Laurie*

Pluto is the planet that describes power. When that planet rules or is placed in the tenth or fourth house and is well aspected, the individual sees that parent as very dynamic, potent, and effective. But with negative aspects to Pluto, he or she may also see that parent as overly forceful or manipulative. With this negatively aspected planet ruling the houses that are descriptive of parental relationships, the parent is sometimes called the "witch parent." If the parent is willful and tricky and if the parent and child continue to stir each other up, a game persists between them. Any attention at all is better than no attention, and both parent and child may use devices that are less than productive to keep a hook into the relationship.

The relationship can represent a tar baby situation, so called for its parallel to the Uncle Remus story. One afternoon, Br'er Rabbit was taking a walk. As he passed a tar baby sitting by the side of the road, he doffed his hat. Tar baby didn't respond. Br'er Rabbit became so enraged at the lack of response that he decided he would teach the tar baby some manners. He punched the tar baby with his fist. Tar baby still didn't respond. Then Br'er Rabbit hit him with the other fist. Finally, he kicked with first one foot and then the other until he was firmly stuck into the tar.

When tricky situations develop between parent and child, it is necessary for the child to go up, around, and beyond the situation in order to ensure his freedom. If the child can learn how to resist buying into or engaging in manipulative and revengeful actions, the relationship may provide him with an opportunity for initiation onto a higher level of consciousness. For wherever Pluto is located in the individual astrological chart is the area where the greatest transformation and initiation can take place. Those are the areas where the individual tests himself to see how he will utilize his own power.

With a negatively aspected Pluto ruling one of the houses describing parental relationships, the parent may have been traumatized as a child, keeping him trapped in a nonproductive and willful "child ego" state. When the child of that parent feels he is being manipulated, forced, or not allowed to express his own child-ego state (he is, after all, the child in the relationship), it is natural to feel some resentment toward the parent. A positive outcome of such an inner struggle comes as a result of an internal wrestling match, like Moses wrestling with the angel. When the individual wins by being able to ignore or let go of the situation, he projects himself onto a higher spiritual level. He has won an internal battle with himself, which frees him to live on a higher level of consciousness. He is then able to project himself onto a higher cosmic level without fear that he will misuse his energy or power.

The part of the body that is stimulated in this parent-child exchange is the entire chakra system and the pituitary gland in particular. With the process of letting go, the individual releases his physical body to operate on a higher octane gas. That gas is prana, and its spiritual energy transforms his automobile into a jet-propelled airplane. When he flies above the clouds, far beyond the smog and obstacles on the earth plane, his perspective of life is very different. At that point, anything is possible.

*Breaking the Script**

*M*an is a creature of habit and change is mostly foreign to life on the earth plane. The difficulties that naturally come with readjustment to new conditions have much to do with maintaining balance between the right and left hemisphere of the brain, and maintaining that balance is one of the prime considerations of living on earth. In order to function under the consistently stressful conditions of present-day life, each individual, perhaps unconsciously, experiments with his own methods of survival, for he is like a gyroscope trying to maintain equilibrium. When a major traumatic event occurs, the system can easily be thrown out of gear.

In evaluating the degree of trauma connected to various stressful situations in life, the highest ratings have to do with making a change. For instance, the loss of a parent, spouse, job, or home can force a person to adjust to a whole new set of circumstances. There can be a difficult period of readjustment to these traumatic situations. Sometimes one person can adjust easily, whereas an-

---

* This term is utilized by practitioners of Transactional Analysis.

other can go through tremendous torture until he is back on point again.

This pull between habit and forced change can be described astrologically when we consider the qualities of Saturn and Uranus. Saturn is the planet that relates to the earth plane, the gravitational pull, and the need for consistency, stability, and security in life. Saturn represents a rooted, settled quality, whereas Uranus describes just the opposite kind of energy. Uranian energy relates to upheaval, unexpected conditions, and the nerve-racking sensations usually associated with such uncertainty. Yet enlightenment and growth only come with change. Stagnant conditions do not foster growth and creativity, but fortunately or unfortunately, life presents many opportunities for each individual to find his own brand of creativity. It sometimes takes creative solutions and courage just to get through each day.

One of the ways an individual can understand the way he handles change is to take a look at the birth process, for that is the first major change a person makes in his life. It is usually quite traumatic to emerge from the safety and comfort of the womb to the colder, chaotic atmosphere outside, and since few people have a conscious memory of the way they make that change, they are not aware of their physical, mental, and emotional reactions. During regression sessions, each person sees exactly how he reacted to his particular situation at the time of entry into life and can correlate the particular stages of that first reaction to the specific reactions he has time after time when change presents itself in his life.

As a person grows, he may become more adept at making changes. He learns how to adjust to the challenges presented to him and finally begins to place his security into the hands of his higher self. At that point he can pilot his vessel through the streams of life with awareness and trust. That ultimate transmutation usually comes as a result of traumas, stress, and change. He may simply get tired of allowing external conditions to debilitate him or worrying over problems that never occur. He finally becomes more philosophical and may be able to develop a greater sense of humor as a result of analyzing his patterns. He accepts his role in life as a problem-solving mechanism and accepts the growth challenges that are constantly being presented to him.

The astrological chart clearly describes what the survival decisions at birth might be. The rising sign, or ascendant, not only indicates the appearance and personality traits of an individual, it also describes how he plans to deal with his future on the earth plane—his modus operandi. Most people make more than one survival decision. In the astrological chart, all of the planets that are placed within the first house, or that make an aspect to the ascendant or to a planet in the first house, describe the varying qualities of early survival decisions. (See Chapter 13.)

The term *script* can describe just what the overall plan of life might be for each individual. Actors follow a script and learn lines that have been written for them by a playwright. Every individual comes into life with a script, ready to portray a role. In the case of life scripts, according to Transactional Analysis the playwright may have been the parents, who had certain expectations for their unborn child. The person himself has chosen a role to play in life, which may or may not be in accordance with the script written by the parents. Sometimes the grandparents, or other powerful family members, have chosen a script for the unborn child to follow.

In the case of royal births, the script is written by the parents, but is reinforced by thousands of subjects who have expectations for the new member of the royal family. The script dictates the individual's behavior and the values he must adopt in connection with his public life. It is very difficult to break a script that has been so tightly written by so many people. One dramatic exception was the former King Edward VIII of England, who became the Duke of Windsor after he renounced his throne in 1936.

Even though David, as he was affectionately called by family members, gave up his crown, he expected to continue serving his country in some meaningful way. In his own mind he was still the king of England, the role he had trained for all his life and for which he was programmed long before his birth. One of the greatest tragedies of his life, in his own eyes, was not being allowed to make a contribution to the war effort. He was exiled far away across the Atlantic Ocean to Nassau, where it was deemed that he would cause the least trouble and embarrassment for the new king and queen, and for England. Second and subsequent sons of kings are given quite different scripts to follow. They are not expected to undergo the training required in order to assume duty as a monarch, but rather to have a good time and stay out of the way.

When a person breaks his own life script or changes the way he automatically tends to react, he releases energy that will enable him to live a fuller, freer existence simply because he begins to realize whether his behavior patterns are productive or nonproductive. He may discover that he has shaped his life according to others' expectations and that there are many new options open to him in the future. Therefore it is important for each individual to analyze what his life script might be and to decide for himself whether that script was of his own choosing or whether his script was written by someone who may not have had his best interests at heart.

An astrological chart can be invaluable in deciding what the life script might be. The beginning of life is described by the ascendant, whereas the prenatal experiences are indicated by the twelfth house. As an example, if Aries rules the ascendant, Pisces rules the twelfth house. The aspects to Mars, the ruler of Aries, and to Neptune, ruler of Pisces, can reveal the way a person felt inside the womb, the conditions of his birth, and the survival decisions he made at that critical moment about how he will behave throughout his life. Planets that are positioned in those two houses can qualify or modify the descriptions.

As an example, acupuncturist Ken Kobayashi was born with Leo rising. He not only remembers his birth, but is aware of executing the birth process by himself. There were midwives present at the time of his birth, but Ken knew what to do and was allowed to take charge of the moment. Not only that, he spoke to his mother the moment he was presented to her and said, "Hi Mom, I'm your baby." (This phenomena prompted several popular song writers in Japan to record the event in music and verse.) With a well aspected Sun in his chart (the Sun is the ruler of Leo), Ken showed his leadership qualities and "kingship" right away. More than that, he was acknowledged as being the boss! He never lacked for recognition during his life and was, in fact, the center of attention (onstage) when he gave a demonstration of his healing potential at the age of 3½. Ken is quite modest about his life and accomplishments. Sometimes a need for extra ego stroking is possible when Leo is on the ascendant. But since he was recognized as the little prince from the moment of birth and was allowed to take charge, he can do so with confidence and joyous self-assurance. With a well-aspected Moon, he was sensitive to everything going on around him prenatally and was carefully nurtured during that formative time in his life (Cancer ruling the twelfth house). This emotional bonding and permission giving enables him to express the compassionate, nurturing part of his nature as well as the dominant leadership qualities. Ken's life script as the little prince was chosen by his parents, but was happily accepted by Ken himself. (See Chapter 19.) Another child born with Leo rising might not be recognized for who he is, would probably not be allowed to take charge so early in his life, and might develop a life script that is similar to being a king in exile, unrecognized in a foreign land.

The therapeutic process helps a person decipher his own patterns and proclivities. A person enters therapy with the idea of changing nonproductive patterns in his life. He can then decide on a more rational level whether or not he is in conflict with expectations projected onto him before or at the time of his birth. At that point, he gains more control over his existence and can begin to make positive, productive choices that are more in line with his own desires and abilities.

A regression session is an especially valuable way of understanding a script that may have been set in motion in this lifetime or centuries before. During that experience, the individual reveals to himself the activities, problems, or guilts that predetermine the kind of script he will act out in the present life. Discovering his reactions and thoughts during the birth process, step-by-step, describes patterns that continue to repeat themselves over and over again. The exact formula set in motion during the birth process describes the way an individual will handle change the rest of his life. He can break the script when he examines the thread of consciousness from the beginning and evaluates whether his decisions work for him or not in the present existence.

If an individual can learn to ask himself the right questions, he can access his own Akashic Records and see for himself what those conditions might have been. The major question to be posed is: "What could have happened in the past that could create such a situation in the present?" The ability to listen for the answer comes with the trust that an answer exists. The mind is the connecting agent to the spiritual self and is the vehicle through which etheric energy and information can pass down into physical expression. If the mind is kept in balance to allow for the passage of pure energy into the system, the body might never be ill. (See Chapter 25.)

P A R T   4

. . . .
. .

Relationship

of Astrology

to Spiritual

Health

Subtle Body Energy

he subtle body is also known as the etheric body or the electric body. It has a direct relationship to the health and energy of the physical body because the etheric vehicle actually underlies the entire physical system. The etheric body actually controls and determines the quality of the life energy of an individual. Its function is to convey lines of electrical force and energy throughout the physical system by way of the seven chakras. These chakras, or spiritual centers, are vitalized by the spiritual vehicle like batteries being recharged. Seven types of energy are distributed throughout the entire human system through these seven batteries or chakras.

There is a counterpart in the etheric body to every part of the physical body, with the exception of the bony structure of the physical vehicle. The nervous system, which medical science can isolate and describe, is a physical network and counterpart of millions of invisible force lines of energy in the etheric vehicle called nadi. These lines of force, which underlie the more substantial body, are isolated into primary lines of energy. The primary lines of energy are called meridians. (See Chapter 18.) Whereas the meridians receive energy from the level of the soul, and carry those impulses throughout the body by way of the unseen lines of force, the nervous system (the physical counterpart of the meridians) receives impulses from the brain (the physical counterpart of the soul) and carries consciousness through the human system via the more tangible network of the nervous system.

The endocrine system is the tangible, physical manifestation of the seven chakras. It governs both physiological and psychological functions of the body, and has, as its primarily responsibility, governorship over the condition of the entire physical organism. (See Chapter 2.) The centers, or chakras, are located in the same general region as the major glands of the endocrine network, except for the root chakra, which relates to the adrenal glands. Those glands are located above the kidneys in the physical body. Each spiritual center supplies the power and life to a corresponding gland that is the externalization of that particular center or chakra. Starting from the top of the head down to the spine, the chakras are the crown chakra (located at the top of the head), the brow or ajna center (located between the eyes), the throat chakra (located at the base of the throat), the heart chakra (located in the center of the chest near the sternum), the solar plexus (located above the navel), the sacral center (located midway between the navel and pubic bone), and the base chakra (located at the base of the spine). The crown chakra relates to the pineal gland and to the fontanel, which remains open for a short period of time after birth. The ajna, or brow, chakra relates to the pituitary gland; the throat chakra corresponds to the thyroid gland; the heart chakra corresponds to the thymus gland; the solar plexus center to the pancreas; the sacral to the gonads or ovaries, and the center at the base of the spine corresponds to the adrenal glands.

The three esoteric systems (the etheric body, the meridians, and the chakras) and the exoteric, or more obvious, systems (the physical body, the nervous and glandular systems) are interdependent. Both systems are responsible for the well-being of the physical body, the development of the psychological quality, and the condition of physical health. The bloodstream, the prime conveyor of oxygen throughout the physical body, is the carrier of the life principle throughout all systems. It also conveys the combined energies of all three systems into the heart, which is the central organ of life.

From an astrological point of view, there is a planetary relationship to the esoteric (hidden, unseen) system and also a planetary rulership for the exoteric (obvious and seen) system. In the esoteric system, the etheric vehicle is governed by the Moon, the meridians are ruled by Venus, and the chakras are ruled by Saturn. In the exoteric or known physical system, the rulerships are different. The physical body, corresponding to the etheric body (ruled by the Moon), is described by Saturn. The nervous system, which corresponds to the meridians (ruled by Venus), is ruled by Uranus. The endocrine system is ruled by Pluto. That corresponds to the chakras, which are ruled by Saturn. (One way to test the theory of these rulerships is to repeat the Saturnian phrase "I should, I must, I ought." These words restrict the flow of energy throughout the chakras. The resultant constriction can be felt, especially in the area of the heart chakra. Now repeat the positive phrase "I choose." The sensation of the resultant energy flow can also be felt in that chakra.)

The transmutation of energy onto the soul level, or from exoteric to esoteric, stems from an individual's conscious decision to begin operating from the higher part of his nature. It involves shifting consciousness by shifting the level of the will. The childish willfulness, which says "I want what I want when I want it," is eventually transformed by the right motivation to the higher will of the soul, which says "I only want what is right for everyone concerned." At that point the individual begins to work on a different level and with different energies.

In light of the astrological significators, it is possible to transmute the activity of the three major exoteric systems by consciously working under the energy of the higher octave planets that correspond to each system. For instance, the transmutation of the physical body energy to the conscious level of the etheric body involves utilizing the positive level of Saturnian energy in conjunction with the higher energy of the Moon. Saturn describes gravity, pressure, limitation in its nonproductive sense; in a more elevated sense it can also describe commitment, a higher sense of responsibility, and destiny. The lower or nonproductive message of the Moon relates to oversensitivity, vulnerability, and emotionalism, whereas the higher message describes compassion. With a commitment to the higher sense of responsibility, purpose of life, and destiny (Saturn) comes greater compassion about the sufferings of all mankind. Physical energy is transmuted above Saturnian pain and limitation onto the higher level of etheric energy, which is an interpenetrating substance. This combined higher energy of Saturn and the Moon are also descriptive of the sufferings of mankind when he is on the earth plane because of his desires or his hunger needs. When an individual develops an ability to rise above his own sufferings, transmutes desire into aspiration, and works in compassionate service to others, he calls higher etheric energy into his physical system as a result of development of higher consciousness. Etheric energy and higher consciousness go hand in hand.

Imbalance within the nervous system, described by Uranus on an exoteric level, causes many physical disorders. Blocked flow of nervous energy may manifest in physical symptoms such as asthma, allergies, rashes, skin eruptions, and nervous disorders. Uranus can even describe autism. In its nonproductive sense, Uranus describes rebellion and impulsive energy; at a higher level it describes a sense of universality and freedom. Venus rules the meridians, nerves, and plexi of the esoteric nervous system. Venus describes complacency, in its nonproductive sense, and the dynamic quality of love in its elevated sense. Love is an energy that is as real as dense matter. Love is such a tangible and powerful force it can promote healing when other methods seem to fail, as if it can draw out diseased tissue and provide a healthy substitute in place of what is eliminated. Universal love that flows from the opened heart chakra toward all mankind also works within the system to lift frayed, stressed nervous energy onto a level where etheric energy can flow inward along the unseen meridians of the body, bringing in a higher level of life force and consciousness.

The transmutation and balancing of the endocrine system and the process of energizing all of the chakras requires working through the higher octaves of Pluto and Saturn. In the nonproductive sense, Pluto describes childlike willfulness. When an individual works with the desire nature to acquire whatever he wants, even at the expense of someone else, he traps himself onto the lower level of Saturnian energy. He sticks himself, like glue, onto the negative level of gravity and possessions. He becomes burdened with his bounty and the additional karma that selfishness brings. If, however, he can successfully release things, people, and conditions that are not productive in his life, he begins to work on the true level of responsibility. He grows from a self-absorbed child into a wise parent to the childlike quality within himself. He refuses to allow anything into his ambience that would damage or abuse the innocence of his inner childlike being. At that point he can become a wise caretaker for mankind. He opens all the chakras to their proper vibratory rate and allows the Kundalini Fire (See Chapter 2) to slowly and consistently rise with great diligence, dedication, and caution (Saturn) to unite inner flame to the cosmic fire. This transformation of energy and magnetism is extremely powerful. Disease must necessarily be burned out with this purifying fire.

True and future healing is brought about when the life force of the soul can flow without hindrance through every aspect of the physical nature. The potency of that flow can then vitalize and eliminate congestions and obstructions that are the source of disease.

The vibrating atoms, molecules, cells, and organ systems of the body all contribute to the unique auric vibration that is radiated by each individual. All thoughts, moods, feelings, attitudes, and values are transmitted through the colors of the aura and can be discerned by psychics and other sensitives who are attuned to seeing those specific colors. The colors emanating from each individual clearly indicate the health of that person.

The etheric body is the vehicle that relates to the highest part of man. It vibrates on a much higher frequency than the physical body and is part of cosmic energy. In fact, Kirlian photography has demonstrated that this higher energy interpenetrates all living matter. Even fruits and vegetables have an aura, the emanation or energy that streams forth from the subtle body. It is clear through Kirlian photography that when fruits and vegetables have been picked, the aura begins to fade, for the life force has been cut off. If a fruit or vegetable has been allowed to sit for several days, the aura markedly diminishes in vibrancy.

In the past, when holy men tried to teach that all is one, the message seemed obscure and too mystical for rational explanation.

But pure energy does exist. It permeates all matter, and as the vibration is lowered and bends around and through shapes, it is refracted into what we can see as colors.

The aura is composed of the emanations of the etheric body. The aura itself is threefold in manifestation. It reflects the condition of the physical body (physical health); the condition of the astral or emotional body; and the condition of the mental body or thought processess. It is through the agent of the aura that we send out vibrations to others. What we say is often less important in relationships than the subtle quality of energy we emanate. It is that vibratory emanation that creates the real effect a person has on his associates. It explains attractions and repulsions that have little to do with personal experience or logical reason. It explains why we fall in love with one person and not with another.

These vibratory emanations carry every thought, word, or feeling that was ever projected by any human being, registering them onto the ethers, where they remain on record for anyone to access, if he or she knows how. This etheric record is called the Akashic Record. Its existence accounts for many psychic flashes and extra sensory perceptions. It explains how some people can give psychic readings for others. I have come to the conclusion that when I conduct a regression session, which enables a person to understand the specific karma he brings into this life, I am actually taking the individual on a journey to his own Akashic Records. In these sessions, pictures of events that have not previously been revealed to the person emerge clearly and easily. I frequently see the same pictures, simultaneously or just seconds before the client, and I am not ordinarily psychic. This journey is an unconscious process on my part, except for my desire to enable a person to see what he needs to see for his own growth. I do not know how the process takes place.

When we begin to study the subtle body energy of a person, we are dealing with energy that vibrates on a level that we cannot see, touch, or taste. In considering the general condition of spiritual health from an astrological point of view, the higher octave planets—Uranus, Neptune, and Pluto—come into play. The position of Uranus in the chart and its relationship or aspects to other planets describes the quality of the higher vibratory, electrical energy carried on the breath, and it indicates how smoothly this higher energy can enter the body. Neptune describes the aura, or the photograph of the esoteric, spiritual body. Neptune's position and relationship to other planets indicates the balance and quality of the aura and the overall condition of the etheric radiation of an individual. A person with a well-aspected Neptune ruling the ascendant or placed in the first house looks like an angel with a glow around his head. This person always photographs like a dream, for his aura produces a gauzelike quality that is easily captured on film. Pluto describes the quality of magnetism inherent in a person's etheric and physical makeup. The aspects to Pluto or its relationships to other planets indicate how a person utilizes that particular quality of dynamic energy. Uranus and Pluto bear the description of the electromagnetic field and how it functions within the esoteric and consequent physical systems. Neptune describes the aura, which is the esoteric picture of that electromagnetic energy field.

Reading the Aura for Signals

*T*he aura reflects the condition of an individual's physical, emotional, mental, and spiritual health. It is actually his electromagnetic vibratory energy in visible form. When the aura is strong and vibrant, it is like a thick white cloud suffused with brilliant colors that surrounds the individual, protecting him from destructive elements in the atmosphere such as radiation from gamma rays and from energy that might not be as high in vibratory level as his own.

The aura is actually the external manifestation of alpha brain waves which exit the body from points around the skull. These points correlate with the T.S. (temporo-sphenoidal) line (see p. 282) and circulate around the body to find entrance through points around the abdomen. The aura, the manifestation of the electromagnetic field, is like a rainbow that is always there but can only be seen occasionally under the right conditions. It can't be seen as readily as one might see a colored photograph in a magazine (which might be described by Mercury), as it takes a higher level of vision or insight to focus in on the finer material of its composition. Therefore, the aura falls under the astrological rulership of Neptune, as Neptune describes insight and a higher level of vision and idealism. So alpha waves, which are produced by the higher vibrations of meditative states of awareness, also fall under the category of Neptune.

To understand more about the electromagnetic vibratory rate, we can use the analogy of a cross of light. The electric light energy, described by Uranus, fuses with magnetic light energy, described by Pluto, and produces man, a column of light on earth. The light that emanates from man is the aura, ruled by Neptune. Neptune, one of the three higher octave planets, sits in between Uranus and Pluto in the astrological lineup.

Think of man in his higher form as merged in the cosmic fire. In the undifferentiated form, as part of the whole, he is nothing but flame or light or intelligence or energy. But imagine an electrical storm, with one spark of that cosmic fire falling away into the lower atmosphere of earth. That spark carries with it the intelligence of the whole cosmic flame, described by Pluto, and comes into a different electrical vibratory rate as it falls through the atmosphere (Uranus) and manifests in a physical vehicle, still giving off the accumulated light energy of his true composition (Neptune), but diffused because of the complexity of the physical vehicle (Saturn). Like a prism, the refraction of color will change depending on the conditions that surround it. So the aura changes and reflects the inner light energy.

The earth plane is the schoolroom or the exercise salon in which everyone is learning to flex his muscles of individuality and to reflect his special brand of light energy. Consequently, there are times when people's vibrations or emanations are distinctly brighter than others. For instance, pollutants in the environment, such as drugs and chemicals, have their own vibrational rate and permeate the atmosphere. If an individual's aura is not bright enough to afford adequate protection, or if a person is especially sensitive to those vibrations and has an imbalance in the electromagnetic fields, the emanations do not afford the intended protection. It is then possible to pick up negative energies that actually catch like steel filings on a magnet. First it is important to keep those alpha waves strong so that the emanation is bright (see Chapter 25—Meditation), and then it is essential to cleanse the aura of anything that might clog or prevent positive etheric energy from reentering the body. Restriction of the positive flow of energy through the etheric system is the underlying cause of lowered vitality or ill health.

Dogs that are trained by the U.S. customs department to sniff out drugs are probably sensitive to the vibratory quality of those drugs as well as just the smell. Some people who are especially sensitive might also be useful to customs officers, but perhaps at the expense of their own health. My own body's reaction to the presence of drugs in the atmosphere is very dramatic. I discovered this quite by accident. I was traveling in a foreign country and was invited to a friend's home for dinner. Later in the evening, two very charming people stopped in unexpectedly. Suddenly I was extremely tired and my body became as heavy as lead. I felt as though I couldn't possibly rise from my chair, much less drive to my hotel. A clairvoyant friend who was present quietly signaled me to go outside for some fresh air. I did so, but with great effort. After a few gulps of the crisp night air, I returned to the dining room. I saw that the two newly arrived guests were graciously offering cocaine to everyone at the table. As soon as it was diplomatic to do so, I made my apologies and left the group.

About a week later, I was having dinner with another group of friends. The same two people came into the restaurant and were seated at a table next to ours. The couple is very likable, and since we all had mutual friends, the tables were joined together. A lively conversation took place and I was having lots of fun when suddenly the woman excused herself and left the restaurant. When she returned a few moments later, my body became leadlike once again. I deduced that she had been outside to make a purchase of cocaine or some other drug. Fortunately, dinner was almost over, and I was able to leave the restaurant soon after the incident. I had this reaction a third time, in a very fashionable restaurant in New York City with an entirely different group of people. Since I knew that no one at our table used drugs even occasionally, I concluded that I must be picking up the energy from someone at a nearby table.

It appears that my aura is especially sensitive to the presence of cocaine and perhaps other drugs as well. Some mechanism in my system shuts down and I am hardly able to move as a result of the sudden loss of energy. Therefore meditation and work with crystals as well as Bach flower remedies, and Vita Florum is as important to my system as water or food, so that I constantly feed the etheric body and create more protection against negative environmental pollutants.

An astrological chart can be an important indicator of the sensitivity of the physical vehicle, as well as the strength of the electromagnetic light field. It can describe how much protection is needed to counterbalance disturbing external conditions. First, look at the ascendant to see its sign placement and whether that sign is earth, air, fire, or water. Then look at the aspects it makes to other planets in the chart to see how those planets modify the quality of the ascendant. Finally, determine the overall balance of cardinality, fixity, and mutability in the chart. A water ascendant and/or strong aspects to water planets in the chart can indicate extreme sensitivity, but overall it is cardinality in the chart that can indicate the least resistance to the physical plane. Obviously, earth planets and fixity describe a stronger physical vehicle and a stronger relationship to the earth plane. Finally, look at the transpersonal planets—Uranus, Neptune, and Pluto. If they are strongly aspecting the ascendant and are in good balance with each other, the physical vehicle can support the energy that is inpouring. But if those planets are in difficult aspect to each other, the natural balance may not be strong enough to easily polarize the vehicle on the earth plane.

It is important to keep the atmosphere around the physical vehicle as pure as possible for the ultimate in physical well-being. Therefore, it is necessary to cleanse the aura frequently and, periodically, to clean out the atmosphere in a room, apartment, or home. There are several ways to do this. The simplest way to cleanse the aura is to take a shower immediately after being exposed to a situation that might carry negative energy. If you live and work in a large city, for instance, you will feel less tired if you take a shower immediately upon returning home after being at work and on the street. This suggestion is not designed to caste aspersions on coworkers or friends, it is simply a device to keep your own energy field vibrant, healthy, and intact. It is an especially important practice for a person with a preponderance of planets in cardinal signs in his or her chart, for many cardinal planets indicates a special sensitivity to conditions and people. This can be even more pronounced if, along with cardinal planets, the ascendant is in a cardinal sign.

One of the most potent methods of cleansing the atmosphere in a room (or a person's aura) is to burn dried sage. Place the sage in a pan that is fire- and heatproof. (Pot holders or a pair of oven mitts should be nearby in case the pan becomes too hot to hold.) The sage is lit and when the smoke becomes heavy, it should be fanned out into the atmosphere and around the body. You can walk around the room or house with the pan of smoking sage; a feather or a feathered fan is a perfect instrument with which to distribute the smoke. It is helpful to say something, even silently, about your purpose in cleaning the atmosphere. You might ask that all negative energy be removed and taken to a place of light where it can be purified and transmuted into positive energy. Rosemary is used for the same purpose in Ibiza, Spain, because it grows in such profusion. It is used by all the country folk in their fireplaces, for it is common knowledge that rosemary is a purifying agent. Burning it on a regular basis keeps the atmosphere pure within the home.

Another method of cleansing the atmosphere of a room is to burn salts, such as Epsom salts or kosher salt, that have been drenched with rubbing alcohol. Please be especially careful, as the flame can become quite high if you use too much alcohol. Be sure to wear oven mitts so that you don't drop the pan. Use a large enough utensil to prevent the flame from coming too near your hands or body. Fire is an excellent purifying agent, but it must be used with great caution.

Wilhelm Reich coined the term *orgone energy* to describe the high vibratory energy, or prana, that permeates the atmosphere. He invented the orgone box to trap some of that energy for healing purposes. Reich discovered that a combination of running water and metal pipes helped trap dead, or negative, energy from the atmosphere and produced a lighter, cleaner feeling in the room. (Since there is a profusion of highly concentrated waves emanating from television, radio, short waves, and other magnetic fields, negative energy can be especially concentrated in areas that are densely populated.) To change the quality of energy in a room, place metal pipes in a bucket in a bathtub and allow water to run over the pipes for several hours. (You can purchase metal pipes from a plumbing-supply shop and have them cut to a length of about a yard. It is helpful to find pipes that are flexible and can bend.) If it is impossible to keep the water running over the pipes for a reasonable length of time, or if there is a water shortage, allow the bucket to fill with water so that the pipes are covered. To prevent stagnation of energy, it is wise to change the water frequently.

When the aura is strong and energy moves freely through the system without hindrance either from within or from outer diminishing agents, colors around the body are vibrant. An individual's condition can be discerned by the colors he emits through the aura, and since the colors and shades of the aura change with differing health conditions, general diagnoses can be made by interpreting those hues. It is possible to develop an ability to see auras that surround other people and to look inside one's own body to determine the color emitted by each chakra.

First it is important to trust one's esoteric vision. If a person has been involved in the practice of meditation, that discipline makes visualization easier. If nothing else, it enables the individual to trust the vision of the inner eyes. If meditation has not been a habit, the development of inner sight may require a little more work and practice. There are preliminary exercises that can help the actual condition of the eyes and eyesight on a physical level, as well as facilitate development of the inner vision.

The first step is to do eye exercises that help stimulate circulation in the area of the eyes. Sit comfortably in a chair and imagine a huge clock placed just a few feet in front of your face. In order to see the numbers, you must make a wide sweeping gaze with your eyes. Start at twelve o'clock and slowly move your eyes toward one o'clock. Then see two o'clock and stretch your eyes to the right in order to focus on your imaginary three o'clock. Begin the downward sweep with your eyes toward four, five, and six o'clock, allowing your eyes to peer straight down at the number six. Then your eyes slowly begin the upward sweep to the left toward seven, eight, and nine o'clock, where your gaze will be stretched as far as possible toward the left. Then bring the eyes upward toward ten, eleven, and back to twelve, looking up as high as possible. Do this clockwise several times and then reverse direction and go counterclockwise a few times.

After you have finished this exercise, close your eyes and gently place your fingertips over your eyeballs without pressure. Imagine energy from your fingers penetrating into the eye, healing and relaxing your eyes. You can very gently massage the area around the eyeball, especially just under the brow toward the center of the forehead. You may feel tenderness or small knots under the bone just where the brows commence in the center of the forehead. Gentle massage of this area with your fingertips helps to stimulate drainage of the sinus cavities, which may cause pressure on the eyes from inside. (This practice is especially beneficial for those who suffer from sinus headaches.) If you have time, put compresses on the eyes to soothe any tension. Dampened tea bags make excellent compresses, as do pads soaked with witch hazel.

The second step is called a confrontation exercise. Sit in a chair facing a partner. The chairs should be far enough apart so that the knees are not touching (the contact might be distracting). Place the hands loosely in the lap and sit in an erect but relaxed position. If you wear glasses, take them off for the duration of the exercise. Look your partner in the eyes. It is necessary to remain unblinking as much as possible. You may discover that your eyes begin to tear in the beginning. Keep looking into the eyes of the person opposite you without staring and without strain.

You may soon begin to see a distortion of your partner's face. Don't break your concentration. Allow the changes to take place before your eyes. If you are sitting opposite someone of the female sex, it is even possible that her face may begin to look like that of a very old man. Just observe without making judgments about what you are seeing, as you are beginning to open up the vision of the inner eyes. You may discover that after a while, tension begins to release, vision clears, and you have widened your peripheral vision. The exchange of energy from one person to another through the eyes can be quite exhilarating, yet calming at the same time. You cannot help but notice new awareness of sensation through your whole being.

After about fifteen minutes of eye contact, take a rest and talk with your partner about what you saw. You may have observed not only a change of features, but colors around the head of the other individual. Each time you repeat the confrontation exercise, you will notice a greater ability to look your partner in the eyes without embarrassment or strain. Try not to work for results, but just continue to focus your attention on the eyes of the other individual. If you need to confine the time limit to five minutes in the beginning, that's fine. Increase the duration of the exercise each time you perform it until you reach fifteen minutes.

If you are working in a group, change partners occasionally to see if your experiences vary. If you are not working in a group, it is helpful to work with the same partner each time, if possible. That way, you will move through any discomforts together, and both of you will be making discoveries at a more mutual rate of speed. After a few sessions of confrontation you will be ready to try the next exercise. Place your partner a short distance away from you with his back to a wall. The space behind him should be devoid of pictures or distractions that would break the line of your vision. Focus your attention on an imaginary spot about two inches above the top of his head. Rest your gaze on that spot until you seem to see beyond the air. You may slowly change your gaze to encompass a wider area around his head, as if you were looking at a halo. You may see an emanation of white that appears to surround your partner's head, and after a while, you may begin to discern colors.

There are two factors that will determine the success you achieve. The first is that each person has his own timing and method of developing a new technique. Try not to be hard on yourself or make judgments about how you're doing. The judgmental process (Saturn) usually obscures progress, much like pulling down a window shade keeps out the light of a bright, sunny day. Suppose you suspect you're only imagining things and you're not really seeing what you think you're seeing. If you negate your own progress, you can't develop in any direction. It is wise to suspend judgment until you've given yourself plenty of opportunity to flex new muscles. If you trust your instincts, you may find that little by little your esoteric vision improves. Your eyesight should keep pace as well. Or perhaps you'll notice no gradual improvement at all until one day the inner eyes suddenly begin to function.

The second factor is the choice of a partner. Your success may depend greatly on the quality of energy that is within the aura of that person. If your partner is ill or has a low rate of vibratory energy, he or she cannot emit strong or vibrant colors for you to see! Before I began to see auras, I practiced all of the exercises I have described and gradually managed to detect faint colors around people if I concentrated on the ability to do so. One evening I went to a Vedanta Temple with friends. The Indian man standing at the podium was wearing a simple white garment. Gradually I saw a beautiful violet emanation around his head that had a very interesting shape. (The color purple is associated with spirituality.) The emanation was wide at the sides, and instead of following the shape of his head in a circular mode, it rose to a peak at the top, similar to the shape of an oriental temple. It was quite beautiful to behold. When the service was over, my friends asked me if I had also seen that color and shape. Individually, we had all seen the very distinct aura of this spiritually dedicated man. The emanation from his being was so strong and the energy in the Vedanta temple was so high that there was very little to inhibit esoteric vision.

Take notice of the aura of the room in which you are practicing. If you have a special place for meditation, you will have already built higher energy into that space, helping you to attain your goal. You can raise the energy level of any room by playing special high-energy music over and over again. Gregorian chants or devotional music carry energy and thoughts of the composer on an esoteric level, which create a vibratory rate particularly helpful for meditation, inner development, and healing. (See Chapter 21.) You may also want to cleanse the space by burning sage, incense, or rosemary. Use an invocation to ask that the room be dedicated for the purpose of higher awareness. (See Chapter 25 on Meditation.)

The last stage of developing the ability to see colors is practiced alone. This time, close your eyes and focus your inner vision on each chakra in turn, starting with the root chakra. Peer inside your own body and try to determine what that chakra looks like and what the color might be. Since these exercises cannot be hurried, please give yourself plenty of time to focus on each chakra in turn without interruption. The true color of the root chakra is red. If you see the color as muddy or dark, you know that an imbalance may have its origin at the very first chakra in the system. This chakra relates to the adrenal glands, which regulate the flow of energy throughout the body and provide extra energy when an emergency arises. If the adrenals are malfunctioning, an individual is likely to feel sluggish and uninspired; other glands of the endocrine system may also be affected.

The root chakra is the center where the serpent fire lies coiled. It is very important that no conscious effort be made to raise the Kundalini as you focus your energy into this center. (See Chapter 2.) The Kundalini Fire is automatically raised from the top chakra downward when all of the centers are cleared of obstruction. To raise this fire prematurely can be dangerous, since upper channels may not be ready for the intensity of the released energy.

Now raise your inner vision to the next chakra in line, which is between the root chakra and the solar plexus, at the midpoint in the area of the belly. It is located near the center of the body, slightly closer to the spine. The healthy color of this chakra, the sacral, is orange. Look carefully with your inner vision to see how clear the color is and what the shape of the chakra might be. If the color is not vibrant, or if the chakra seems inactive, the origin of imbalance or health problems may come from organs located in that area of the body, specifically the reproductive organs. The sacral center relates to the reproductive organs and sexual urges. Sexual desire is the exoteric urge for union that reflects the esoteric desire for union with the soul. (See page 113 on Mars and sexual energy.)

The next area of attention is the solar plexus. This chakra is located in the center of the body, above the navel but well below the shoulder blades. This is the seat of emotions and desires. A vital goal in life is to transmute all manner of desires—good desires, selfish desires, wrong desires, and spiritual desires—into aspiration. The solar plexus chakra is a very powerful center and is apt to be out of balance in many people because it is the recipient of all emotional reactions. The emotional body is the hardest to control since it relates to the astral plane, and the solar plexus area is constantly being bombarded with energy from that plane of activity. The individual solar plexus is also connected to the collective solar plexus, which means that the emotional reactions a sensitive individual experiences may be reflections of all the emotional reactions that might be floating around in the atmosphere. Many mediums and psychics work through this center rather than through the ajna or third eye. The solar plexus is the center that relates to the stomach, liver, and pancreas. It is not a coincidence that many mediums and psychics have diabetes or hypoglycemia. The entire area below the diaphragm can be in a state of constant turmoil if this center is out of balance. Its natural color is yellow. Make note of the hue and clarity of this chakra as well as its tone and condition. Many weight problems stem from disturbance in this area of the body, not from real hunger. With some attention to creating balance in the solar plexis center, problems relating to digestion, elimination, and assimilation can be alleviated.

Next comes the heart chakra, which is located in the center of the body between the shoulder blades. When this chakra is open and in balance, the heart radiates the energy of love. Personal love, romantic love, and mother love are normally felt in this part of the body, but when the heart chakra is fully energized, there is a sensation of universal love that radiates a magnetic quality not only into the individual system, but out to mankind and through-out the cosmos. The life force works through the heart, utilizing the bloodstream to carry love, the life force, throughout the phys-ical body. Consciousness, which is different from love energy, works through the brain, using the nervous system. Energy that is magnetized through the heart chakra becomes available for heal-ing oneself and others, and has a regenerative quality. With focused awareness and renewed sensations in the area of the heart center, pure feeling is often transmuted to thinking with the heart. Ac-cording to Alice Bailey, "as a man thinketh in his heart, so is he."

One of the meditations taught by Tibetan lamas involves the repetition of a mantra and visualization of the words of the mantra revolving around the heart chakra, like carousel animals revolving around a merry-go-round. Another meditation, taught by an es-oteric school, involves concentration of attention on the heart chakra from the back, focusing on the point between the shoulder blades.

The heart is the central organ in the body. Its astrological coun-terpart is the Sun, the center of the solar system and the spiritual source of light and love. The opening of this center allows for greater attention toward group consciousness. The awareness of the personality is superseded by a broader awareness that includes all mankind, rather than separation of one man from another. The full meaning of the Sun in astrological terms, as it relates to kingship or to executive capacity, is transmuted so that the individual becomes aware of his connection, through love, to all mankind.

The heart chakra relates to the thymus gland, one of the parts of the endocrine system that influences the immune system and regulates physical growth. From a psychological perspective, imbalance in this gland seems connected to irresponsibility or amorality. If this gland is stimulated and balanced, an increased sense of responsibility, leading to service toward mankind, appears to be the result.

The color of this chakra is green. As you make note of the hue of green, you can also determine whether the heart chakra feels relaxed and vibrant. Next to the solar plexus, the heart chakra is the area of the body that takes most of the brunt of trauma or pain. It is absolutely essential that this area vibrate in balance. The closing off of this center, with the resultant closing off of love, points the way toward later problems with the heart. The heart muscle is much too fragile to bear the brunt of accumulated trauma and tension. (See Chapter 21 on Color.)

Next in line is the throat chakra, which is considered to be the power center. This chakra is located at the back of the neck and reaches upward into the medulla oblongata, involving the carotid gland and downward toward the shoulder blades. This chakra is the first of the triad of chakras leading into the head. Just as the neck is a connecting bridge between the body and the head, the throat chakra is the connecting bridge between lower-body functions and functions of the head. This is the chakra through which intelligence is creatively focused and released. Thoughts become creative and powerful when they are spoken or expressed. What we say carries the power of our thought whether that is for good or for ill, for this chakra registers the intention or creative purpose of the soul. Be wary of gossip, as that is a particularly negative use of vocal power and can condition the quality of energy transported through the throat chakra. Blocked energy in this area of the system may be apparent with physical symptoms such as choking, coughing, difficulty in swallowing, or lack of ability to verbalize ideas.

This center relates to the thyroid gland. The thyroid gland regulates the general metabolic activity in the body and balances the distribution of food, fuel, and energy throughout the system. Look inside to see the shape and character of this chakra. Its color is blue. The shade of blue should be vibrant yet soft in hue.

The ajna, or brow, chakra is located in the center of the forehead just above the eyebrows. This is the chakra that relates to the pituitary gland, the central organ of the endocrine system. This center also relates to the opening of the third eye. The chakra has two wings that spread out to the right and the left of the head. These wings are symbolic of the two paths in life, just as they relate to the two halves of the brain. The left hemisphere (Mercury) describes the way of matter or materialism, and the right hemisphere (Neptune) relates to the way of the spirit. Neither is any good without the other. The brow chakra is the integrating point between the right and left halves of the brain. The activation of this center releases powerful idealism and fosters insight. It allows for expression of imagination and desire in the highest sense. (See Chapter 10, Dr. Chrane.) These are the dynamic forces behind all creation. When these energies are out of balance, any feelings of despair and resultant illness may be related to the sense of separation from one's higher self.

There is a stream of light that descends downward from the crown chakra to cross the two streams of energy or light emanating from the brow center. This cross of light symbolizes man's struggle to live within the confines of matter while he activates and creatively manifests the higher will of the soul. Creating a balance of these streams of light keeps an individual upright and receptive to the higher energies that course throughout his system. Inspiration flowing downward into the system from the crown can then be directed outward toward mankind, expressed through the throat in a creative fashion. This energy source is utilized and revealed to mankind through inspiration which leads to creativity. In this way man can be freed from the heaviness of the cross of materialism he bears in life. The balance of energy streaming from above, integrated with emanated energy, creates a dynamic electromagnetic field and relates to a higher level of psychic ability and inspired perceptions. Activation of this center releases true inner vision (see Chapter 17 on Alignment of Body Structure, Exercise; and Chapter 25 on Meditation.) The color of this chakra is indigo.

Check to see the clarity of the color as well as the overall condition of the chakra.

Finally, the crown chakra is located at the top of the skull. It relates to the pineal gland which is crystalline in its composition. The pineal gland is thought to control the hormonal time clock that inhibits sexual maturation until puberty. It is located at the area of the fontanel, the soft spot in a baby's head. The pineal gland is active during infancy until the indwelling soul is fully anchored in its physical body. At that point, the fontanel has also closed, prohibiting the premature exit of the spirit. This gland becomes active again when man chooses by his conscious will to enter the final stages of divine expression and decides to be an agent for the accomplishment and expression on earth of the higher will of the soul.

When this chakra is fully vibratory, it registers divine purpose and is the center where the energy of will, of consciousness, and of creativity meet. The goal of all meditation is to activate the entire system of the centers so that energy from the etheric body and from the ethers can stream downward through crown chakra, the highest point in the esoteric glandular system. Its activation reinforces and comes about as a result of the connection that is made with the higher self. The crown chakra may not be open and active in the majority of people at this time. However, even if the chakra is not fully activated, there is some semblance of vibration and color residing there. The color of this chakra is violet or purple.

Each of the chakras emits a color into the auric field of the body. If energy is lacking in one or more of the individual chakras, it is helpful to visualize the corresponding color, which can then be sent into the appropriate parts of the body through meditation. (See Chapters 21 and 25.) Greater balance can be achieved in this all-important esoteric glandular system by consciously attuning the inner vision toward each center in turn, with the intention of energizing and releasing blockages that might inhibit the fullest expression of etheric energy into the physical system. It is helpful to keep a periodic record of what the characteristics of each chakra appear to be and to note what changes may occur. Charting your own inner energy, as seen through the chakras, can finely attune your ability to energize your physical system.

PART 5

Types of Therapies

Alignment of Body Structure, Exercise

*A*ll of the Universe is energy. Energy moves, pulsates, and swirls throughout all levels of existence. It also moves throughout the human system. Blood flows through the heart and veins, food moves through the alimentary canal, and electrical currents move throughout the brain and nervous system. Good health depends on that movement, for as long as energy continues to bathe each part of the system, stagnation and toxicity cannot easily poison or contaminate the organs and various systems of the body. Keeping the continual flow of healing, vitalizing energy bathing the system without blocks or interruption is the true key to the fountain of youth. If cells, organs, and all systems are continuously regenerated with proper stimulation, a person cannot grow old in the traditional sense.

Dr. Virgil Chrane, a chiropractor with a private practice in Dallas, Texas, reveals some interesting statistics in relationship to the physical body. The human body is composed of approximately one hundred trillion cells. These cells are in a constant state of division and multiplication. The energy necessary for this division is enormous. As an example, red blood cells are replicated every ten to fifteen days, heart cells are replicated every three months, new liver cells are made every six months. According to Dr. Chrane, the spinal cord and nervous system are renewed every seven years. It is interesting to note that Uranus, which rules the spinal column, nervous system, and neurological functions of the brain, transits each astrological sign every seven years.

On an atomic level, the physical body is a whirling force field of vibratory power and the number of atoms in a human body is staggering. Yet, if the space *between* the atoms were removed, a person would be the size of a barely visible pin prick. The relationship between space and mass in the human body is estimated to be some two hundred billion to one in favor of space, so the human body is mostly space in various stages of vibration.

On a physical level, there are two hundred and forty-four muscles that attach directly to the spinal column, with over one thousand possible directions of pull. Muscles move bones, so healthy muscle tone is the basis of proper structural alignment. Therefore, it is essential to have a balanced flow of energy into the muscular structure to maintain that important muscle tone.

Dr. Chrane also describes how tension, indicating blocked energy, relates to structural imbalance. (See Chapter 10.) Imagine a broom handle, balanced on a base, and held in place on that base by equally taut rubber bands. Consider what would happen if one of the rubber bands were to become slack and weak. Obviously, the normal rubber band would contract and shorten. The tightened rubber band would pull the top of the broom handle to the tight side and the broom handle would no longer be upright. In this analogy the broom handle relates to the spine and the rubber bands relate to muscles, so when muscles become tight and tense, the spine and the whole structural balance of the body is pulled to the tight side. However, it is actually the other side of the body that is weak.

Physical exercise is one way that energy can be stimulated to move throughout the whole system, but unless the physical body is in proper alignment to begin with, exercise may only exacerbate the condition of imbalance. The skeletal structure, which is the basis of the whole physical makeup, is like the beams that hold up a house. It is important that those beams are strong and straight. When the skeletal balance is maintained, all of the internal organs can fall into their proper position without being squeezed or

pushed up against one another. Therefore chiropractic adjustments, as an example, can ensure that proper structural alignment
is maintained.

For perfect health, the flow of energy must exist not only in the
physical body, but on all levels of man's constitutional makeup.
Energy flow begins on the highest of these levels, the etheric,
represented by all of the transpersonal planets—Uranus, Neptune,
and Pluto—and since that level is most buoyant in its structure,
fewer obstacles to energy movement are encountered there. (See
Chapter 2.) Energy filters down throughout all the vehicles, changing in its density and ease of movement over the course of the
downward flow. The physical body, the most dense vehicle of all,
represented by Saturn, is where blocks to the flow of energy finally
become apparent, like rocks damming up the flow of water in a
stream. So the symptoms of congestion in the other vehicles can
manifest in the physical body. A person may become tired or stiff.
His back may ache or he catches a cold. These symptoms come as
a result of daily stress, but may also be the surface revelation of a
lack of flow of energy on some other level.

In an astrological chart Saturn describes not only the blocked
energy on a physical level, but also in the external conditions of
life. So external pressures help create physical tensions as well.
But since Saturn also represents karmic conditions, or blocks that
we bring into this life, it describes physical symptoms that may
manifest as a result of karma-related stressful conditions, as well
as the everyday stress of life on the earth and physical symptoms
that have their cause in past-life experiences. Many new-age chiropractors, and Dr. Ilan Bohm in particular, are able to determine
the level on which the imbalance occurs in the system, as well as
which part of the body may be out of balance. Because we live in
a world where gravitational pull (Saturn) constantly works against
buoyancy and lightness (Uranus), it is important that the physical
structure remains in balance. It is then easier to resist complete
capitulation to gravitational pull (Saturn) and the lethargy that
eventually results in sickness or death.

FOUR CATEGORIES
OF BODILY FUNCTION

There are four main categories of bodily function that need to be stimulated by exercise or by properly concentrated use of mental energy. Each of these prime functions relate to the four elements— earth, air, fire, and water. Everything on earth is composed of one of these elements. However, man's constitution incorporates all of these elements in varying proportions. The four catagories are:

EARTH ....skeleton
AIR ....head and brain
FIRE ....heart and circulation
WATER ....digestion and elimination

An astrological chart can determine the exact degree of each element in an individual's system and can indicate which bodily system may be out of balance. (See Chapter 9.) For instance, an even balance of elements in the body would be indicated by having three planets in each element. You can incorporate the ascendant and midheaven, as well as the North Node, in this evaluation. (If you do not have a copy of your chart that includes those points, see the Appendix for information about obtaining a copy.) In that case, there would be four points in each element. If there is a lack of earth (let's say only two earth planets, as an example), the physical structure (or skeleton, bones, and teeth) may need special attention. If there is a lack of air, special attention should go toward the head and brain. This is also true if there is an excess of planets, or points, in an element. (Obviously if there is a lack in some element, there will be an excess in others.) The idea is to rebalance the natural quantity of energy (described by the balance of elements) into specific parts of the system by giving that section of the body some extra help. This method of diagnosis, and the subsequent proper exercise to increase energy into a specific part of the body, can help prevent ill health or malfunction of bodily systems in later years. In youth, a person's natural vibrancy can mask an imbalance in certain parts of the body. An astrological chart can be important in determining health and balance with children, as an example, to prevent unseen conditions from gaining a foothold that may surface in later years.

So it is necessary to attend to proper alignment of the skeletal structure, which relates to the earth element; stimulation of the brain and nervous system, which relate to the air element; vitalization of the heart and circulation, which relate to the fire element; and direction of energy into the organs of digestion and elimination, which relate to the water element.

STRUCTURAL BALANCE AND THE EARTH ELEMENT

Saturn represents the skeletal structure. That rulership includes the bones, teeth, and production of calcium in the body. Saturn describes the earth plane, gravity, and the physical body, which is the vehicle we utilize while on the earth plane. The battle between buoyancy of spirit and gravity of life on earth can best be described using the analogy of a helium-filled balloon. If an individual has a great deal of air energy, or Uranus on the ascendant (or in the first house), as an example, the desire to float away is sometimes overpowering. This can also be indicated in an astrological chart if there is a lack of earth or if Uranus is in difficult aspect to a planet ruling the ascendant or placed in the first house. To prevent its floating away into space, that vehicle (the balloon) must be held down to the ground by ropes attached to sandbags. A certain amount of strain is placed on the ropes that connect the balloon to the sandbags. Those ropes can serve as an analogy for the skeletal structure, straining to maintain balance between the weight of the sandbags and the human spirit, which attempts to soar beyond its fetters. So Saturn describes external restrictive conditions that can actually serve as a positive restraint or stabilizer, forcing us to remain on earth. But when Saturn has many difficult aspects in an astrological chart, it is a strong indicator that it is the skeletal structure that takes most of the strain when dealing with stressful or restrictive external conditions.

Since almost everyone on earth has some karma to work out,

as well as many daily stresses in the present life, almost everyone experiences some physical difficulties at one time or another. This is especially true when Saturn rules or is placed in either the first or the sixth house of health, or is close to the ascendant in the twelfth house. (This can also be indicated by Saturn in difficult aspect to another planet that rules or is placed in the first house, or that rules or is placed in the sixth house of health.) When an individual has Saturn heavily aspected in the natal chart, the bony structure, including the teeth, may need extra attention. As an example, an individual with Capricorn rising, or with Saturn in the first or sixth houses, may have more rigidity in his skeletal structure than someone with a different rising sign, and may, therefore, be more prone to the development of arthritis or lack of calcium in the body, or to problems that exist with teeth (see T.M.J. syndrome, p. 286). Since arthritis can manifest with calcium deposits (Saturn) in the joints, spinal adjustments and exercise can help keep the body limber and prevent such an accumulation from occuring. Diet is also important in the treatment of arthritis (see Chapter 20), as well as proper dentistry. Early prophylactic measures can be especially important in preventing physical problems that relate to these conditions.

In our present society, exercise has become almost a religious ceremony. It is considered a character weakness if one does not jog, ride a bycycle, attend exercise classes, or at least spend time before the television set with one of the video fitness personalities. However, the true benefits of exercise have little to do with the way current fashion trends portray them; that is, the effect exercise has on beauty of form, as an example. One prime benefit of physical exercise is it stimulates the release of endorphins into the brain. Endorphins are natural opiates that sharpen mental alertness. So there are specific exercises that stimulate the mind and the internal organs as well. But the combination of concentrated, directed thought with specific exercises can magnify the amount of energy sent to those specific areas. (See discussion of water element, p. 291.) The benefit of such directed energy considerably increases the results.

Chiropractic Adjustments

Chiropractic treatment is mainly ignored and often scoffed at by the medical community at large. Yet in the 1940s a group of doctors from Harvard University investigated stories of miraculous cures, some of them as a result of spinal adjustments, that came about as a result of readings from a psychic named Edgar Cayce in Virginia Beach, Virginia.

Cayce became well known to the public when a book about his life and work was written by a college friend of his son, Hugh Lynn Cayce. The book, entitled *There Is a River*, was written when Thomas Sugrue, a devout Catholic and a skeptic, went to Virginia Beach to prove that Edgar Cayce was a fraud. After observing Cayce's ability to put himself into a trance and diagnose illness at a distance without ever seeing or talking to the person contacting him, Sugrue became a champion of the gentle, modest man who wrought such miraculous cures.

In his trance state, Edgar Cayce would diagnose the condition of the person requesting his help and suggest treatment. The treatments Cayce suggested utilized natural ingredients or methods and sometimes seemed too simple to be effective. He had cured his wife of tuberculosis, as an example, by prescribing inhalation of fumes from ordinary ingredients that were put inside an oak keg. One request for help came from the parents of a beautiful little two-year-old girl who was born quite normal, but had increasing debilitation with motor skills and brain function as she grew older. In fact, she had been examined by specialists who feared she was retarded and gave no hope for improvement of her condition.

Cayce went into his usual trance, first loosening his tie, taking off his shoes, and lying down on a table. His secretary followed her usual pattern of reading the letter of request and, with pen poised, preparing to take down the diagnosis and treatment given by Cayce. In his trance state, Cayce spoke in a voice that was deeper than his own. He seemed to see inside a body, as if he were able to tap a universal X ray of a person's makeup. In this instance, he told the child's parents that she had fallen from her carriage when she was about six months old and had injured her spine, blocking energy going into her brain. He recommended a simple chiropractic adjustment of a particular vertebra. This treatment alone corrected the situation. Within a short period of time, the parents joyfully wrote to report that their little girl was relearning all she seemed to have forgotten and her motor skills were improving day by day. She was eventually back to normal as a result of realigning her spine.

In recent years, many new techniques and diagnostic procedures have been incorporated into the traditional chiropractic practice of adjusting the spine. As an example, kinesiology, or muscle testing, acupressure, acupuncture, hand and foot reflexology, hands-on healing, and stroking of the aura are frequently combined with spinal adjustments. Dr. Ilan Bohm, a chiropractor with a private practice in New York City, is one of those special and gifted new-age doctors who works on the etheric body while at the same time giving other forms of treatment. Therefore, he can determine not only the *cause* of a problem but the *level* on which a problem originates. In describing the many systems of diagnosis and techniques he incorporates in his work, Dr. Bohm explains that a relationship exists between every muscle and every organ in the body. This relationship is the basis of an especially accurate diagnostic tool called applied kinesiology (see Chapter 18). Dr. Bohm also uses the oriental method of diagnosis through the pulse, as well as diagnosis by feeling the line at the base of the skull, called the T.S. (temporo-sphenoidal) line, where the dura mater exits the spinal column and enters the head. This T.S. line reflects and pinpoints areas of tension along the spine.

Dr. Bohm also works with acupuncture points in the ear, which are related to internal organs and body functions. The treatment through the points in the ear is called anatomic auricular therapy. The ear is shaped like a fetus in the womb, and the acupuncture points around the outer rim and the inner visible surface generally relate to the position of the organs if a fetus were lying in that position (see Chapter 19). The eyes also reflect conditions of the internal organs, because specific areas of the eye relate to specific organs, and a system of diagnosis called iridology can reveal sources of physical problems. If eyesight is less than perfect, it may be a clue that internal organs, especially the kidneys, may be out of balance. Dr. Bohm also uses crystals to facilitate the healing process. A sophisticated set of crystals, in his office, are calibrated to match the frequencies of many internal organs. (See Chapter 22.)

In describing the most important advantages of chiropractic treatment, Dr. Bohm points out that there are holograms all over the head which relate to body parts and internal organs. This enables a diagnosis to be made about many conditions in the body. He stresses that the importance of chiropractic adjustments has to do with circulation of the spinal fluids into the ventricles of the brain.

Although Mercury describes the practical mental processes, Uranus describes a particular quality of mentality that may be associated with a potential for genius. Uranus indicates special awareness and inventiveness, so if the spine is in balance, a higher degree of Uranian energy can reach the brain and may produce unusual mental results. But since Uranus describes the nervous system (and its esoteric counterpart, the meridians), as well as the area inside and around the bones of the spinal column (the covering of the spine, called the dura mater) and the spinal fluid inside the spinal column, it also describes skin and the membranes that lie inside and around the bony structure of the rib cage (including skin and the membrane of the lungs, which carries oxygen). So Uranus describes the "higher octave" of the nervous system as well as the "higher octave" of the breathing mechanism.

The spinal fluid lies inside a series of membranes called the meninges, which cover the spinal canal in three layers like an insulated electrical cord. The spinal fluid must circulate into the ventricles of the brain for the body to function. When vertebrae go out of position, there is a torquing of the sleeves of the dura mater (the outermost layer of the meninges, the "skin" of the spinal column) which prevents the spinal fluid from circulating into the brain. Imagine a trunk of a tree with many branches, covered by a sweatshirt. The branches are where the nerve roots lie. When one of the bones of the vertebrae goes out of position, it chokes off the sleeves so that toxins can accumulate. Then this torquing causes aberration of nerve impulses and produces pain and discomfort, if not more serious neurological conditions.

Dr. Bohm explains that there is one continuation of tissue that goes from inside the spinal column into the head and compartmentalizes inside the skull, creating three major sections which house the brain. The dura mater (this single tissue) then exits around the base of the skull and goes around the head, creating the covering outside of the skull. The temporo-sphenoidal line is the line at the base of the skull where the one tissue exits. So there is a reciprocating tension that occurs between the area of insult inside the spinal column and the area around the T.S. line. If there is a torquing of the vetebrae along the spinal column, there will be resulting tension on the head as it exits along the T.S. line. So it is possible to feel the tension on the skull because of the attachment and know exactly where the torquing occurs on the spine and which organs in the body may be affected.

Ma Roller

A Ma roller, a wooden device that looks somewhat like a rolling pin with two raised ridges, can be helpful in keeping energy moving along the spinal column. This device, shaped to go along the spinal column so that it stimulates the muscles on either side, can be purchased in most health food stores and can be very effective in keeping blood circulating into the muscles that run from neck to buttocks along the vertebrae. With increased circulation of blood to those muscles, the nervous system is also bathed in energy, so the benefits of using this device can be multifold.

Ma rollers do not come with instructions, yet the use is obvious. The roller is placed on the floor (a carpet facilitates its use) underneath the spine. The raised section of the roller should touch the points between the vertebrae, stimulating each one in turn as an individual lies on top of this roller. It is beneficial to roll very slowly over this device, allowing plenty of time for the muscles to be stimulated. As the body relaxes around the pressure, the muscles are benefited by the stimulation.

It is important to roll from the top of the spine down, placing the body with the neck on the roller first, then slowly rolling each vertebra in turn over the roller until the base of the spine is reached. (In the chapter on meridians, you will note that there are specific directions for stimulating energy along each meridian so that the body is energized, not de-energized. The meridian down the back must be stroked from the top down. Otherwise a decrease of energy will result. The contrary is true with the meridian in the front of the body. That meridian must be stroked from bottom up. That is the meridian that stimulates energy into the brain, just as the back stimulates the flow of nervous energy, which also benefits the brain.)

Yoga Exercises

One type of exercise that is especially beneficial to the spinal column is the practice of yoga. Yoga exercises can be particularly important for a person with Capricorn rising, or with Saturn in the first or sixth house or aspecting another planet that rules or is placed in those houses. In addition to increasing skeletal flexibility (see Chapter 5 on Saturn), yoga stretches also stimulate internal organs and glands, keeping them vital and functioning. There are literally hundreds of yoga positions, each one specifically designed to stimulate energy and direct it into a particular organ or part of the body. Therefore, these exercises should be learned under the tutelage of a competent instructor. (With proper instruction and supervision, the student will avoid straining muscles.) These exercises must be practiced slowly and with intense mental concentration. No other exercises are quite so effective in keeping the spine flexible and the internal organs regenerated and vital.

One yoga exercise is called the plough. Lie on the ground on your back and lift your feet and legs straight over your head. Then lower them to touch the ground behind you. Your back gradually lifts off the floor, bending to accommodate the stretch. The energy shoots along the spinal column, bathing the nervous system with increased flow of blood. The circulation of that energy can benefit the whole system. It may take some time to achieve the flexibility necessary to do this exercise to its full potential, but when it is done properly, benefits accrue not only to the spine and the nervous system, but also to the thyroid gland. The bent neck stimulates the gland, increasing hormonal output. With increased movement of energy through the body, a feeling of exhilaration and well-being is noticeable almost immediately. Although daily practice of yoga exercises maintains flexibility of the spine, if stiffness is pronounced, especially at the beginning of the discipline, an adjustment by a competent chiropractor may be very important.

T.M.J. Syndrome

The human skeleton is a most sophisticated and intricate design of hinges and connections that allows for flexibility and free movement of the body. Part of the maintenance of perfect balance of the skeleton depends on proper dentistry. It is as important for overall health of the body to make sure that teeth are properly aligned as it is to maintain flexibility of the spine, for the teeth and spine are connected. (Both are ruled by Saturn.) One important hinge, which is often overlooked until problems are painfully overt, is the jaw. Part of the way the balance of the jaw is maintained is with a proper bite or proper alignment of the way teeth come together, called occlusion. If the teeth do not occlude as they are meant to, the jaw accommodates by shifting ever so slightly to allow the teeth to grind food more efficiently. If the jaw shifts, the whole body begins to adapt, putting pressure on the physical structure and the internal organs. Resulting tension from the imbalance of the physical structure produces internal malfunction that may not be readily diagnosed. That's why dentistry (Saturn) is important in maintaining proper structural balance (Saturn), which in turn improves the health of internal organs.

One physical disability that can occur as a result of imbalance in the physical structure is the shifting of the jaw. This condition is called temporomandibular joint dysfunction, or T.M.J. syndrome. This can also occur as a result of improper dentistry and may be more prevelent than is commonly recognized. This syndrome can cause imbalance of the whole skeletal structure and many physical problems. In this instance, the jaw becomes somewhat permanently misaligned and can cause pain and discomfort, as well as more serious conditions that come with malfunction of internal organs. One clue that such a misalignment of the jaw exists is a clicking sound that occurs while chewing. Other clues are frequent headaches and awakening in the morning with a stiff jaw. Excessive wax in the ear may also be a clue that some misalignment of the jaw exists. If this goes undetected, the jaw may eventually become arthritic or simply cease to function.

It is necessary for food to be properly masticated by the teeth to release nutrients into the system. Food must be well chewed and broken down in the mouth because the *stomach has no teeth*. The digestive tract depends on that preliminary food processing, as some nutrients are first absorbed into the body through the mouth. Other nutrients assimilated in the stomach can be easily absorbed only if food is well masticated. Unchewed bits of food can also cause problems with organs of digestion and elimination. The jaw, stomach, and digestive tract are not the only parts of the body to be affected if this occurs. When the body begins to shift to one side or another, even very slightly, stress is put on organs without a person's being consciously aware of this, and serious health problems can develop many years later as a result of the lack of proper occlusion of the teeth.

MENTAL ENERGY AND AIR ELEMENT–STIMULATING BRAIN-WAVE ACTIVITY

We have already established the relationship between the hands and fingers and mental activity (see Chapter 5 on Mercury) and we have noted how Uranus relates to mental activity (p. 259), and we have noted that if a thumb is lost, brain waves can become scrambled. But the opposite side of the coin also exists. For example, when a baby sucks his thumb, he is actually stimulating brain-wave activity. Animals automatically chew on their toes, and while we cannot prove what mental activity that might stimulate, it seems clear that natural instincts among human beings and animals may have a deeper effect on health than may be readily apparent.

Next to the prime importance of proper structural balance, which allows natural body functions to stimulate mental alertness, by far the most effective exercise for stimulating brain-wave activity has to do with use of the pairs of limbs: the arms and legs. I have described the cross crawl exercise (Chapter 5 on Mercury) and indicated that it is more beneficial to stop in the middle of a busy day for a brief moment of the cross crawl exercise than taking a coffee break. The energy that is stimulated by this exercise brings an immediate sense of mental alertness and can therefore be very important in dealing with depression. (Also see Bach flower remedies, Chapter 20.)

Cross Crawl

It is essential for a baby to learn to crawl before he learns to walk, for the act of crawling stimulates the development of brain waves. Tests indicate that if a baby has skipped that all-important crawling stage, he may have later learning disabilities. The cross crawl exercise simulates a baby's crawling stage when his brain waves are being developed. Thus the exercise continues to stimulate energy into the brain. This exercise can be done standing in place or while walking and running. Lift one leg quite high, with the knee bent, while the opposite arm, with bent elbow, is raised. Both the leg and the arm are bent at knee and elbow to form an angle. Then lift the opposite leg and arm. After doing this for a few minutes, you will feel a new sense of energy in the head, affecting the thought processes in a positive way.

There is an even better way of doing the cross crawl than standing still on a floor. Try combining this exercise with bouncing on a rebounder by incorporating arm movement while bounding on one leg at a time. A rebounder is a small trampoline that allows one person to jump up and down, with resistance from a springy substance at the floor of the rebounder. This exercise has a variety of benefits. For one thing, the resistance provided by the rebounder stimulates muscle tone. Bicycling can also stimulate brain-wave activity, but only the legs are involved, not the total movement of arms and legs.

Exercise for Dyslexia

The relationship between the muscles and the organs is not the only reciprocating system in the body. We have discussed how the brain (described by Mercury in the astrological chart) relates to the pairs in the body, especially the arms and legs (also described by Mercury), and how Uranus relates to inspirational mental energy and to the nervous system. And since Uranus describes the meridians in the body, when Uranus is in difficult aspect in an astrological chart, dyslexia may present some problems. Dyslexia is actually a case of reversed meridians, but the possibility of learning or reading disorders, with resulting emotional reactions, is the most serious result of this condition. Sometimes the disability is very slight and may result only in a tendency to reverse numbers or letters. The possibility exists that with dyslexia, an individual is more polarized on a spiritual level of existence than on an earth level; he can read the rules of spiritual existence, but he can't read those of the earth plane. He can be living the mirror image of himself. On a subconscious level, the desire to float back to the freedom of the etheric levels of existence creates a resistance to energy flowing correctly through the meridians. The reverse may be true. If meridians are reversed it may also create a sense of wanting to leave the body because of the lack of feeling of harmony.

The Oriental theory that the meridians are formed first in fetal development seems to find correlation in recent developments in the treatment of dyslexia. The Listening Center, a clinic in Toronto, Canada, treats dyslexic patients by using a variety of techniques designed to reprogram conditions that were prevalent in the womb. Among other techniques, they play the sound of the mother's voice as it might have been heard by the fetus in the womb. They have obtained very positive results with this prenatal therapy. Sigmund Bereday has obtained miraculous results with dyslexic patients in a few sessions with his biofeedback performance synchronization. (See Chapter 1.)

In his book *Touch For Health*, Dr. John Thye describes a simple five-minute exercise which reverses the meridians in the body and has a definite effect on brain-wave patterns. This simple exercise enables a person to stimulate and rebalance brain function by placing their hands and legs in a particular position and sequence. First, sit erect with the feet on the floor. Next, place the left heel on top of the right knee. (The left knee will be bent out to the left side at an angle.) Then put the right hand over the top of the left foot, and finally cross the left hand over the right wrist to grasp the left foot under the arch. (You will note that the wrists are crossed, with one hand on top of the foot and the other covering the bottom. If you have the hands placed properly, the left wrist lies above the right wrist.) Sit like this for a few minutes and then uncross the legs, replacing the feet on the floor (not touching). The final stage is to place the fingertips together and hold them in that position for another few minutes. The results of this simple exercise are quite miraculous. The correction can be checked through the technique of kinesiology. (See Chapter 18.) In my own experience, when I eat something that creates imbalance in my blood-sugar level, I find that I reverse letters and sometimes words while I am writing. By taking a short break to do this exercise, the problem no longer exists. I have also found that if I am mentally fatigued, the exercise stimulates more energy into the brain.

CIRCULATION AND FIRE ELEMENT

Rebounding is not only important for increasing blood flow in the body and benefiting the circulatory system, it is the best way to stimulate the lymph system, which has no duct to the outside of the body (as do the systems of digestion and elimination). The condition of the lymph system is important for it is the system connected with immune functioning. The lymph nodes store and produce lymphocytes. The T cells, one variety of lymphocytes, are important in the fight against cancer and viruses, as an example. B cells are another variety of lymphocytes which produce anti-bodies that are necessary in the fight against AIDS. Keeping any of the body fluids in motion helps prevent the accumulation of toxins and keeps the system working. (There are many factors in prevention of cancer and AIDS, so it should not be assumed that rebounding will prevent such diseases from occurring.) Ten minutes a day on a rebounder exercises the muscles, organs, lymph system, brain, and helps keep the skeletal structure in balance. This is partly due to the stimulation of muscle tone which allows the vetebrae to remain aligned, but it prevents damage to the spine and bony structure, as might happen with jogging on a hard surface, since the base of the rebounder gives with body weight.

As we have noted, proper physical alignment is a prime prerequisite for keeping the enthusiasm high (Jupiter) and for tapping the higher consciousness. Inner balance cannot be achieved if the body is not balanced.

DIGESTIVE ORGANS AND WATER ELEMENT

One of the most sensitive areas of the body is sometimes called the "breadbasket." That area incorporates the prime organs of digestion, the stomach (ruled by the Moon) and gall bladder; and the organs of detoxification, the liver and kidneys (ruled by Jupiter), and the organ of assimilation, the spleen (ruled by Uranus). The spleen is the central organ where the spiritual network hooks up to the physical network, as it connects the etheric body to the physical vehicle. The splenic chakra is located just above the root chakra, halfway between that chakra and the solar plexus. But the spleen also relates to a center between the shoulder blades where spiritual energy pours into the physical body. So any problems that occur in the area of the body called the breadbasket are not only related to the daily task of processing food, but to the assimilation of the myriad energies that pour into the body through the spiritual network. This is why the stomach often takes the brunt of external (especially emotional) problems. It is so closely related to the location of the spleen and the possibility of congestion when higher energy attempts to enter into the body. The point of contact between spirit and matter can be like an electrical wire shooting off sparks if it is not properly grounded.

Many people suffer from obvious digestive problems, but other conditions such as diabetes, hypoglycemia, allergies, eye problems, and even senility may have their roots in imbalance of that area of the body. It has become increasingly apparent that almost everyone who works with psychic energy suffers from hypoglycemia or diabetes. This can include astrologers, numerologists, psychics, therapists, and almost anyone who counsels or gives comfort to those around him. Spiritual energy is the commodity that is most necessary for that kind of work, and therefore the drain on that area of the body is enormous. As we have noted, it is essential to treat not only the physical body, but the emotional and spiritual vehicles as well, so exercise is important in preventing blocked energy. Proper diet, herbal remedies, cell salts, Bach flower remedies, use of crystal essences, acupuncture, color, and sound are also extremely effective when working with this particular area of the body.

Ken Kobayashi, Japanese acupuncturist who maintains his Natural Remedies Center in New York City, as well as a country retreat for his patients in upstate New York, taught me an exercise for purifying the liver and inadvertently the whole breadbasket area. He stressed its importance for everyone, but especially for people who work with psychic energy. It is extremely beneficial in the prevention of disability of the organs in that area of the body, as well as for relieving the feeling of being drained after counseling sessions. This exercise incorporates the hands (Mercury, as related to Gemini and the pairs in the body), the eyes (Neptune), the liver (Jupiter), and the mind (Mercury).

The exercise is done in this way: The right hand is placed on the liver (located just below the rib cage on the right side), while the left hand is held aloft at an angle (much like the angle of an airplane taking off) with the palm up. The eyes must be focused on the palm of the left hand throughout the exercise. First, rub the palms of the hands together to stimulate heat and energy. Then put the hands in position and focus the eyes on the left palm. As you breathe in through your nostrils, gently press the right hand over the liver, pushing it slightly in and up. As you hold your breath, focus the mental attention on the area behind the navel and visualize purifying energy swirling throughout the whole area of the stomach and liver. The head should feel cool as energy leaves that part of the body and is directed into the area of the breadbasket. Next, release the breath through the mouth and release the pressure of the right hand on the liver. This exercise should be done in yoga position (sitting on a flat surface, with knees jutting out to the side) and should be done seven times in each session. Sessions should be done twice a day. You will feel the benefits immediately and may even burp quite a lot just after you've completed the exercise.

In astrological terms, the connection between the eyes (Neptune) and the liver (Jupiter) can be explained when we consider the ancient rulerships of Pisces. It was thought that both Neptune and Jupiter ruled that sign. Many astrologers still make a connection between those two planets and in this instance, those rulerships would seem to apply, for Ken stressed the physical connection between the liver and the eyes.

Ken described an incident that occurred when a young woman called him at his Natural Remedies Center from Japan. She was worried about her father, who was suddenly forgetful and irrational in his behavior. Ken was unable to treat him with acupuncture from that distance, but he was able to send the young woman enough herbal mixture to treat her father for a month. Ken had diagnosed the problem as relating to the man's kidneys and was able to make a connection between the onset of senility and the kidneys because of his years of experience, as well as his own psychic sense. Within the month, the young woman called again to say that her father was completely back to normal. Once again the relationship between kidneys and brain can be shown astrologically, as Neptune rules the right hemisphere of the brain and is the coruler of Pisces along with Jupiter.

So once again, the relationship between bodily functions (in this instance the liver and eyes and right brain) can be described astrologically. Ken indicated another way that such a relationship exists. He said that after doing this exercise each morning and evening, a person will be so enthusiastic and happy, he will awaken in the morning and joyously say "Oh isn't it wonderful, it's raining," or "Oh look, the sun is shining." Jupiter rules enthusiasm and joy, as we know.

Modern astrological practice tends to assign one planet to each sign. Two new planets are expected to be discovered, which will allow Mercury and Venus to rule only one sign each, not two. In addition, the comet Chiron was discovered in 1977 and has been related to the sign of Virgo. Although in-depth research is not yet complete, Chiron seems to relate to health conditions in particular, since Virgo is the natural ruler of the sixth house of health. With more time and research, we will be able to determine exactly how Chiron describes health in the body, but Chiron appears to be another bridge between the earthbound planets and the higher vibration of Uranus. Its orbit is between Saturn and Uranus. As we make more breakthroughs in natural healing techniques, Chiron is emerging more dramatically on the scene of the astrological community. Coincidentally, health consciousness and health industries began to gain favor around 1977. With Chiron now in the spotlight, it is time for health matters to come to the fore of world attention.

Kinesiology (Muscle Testing)

*A*pplied kinesiology is a diagnostic system that depends on the strength of specific muscles to indicate physical imbalances and the weaknesses of organs. It is primarily used by new-age healers, chiropractors, and massage therapists, but it can also be used by ordinary individuals to determine many things about their physical reactions to the immediate environment. This system of testing indicates individual allergic reactions to substances, for example, but even more amazingly, it can accurately reveal the quality of energy exchange between people and how a specific person can affect your general health and well-being.

This method of testing is not a mystical process; it is based on extensive scientific research that was conducted by two embryologists, the Drs. Kendall, who specialized in research concerning cellular activity. These doctors discovered a process of cloning that occurs with cellular growth which they called *mitosis*. They also discovered a particular cellular activity which they termed *differentiation*. When the original cell (called a germ cell) divides, and the process of differentiation begins, these divided cells become specialized. In other words, they become hair, or blood, or fingernails, as an example, and will remain specialized as hair, blood, and fingernails throughout the life of the cell. But the Drs. Kendall also discovered that in the process of differentiation, one branch of that specialized cell becomes an organ and the other branch becomes a muscle. So both organ and muscle originate from the same germ cell. Therefore, a relationship exists between the organ cell and the muscle cell, much like the relationship that exists between twins. There is a symbiotic connection after the pairing off of the cells that is never broken. So when a particular muscle is weak, it also indicates a weakness that exists in its related organ. As an example, the hamstring muscle relates to the large intestine, and the quadriceps muscle relates to the small intestine. When an individual has an intestinal virus, for instance, energy is also depleted in the quadriceps muscle, and the individual experiences weakness in his legs.

A similar symbiotic connection has been observed in studies concerning twins. In the instance of identical twins the fertilized egg, expected to produce one fetus, divides to produce two. Identical twins seem to follow the same patterns and develop the same characteristics whether they are raised together or not. It has been amazing to find twins who were separated at birth and had completely different environmental conditioning during their formative years, and discover that they gravitated toward the same profession, bought the same kind of house at the same time, and drove the same kind of automobile. These twins married in a generally similar time frame and had the same number of children. One case of a strong symbiotic connection between female twins revealed that when one twin became pregnant in California, her sister had morning sickness in New York. Twin friends of mine continually upset their dance teachers, who would be sure they were playing games. Even though they might be in different parts of the room, or at the opposite ends of a line, they would make a mistake in their dance routines at exactly the same time.

There are forty-two pairs of related muscles and organs, and there is a specific method of testing each muscle in order to determine the condition of the related organ. Some of the muscles are tested by putting pressure on arms, whereas others are tested by pressure on legs. The process is exact and somewhat complex, but the method can be learned with a minimum amount of time if the interest is strong. In his book *Touch For Health*, Dr. John Thye describes such testing and augments the description with photographs and illustrations.

However, there is a simple method of testing that can be easily learned by almost everyone. This kindergarten version can accurately indicate individual reactions to substances and to people. The method requires two people working together and utilizes only the arm. One person stands erect and holds one arm straight out in front of the body with the palm down. The other person stands to the side of the first person and also holds his arm out in front of his body. He then places his wrist above the wrist of the person to be tested, with his palm downward, and applies enough pressure to determine their mutual strength. There should be equal tension, with the original person easily resisting the downward force of person number two. (If the second person is much stronger than the person being tested, he will have to adjust the amount of pressure he exerts in order to create that equilibrium.) When you have established the amount of pressure the partner can exert without forcing the arm of person number one downward, the testing can begin.

Choose a substance that you know is detrimental to your system. I might choose a bowl of sugar, as an example, knowing that my system reacts badly to that substance. Someone else might choose salt, or a bottle of whiskey, or a bottle of milk. Hold that chosen substance in front of your solar plexus (stomach area) with your other hand and ask your partner to begin putting pressure on your outstretched arm. If the substance is detrimental to your system, you will not be able to maintain the outstretched position. Your arm will be very weak. However, if the substance is beneficial, your arm will be very strong, and you will easily be able to resist the pressure exerted by the other person. This can be especially helpful if you become aware of digestive problems, as an example. You may not know what you are eating that is causing indigestion or gas, but with this method it will be easy to determine what should be eliminated from your diet.

It is most interesting to determine how you react to the people you associate with on a daily basis. You may not know that someone is actually detrimental to your energy field, but you may discover that whenever you are around a particular individual, you feel tired or depressed. That person may not intend you harm, but may have a weak energy field of his own which drains your own vitality. The opposite is also true, as some people seem to energize you without their doing anything special.

This kind of testing must be conducted with a sense of responsibility, as the use of such a technique to give you an excuse to make a judgment about someone could cause you to harm them or create karmic bonds (obligations that will have to be resolved in the future). Criticism or judgment about another person can stop your own development, as it erects a wall between you and another human being. You don't have to love everybody on a personal basis, but your willingness to allow everyone to resolve his personality difficulties, or life conditions, in his own way frees you to do the same. Your purpose in determining how another person affects your own energy system is to help you determine whether a close relationship will be productive or nonproductive to your own health and energy. With knowledge of how your body reacts to another person, you can choose to be with that person or not, depending on your ability to deal with additional stress at any given time. If you are depleted by a particular association, you may need to be in a very happy mood and in peak physical condition when you are around that person. In that way you can emerge with a positive feeling.

This type of testing can be especially helpful if you feel that you are working in a job situation with someone whose energy might be detrimental to your efficiency. It may be important for you to find a way to remove yourself from close working proximity, if such were the case. It becomes clear that even being around the energy field of some people can energize us, whereas other people tend to drain us. As an example, on a personal level, love relationships go through a variety of stages. No one person stays exactly the same every moment of every day. However, if another individual weakened your system all of the time, it would be very difficult to maintain a close relationship with that person without giving up some of your own strength or getting sick. Then you are doing an injustice to yourself, a situation that carries as difficult a karmic burden as if you were harmful to someone else. (See Chapter 5 on Sun.)

Energy exchange between two people is easily determined

through comparison of their two astrological charts. One of the most important functions in knowing your own astrological makeup is to help you understand the specific way in which you interact with other human beings. (Transactional Analysis is a form of therapy which uses that premise as a basis for its theory. In my work with Marion Weisberg, a T.A. therapist, we found tremendous value in combining my interpretation of the astrological chart with Marion's brilliant ability to heal the condition through her expertise with T.A. techniques. In T.A. terms, the way you've learned to communicate early in life is the way you continue to communicate with other people throughout life until you break the script. See Chapter 14.) Usually, our first instincts about a person can tell us who to avoid and who to let into our lives, yet we rarely pay attention to those first impressions. After testing the relationship through kinesiology, you may want to know more specifics about your attraction to or repulsion by another person. At that point, comparison of the elements in your two charts can be a strong indication as to how you will affect each other. For instance, if two people each have an abundance of water, they may not be able to nurture each other. They may keep each other feeling drained, drowning each other in emotional reactions. If one person has an abundance of earth in his chart and the other is lacking earth, for instance, the earthy person may feel he is always shouldering most of the burden. Lack of balance between the air in two charts indicates whether or not two people will have an intellectual rapport. Intellectual or mental compatibility is obviously very important in a relationship. Too much fire in both charts can also create a depletion of energy, as fire needs air and earth to keep its flame high. Water puts out fire, so with an overabundance of fire in one chart and water in another, the water person may act like a squelcher, in spite of his best intentions.

The second best way to determine an exchange of energy between two astrological charts is to look at the compatibility of the sign position of the Sun, Moon, and ascendant in both charts. The two Sun signs do not have to be in harmony, as an example, if one Sun sign position is in harmony with the Moon sign position (or the ascendant sign) in another. The best balance is to have three sign placements in harmony with three sign placements in the other chart. Two and two is workable, but with only one sign placement in harmony with one in a second chart, the energy exchange would be most difficult to reconcile.

The final method of comparison of two astrological charts is to compare the exact degrees that exist between the planets in the two charts. If there are twelve matching aspects, within one degree of the match, there is a definite long-lasting tie that will allow each person to grow at his own rate of speed and in his own direction, without pulling the relationship apart.

When you are using the method of kinesiology to test relationships, test yourself by simply thinking of a person you love and who makes you feel very happy. Ask the person who is working with you on the test to determine the strength of your resistance to the pressure he exerts. In this instance, your arm should remain strong. Next, think of someone who you suspect may not have your best interests at heart or who might upset you. When your partner puts pressure on your wrist this time, your arm will weaken if you are accurate in your evaluation of the association. Finally, think of someone of whom you are not sure. You may sometimes feel strengthened by this person, but at other times you feel unsure that the association is a positive one. You can get a very accurate picture of just how this person affects you and whether the upsetting times are only momentary, possibly due to stressful events in their own life.

Kinesiology is really a way of reading your own subconscious mind. Each individual has all the answers he needs within himself if he only knows how to listen for them. In astrological terms, the planet Mercury relates to thought processes and the analysis of a situation. Mercury also describes the pairs in the body, including the arms. The relationship between the mind and the strength of the arms can be clearly established through this method of testing. Mercury's message is that if we can trust our inner knowledge, we have all knowledge within ourselves, but since most of us come into the earth plane to complicate matters, we need techniques that relate to Mercury in order to learn that we already know many things! But after all, the earth plane is the school where we can expand, explore all possibilities, examine many potentials and facets of the same thing, and differentiate the quality of knowledge in order to finally choose the simplicity of listening to ourselves.

Dr. Ilan Bohm (with Gemini rising) demonstrated another technique for testing inner knowledge. This one can be done by your-self. In this situation, responsibility must also be a motivating factor or your answers may not be accurate. The mind will not lie to you, but it will answer the exact question you ask. First, place your fists together in front of you with the fingers touching. Turn your fists so that the thumbs are outstretched and pointed away from your body. Then enclose one hand over the other, so that the thumbs are lying close together. First, request that your higher self and mind will give you accurate information. Choose one thumb to be the "yes" thumb and the other to be the "no" thumb. (You must test this out after you've asked for an accurate reading by asking which thumb will be the "yes" thumb.) If you get a tingling response in the left thumb, that will be your "yes" thumb (and the other thumb will obviously be the "no" thumb). The response may be anything from a tingling sensation to the thumb actually jumping out, one slightly in front of the other. Try asking yourself questions that can be confirmed to be sure that you are getting an accurate reading. Practice makes perfect with this technique, so keep exercising your responsible position in getting your own inner answers.

There are many ways to tap the subconscious to get answers or confirmation of what you already know or suspect. Eventually you may be able to develop more of your inner sense and get answers without using any techniques at all. An ideal goal is to work toward more trust in your own inner instincts, developing an ability to get a quick response from any question you might ask. It is im-portant to know that you do have inner knowledge and instincts that guide you. The more trust you can develop in your own inner guidance, the easier it is to trust that life will always provide exactly what is needed in outer conditions and events.

Acupuncture, Acupressure, Meridians, and Hand and Foot Reflexology

ACUPUNCTURE

In the early sixties, a new system of treatment arrived on the scene in the United States. This strange new technique came primarily from Korea, at that time, although the system was quite common everywhere in the Orient and had been practiced there for many centuries. Along with an unfamiliar name came some unbelievable stories. There were tales of women having given birth without any pain at all. There were pictures of people undergoing difficult operations, wide awake and smiling. They had been given no anesthesia, and they suffered no pain. This new technique was called acupuncture. Acupuncture was talked about, written about, and caused an enormous amount of controversy among the medical profession and with the general public.

A major controversy emerged over whether acupuncture could or should be legalized in the United States. In the beginning, the practice was thought to be akin to quackery. But by the mid-seventies the medical community could no longer ignore the fact that acupuncture is enormously effective in connection with pain control. The American public finally got used to the idea that acupuncture is a viable treatment for many maladies. The legal system decided to give it sanction.

No one seemed to realize that it was an insult to approach age-old Oriental methods of healing with such doubt. With a rather superior manner, practitioners in the United States adopted a wait-and-see attitude toward a technique that has proved effective for thousands of years in the Orient. The cures that are effected by acupuncture with relative simplicity are far beyond what traditional medicine has been able to accomplish through surgical methods. In this country, if the gall bladder or spleen, as an example, are not functioning, they are simply removed. How easy it might be to use acupuncture to attempt to restore energy flow into the organ before it is completely defunct and such drastic steps are necessary.

According to the results of tests conducted in Korea in the 1960s by a team of researchers headed by Professor Kim Bong Han, the meridians, the etheric counterpart of the nervous system, are formed earlier in human beings than the vascular and lymphatic systems and are not interconnected. It was the conclusion of the researchers that the organized structure of the etheric body (meridians, chakras) precedes and guides the development of the physical body. The Chinese call etheric energy "ch'i" and believe that it enters the body through acupuncture points and flows to deeper organ structures through the meridians. Along with the twelve main meridians in the body (the thirteenth is the main energizing meridian for the whole body, not specifically related to an organ), there are twelve major categories of acupuncture points, just as there are twelve astrological signs. For every organ there is an energetic flow through two sets of meridians, and each meridian has a yin side and a yang side. Therefore, the meridians in the body also fall under the category of pairs in the body, just as we have a left and right hemisphere to the brain, two eyes, lungs, arms, and legs. The pairs (Mercury as related to Gemini) are important in connection with healing, for it is through finding proper balance between the pairs that vitality and energy are restored to each organ of the body.

Each system of therapy we are discussing works directly on a specific or on several levels of the human system, whether that is the physical (Saturn), mental (Mercury), emotional (Moon), or spiritual (Uranus) level. Imbalance first occurs in the etheric body and filters down into the physical system, manifesting as pain or disability in perhaps a seemingly unrelated part of the body. Acupuncture effects cures first on the etheric level by helping to regulate the flow of energy in that body, but then it also works on the physical body, because it directs energy to penetrate immediately and directly into the organ that is being treated. Since each meridian relates to a specific organ and regulates the flow of energy into that organ, work that is done on the etheric level actually manifests and benefits the entire physical system. (See Chapter 2.) So the diagnosis of the true cause of illness is very important, because most symptoms are only an external manifestation of imbalance of a major organ. Traditional medicine generally treats symptoms without looking into their underlying causes, which might exist on the etheric level.

Oriental doctors utilize many systems of diagnosis, including taking the pulse in five different ways. The determination of the specific acupuncture points that will affect rebalancing of energy and bring a resulting cure is very complex. When acupuncture is utilized, it is possible to find and rebalance the disruption of the routes of energy on the etheric body level much earlier than could be done through traditional methods that treat only the surface manifestations of a problem. This is reflected in the quality of energy described by Uranus and Saturn. Uranus, which rules the meridian system, has a higher rate of vibrational frequency than Saturn, which rules the physical system.

There are many techniques that relate to acupuncture which can be utilized for healing. First is the use of needles or electrical stimulation along the acupuncture points that can reverse severe symptoms of energy imbalances. Since the study of acupuncture is extremely complex, and there are some points that strengthen the system and others that weaken it, it is important to find a practitioner well versed and experienced in the procedure.

As we have noted, the meridians in the spiritual network correlate with the nervous system of the physical body. Energy flows through the nervous system to and from the brain (see Chapter 16), and brain impulses direct all the automatic functions in the body, like an automatic pilot. The heart beats without our conscious thought; the impulse and signals are directed by the nervous system. If there is a disruption of energy in the brain and nervous system, as example, there is resulting dysfunction of the motor system of the body. Energy flows through the meridians from the etheric levels and sustains the chakra system, the batteries of the etheric body. The etheric body is the underlying electrical system from which all illness originates. So cures of the physical body do not erase the malfunction from the spiritual network. Physical malfunctions inherited from past lives, as an example, are merely massaged by allopathic methods of healing. If an imbalanced condition occurs due to restimulated patterns on the etheric level, operations do not take care of the problem. The imprint remains to surface again and again. But physical malfunctions are permanently rebalanced when methods that work on the subtle body level are used, depending on the severity of the damage done by blocked flow of energy.

Ken Kobayashi, a Japanese acupuncturist with a private practice in New York City, describes acupuncture by talking about the energy system. He says that, usually, energy stays inside the body and spreads all through the organs. He points out that the organs have their own energy, or frequencies, too. The meridians are like the pipes between organs, so if we touch a meridian point, we can touch inside the organ. For example, constipation occurs because the bowel doesn't produce enough mucus, so the bowel is hard. The acupuncture point at the center of the head connects to the intestines, but also to the central nervous system. That is the master socket. So we can't touch inside the intestines, the source of the problem, but we can touch the head. When that point is touched by acupuncture, the sound of rumbling in the intestines occurs right away. Ken showed me that stomach acupuncture point #36 (the point that connects the stomach and gall bladder) is located on the leg at the side of the knee. He says if someone has gas or something stuck in the stomach and you put an acupuncture needle in that point, you'll hear a gurgling sound within two seconds.

When I asked Ken about using acupuncture to cure sexual dysfunction—especially impotence, as medical science has not yet found a way to restore sexual potency once it is lost—he mentioned that blocked sexual energy is especially high in New York City, as stress plays such a large part in this condition. But he said that this dysfunction relates primarily to the kidneys. One kidney point is just under the navel and is a life point. If that area of the body is soft, something is not right with the system. In astrological terms, Mars rules sexual as well as creative energy, which is the life force. And Mars rules the adrenals, which sit on top of the kidneys. If adrenal malfunction is evident, a lack of energy results in lack of drive, whether that be in creative areas or in terms of sexuality.

Ken treats sexual dysfunction by starting with the central nerve, to calm the person. He points out that nervous people are prone to this condition and theorizes that impotent people are more sensitive than others might be. He also points out that the blood in nervous people is especially acid. (Mars rules the blood as well as the adrenals and sexuality.) To determines why the kidney is weak, he checks the liver. Sometimes blocked sexual energy is physiological, and like having to urinate a great deal, ejaculation is quick. He points out that if that continues for many years, impotence is likely to occur (but exhaustion also contributes to the condition).

Ken describes a man as being like a tree. The sap in a tree comes from the roots, rises in the trunk of the tree to make maple syrup or beautiful flowers. He says human beings are the same. Energy is like the tree's sap and stays inside the sexual organs, and also near the navel. The sap can be used up with worry, thinking too much, or talking too much, and if a person uses up lots of sap every day, he will lose sap in sex organs as well.

In Ken's experience, when the liver, kidney, and natural immune system are rebalanced, it is easy to restore sexual potency. Mars describes sexuality but also rules romance, and Ken comments that many women experience a diminution of sex drive after menopause. While a woman still wants romance, she doesn't necessarily desire sexual activity. However, if that woman should fall in love, her sex drive increases immediately.

Ken Koyabashi was an extraordinary person from the very beginning of his life. He remembers his birth quite clearly and actually spoke to his mother as soon as he was born. He said, in Japanese of course, "Hi Mom, I'm your baby." There were many witnesses present who not only saw him birthing himself (Ken said there was a midwife present, but she didn't interfere when she saw that he knew exactly what to do), but also heard him say hello to his mother. Later on a composer wrote a song to commemorate the phenomenon.

Ken began his mission as a healer when he was only 3½ years old. His father was a well-known physician in Japan, and he wanted to conduct an experiment to see if the pure energy from a child, who knew nothing about medicine or the physical body, could effect cures. He called together about eight hundred prominent doctors and professors to an area like a baseball field. He used Ken as the subject of the demonstration simply because it was convenient to use his own son. (Ken had also shown an ability to heal little chickens who were sickly. He would say to the chicks, "Don't die. It's okay if you die later, but at least taste what life is all about.") Ken remembers being in his father's arms and thinking it was a very big party. After apologizing to Ken for putting him through this test, Ken's father asked him to do a favor. He introduced Ken to a woman whose baby didn't nurse enough and whose breasts were very sore and swollen. He told Ken not to touch her breasts and explained that her baby didn't drink her milk. Ken remembers that the lady's husband was quite upset over this test and wanted a doctor. Although he wasn't afraid, Ken really didn't want to participate in the demonstration. It was due to the lady's request that Ken was willing to do what his father wanted. His father's words were, "You can cure her."

The lady helped him by first telling him that he had nice eyes and he could do it. Ken said, "She had a mind to believe." He automatically rubbed his hands together and felt his fingers burning. At that point he felt he could cure her and asked heaven what he should do. He touched her shoulders very lightly, and with the lady's comment that it felt comfortable, he knew he should touch her neck. (He had also played with rabbits, holding them by the ears and neck. Now Ken knows that the neck is connected to the whole nervous system.) At that point his hands began to move automatically and he massaged her fingers. He had watched dogs and cats biting their paws, and not being able to bite her hands, he massaged them instead. (Now Ken knows that the fingers are connected to the brain, which sends messages into the body through the central nervous system.)

Ken was a wise child and asked permission to touch her legs.

Then he began working on her back with small hands that had no strength. However, the energy from his hands was enough. (Ken was used to walking on his father's back and also knew he couldn't do that with the lady.) Finally his father said that was enough, and the lady's breasts began to discharge milk as her nervous system relaxed. The baby nursed eagerly, and the lady was hungry, very happy, and grateful. Ken's father picked him up to the applause of eight hundred people. There was a small repercussion, however. At the party afterward, people kept giving Ken sips of saki without his father's noticing. Ken remembers being drunk and hung over for at least a week afterward.

Ken actually relaxed the lady's body by sending energy into her nervous system so that she could then heal herself. Acupuncture and all natural healing work on the principle that the body heals itself if the energy within the system is abundant enough. If the energy is not abundant, it can be restored by touching the right spots on the meridians either with needles or with the hands (see acupressure, page 310). Uranus rules the nervous system and also describes a natural healer in the astrological chart, especially when Uranus rules or is placed in the eighth house, the sector that describes the kind of energy that can be sent out to the rest of humanity.

For three years I conducted conferences on healing techniques of the new age at the Hotel Hacienda, the most beautiful hotel in Ibiza, Spain. Ibiza, the second largest Balearic island in the Mediterrean, is known by many European doctors to be a healing island. For instance, after a terrible accident which resulted in severe burns to his body, the race-car driver Nicki Lauder was told by a German doctor that it was necessary for him to move to the island of Ibiza if he wished to live. There are many reasons for this commonly held theory. First, it is considered to be the opposite end (positive pole) of the Bermuda Triangle. There is a particular section of the island called Es Vedra, where a mountainous rock juts out of the water. It is a spectacular sight, but far more important than the visual pleasure one finds when driving down a winding road toward the beach is the sense of energy that shoots up around that spot. With any degree of sensitivity, a person can feel the flow of energy in the same way he might feel air currents blown along by the wind.

When I presented my ideas for the conferences to Sr. Ernesto Fajarnes, the director of the Hotel Hacienda, he was extremely cooperative and generous. In fact, "El Jefe" (the chief) was quite excited about my using the hotel facilities. His enthusiasm was made clear to me when he told me his story. For some time, Ernesto had had blindingly painful headaches. In fact, he had lost sight in one eye and wore an eye patch. He was told he had a brain tumor and an operation might or might not be successful. Without an operation and biopsy, there was no way to know if the tumor was benign or cancerous.

Ernesto, a Scorpio with Virgo rising, is endowed with an exceptionally high level of intellect and abundant energy. He lives a full and dedicated life in Ibiza. He is extremely sociable and has friends all over the world. In the wintertime when the hotel is closed, Ernesto teaches and manages a hotel school he founded. In the summer, he is the director and chief personality at the hotel, not only overseeing all hotel activities, but greeting people who come back year after year to spend time in this very special place. He loves the island of Ibiza and is involved with the office of tourism, and in his spare time, he dedicates himself to his family. To have a disability and to suffer so much physical pain was not in Ernesto's grand plan for life.

Ernesto had consulted specialists at New York University, in New York City, who kept him apprised of the condition of the tumor. But before he had decided whether or not to risk an operation, he met Dr. Ramamukti Mishra. Dr. Mishra, who has an ashram in upstate New York, had quite a following on that Scorpio island of Ibiza and was a frequent visitor. He met Ernesto and began to treat him with acupuncture. At first, the severity of the headaches diminished, but with each successive group of treatments, other symptoms began to be relieved. Ernesto's eyesight returned, at least to a degree that enabled him to do away with his patch, and his energy returned. Ernesto has made subsequent yearly trips to New York to consult with the medical specialists and to be examined with the aid of the most sophisticated technical equipment available. His doctors are quite astounded, as the tumor has shrunk from the size of a fist to the size of a pea. At the latest report, the tumor could hardly be detected at all. Ernesto talks with great exuberance about his "guru," Dr. Mishra, and about the wonders of acupuncture.

I also had a personal experience with the wondrous healing that occurs with acupuncture treatments. In 1972, I impulsively picked up a very heavy potted tree and moved it to another location. I felt an instant hot twinge, like someone had punctured my back with a red-hot needle. I began suffering intense back pain, which continued through many months of treatment with an orthopedic surgeon. Nothing other than complete bed rest could ease the pain. It was necessary to slide sideways out of a car to avoid going into spasm. At one point, the sciatic nerve was affected, and I spent one night crying with pain, unable to sit, stand, or lie down.

Finally, I heard about a Korean doctor who was brought to California to teach acupuncture at UCLA. Fortunately, I was able to obtain an appointment with him. At the first session, he placed me facedown on a therapy table and did something to my back. I felt absolutely nothing, not even a pin prick, but I knew he had inserted some acupuncture needles in my back. After a while of total relaxation on the table, he heated the needles, and I felt a warm glow. Then he removed the needles and I was told to go home, rest, and return in a few days. After the first treatment, I fell into a deep sleep, almost like a trance state. It was extremely refreshing. During the night I felt a wave of pain lift from my lower back and rise to the upper section of my body. I had three treatments in all, the next two being administered while I was sitting in a chair, facing backward. These times, the needles were inserted in the upper part of my back. After the last treatment, I felt the pain lift completely out of my body, and it was permanently gone.

A C U P R E S S U R E

As we have shown in the story about the 3½-year-old Ken, it is also possible to use a technique called acupressure, which is applied manually on the acupuncture points along the meridians. This technique is helpful if there is some mild imbalance in function of organs, such as a headache or momentary indigestion. It is also

Stroking the Meridians

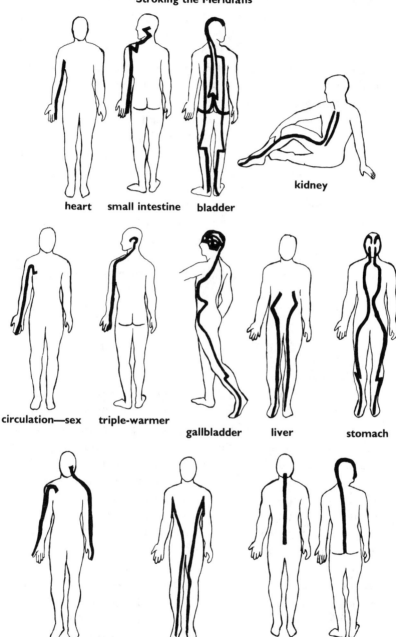

heart   small intestine   bladder

kidney

circulation—sex   triple-warmer

gallbladder   liver   stomach

lung   large intestine   spleen   central governing

extremely effective to stimulate the flow of energy along the meridians, by using a technique called "touch for health," thoroughly described in the book *Touch For Health*, by Dr. John Thye. This technique incorporates the manual stroking of each meridian in a specific way to facilitate a dynamic flow along those lines. (See Chart, p. 311.) This technique is especially effective when health is generally good, and prevention is a prime motivation.

It is also possible to "hold" certain points, without any pressure or instrument at all. The energy emitted from the hands releases energy that stimulates the points and induces healing. (Theoretically, high energy is pulled into the body from the energy fields surrounding the body through the left hand and is released back into the atmosphere through the right hand. Many people wear watches on the right arm, the arm where the energy is leaving, instead of on the left arm, where the energy is entering. These holding points are also clearly illustrated in Dr. Thye's book *Touch For Health*. See illustration for lines that relate to the meridians.

FOOT REFLEXOLOGY

Each organ and part of the body has a reflection point in both the hands and the feet. It is possible to stimulate energy to various parts of the body through energizing these points. Some knowledge of the exact placement of these reflex points in relationship to each organ is required if specific benefits are desired. However, it is possible to give the feet a thorough going over, massaging the whole area without knowing which point is affecting which part of the body. Good health and energy can be assured simply by taking the time to work on the feet each night, applying rich, aromatic lotion during the process.

One of the most pleasant of sensual delights is to massage the feet of someone you love while they are massaging your feet. It is a great way to show tenderness and affection. Even if a day has been difficult and you are tired, this process restores energy while relaxing you before sleep, instead of letting the problems of the day sink in on a deeper, more subconscious level. It is also a good

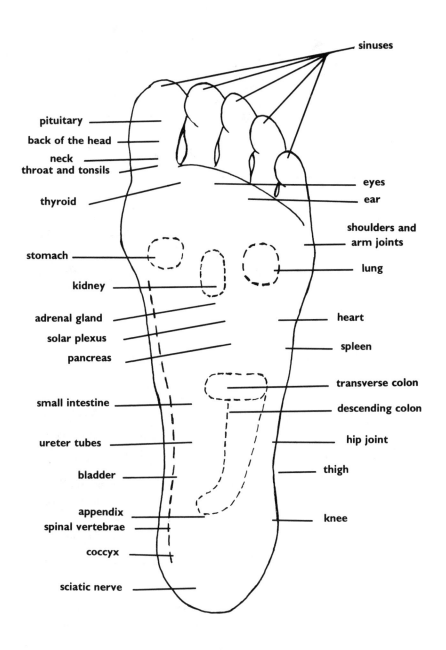

sinuses

pituitary

back of the head

neck

throat and tonsils

thyroid

eyes

ear

shoulders and
arm joints

stomach

lung

kidney

adrenal gland

heart

solar plexus

spleen

pancreas

transverse colon

small intestine

descending colon

ureter tubes

hip joint

bladder

thigh

appendix

spinal vertebrae

knee

coccyx

sciatic nerve

Foot Reflexology Points

Left Foot

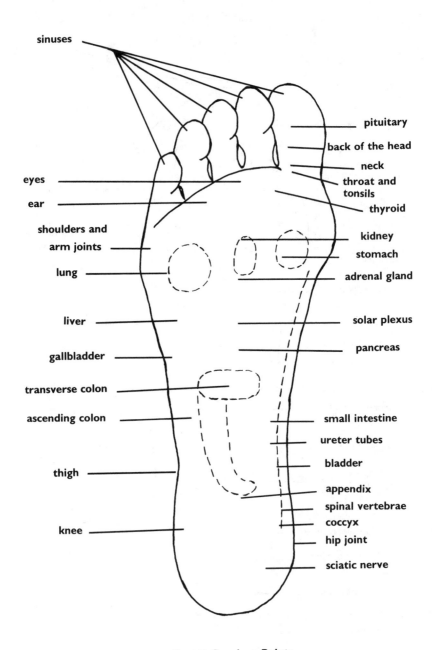

Foot Reflexology Points

Right Foot

idea to rub a baby's feet to stimulate healthy development of each organ from the earliest stages of life. And it is a wonderful way to express your affection to your child.

The reflex points for some of the organs or parts of the body are located in both feet, but some are only located in one or the other foot. (Refer to the diagrams on pp. 313–14 to locate the exact positions of the reflex points.)

With a small amount of study, it is easy to learn these reflex points and what organs of the body they correspond to, and to begin to feel a physical response there when energy begins to flow. There are special sandals that can be purchased in health food stores or stores that cater to new-age healing that will stimulate all the points while you are walking. This is an excellent way to remain in a healthful mode if you are really too busy to give yourself a foot massage.

HAND REFLEXOLOGY

The points on the hands correspond to the points on the feet. (See charts on pp. 316–17 for reflexology points on the hands.) I've always found that I can spend more time massaging my hands than my feet, as I can stimulate the points while riding in a cab, sitting in a restaurant, or in the company of other people. It is a bit harder to take off your shoes and socks to work on your feet in a public place. You can also use a tool of your choice for stimulating the points on the hands. My preference is to use something metal, as it relates to a Mars quality of energy, beneficial in my chart. There are Chinese metal balls available for this specific purpose, but the blunt end of a spoon will do nicely. A crystal works wonders too, especially if you have programmed that crystal for healing. However, if you have a sensitive sign ruling the ascendant or the sixth house, you might prefer using a small rubber ball, which will stimulate all the points as you are rolling it around in your hands. There are specific balls manufactured for the purpose of hand reflexology. The hard rubber points put more pressure on the reflex points.

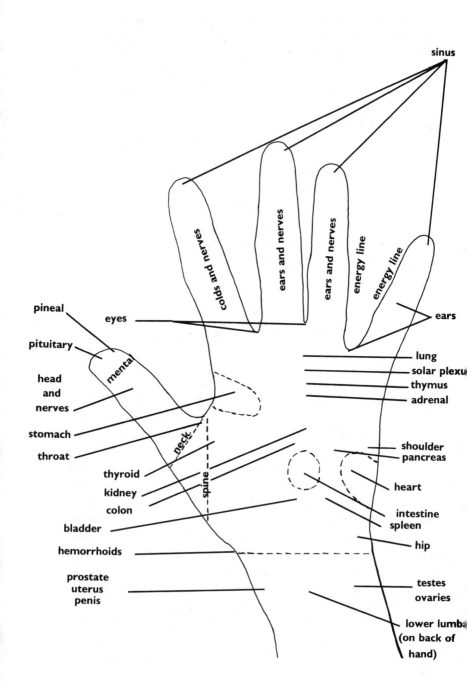

Left Hand, Palm Up

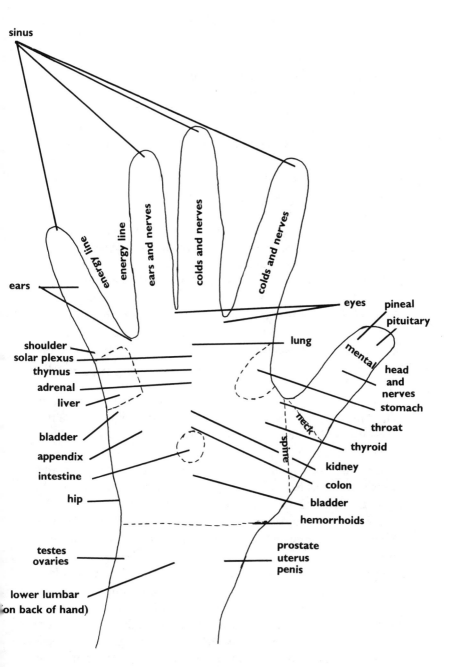

sinus

energy line

energy line

ears and nerves

colds and nerves

colds and nerves

ears

eyes   **pineal**

pituitary

mental

shoulder
solar plexus
thymus
adrenal
liver

lung

head
and
nerves
stomach

neck

spine

throat
thyroid

bladder
appendix
intestine
hip

kidney
colon
bladder
hemorrhoids

testes
ovaries

prostate
uterus
penis

lower lumbar
(on back of hand)

Right Hand, Palm Up

Another great trick is to have clothespins handy for massaging the ends of the fingers; this is the area that controls the sinuses. If you have sinus problems or allergies that clog the sinuses, you can find instant relief through this method. I prefer using clothespins over any other method, because my own hands are not strong enough to produce very much pressure, and I am often too impatient to work on my own hands long enough to have very much benefit. Just as it is beneficial and delightful to have someone else working on the feet, so it is with the hands. If there is any weakness or imbalance in your own system, it is difficult to direct your own energy in a way that will ultimately bring relief. The exchange of energy between two people can accomplish a lot more than simply working on your own hands.

There is a point between the thumb and first finger, just beyond the web of the hands, that will cure headaches. If there is enough tension to cause a headache, you will feel a slight swelling or puffiness in that area of the hand. A clothespin placed on that spot will do the trick in no time. A few years ago, before going on *Kelly and Company*, a terrific television talk show emanating from Detroit, Michigan, I was in the "green" room watching a doctor who preceded me on the show. He apologized to the audience, on the air, for being less than his best that day, as he had awakened with a terrible headache.

At that time I always carried my clothespins around with me. When the doctor came off the show, obviously in a lot of pain, I asked if I could attempt to cure his headache. He was a willing subject, and to his great astonishment, after a few moments of wearing the clothespins on the webs of his hands and on the tips of his fingers, his headache was gone. We decided his case would be a good way to illustrate the technique on the show, so the doctor walked on again with me, wearing the clothespins on his fingers, and announced to the audience that his headache was gone.

As with many techniques that deviate from what we think of as normal systems of healing, it was fine to talk about the clothespins, but not fine to really take them seriously. I am always a little saddened when I think of how many people could avoid so much pain and suffering if some credence were given to these simple and sometimes down-home methods of treatment. Hand and foot reflexology, as well as the stroking of the meridians through the "touch for health" techniques, if practiced on a daily basis, can do so much to keep everyone healthy before serious illness has a chance to set in.

MASSAGE

Just as with exercise, massage can be conducted on many levels. Usually the purpose of a massage is to loosen tight muscles and bring greater relaxation to the individual, especially if that massage takes place in a gym or just after strenuous exercise. However, massage can serve a much deeper purpose. If the person giving the massage has the intention or motivation of healing the body, he can accomplish miracles.

One of the most beloved masseurs in New York City was Dr. Harold J. Reilly. Harold J. had been a trainer for prizefighters and later traveled with an opera singer to keep him in peak condition while on the road. After he grew tired of traveling, Dr. Reilly opened his own health center on the top floor of a building in Rockefeller Center in New York and attracted many radio and television executives, among others, from the vicinity. But suddenly clients were coming to him who had been recommended by someone named Cayce who lived in Virginia Beach, Virginia.

Dr. Reilly was mystified, as he had never heard of this person and couldn't imagine how the gentleman even knew his name. Finally Reilly took a trip to Virginia Beach to meet the extraordinary psychic healer Edgar Cayce. Cayce could diagnose illness at a distance when he was in a trance state, and he prescribed very simple but unusual therapies for those times, the 1940s. He often recommended specific massage to parts of the body and spinal column. At other times, he recommended electrical treatments. An extensive library exists in Virginia Beach at the Association for Research and Enlightenment, the Cayce Institute, which incorporates all of the readings Cayce conducted throughout many years and the specific treatments for a huge variety of illness and maladies.

Evidently, Dr. Reilly was working on a higher level of consciousness with his healing massage than, perhaps, even he was aware of, because Edgar Cayce was told, in his trance state, to send certain people to Reilly's gym for treatment. I had the rare pleasure of meeting Dr. Reilly in the early sixties and began going to him as often as possible for his special brand of healing massage. Dr. Reilly often invited me and two of my friends, along with our children, to his farm in New Jersey where he fed us organically grown vegetables, pampered us with fresh air and loving kindness, and gave us his special brand of healing massage. Dr. Reilly wrote a comprehensive book on healing entitled *Edgar Cayce Handbook for Health through Drugless Therapy*, published in 1975 by the ARE Press.

Most recently, in Ibiza, Spain, I was treated to another very special kind of massage given by an American nurse now living on the island named Mudra Griebal. Mudra was a participant at the first "Healing in the New Age" conference that I coordinated in 1984. (It was primarily because I met so many people like Mudra now living on that rare and special island and possessing extraordinary healing talent that I decided to present such a conference.) I asked Mudra if she could describe what she does that makes her massages so healing. She responded by telling me that she uses a variety of tools, but that she mainly trusts her own inner sight. Mudra stressed that she doesn't heal, as she is only an instrument, and that the client must accept the responsibility for his or her own healing. However, before beginning a massage, Mudra offers several prayers. She offers herself as a vehicle for healing and asks that her higher self touch the higher self of her client. As she asks for guidance and protection, calling in the light of love of many masters, she asks that each person will live in health and that no harm can come to the person through thought, action, or deed.

As with all healing, Mudra understands that the integrated energy must take place throughout all the bodies. She uses such tools as Bach flower remedies, crystals, stones, and specific aromas and essences. She works with diet, breath, and sound. During the massage she may bring in external sounds such as the ringing of Tibetan temple bells, but she also encourages the client to emit his own sounds. As with my regression sessions, Mudra feels that self-forgiveness is the greatest healing force of all.

Mudra was able to demonstrate her work during a session she conducted with a ten-year-old boy named Lucas. Lucas is quite a special young man. He is the son of Bob and Estela, both midwives on the island. Bob, now deceased, was an American who had established such a reputation throughout Europe that many famous actresses would travel to Ibiza during their pregnancies so that Bob could deliver their babies. Estela, the daughter of an Argentinian doctor, began to work with Bob and has continued the practice alone since his death. (One of her special techniques is to talk to the babies as they are being born, giving them instructions, guidance, and reassurance so that their entry into life will be as easy and pleasant as possible. Estela's babies recognize her many months later, when she might inadvertently see them, and always give her a big smile and acknowledgment.)

Lucas asked that he might be given a massage by Mudra, as he had some pain in his body. Mudra gave Lucas a green scarf and two green-blue egg-shaped stones to hold in his hands during the massage. Then she did her own preparation with her prayers and affirmations. Lucas was asked to choose the master he wanted to work with. Mudra commented that she saw a dent behind his solar plexus and a bump between his shoulder blades. There were bumps in front of both shoulders and bumps in front of his head. There seemed to be pain involved in the areas she described.

Mudra instructed Lucas to watch his breath enter and leave his body and taught him how to breathe during the session. Next Mudra began to guide Lucas through a visualization of how his body looked. She asked him to identify the places that hurt and told him to breathe into those spots. She then asked him to let a sound emerge from that place. In one instance when she asked Lucas what the painful spot looked like, he replied that he saw the color turquoise and that he saw a stick going through his body that was red. As Mudra began to massage that area, he began to see a round ball above the turquoise, and then the red passed down into his lower back.

One of his most interesting observations occurred when he saw an orange triangle moving around his body. Mudra asked him what that triangle might say if it could speak to him. Lucas replied without hesitation, "It says this is my place. He's moved around and found the right place and is home!" Then when he saw a smaller green triangle, Mudra directed him to breathe into his heart and instruct it to expand on both sides. (Green is the color of the heart chakra.) Lucas volunteered that the triangle had become a flashing green rectangle now. When Mudra asked him to listen to what the rectangle might say, he answered, "The rectangle says the brain sends the flashy green rectangle messages, and it does what the brain says to do. I trip over and the brain says put your arms forward to keep from falling over and smashing your face. . . . All of your left arm is given full choice and (the brain) says the right one had been used a lot."

With a lot of glee from Mudra and Estela, who knew what Lucas was learning about the balance between right and left hemispheres of the brain, Mudra suggested that perhaps if he used his left arm more, he might bring better balance to his brain. Then Lucas began to see many colors emitting from his body, especially where there had been pain. He realized he could direct the colors to move to the parts of his body where they belonged. He also learned not to be fearful of falling down and hurting his face.

Estela, Lucas's mother, observed a shape above Lucas's head that she described as a light bulb or an inverted uterus. She described the vivid colors she saw coming from his body and then saw what she described as baby chicks around his throat chakra. Her realization was that when Lucas was sleeping, he kept his head tucked down, and she felt he was closing his shoulders so that the heart chakra was blocked. She commented that if she, as his mother, had tried to suggest some things to him, he might not listen, but what he experienced from the massage and saw for himself he would not forget.

I had already set up and interpreted Lucas's astrological chart for his mother several years before that time, and indeed what Lucas saw in his session with Mudra was exactly what his chart indicated about blocks to his body. Lucas was born with his Sun in Capricorn (Saturn) and with Leo rising. When Leo is on the ascendant, Saturn rules the sixth house of health. Pressures exerted structurally and psychologically cut off the flow of energy. (See Chapters 5 and 6 on Saturn, and Leo ascendant.) But with Leo rising, the particular area of the body that can be affected early in life is the heart chakra, and therefore the heart.

It is very important to work with children early in life to prevent those blocks from setting in on a permanent basis. You can give your child a massage simply by awakening him or her with a loving back rub to stimulate energy along the spinal column. What better way to prepare a child for a productive day at school. It seems a far better way to prepare him or her for receptiveness and joy in learning than the typical, "Hurry up, you're going to be late."

And please don't forget your adored animals. Any of the above-described techniques work on animals equally well. My daughter Diane was able to use acupressure to relieve, to a great extent, the pain and stiffness in the lower back and hips when her beautiful Sagittarian Doberman, Sabrina, began to get older. My adorable Samantha, an Aries with Gemini rising and Moon in Leo, expects her nightly massage and emits little sounds of pleasure as she falls off to sleep.

Diet, Herbs, Bach Flower Remedies, Vita Florum, and Cell Salts

DIET

The subject of diet has been researched, discussed, and written about from almost every possible angle. Even Nostradamus himself described diet as it related to astrological signs. This topic could fill many books by itself, so we will touch lightly on the high points of diet as it relates to the astrological chart.

The United States has become increasingly diet conscious, with myriad theories as to how diet affects the physical system. For the most part, *diet* usually means a program for the loss of weight, but in reality, the word describes the variety of combinations of foods one puts into the body for the sake of energy conversion and for health. If proper diet is really taken into consideration (that is, the analysis of the intake of food from the point of view of what will produce better energy and health), the body should neither be too thin nor too fat. However, there are many reasons why under-weight and overweight conditions exist.

As we have noted, man is a column of light. In reality, each human being is a spark of the divine cosmic fire descended into earth for the purpose of augmenting the flame. Eventually his mission is to return home with experiences that will enrich the whole. His earthly experiences cause his individual flame to grow brighter, flicker, or grow dim. It is the right of each person to decide whether he wishes to shed any light at all, and if he so chooses, how he can best shed his own particular quality of light into the shadows of earth. The earth plane has no light of its own, except that from the heavens, man's inventions, and man's individual cosmic light.

What we consume in the way of food has a great deal to do with whether the instrument (the physical body) is translucent or whether it becomes opaque. The specific foods that can be tolerated and utilized by each human being can be different. The balance of elements in an astrological chart can give clues as to what each person's system requires and can tolerate. For example, an individual with many earth planets in his chart may be able to digest a greater preponderance of earthy kinds of food, such as meat, potatoes (starches), and root vegetables. But an individual with many air planets may need to eat very light foods that would relate more to air energy. Those foods might be sprouts, lettuce, asparagus, and foods that contain sunlight and chlorophyll, such as flowers. That rule in itself is too simplistic, however, because the health patterns revealed through looking at the overall astrological chart can indicate digestive patterns or predispositions to food allergies.

Regular consultation with a specialist in nutrition can be essential in determining what factors are important for each individual system. Dr. Elizabeth Dane, with a practice in New York and in California, considers not only specific foods for an individual system, but the supplements and other digestive aids, as example, that keep each person in healthful balance for peak energy.

Man is not only a column of light, but according to the late Neil Michelson, an astrologer, his physical makeup can be likened to a garbage disposal. What he puts into his system must be processed and then disposed of! If he inadvertently drops a fork into the garbage disposal, he must stop the machine, fish out the bent fork, and push the reset button. Finding the foods that are right for each individual system can be somewhat like that.

One experience illustrated this for me quite clearly. One day I was driving my car along a road in upstate New York when I saw a man walking in the opposite direction. He had white hair and beard, was wearing saffron-colored robes, and was barefoot. His face was quite young and beautiful, although I could guess that he was not a young man. I stopped my car and asked if he wanted a ride. He gestured that he was going in the opposite direction, but I turned the car around to pick him up anyway. I suspected that he had taken the vow of silence by the way he responded to my question, and I was correct in that assumption. He wrote a note telling me his destination, and I told him I would take him there, but that we would go a different way. Actually, this entailed driving almost twenty miles over the road he had just walked. I thought of my reaction if I had hiked those many miles and was then driven back over them again, but he smiled and indicated the route would be fine. I realized that this beautiful man had neither been extremely grateful that I had picked him up, such as I might have been, nor did he seem to expect it was his due. It was clear that he walked in the pure light, and whatever happened was exactly correct for that moment.

After a while he dozed off, and I realized that if he had taken the vow of silence, he had probably also taken the vow of poverty and might be quite hungry. I had just shopped for dog food, diet cola, and a container of ricotta cheese. There was not much of a selection to offer him, but when he awakened I asked if he would like some cheese. When he accepted, he read the words printed on the side of the container with great care, and I understood very clearly that if it had contained anything detrimental to his system, he would have declined even if he had not eaten for days. What a lesson for me! Much of the time I eat on the run, grabbing whatever I can find that will satisfy my hunger pains of the moment. Many people rely on fast foods to meet the hectic pace and stress of the times. These foods can be just like dropping the fork into the disposal.

Edgar Cayce prescribed some foods that are important for every-one to consume each day. For example, the daily intake of gelatin is valuable in keeping the colon lubricated. This is particularly true for a person with Virgo rising or ruling the sixth house, since Virgo is the sign that relates to the colon. But it is valuable for everyone to keep the colon in good working order, as it has many twists and turns that can collect food deposits, which in turn produce toxins. (Along with gelatin, regular colonics keep the colon clean and the brain stimulated.) Cayce also recommended eating five almonds a day to prevent cancer. He also gave a recipe for a breakfast meal called "mummy food," because it was found in the tomb of an Egyptian mummy. The combination of cornmeal, figs, dates, and raisins provides the energy at breakfast that charges the body for the whole day.

Drinking quantities of Aloe Vera juice is also excellent for keeping the system lubricated and in balance. Research efforts connected to the ingestion of Aloe Vera reveal amazing progress in treatment of everything from a simple cold to the most severe diseases, especially when used in conjunction with other methods of treatment.

After all the diet books have been read and reread, one major factor stands out. The intake of food must match the level the body is capable of processing and burning up in energy. This ratio is called the metabolic rate. If the metabolism is slow, the body burns less converted fuel, and the food intake must necessarily be less and more qualified in type. An astrological chart can give clues about the quality of the metabolic rate. Fire signs, as an example, burn food at a high metabolic rate and may need extra protein to fuel their zestful energy.

The extra factor that will enable a person to eat more food is the amount of exercise he gets, for exercise helps to burn food faster. If the metabolic rate is high, food is naturally burned at a faster rate and a person can eat more without any possibility of excess fat stored on the body frame, but he must still be aware of what his system can easily digest.

The astrological chart can describe diet and proper food for each person in several ways. First, the ascendant describes body type, which determines the kind of food that is appropriate to the individual and how the physical body will relate to the environment, including food. Second, the astrological sign placement of the sixth house describes health in general, but also the organic balance and inherited genetic factors. It also describes how one digests and absorbs food into the body. That, in turn, predescribes the natural selection of food and whether that selection is wise or not. The sixth house can indicate how one actually consumes the food. As an example, with Virgo ruling the sixth house, it is important to analyze the kind of food that can be easily assimilated into the system. Virgo rules the intestinal tract, so the foods that are chosen need to stimulate the digestive process that occurs in the intestines in order to maintain a healthful balance in the system. Virgo describes the way the mind works, therefore it behooves the individual with this house placement to choose brain foods such as fish, sardines in particular. Mental processes such as worry, fear, and doubt will affect the digestive process more in a person with this house placement than someone else, as an example.

If an individual counts the number of planets in the chart that relate to each element, he can determine whether he has enough of earth, air, fire, and water in his system. He may need to balance those elements by choosing foods that relate to those elements. Protein, root vegetables, and meats relate to the earth element. If a person is lacking earth in his chart, he may need to choose foods that help the grounding process, considering what his digestive process can assimilate. People with earth signs on the ascendant may need to consume extra protein in the form of meats to fuel their heavier, earthy structural nature.

Fruits relate to fire signs. With lack of fire in the chart, the individual may need to consume protein and fruits that are energizing, even red in color, whereas air relates to flowers and more delicate plants. With either an abundance or a lack of air in the chart, the individual may require brain foods, such as fish, to stimulate intellectual processes. But air signs, especially Aquarius, have a better chance at becoming airarians (people whose systems can subsist almost entirely on oxygen and who can thrive on small amounts of food). Air (oxygen) is a basic food substance for these signs. Herbs and plants grown aboveground are important to stimulate the systems of air signs. Sprouts can be a valuable source of nutrients as well. If the individual is a water sign or is lacking in water, he may require plants that contain more water, such as zucchini, squash, cucumbers, tomatoes, and melons. If there is an excess of water in the system, these foods may produce allergic symptoms, and foods that are natural diuretics can be important to keep the tissues from collecting excess fluids.

Determining a proper and comprehensive diet from an astrological point of view requires an analysis of the entire chart; not only the house positions and the elemental placement of the Sun, but the aspects of all the planets and their placements. The planets describe and indicate the body processes, the organic strengths and weaknesses, and how they relate to the quality of diet. The planets also describe foods such as sugars, starches, fats, dairy products, vegetables, proteins, and carbohydrates. Jupiter rules fats, for example, whereas Venus rules sugar. The Moon rules milk and dairy products, and Saturn describes calcium and gelatin. Neptune describes drugs; Pluto describes stimulants. Planets can describe vitamins, enzymes, steroids, and general body chemistry such as acid-alkaline balance.

Kinesiology can help to determine which foods energize the system and which ones might deplete or clog it up. (See Chapter 18.) Another determining factor in the proper assimilation of food into the body is proper mastication. Food must be thoroughly chewed in the mouth before it passes down into the alimentary canal and then into the stomach as the stomach has no teeth! Preliminary digestion of some nutrients also occurs in the mouth, so the food must stay there long enough for that process to take place. Proper mastication has to do with how the teeth meet in the chewing process. Therefore, an important planet to consider in the chart is Saturn, which rules not only the teeth themselves and the calcium contained within, but also the body structure and especially the jaw, which allows the teeth to meet. Since Saturn describes the skeleton, if the body alignment is out of balance, the whole intricate mechanism of food absorption is thrown awry.

For people who are trying to lose weight, regular trips to a highly qualified chiropractor may be essential to set the whole process in motion. Not only is the body structure important for proper assimilation of food, but treatment by acupuncture can stimulate proper production of the secretions of the digestive organs that allow the breakdown of foods to take place. If more energy is created in the body by reducing stress and tension in the frame, and by inducing energy to flow properly through the meridians, there is less need to eat the wrong foods just to satisfy the sensation of hunger. Saturn also describes discipline and the attention needed to curb compulsive food consumption.

People who tend to be overweight may also be lacking the color blue in their systems. (See chapter 21.) Blue is the color of the throat chakra, which relates to the thyroid gland. The thyroid regulates the metabolic rate in the system. Therefore thinking, wearing, and ingesting blue can be beneficial in stimulating the thyroid and consequently the metabolic rate. (See Chapter 22.)

The next area to examine in the astrological chart is the Moon, which rules the stomach and the digestive processes. The Moon also describes the emotional need to put food into the mouth. It indicates the areas of life that create a sense of vulnerability, hurt, or feelings of abandonment, which so often predates eating disorders. It is fairly obvious that overconsumption of food is often a substitute for being nurtured in external areas of life. This means emotional response from people in personal areas, but can also include job fulfillment, relationships, and familial situations. Loneliness, oversensitivity to environmental conditions, and stress can certainly lead to food intake that is not carefully thought-out.

The placement of the Moon in the natal horoscope, as well as the sign through which it is currently progressing, describes the quality of emotional response one receives, and indirectly, the kind of eating habits that relate to a specific time in life. The placement of the Moon in the chart can also indicate whether or not food allergies exist. If a person has Cancer rising, or Aquarius on the ascendant (which places Cancer on the cusp of the sixth house), the Moon and its phases have direct bearing on the individual's emotional connection to food.

Food can also represent pleasure, so the need for pleasure in life may lead one to be attracted to certain types of foods. A look at the astrological chart can help determine which foods can bring pleasure as well as increased health and vitality into the physical system.

As a general rule of thumb, determine the sign that rules the ascendant (and take into consideration any energy described by planets positioned in that first house). Then determine the planet that rules the sixth house of health. Next, analyze the element that comes into play as a result of the sign placement of those planets.

ELEMENTS	SIGNS
Earth	Taurus, Virgo, Capricorn
Air	Gemini, Libra, Aquarius

Fire ....Aries, Leo, Sagittarius
Water ....Cancer, Scorpio, Pisces

There are four major categories of bodily function that can relate to these four elements. The building of bones and prevention of calcium deposits in the body relates to the earth element. Mental stimulation and the proper balance of the nervous system relates to the air element. Stimulation of metabolism and circulation relates to the fire element. And regulation of digestive and elimination systems relate to the water element.

Earth Signs

Earth signs need bone-building calcium and protein. The foods that stimulate the building of bone are milk, cheese, meat, or vegetable protein (brown rice and beans are a fabulous source of vegetable protein). The prevention of calcium deposits in the body, however, depends on keeping the acid-alkaline balance even in the system. One teaspoon of apple cider vinegar mixed with honey in a glass of water upon arising will maintain that balance and prevent arthritis (*Vermont Folk Medicine*). Lemons also help maintain that balance. Earth signs are more easily able to digest meat protein than other signs, as a general rule, but it is wise to avoid fatty meats, such as pork.

Air Signs

Since air relates to mental energy and the nervous system, it is important for air signs to consume foods that stimulate the brain and nervous system. Sardines, oysters, and seafood in general are considered to be brain foods. Any food rich in vitamin B-12 is beneficial for the nervous system and can be found in meats, soybean products (tofu is a good source of soybean), swiss cheese, pickled foods, livers, and cottage cheese. Lettuce, sprouts, oranges, celery, and almonds are particularly good for air signs, as they stimulate mental energy as well as the nervous system. Sprouts can be grown at home quite easily and are delicious when combined with salads.

Fire Signs

The element fire relates to the circulatory system. Therefore, foods that purify the bloodstream are beneficial, as well as anything connected with movement of energy throughout the body. Fats, eggs, ice cream, and foods high in cholesterol can damage arteries and should be consumed in moderation. Vitamin E is essential for healthy blood, as it enables the blood cells to absorb a greater amount of oxygen and helps prevent high blood pressure. Foods high in Vitamin E are wheat germ, sunflower seeds, salmon, peanut butter, mushrooms, parsley (for purifying the blood), cabbage, asparagus, carrots, broccoli, avocados, and spinach. Turkey meat also contains Vitamin E. The best blood purifier of all is garlic. In fact, a stew of garlic cloves and onions can be a fabulous cure for the flu, bronchitis, and colds. This combination is very effective in helping to keep blood pressure stabilized. However, you may need to hide away while you are consuming this stew, unless you have very loving, tolerant friends. Certain foods can help prevent anemia, such as artichokes, dandelions, spinach, and watercress.

Water Signs

Since water signs relate to the digestive and elimination systems, soothing foods and natural diuretics can help prevent water retention. Foods high in potassium are very beneficial. (Potassium sold under the name KM gives concentrated dosages to supplement the diet. However, dosage should be supervised by a health professional.) Potassium aids in the elimination of water from the tissues and reduces allergic reactions to foods or substances in the air. It also activates the production of digestive enzymes, which help process the food before elimination. Foods high in potassium are strawberries, asparagus, cantaloupe, bananas, almonds, potatoes, sesame and sunflower seeds, and tuna fish. Any water foods such as watercress and watermelon are beneficial to water signs. Since water signs can tend to gain weight as a result of fluid retention, the drinking of eight glasses of pure water every day keeps the kidneys flushed and prevents edema and toxicity in the system. Foods can act as diruetics as well. They are radishes, celery, cucumber, parsley, oats, asparagus, and kidney beans. Certain foods act as digestive aids. They are rhubarb, papaya, oats, carrots, and oranges.

H E R B S

Historically, the Chinese have been the only people to develop an organized method for recording and documenting foods and their effects on the human body. Whereas most civilizations have used herbs to some degree (usually only one to two hundred varieties), over the last five thousand years the Chinese have developed a working knowledge of thousands of herbs. In the ancient Chinese culture, the court physicians guarded the Chinese emperor's health, while the twenty thousand or so people who lived in the palace compound acted as guinea pigs, becoming human laboratories that allowed them to develop their knowledge. Physicians utilized tools such as acupunture and foods, watching and learning which methods worked and which ones did not. Chinese physicians became the world's experts on healing plants and on the body itself. Their experiments on how blood circulated, as an example, led to their extremely sophisticated method of diagnosis through the pulse.

Some of China's best medical ideas came from the priests as well as the physicians. The priests were well versed in martial arts, and therefore their prime concern was how substances affected physical strength, stamina, and energy. They were also concerned with purity of thought, mind, and spirit, which they felt was directly related to the intake of specific foods to stimulate mind and spiritual processes. They were concerned with substances that would heal the bruises, torn muscles, and general trauma associated with the martial arts.

The formulas for the herbal healing combinations, which became famous throughout China, were kept hidden within the temples. Although they were used to treat the emperor as well as the elite among them, even the emperors had no access to the information.

According to Dr. Tei Fu Chen (a licensed pharmacist, research biochemist, herbalist, and personal physician to Chiang Kai-shek), about three hundred years ago, the emperors captured the Shao Lin temple and placed the formulas in the emperor's library along with other manuscripts of healing arts. When the Boxer Rebellion took place in the early years of the present century, the palace was pillaged. However, the manuscripts were carefully hidden with the Chen family, who utilize these valuable formulas to this day in connection with healing. The information was used to feed the Chen family during the last three generations.

Herbs are classified in three major categories. First there are poisonous herbs. Second, medicinal herbs that control body functions in much the same way as drugs commonly used in the medical profession today. (Digitalis, as an example, is an herb that commonly grows in gardens but is critical in treating certain heart conditions.) The third category is food herbs. These herbs do not control the body, but feed the glands, organs, and system, as well as aid in repair and proper functioning and self-regulation.

The subject of herbal medicine is so vast we can only scratch the surface here, but it is possible to examine four of the basic principles. The first is that herbs give concentrated nutrients that are readily assimilated by the glands and organs for use in tissue repair and regeneration. The second major principle is that herbs provide precursors for the glands and organs to use in their manufacture of key hormones and enzymes. Thirdly, they provide basic elements which give energy and oxygen at atomic and molecular levels. Herbs work on the etheric energy system. And finally, herbs provide substances which feed the basic energy cycles in the body's metabolic process to liberate energy, heat, and oxygen.

Dr. Chen believes that herbs are especially important because they fortify the body against the constant barrage of negative outside influences. The basic philosophy behind herbal remedies concerns the regeneration of the energy system, which can then effect its own healing. Over an extended period of time, poor nutrition can cause a degenerative cycle within the body. Western society uses the device of substition, or a controlling substance such as drugs, to stimulate the diseased function. Substitution can give temporary aid, but the patterns still exist on the etheric imprint of the body. Only a regeneration of the system really solves the problem. This can be done with therapy, such as acupuncture, that affects the etheric body and with the use of substances that heal on that level. Herbs are one of the substances that can correct imbalance and restore functioning of cells. Traditional medicine usually adopts the course of removing and replacing a weak organ. This is due partly to the lack of information about the etheric body and the substances, such as herbs, that really do repair damaged tissue, and also to the lack of trust in such simple remedies.

The astrological chart is an extremely valuable tool to use in the diagnosis of imbalance of organs and especially to determine the condition of the etheric body and its webbed network of associated energies. Uranus is the key planet in the individual astrological chart which indicates the condition of the etheric body and its connection to the physical mechanism. But once again, consideration of the elements and of the planets that rule the ascendant, that are placed in the first house, and that rule the sixth house give a general rule of thumb as to which herbs are most beneficial for the individual system.

Natural herbs also can be related to those four categories of body function. Herbal rememdies are not only beneficial, but can act as natural condiments when combined with other foods.

Earth Signs

The prevention of arthritis is important for earth signs, as the accumulation of calcium deposits quickly upsets structural balance and can be very painful. Herbs that help prevent arthritis are burdock, cayenne, horseradish, wintergreen, black currant, alfalfa, comfrey, garden violet, and buttercup. Edible flowers such as violet, buttercup, and pratalina (a type of daisy), combined with dandelions and feather ferns make a very unusual and tasty salad that is beneficial for earth signs.

Air Signs

Air signs need stimulation to the brain, especially as it relates to the nervous system and oxygenation of the system. Herbs that are especially helpful for nervous conditions are catnip, blue vervain, chamomile, jasmine, lavender, pansy, peppermint, periwinkle, rosemary, sage, savory, thyme, and wild marjoram. Herbs that benefit the lungs are chickweed, saffron, cowslip, anise, barley, catnip, eucalyptus, fennel, heather, horehound, and licorice,

Fire Signs

Good circulation and blood pressure is important for fire signs. The herbs that benefit anemic conditions are alfalfa, barberry, fenugreek, gentian, comfrey, thyme, and nettles. Herbs that benefit high blood pressure are rosemary, lavender, heather, hawthorne, and anise.

Water Signs

Herbs that benefit digestion and help alleviate any stomach problems are black mustard, anise, chamomile, caraway, coriander, dandelion, dill, eucalyptus, fennel, gentian, goldenseal, horseradish, juniper, lavender, magnolia, nutmeg, parsley, peppermint, wild ginger, white mustard, sweet marjoram, savory, sage, and rosemary.

BACH FLOWER REMEDIES

Of the therapies that work on more subtle levels, one of the most amazing is the group called the Bach flower remedies. These remedies were discovered by an English bacteriologist, Dr. Richard Bach, when he found that by ingesting the essence of a particular flower, he could simulate in himself the emotional state of mind that the flower could cure. He began to follow the homeopathic branch of medicine, which treats like with like. (See Chapter 1.) In 1930, after twenty years of practicing traditional medicine on Harley Street in London, Dr. Bach gave up a lucrative practice to perfect his new method of healing.

The prime difference between the flower remedies and other ingested substances is that they work on the mental level, effecting a cure by dealing with the state of mind of the individual. The remedies help a person overcome the worry, fear, or depression that can hinder recovery.

Dr. Bach was a pioneer in the study of the relationship between emotional stresses and physical illnesses. Originally, he found seven categories of illness and produced vaccines that related to each type of bacterial illness. Later on, that discovery led him to his original twelve flower substances. Those original twelve substances seemed to cover a wide range of emotional reactions. After devoting himself to a full-time search for more plants that would relate to negative states of mind, he expanded the number to cover a range of thirty-eight negative states of mind. He designated one flower remedy for each of the most common negative states of mind or moods that can afflict a person. He divided these remedies into his original seven major categories under the following headings: fear, uncertainty, insufficient interest in present circumstances, loneliness, oversensitivity to influences and ideas, despondency or despair, and overconcern for the welfare of others.

The story of the development of his theories is a fascinating one. Dr. Bach was treating patients with chronic gastrointestinal illnesses and discovered that by vaccinating the patients with minute doses of the specific bacteria related to their particular form of illness, he could produce significant improvement. At about the same time, he read of Dr. Samuel Hahnemann's work in homeopathy, which presents the hypothesis that one should treat like with like. Dr. Bach progressed from injecting small amounts of toxin into the system of his patients to preparing homeopathic concentrations of his vaccines that could be given orally. Coincidentally, Dr. Bach began to notice that his patients, who were ill with one of seven types of bacterial infection, displayed specific personality types and temperaments. He was able to relate a specific type of personality with each of the seven types of illness. He experimented with giving the patients one of the seven types of vaccines, now called Bach's nosodes, which he related to each of the personality categories. He began to ignore the physical symptoms and treat only the mental and emotional disorders of his patients. He researched matching patients with the nosodes that matched their emotional nature. He achieved significant results with this method of treatment that far exceeded his expectations.

The next development came with his awareness that the people belonging to the same emotional category did not necessarily have a predisposition to the same disease. However, regardless of the disease, the patients in each category reacted to their disease in the same way. He began to link mental and emotional states to the remedy most likely to cure any disease related to that state of mind. He didn't like putting toxins back into the body and felt there must be something in nature that duplicated the vibrational energy level of the emotional or mental disorder.

Bach understood the relationship of the higher mind to the magnetic qualities of the higher subtle bodies. He himself was psychic and was extremely sensitive. Eventually, he was unable to live in London because of all the conflicting energies around him. After an illness that almost caused his death, Bach moved to the country and discovered that he could merely touch his lips to the morning dew from a particular flower and he would experience all of the physical symptoms and emotional states that particular flower essence was the antidote for. He was able to obtain vibrational tinctures by placing flowers in water in the sunlight. It was sun that seemed to charge the water with the specific imprint of the flower's vibratory level. This seems to confirm that prana, the higher etheric oxygen or ether found in sunlight, is indeed an important factor in the energy of the etheric system. Dr. Bach was evidently operating on a very high virbatory level himself, as he had an almost psychically sensitive reaction to the flowers. He used his own energy system as his tool for what might work with others.

It seems significant that in the beginning, Dr. Bach found seven types of bacteriological illnesses, seven being the spiritual number that relates to the esoteric plane, and then found twelve flower remedies that relate to the twelve astrological signs. In his book *Heal Thyself*, Dr. Bach discussed the traits he felt were the primary causes of disease. These traits were seven in number, relating to the seven categories of illness. He cited pride, cruelty, hate, self-love, ignorance, instability, and greed as the seven major categories that could cause illness in the physical system.

Considering only the original twelve flower remedy categories, we can find a correlation with each astrological sign. For a clue to flower remedies that might be beneficial to each individual, it is necessary to consider the sign in which the Sun was placed at birth, as well as the sign of the Moon and Mercury, since the remedies work in conjunction with mental and emotional processes. You might also consider the sign that lies on the cusp of the sixth house of the individual chart. The flower remedies can be further categorized, associating all thirty-eight remedies to more subtle personality traits in conjunction with each astrological sign or the patterns that are described by the aspects in the chart.

The twelve outstanding states of mind (i.e.: the emotional states the flowers can cure), according to Dr. Bach, are fear, terror, mental torture or worry, indecision, indifference or boredom, doubt or discouragement, overconcern, weakness, self-distrust, impatience, overenthusiasm, pride, and aloofness. In his book *The Twelve Healers of the Zodiac,** astrologer Peter Damian writes about his choices for the association of each flower remedy to each astrological sign. It may be important to conduct your own research into the remedies that work best on an individual level and consider where the associated astrological sign is positioned in your individual horoscope—that is, ruling the ascendant or the sixth house.

Mr. Damian relates clematis to the sign of Cancer. As an example, in my personal experience, clematis is a remedy that brings about a general feeling of well-being in my life and energizes my system. Although I am a Scorpio, I have Cancer rising. (Chicory, which Mr. Damian relates to the sign of Scorpio, is not one of the remedies that seems essential for my system.) Agrimony, which Peter relates to the sign of Sagittarius, is very important to my system, and I have Sagittarius on the cusp of the sixth house. But, if I had to choose only one flower remedy that I should never be without, I must confess it would be impatiens. It doesn't take much

* York Beach, ME, Samuel Weiser, Inc, 1986; and under the title *An Astrological Study Of The Bach Flower Remedies*, Essex, England; C. W. Daniel, 1986, p. 37. Used by permission.

of a stretch of imagination to associate that remedy with a characteristic of impatience in a person's makeup—an Aries trait. Although I have Cancer rising, my Moon is placed in the sign of Aries and is conjunct Uranus, also in Aries. The combination of the rising sign and the sign placement of the ruler of the rising sign seems to be especially significant in my own experience.

The flower-remedy/zodiac-sign associations Mr. Damian makes are:

Aries with Impatiens
Taurus with Gentian
Gemini with Cerato
Cancer with Clematis
Leo with Vervain
Virgo with Centaury
Libra with Scleranthus
Scorpio with Chicory
Sagittarius with Agrimony
Capricorn with Mimulus
Aquarius with Water Violet
Pisces with Rock Rose

It is interesting to note that Bach flower remedies are completely safe to administer to children. The essences contain a minute amount of the actual flower substance, yet the biological imprint makes a profound difference in the emotional and mental well-being of an individual. It is also important to dilute the substances with only a drop put into a whole glass of water. As with many homeopathic remedies, less is more. The rationale that the remedies might act as a crutch or excuse for a young person to avoid control of his own emotions is invalid, simply because the remedies enable a person to exist on a higher level. If the psychological blocks are removed (such as worry, fear, and anxiety), a child is free to explore his talents and potential without that devitalizing emotional overlay. Imagine how wonderful it might be to undertake major exams in school without the all-encompassing anxiety that usually goes hand in hand with such pressure. Examinations have been criticized as standards for evaluating intellectual achievement because, many times, it is the student who can remain calm who scores the highest grades.

As a word of caution, however, Bach flower remedies are usually preserved in a minute amount of alcohol. It would be wise to use applied kinesiology to see if that infinitesimal amount of preservative would affect the condition of alcoholics, as an example. It is possible to make your own flower essences without any alcohol once you have determined which ones are beneficial for your system. It is then necesary to refrigerate the essences to avoid spoilage.

A good general rule is to test the essences that tend to energize the system through applied kinesiology. (See Chapter 18.) Place the bottle of essence over the solar plexus while another person tests the strength of your arm. If the arm remains strong, the essence is beneficial. If the arm is weakened, try the next essence to determine the best formula for your particular system or momentary symptom.

Vita Florum

Vita florum, meaning "life's flowering," is a remedy that is also derived from flowers. Unlike the Bach flower remedies, it requires no diagnosis, as vita florum consists of just one preparation. The single preparation acts as a battery for the whole system, from the etheric down through the physical, and contains a very approximate form of the causal energy, or the etheric energy, which is the "idea" that underlies every physical thing.

Vita florum was discovered by Elizabeth Bellhouse, a former practitioner of Bach flower remedies in England. She began her practice in 1945, and by the time the new formula was revealed to her, she was the foremost practitioner of the Bach remedies in England. Mrs. Bellhouse states that she received the formula through a miraculous revelation from Maria and Christ, and that it included all the technical information she needed to produce and handle vast quantities of vita florum, from the gathering of particular species of flowers from their far-flung locations to the distillation and bottling of the essence.

Vita florum has been recognized by the United Kingdom's Ministry of Health as essentially spiritual in nature. One British doctor commented that vita florum has the potential to heal everybody and everything. As with any powerful healing agent that works on the etheric system, there are incredible, almost miraculous stories of how the remedy has affected illness and infirmity of every kind. The confirmation of the healing power of this remedy has been documented, and its vibratory rate has been recorded on spectrometers and voltmeters. Dosages of vita florum have been known to improve memory and eyesight, relieve back pain, relax muscles that caused a twisted ankle and foot, and bring about new levels of consciousness and awareness on a spiritual level.

Kirlian photographs have shown the rapidity of the curative effect of vita florum. As an example, the corona (or aura) of a fingertip of a sick person was photographed before and after treatment with this remedy. In four successive pictures the change in the emanation around the finger, from the untreated sick stage to three minutes after application, is quite dramatic. In the first picture the emanation around the untreated fingertip appears broken and quite ragged, with some pieces completely missing. In the second picture, taken immediately after an application of vita florum, the dark emanation appears to be filling in rapidly. In the third picture, taken one minute after application, the aura or corona is almost completely intact, and in the final picture, taken three minutes after the application, the aura is strong and solid around the fingertip.

There are seven forms in which the essence can be obtained. There is water to be taken internally in drops or in a bath; a tablet which has the required five drops already premeasured; an ointment which is applied on the various chakras (and should always be applied to heart, solar plexus, and navel); a lotion to be applied on the face or as a gargle; a massage oil; a salve for rashes or to be applied to nails; and a powder which is the most potent form of all. The powder can be shaken into shoes and spread on bed sheets for a delicious, protected, inspired sleep. There is a lotion which can be added to bathwater to counter fatigue or the onset of a cold or flu, or just to relieve aching muscles. The ointment can be applied over the solar plexus and heart to counteract the effects of jet lag, as an example.

When I tested vita florum, I experienced an immediate change in my system. I noticed that instead of *feeling* the effects of pressures in my work and home environment, I was suddenly able to *see* the situation and even read the thoughts of a person who was angry, rather than feel the effects of such anger. I noticed a renewed concentration and calm that I have not experienced since I was a child, even when I was under heavy Saturn aspects that usually spell a day or so of fatigue.

CELL SALTS

Biochemical cell salts, which are needed by the body to maintain the proper function of all cellular life, fall into the category of homeopathic remedies (like treating like). They also work on the subtle body system and have been widely used in European countries to maintain good health and physical condition. Luckily, the United States is now beginning to acknowledge this method of treatment, and these substances can now be found in health food stores on this side of the Atlantic.

Once again, the number of existing cell salts is twelve, just enough to relate to the twelve astrological signs. The fact that this number recurs in remedies that work on the subtle body level is an interesting confirmation of the divine order of the Universe.

Cell division is one of the first processes that takes place in the development of the fetus. Cells divide and reproduce themselves at varying rates throughout the lifetime of the human being. It may well be that the deteriorating quality of the reproducing cells is the cause of the downward spiral of aging. As we have seen, certain cells become specialized cells. They are cells of hair, nails, organs, etc., and each cell has an imprint or template that describes its special characteristics. When the cells begin to wear out, the necessary ingredients for replacement are enzymes composed of proteins, vitamins, and minerals. If these ingredients are prevalent in the diet, the cell can be replaced, but if those substances are missing from the body, the cell dies. The primary function of the cell salts is to supply the body with the necessary ingredients to replace worn-out enzymes.

In his book *How to Use the Cell Salts*, astrologer Robert Carl Jansky has devised a formula to determine which cell salts fit your particular body chemistry, as related to the astrological chart. He combines the cell salt that relates to the Sun sign, the Moon's south node, the rising sign, and the sign of Saturn's position. He suggests taking ten cell salts daily, allowing them to dissolve under the tongue. The ten tablets are made up of two tablets of each cell salt that relates to each of those astrological points, except the Sun. Mr. Jansky suggests taking four of the salts that relate to the Sun's placement in the chart.

Mr. Jansky's cell-salt/astrological sign relationships are:

Aries to Kali Phos. (potassium phosphate)
Taurus to Nat. sulph. (Sodium Sulfate)
Gemini to Kali Mur. (Potassium Chloride)
Cancer to Calc. Fluor. (Calcium Fluoride)
Leo to Mag. Phos. (Magnesium Phosphate)
Virgo to Kali Sulph. (Potassium Sulfate)
Libra to Nat. Phos. (Sodium Phosphate)
Scorpio to Calc. Sulph. (Calcium Sulfate)
Sagittarius to Silica (Silicon Dioxide)
Capricorn to Calc. Phos. (Calcium Phosphate)
Aquarius to Nat. Mur. (Sodium Chloride)
Pisces to Ferrum Phos. (Iron Phosphate)

I suggest the careful reading of Mr. Jansky's treatise on the cell salts and experimentation of the effectiveness of these biochemical salts on your own system. Once again, the system of kinesiology is especially effective in determining the exact ratio of the specific salt for your own highly individualized system.

Color and Sound

C O L O R   A N D   T H E   E L E M E N T S

Color is generally thought of as something to appeal to the physical senses. But we also know that color can affect emotional and psychological balance. As a result of the small amount of research conducted with color therapy, some hospitals have attempted to incorporate the healing tones of green into their decor, but usually the shades chosen are far from the ones that will stimulate healing. Very few scientists or doctors take the subject of color healing seriously, nor do they do serious research on colors that will have an effect on the human system. Interior decorators, as a group, are more cognizant than doctors of the influence of color on moods, as an example, but the approach is more from an aesthetic point of view than an interest in the real healing power of color. Specific colors stimulate a specific kind of energy, so the awareness of how color can affect particular people might be a factor in creating the kind of environment that will stimulate family harmony and happiness.

Man is a veritable rainbow of color. Essentially, he is a spark of light energy, broken off from the whole belt of the spectrum of cosmic, fiery light energy described by Pluto. As we have noted in our discussion of the aura (Chapter 16), man carries that light consciousness into the darkness of the earth plane. Before Edison and electricity, the earth plane, essentially a plane of darkness, had only the light from the Sun, Moon, planets, and stars—all heavenly bodies.

Color is merely a specific refraction of light as it bends around obstacles that diffuse its pure beam. As light comes into denser levels of existence and hits more things in its path, it differentiates into color. Each color and shade is a reflection of different rates of vibrational levels. As a column of light, man carries the same colors in and around his energy field or aura and reflects specific colors depending on the vibratory rate within his system. Each color, with its different rate of vibration, relates to a specific chakra and organ in the body. Starting at the root chakra and continuing upward to the crown chakra, the colors and their relationships are as follows:

> Root chakra—red (sexual organs)
> Sacral center—orange (spleen)
> Solar plexus—yellow (stomach)
> Heart center—green (heart)
> Throat center—blue (thyroid)
> Brow chakra—indigo (pituitary)
> Crown chakra—purple (higher mind, brain)

Each person emits specific colors from his energy field that describe the conditions of his life and his state of well-being. This reflected flow manifests in an aura or emanation around the head. Since the quality of each color in the aura (Neptune) can describe the condition of the related organ, so color therapy can facilitate the rebalancing of the system. This is accomplished through a process of visualization (Neptune). Since a person projects the colors that relate to the organs, he can also put a greater degree of color into that organ if he has not been able to maintain a perfect state of health and balance.

Thought patterns can create color emanations from the body as well, but this may not be conscious everyday thought. Because muscles, organs, and chakras can be the recipients of stress, the level of consciousness of each organ relates to thought patterns. And because man is like a gyroscope, constantly adapting to life circumstances that are unconsciously created by his higher self to facilitate growth, he projects different qualities of energy, vibratory rate, thought, and colors from the chakras as he learns to flex his spiritual muscles. There may be a lack of a specific color in his aura, depending on his daily state of being, or there may be weakness in color emanating from a particular chakra which would describe a weakness in the physical system. With diagnosis of the problem, it is possible to infuse more color into that area of the body by visualizing, imagining, or pulling in more of the color from the unending source of color (representing energy) of the universal supply house.

In Chapter 25, I describe a color meditation that charges and energizes the physical system by augmenting the colors in the chakras through visualization. However, to determine what colors might be especially important for your particular system, take a look at the balance of elements in your astrological chart. You can compensate for any imbalance of elements in your chart by working with the color associated with that element.

Earth relates to brown tones, air relates to blue hues, water relates to green, and fire relates to red. Analyze the amount of each element contained in your individual chart and then relate the colors to those elements. If you are lacking fire or feeling tired, as an example, take a few minutes to energize the system by thinking red or visualizing the element fire. You can also visualize the color red, wear it (in clothing and in jewelry), surround yourself with it, drink it (in the form of crystal essences), and eat it! If you are lacking water or feeling thirsty, you can drink a glass of water as well as visualize the water element or the color green penetrating your whole system. If you lack the air element or are using an extra amount of intellectual energy, you can benefit your system by thinking blue. And finally, if you lack earth or need to ground yourself or develop more practical habits, think brown or earth tones.

In Atlantis, priests and priestesses were really healers, and their temples were designed to use color, sound, and many other elements so that healing could take place. When the healing occurred, spiritual living was automatic. There was no need to intellectualize religious theories, or proselytize, as true healing, which can only occur when all vehicles are in balance, polarizes a man onto the level of spiritual existence. He experiences a connection with his soul and automatically is attuned to energies that exist on that level. If we could adopt the positive qualities of the Atlantean life and avoid the pitfalls that occurred in that highly technological society, we could once again bring forth the sophisticated systems and knowledge that were in existence then.

In the late seventies, I was lecturing in a small midwestern town. A lovely young woman asked for a private appointment in order to do a past-life regression session. When she reviewed a past life, she saw herself in an Atlantean temple and began to describe specific techniques that were connected to healing in those days. She described in detail the use of crystals, and even more importantly, the construction and shape of the room where she was working that allowed light to beam down through an aperture. The light diffused into specific colors that she focused on different parts of the body, depending on the illness, to effect healing.

When this young woman finished her session, she was as startled as I had been over the details and quality of information that she revealed. Although I have conducted thousands of regression sessions over the years, I have never forgotten this lady and her sophisticated knowledge of color healing, which had been completely lost to her in this lifetime. In fact, this lady worked in a factory in the small town where she lived. When we discussed her real potential, I asked her why she was working in a factory. She told me that the hours suited her present schedule, as she was intensely involved in relearning the healing techniques that she had been expert in administering in Atlantean days.

Imagine my surprise when I read an excellent book by Dr. Richard Gerber, *Vibrational Medicine*, and discovered a passage that described the treatment of disease in Atlantean days. Dr. Gerber quoted from *The Revelation of Ramala* by Neville Spearman, who said, "In instances of disease or illness, the Atlanteans recognized that the source of the disease lay not in the physical but in a higher body. Therefore they always cured the higher body, not the physical. If a person was ill he was taken to a place of healing, a temple, and placed in a healing room. This room was constructed of a certain type of stone, of crystal, and was so shaped and angled that the power of the Sun was diffused into beams of different-colored cosmic light and energy. The person was then placed in the middle of the room, depending upon the nature of his illness, so the correct rays of light, and therefore color, were directed onto him.

"Also, of course, the priests of that time, being evolved souls with a high degree of consciousness, could look at the Akashic Record of the person who was ill, for illness is not necessarily only of one's present life, but can stretch back through many previous lives. They could cure, or attempt to cure, the true cause of the dis-ease in that person." The description written by Mr. Spearman was exactly the description given by this lovely lady in her regression session.

Color healing can take place without sophisticated construction of rooms or equipment that beams colored light onto different parts of the body. The use of the mind to visualize color and then to project specific colors onto or into the body is equally effective.

When I do regression sessions, I ask the individual to look inside his body when he is describing emotionally upsetting events, especially those that took place in childhood, to see where he is most likely to tense his body during moments of stress. During stressful incidents in the present, the individual is prone to tense those same areas of the body. This constant wear and tear on the same organ or body part can, over time, create imbalance. More often than not, the tension or gripping occurs in the stomach or the heart. (Sometimes the person sees himself feeling pain in the chest or throat, even arms or legs, but those two areas of the body seem to be hardest hit in most people.) When the person has located the area of gripping, I suggest that he or she begin to visualize color into that part of the body. I suggest the use of a small ball of color, the size of a cotton ball, of a special hue to be projected mentally into that part of the system. I suggest (these are not hypnotic suggestions but recommendations) that the color be projected inwardly to the level of the chakra system.

Most people have no problem discovering where a chakra is located. The color stimulates a sensation or feeling of the exact location of centers in the body that are not found with X-ray machines. In the choice of color during the regression sessions, I trust my instincts and ability to sense rather than see the condition of the chakra, to prescribe specific colors. However, I suggest to the individual that he try out different colors for himself to see which ones create more energy or feeling of harmony.

Testing with kinesiology can give an accurate indication of which colors are lacking in the system, and a look at the astrological chart can also reveal a lack or imbalance in one color or another.

It is not uncommon for a person to gravitate toward specific colors to wear depending on different moods. However, there are some colors that need to be avoided under certain conditions. One of those colors is black. Not only is black associated with a black mood, or depression, but black is an unhealthy color to wear if a person has a very sensitive nature. The color black absorbs, whereas white reflects. If a person is very sensitive, he may not even want to wear black to a funeral; it would be too easy to absorb all the anguish and sadness of the bereaved family, as an example. White is an excellent color to wear during meditation or during any activity that could use a spiritual helping hand, as it can attract more light and reflect outwardly any debilitating influences in the atmosphere or environment.

Spiritual development is aided by wearing a white scarf over the crown chakra during meditation. Each person is sending a beam of light out into the atmosphere, and with the purity associated with the color white, and the activity associated with prayer, inspired reading, or meditation, a person can attract high beams of energy and highly evolved spirit guides to act as a protective force on the path toward enlightenment (or more light, therefore color, energy).

SOUND
. . . .

Music and sound are described by the planet Uranus in the astrological chart. If a person has Uranus on the ascendant, or ruling the rising sign in his chart, or similarly related to the sixth house of health, music may be one of the most important therapies in connection with the healing of his system, for Uranus rules the nervous system in the physical vehicle and the meridians in the etheric system.

With a strong Uranian characteristic to my ascendant (my Cancer rising hooks into my Moon conjunct Uranus in the sign of Aries), I survived a very difficult childhood by studying classical music (playing the piano and singing) from the age of four until my college years. Music, ruled by Uranus, has the same vibratory energy field and characteristic as astrology. John Addey devised his whole system of astrological harmonics on the same principle as harmonics in music. It is now quite clear to me that I became an astrologer only when my musical career was thwarted.

During the early sixties, I joined a group of actors in an organization called Bedside Network. We traveled to nearby veterans hospitals to entertain the patients. Old radio shows were taped, with some actors and many patients playing the various roles, and other actors filling in as technicians and directors. These taped radio shows were played back during the week over the hospital loudspeaker system. There was an exception, however. There was only one group who went into the mental wards, and instead of using radio scripts, music was the activity of the evening. Naturally, I gravitated toward the music room and the mental patients. I was, even then, extremely interested in the effect of music and its place in healing. I was especially fascinated by the way music could stimulate the mind. Instead of singing to the patients, we encouraged them to get up in front of the microphone to sing. We would sing along if the person needed a support system, but most of the time, the mental patients were very eager to express themselves by singing. After their solos, the pianist and I would play back their recorded songs. The looks on their faces was a joy to behold. The music activity was actually used by the staff psychiatrists to help them evaluate the progress of the patients. Week after week, we watched patients getting stronger. Their participation in the music room was a clear indication of their well-being.

There was one notable exception. A man we will call Andrew was in what appeared to be a semicatatonic state. He had white hair and looked to be about sixty-five years old. Andrew never moved from his chair. He held the sheet music and occasionally would mumble a song into the microphone, but his participation was minimal. During one period of time when I was traveling with a Broadway show, I was missing from the music room for about nine months. When I returned, a personable young man was helping set up the chairs, and he greeted me as if he knew me. Since I had a rather blank look on my face, one of the attendants pulled me aside to explain. "Don't you recognize Andrew?" he asked. I was amazed at the difference in his looks, manner, and personality. The psychiatrists reported later that music therapy had played a large part in the transformation that had taken place in Andrew's life.

Music has a rate of vibration that reaches into the physical vehicle because it can establish a resonance between the vibratory rate of the chakras and organs. Sometimes music transcends the physical senses. As an example, people who are deaf can sense the vibrations of music without necessarily being able to hear the pitch and cadences of a melody.

John Beaulieu wrote a book entitled *Music and Sound in the Healing Arts*. John uses music in connection with therapy, and one of the devices that he finds particularly effective is tuning forks. According to John, "Tuning forks provide a simple and effective method for activating the overtone series in meditation and healing. Listening to pure Pythagorean intervals is a method of attunement with sacred sound. Through the act of tapping two tuning forks together we can hear sacred ratios. These ratios are found in nature and are considered by the ancients to be a fundamental part of the human soul or psyche. Each interval can potentially awaken within us a deep universal archetype." John also explains how certain musical intervals create a sympathetic response or resonance within the human mechanism.

It was Barbara Gess, my editor, who introduced me to an amazing demonstration of the effectiveness of John's tuning forks. Over the Thanksgiving holidays, I invited many guests to join me for the long weekend. One of those guests was my former mother-in-law, a Scorpio, who is incredibly vibrant at the tender age of ninety. She has not lost her sophisticated bearing and cultured appearance. She is easily excited and curious about people and things that are new and interesting. Her biggest drawback, at this point in her life, is debilitating back pain that prevents her from gadding about as she is used to doing. The trip from Washington, D.C., to Columbia County, New York, was extremely difficult for her to undertake. After riding on a train by herself to New York and then, with only a day or so in between, driving in a car for two hours, she was feeling quite weak. She was gracious and sociable for the first day, but I noticed she disappeared frequently to retire to her room.

Barbara, who is a musician as well as my editor, was a guest over the weekend and luckily brought her tuning forks to demonstrate their effectiveness. First she demonstrated the tuning forks by healing me. One of the biggest physical problems with writers is lower back pain. I have been free of back pain for many years, but when I spend hours hunched over the computer, the pain is sometimes agonizing. My back pain had been aggravated by the recent move and my hurried unpacking of lots of boxes. When Barbara finished her treatment on my system, I was completely free of any pain in any part of my body, and in fact, I experienced a tremendously exhilarating feeling of euphoria.

The real test was her treatment of my mother-in-law, who has a degenerating condition of the spine not uncommon at her age. Barbara gave her a session with the tuning forks, and when she arose from the bed where she was treated, she was amazed that her pain was gone. For the rest of the weekend, she exhibited an energy and vibrancy that was clearly missing when she arrived. After returning home to Washington a few days after the Thanksgiving weekend, she remarked to a friend, "What did that lovely girl do to me? I haven't had even a twinge of back pain since her treatment, and before that I was unable to move without painkillers." This vibrant lady has Virgo on the ascendant, which puts Uranus on the cusp of the sixth house of health in her astrological chart. Music is clearly the tool to be used for healing her system, as is any technique that relates to the higher level of energy that will affect her neurological or nervous system.

The relationship between tone and color and astrological signs has to do with the harmonics of the vibrational rates of the organs. The fifth harmonic is the one used to indicate conditions of health in the chart, and the fifth harmonic on the tuning forks is the interval related to healing of the physical body.

Each astrological sign has a counterpart relationship to a particular musical note. It is possible to compose a symphony of your own astrological chart by relating it to the appropriate musical notes. Aries relates to the note and key of C. Aries is the first sign of the zodiac and middle C is the first note in the primary musical scale of C. Taurus relates to the first black note on the piano, or C sharp, as well as to that musical key (on the keyboard of a piano). This is also D flat in the musical scale. Gemini relates to the key of D, and that note, D, is the third note on the keyboard, counting the black keys as well. Cancer relates to the musical note of D sharp (or E flat), the fourth key on the keyboard of a piano, whereas Leo relates to the musical note of E. Virgo relates to the note and key of F, and Libra relates to F sharp (or A flat). Scorpio relates to the key of G, and Sagittarius relates to G sharp or A flat. Capricorn relates to A, Aquarius to A sharp or B flat, and Pisces correlates to B. We are then back to middle C and the first sign of the zodiac, Aries.

Each note on a piano can be the beginning note of a musical scale, using the black keys to make the intervals between notes correct. You may try composing your own symphony by selecting the most prominent planets in your chart and correlating them to their individual notes. You may want to start your symphony with the sign that rules your ascendant or emphasize the note that relates to an element that is strong or weak in your own chart. You can determine the amount of elemental energy for your symphony by adding up the planets found in the signs that relate to each element and pull out the notes that relate to that same formula. As an example, with a lot of fire and water in my own chart, and only two little earth planets, I can stabilize my physical vehicle (related to earth element) by humming or playing the notes of D flat (Taurus), F (Virgo), and A (Capricorn). Or I can examine the sensitivity of my Cancer rising combined with the nervous quality of Uranus and find a protective note in E flat (Cancer) and B flat (Uranus) combined with C (Aries). My Moon and Uranus are positioned in the sign of Aries. You can also stress the note that relates to the planet ruling or positioned in the sixth house of health.

Particular pieces of music are inspirational. As an example, the Gregorian chants produce powerful musical vibratory rates. These chants are usually based on the interval of a fifth, and the fifth harmonic is the one associated with healing and balance in the body. Consider too the origin, the meaning of the words, and the source of those chants, and you can see how they can propel an individual into a state of attunement. Musical compositions carry the essence of the vibratory rate of the composer. There are groups who protest certain words in currently popular recordings, whereas they might be more concerned with the subtle vibrations of the groups that are being propelled into the air waves. Usually the words relate to the energy fields as well, but it is the vibrations that can creep into the esoteric nervous system that might be even more damaging.

CHAPTER 22

Crystals and Gems

CRYSTALS

In this exciting period prior to the true dawning of the Aquarian Age, crystals are regarded with interest and respect. However there may not have been such positive properties associated with crystals in Atlantean days. As legend has it, crystal power became a dreadful weapon of destruction at that time. It was wrongful use of crystal power that was credited with the sinking of the vast continent of Atlantis beneath the waves of the ocean.

Every religion has its story of a great flood or cataclysm. The biblical story of Noah and his ark certainly describes that kind of cataclysmic event, but since no other records exist that we know of, it is difficult to know exactly what happened at that precarious time in history. However, when similar stories circulate from many sources, it is hard to pass them off as mere myth. Such is the case with the story of Atlantis. One of the prime sources of the Atlantean story and the events that led to the destruction of this major civilization is the work of Edgar Cayce. According to Cayce, two rival political factions emerged to fight each other over the use of crystal power. Some sources say that it was the Sons of Light attempting to triumph over the Sons of Belial for control of that important source of energy. The end result was that the level of power emitted by the crystals was strong enough to disrupt the balance in the atmosphere and consequently caused earthquakes. The vast continent of Atlantis broke up into smaller islands, most of which eventually sank beneath the waves. Some parts of Atlantis, which spanned the area we now know as the Atlantic Ocean, still exist. The areas around Bimini and the Canary Islands off the coast of Africa are probably the remnants of the opposite shores of that huge chunk of earth. Residents of the Mediterranean island of Ibiza, located off the east coast of Spain, also believe that the magical Balearic island was part of that vast continent. The energy is so high in parts of the island that it literally shoots up from the earth.

According to Edgar Cayce, some of the land that once made up Atlantis would begin to rise off the coast of Bimini during the decade of the sixties. Even though land has, indeed, been sighted on the ocean floor, and what appear to be the remains of temples have been explored by deep-sea divers, many people still consider the story of Atlantis a myth. But it may be important to take the stories seriously, because crystal power in Atlantean times was like the atomic power of today.

In modern times, crystals are the most important component in the manufacture of computers. Microchips that store vast quantities of information are really crystals. (Silicon Valley, the area in California that has spawned the greatest number of computers, is so named in honor of crystals. The crystals used in manufacture of computers have been homegrown, however, and have been charged with very precise added elements to produce variants of natural crystals more suited to use in computers.)

The crystals used for healing are quartz crystals, which grow naturally in the ground. Silica, probably the most abundant mineral on our planet, is the basis for sand, which we melt to become glass. In its crystalline form, silica becomes quartz. Crystals were formed by the slow-cooling molten silica as the earth was being formed. The bubbling molten silica was pushed to the earth's surface and began to change in structure and form the beautiful shape of the crystals we see today. Those crystals are exactly the way they were formed hundreds of thousands of years ago.

Every molecule contained in the quartz structure is exactly like the whole crystal, so the whole crystal is a macrocosm of its molecules. In many natural structures the whole is like every other particle contained therein, but this formation particularly explains the resonance that occurs between groups of crystals. A small crystal can take on the exact properties, characteristics, and power of a crystal many times its size. Therefore, even a small crystal can be programmed with powerful energy, like programming a computer, and can act like a battery to facilitate healing. Crystals can assist with meditation, help increase psychic abilities, increase energy, relieve headaches, balance the aura, and increase the ability to communicate by thought transmission, where the vibratory energy moves to any distance, free of obstructions and misunderstandings (the Plutonian-cosmic level). Crystals act like a magnifying instrument and a transmitter. Crystals are used in radios, as an example, because of their ability to transmit and receive.

If a person inadvertently puts his favorite quartz crystal next to his computer, he may discover that his sophisticated computer programs become scrambled. If you can imagine the powerful use of crystals in connection with computers and radios, you can conceive of the vast amount of good that can be done through the use of them in healing. This concept relates to the ability to bring energy from a cosmic level, described by Pluto, into a level where high energy can be transmitted into the specific energy fields of individuals. The practice of radionics, (see Chapter 23) as an example, uses crystal energy and frequencies to effect healing at a distance, described by Uranus. The cross of electromagnetic energy of man's light body (see Chapter 16) is analogous to the essence of the crystalline energy fields. If an individual can imagine himself as a giant crystal, he is a walking, living, breathing light giver and an agent of healing to everyone with whom he comes in contact, and he needs no other device to bring energy into manifestation. However, as in everything that operates on the highest frequencies of nature (that is, on the etheric, Plutonian level), any use of such a powerful instrument must be accompanied by high motivation and a sense of responsibility. That is a prime requisite in the use of crystals and cannot be stressed strongly enough. Crystals will reproduce exactly what is programmed into them. If everyone used their crystals to create more harmony on the earth plane, you can imagine the force for good that could be created. But imagine also what might happen if negative people, with the intent to do harm, programmed their crystals to that effect.

When a large group of people gather together to protest a social situation, such as a march on Washington to protest inequality or a rally in Malibu to protest the pollution of the earth, public opinion begins to change. If, as well, people gather together in thought, as in meditation with crystals, at a specific time and place, the same concentration of energy can occur and even more powerful benefits accrue. This gathering on the etheric level can take place by working with crystals that are programmed to heal people and specific conditions.

Powerful changes on earth can be effected if everyone reading this book, as an example, would spend a few minutes each day working to heal conditions that are negative and destructive. This can be accomplished by working with a crystal that you program to ensure enlightenment, love, peace, and well-being for each and every human on earth. In this way, each person creates a powerful aura within which only positive results can occur. This involves seeing the ideal conditions for each and every person through the powerful tool of visualization (Neptune). Since whatever thought or deed each individual sends out to humanity must return like a boomerang to the sender, only positive results can occur in life. But the important thing is that the motivation is for the welfare of others, not oneself. The personal benefits come as a result of that motivation.

When Pluto is positioned in, or rules, the twelfth house in an astrological chart, the individual already has a natural, powerful, dynamic ability to transmit thoughts on a subconscious level. They may be totally unaware of such potent psychic energy, and there is where danger can occur. It is essential for a person with this house placement to be aware of their power for good or ill. With high motivation, their thoughts will always be positive and uplifting, and these individuals can act as instruments for the awakening of mankind. Their inner thoughts are the very tools that can be used for healing. But if they carry anger, ill feelings, and malefic intent, their thoughts are just as powerful in causing disharmony. A sense of the responsible use of the mind must be ingrained from childhood with this kind of house placement or position of Pluto in the astrological chart. Without knowledge of such power, much ill health and many difficult conditions can occur, even to the individual himself, if he is unaware of what he is sending out to others, for Pluto acts like a boomerang. If a person with such an already potent mind used crystals to augment what he possesses quite naturally for the welfare of others, he would carry within him a very special motivating force for good on earth. Since ignorance is no excuse and thoughtless actions against other people carry a heavy karmic penalty, these people in particular must use their crystals with loving care and respect, as should the rest of us.

Many people who formerly lived in Atlantis are back on earth again, and we are beginning to reach the level of technology that was achieved in that highly sophisticated society. There are still some things that are waiting to be rediscovered, though. (In Atlantis there was a flying machine called a Valix, which could easily climb to other planets and just as easily plummet to the depth of the seas. We are slowly aiming for space travel with NASA programs, but such a vehicle for common usage seems far off. There are tales of earthships that caused the huge craters that exist in certain locations on earth and can be spotted from the air. These tales do not seem so farfetched now, in light of the blast-offs of rockets from Cape Canaveral in Florida.)

During regression sessions with former Atlanteans, the stories and detailed descriptions that emerge from people with very different earth-plane experiences dovetail exactly. One young lady began to describe what she saw in her mind's eye with great hesitancy. She had never read about Atlantis, yet when encouraged to relate what she saw, her descriptions were exactly as many others have been. She even described the buildings and construction materials that are so different from our present materials and types of architecture. When so many descriptions and stories match exactly, there can be little doubt that these things existed.

Many people who used crystals regularly in Atlantean days are back on earth. We have a second chance, now, to use that same powerful tool to bring about positive changes on earth, rectifying the damage that was done so many centuries ago. With the commitment to effect healing with positive energy, thought forms, and actions, crystals are incredibly effective tools to use for healing. Each crystal develops a "personality" of its own. I have many crystals that I use for different purposes, including one which can be used to energize the whole chakra system.

You can do this too by attaching a fine cord around the middle of a crystal and programming it for healing. This is done by projecting your thoughts and purpose into the crystal by first being clear in your own thoughts. So think of what you want and then blow that thought into the crystal with your breath. Before you program the crystal, give it a bath in saltwater and, if possible, place it in sunlight to clear away obstacles or negativity that prevent free-flowing energy swirling throughout the etheric system. (It is the intent of your thought, sent out with each breath, that programs the crystal.) Place the crystal over each chakra in turn, starting at the root chakra, and allow it to swing freely above each chakra for several minutes. The crystal will indicate when the blockage is cleared by ceasing to swing. As the crystal moves upward along the chakra system, the individual being healed feels energy moving in his body. You can effect healing in your own body by practicing this technique while lying on your bed, swinging the crystal above you.

If I am working on someone else, I ask them to lie facedown on a bed and I work on the chakras from the back first. Then I ask them to turn over and work on the front of the body. It is best to start from the root chakra and work upward. To energize the brain, you can use your hand to sweep energy upward from the root chakra to the head. If you move in the reverse order, you de-energize the brain.

A crystal can also be a very effective tool for protection. I slept with a crystal in my left hand for many years, and it allowed for deep sleep without any anxieties or nightmares. In this case I would program the crystal to protect me from any negative energies or thought forms that might happen to float by when I was not awake enough to detect them. Sometimes if I had forgotten to pick up the crystal, or if I fell asleep before I expected to, I might have awakened in the middle of the night knowing that something was different in the energy of the room.

Sleep can be an important learning time as well. There are some crystals, called record keepers, that contain much information from Atlantean days. These records can once again be revealed to people who are receptive to such information and who are pure of heart. The time of sleep can be especially important for information to come into the subconscious mind. This can be accomplished by holding the record-keeper crystal in the hand or by placing it over the brow chakra. Record-keeper crystals can be recognized by a small triangle embedded on the surface of the crystal itself. (Katrina Raphaell describes record-keeper crystals and their use in her book *Crystal Enlightenment*, published by Aurora Press in Santa Fe.)

Finally, a crystal can be used to send special messages of love to family and friends. Use a special crystal, programmed to transmit those positive messages, and hold the crystal in your right hand. Think of what you wish to transmit and blow the message directly into the "face" of the crystal. One breath will do it. Then turn the face of the crystal in the general direction of the person you wish to receive the message and let the crystal do its work. Crystals can also be calibrated to send energy on a specific vibratory level, much as the radionics machine is able to send vibrations on a specific frequency to a specific person. Crystals can also be calibrated to match the vibratory rate of each organ. Dr. Ilan Bohm, a chiropractor in New York City, has a set of crystals in his office that are so programmed. He uses his crystals in conjunction with other techniques to affect healing to a high degree.

Just as with other techniques, you can use crystals on a simple level, but you can also learn more sophisticated techniques. If you wish to do so, there are many excellent books and teachers. One such inspired teacher, Katrina Raphaell, writes about crystals and their use in *Crystal Enlightenment* and *Healing with Crystals*, both published by Aurora Press. Another expert on crystals is an attractive blond Iroquois lady named Oh Shinnah. I first met Oh Shinnah after attending a large healing conference in Washington, D.C., in 1981, sponsored by the Sufis. The Sufi master Pir Vilyat Khan was present to lead the group in a color meditation each day that set the stage for the most peaceful, though massive, group situation I've ever encountered. After Dolores Kreiger discussed her work of teaching hands-on healing to hospital-staff nurses, she mentioned the workshops conducted by Oh Shinnah on crystal healing.

Oh Shinnah was called into life on a wave of crystal energy. Her mother and father went to a special mountaintop and laid their crystals out to call in a special spirit to be their child. (Many people ask Oh Shinnah if that was all that was needed to bring her in, but she laughs and says she was conceived in the usual manner.) This thoughtful, loving invocation and careful preparation is reflected in her astrological chart, as she has three grand trines! (Grand trines describe a level of protection that is assured throughout any situation that might occur in her life.)

Oh Shinnah underlines the necessity of dispelling "glamour" when dealing with practical subjects. A no-nonsense manner is necessary when one begins to work with high etheric energies, as there are so many incorrect assumptions about the usage of crystals. So it is important to be properly instructed in the care and feeding of your special high-energy tools. Any qualified teacher will give instructions about the original selection of crystals for each purpose and how they should be cared for in order to protect the high vibratory quality. Different types of crystals possess different properties. Rose quartz, a beautiful shade of pink, is especially helpful in healing the heart, as an example.

GEMS

Gemstones carry vibrations in the same way that crystals do, except that they operate on different frequencies. Some gemstones work on the physical level, some on the mental, and some on the spiritual. Diamonds, as an example, are very pure stones and work on the spiritual level. There is good reason that they are so often set in engagement rings, as diamonds carry the purest quality of spiritual energy needed to unite two people in life.

Jade is a particularly important stone to wear as it affords tremendous protection. My favorite jade story was also a story of loss to me. I had been given a beautiful imperial jade ring with a vibrant green color by someone I loved very much who died. The ring was special and I always wore it on my right hand. One day I was walking down Broadway in New York City and stopped to look at some bags that were being sold by a street merchant. After a quick look I decided that I wasn't interested in what he had to sell. As I walked away, I felt a stab in my back between the shoulder blades. I quickly turned around, but no one was behind me. However, the young man who was selling the bags was glaring at me with tremendous anger. I continued walking, but shuddered to think how real that stab had felt to me. I must have been the hundredth person to walk away without purchasing something, and his anger had built toward people in general. When I arrived at my destination, I happened to glance down at my jade ring and saw that the stone was gone. The jade was perfect, with no cracks, and it was set tightly in the ring, so there was no danger of it falling out. However, legend has it that jade will crack before a person will. I was very sad to lose that beautiful stone, but very thankful for the protection it offered. This has happened in several other instances when I have lost pendants of lapis lazuli and other jewelry. Lapis is another very protective stone, working on a mental level.

When you are selecting any crystal or gemstone, take some time to hold it in the palm of your hand. If the stone feels cold or cool, that is not your stone. It should feel quite warm, indicating that the vibrational level is stimulating the vibrations in your own palm. Gems are not only beautiful, they are important tools for balancing energy. Familiarize yourself with the qualities that you want to develop within yourself and select a beautiful gem to assist you in attaining your goals.

There are specific stones that relate to astrological signs, but it may be that there are qualities that you wish to develop beyond what is indicated by your Sun sign. The stone relationship to a particular astrological sign can be indicated by the characteristics associated with, or to be developed in connection with, that sign.

SIGN	STONE	CHARACTERISTICS
Aries	bloodstone and diamond	courage
Taurus	sapphire and turquoise	self-love
Gemini	agate and chrysoprase	loyalty
Cancer	moonstone, emerald, and pearl	protection

Leo	amber, tourmaline, and sardonyx	radiance
Virgo	jade and carnelian	fluency
Libra	opal, coral, and lapis lazuli	universal love
Scorpio	aquamarine, lodestone and beryl	wisdom
Sagittarius	topaz and chrysolite	joyfulness
Capricorn	ruby, malachite, onyx and jet	strength
Aquarius	zircon and garnet	enlightenment
Pisces	amethyst	vision

The color of the stone can have a great deal to do with balancing energy in your body and in the chakras. As an example, the color red is the color of the root chakra, located at the base of the spine. Red-colored gemstones benefit conditions that relate to the blood and can stimulate energy throughout the system. Red stones include the ruby and the garnet and relate to the fire element and specifically to Aries energy.

The second chakra is the sacral or splenic center. The color of that chakra is orange. Citrine and carnelian fall into the category of gems with an orange color. These stones are particularly effective in clearing any congestion in the lungs and for eliminating toxins in the colon, gall bladder, and liver. Carnelian is a mental stone and is effective in removing blocks to communications. These stones relate to the air element and especially to Gemini and Mercury in the chart.

The third chakra is the solar plexus, and it relates to the stomach area. The color of this chakra is yellow. Yellow stones include topaz, golden citrine, and golden beryl. These stones relate specifically to digestive problems, but because intellectual work utilizes the color yellow, these stones stimulate brain activity. They relate to the water element and specifically to the sign of Cancer.

The next chakra is the heart chakra and its color is green. Green stones are emeralds, green tourmaline, and peridot. They help increase vitality and build muscle tissue. Basically, green stones restore tired nerves and can be helpful with romantic or emotional problems and high blood pressure. These stones relate to the fire element and specifically to the sign of Leo.

The throat chakra, located near the thyroid gland, relates to the color blue. Blue stones are aquamarine, celestite, azurite, blue topaz, and some opals. These stones can be used, in general, to benefit thyroid conditions, laryngitis, or sore throats, and can help with depression. People who are overweight may have too little blue in their systems, so these stones can help balance out the system by infusing more blue energy. These stones relate to the air element and specifically to Taurus.

Indigo is the color of the brow chakra, and it relates to the pineal gland and to psychic energy due to its location at the third eye. These stones are sapphires, lapis lazuli, and dark aquamarine. They can help filter out radiation and benefit problems with the eyes, ears, and nose. These stones can be sleep inducing as well. Since dark blue gemstones relate to psychic energy, they relate to the water element and specifically to the sign of Pisces.

Violet is the color of the crown chakra, which relates to the pituitary. Amethyst and violet garnets are particularly important to wear for transformation onto a higher level of spiritual consciousness. They help with splenic disorders, bladder and kidney problems, and in any mental disorders. These stones also relate to the water element and specifically to the sign of Scorpio.

Rose quartz falls into the category of a red stone, but it is especially beneficial in healing the heart. It can also be used to soothe, calm, and relax people with strong Leo in their astrological charts.

There are several companies that produce distilled, liquid stone essences. These liquids can be used in a manner similar to Bach flower remedies. Bottles of the distillation of stones should be tested by using kinesiology to determine which will be most beneficial to an individual imbalance of the system. The tinctures are very powerful, however, so caution must be used regarding the amounts that are consumed. As an example, herkimer in liquid form can create a feeling of spaceyness. Do not take herkimer when driving a car or using machinery, as an example. These essences can be purchased in New York City from Gemmed Stones and from Oh Shinnah at the Center for Grandfather Coyote in Florida, or you can make your own by placing your gemstones in distilled water and in strong sunlight for six to eight hours. The essences need a drop of brandy to act as a preservative.

Radionics

$\mathcal{R}$adionics is a method of healing that is quite familiar to Europeans but is still relatively unknown to Americans. The fact that its popularity has not yet crossed the Atlantic Ocean may be due, in part, to the fact that it seems too mystical to be substantive. Radionics treatment is based on relating to, and working with, the vibratory rate of the energy of the subtle body. The diagnosis and treatment of illness through radionics does not depend on close proximity of the patient to the healer; these cures are effected from a distance.

The system of radionics relates to the planet Uranus and Pluto. Uranus describes the vibratory patterns of radionics, but Pluto describes universal consciousness and matters that are affected on a level where there are no obstacles. (See Chapter 25.) Many dedicated researchers have been able to tap the concept of a universal stream of energy and have devoted their lives to bringing scientific proof to this theory. Wilhelm Reich, as an example, coined the term *orgone energy* to describe this universal source of energy, yet the scientific community had a hard time accepting his theories. (Although science is ruled by Uranus and works on a level that might be described by that planet, the scientific method can be described by Saturn. In other words, the potential for enlightening results can come through science, yet sometimes the rigid methodology necessary to bring proof to these inspired theories can delay or block the results.) The bridge between higher scientific research (Uranus) and the methodology (Saturn), and the comprehension of the cosmic principles that need no proof (Pluto), comes with the ability to trust (Neptune) on a higher level of conception. To be able to accept cosmic principles without fear of contradiction means that research must be conducted; only when those findings have been proven beyond a doubt can they be accepted into society without skepticism. But it still requires faith. This seems to be the bridge that many people cannot cross.

Certainly in the United States people have been hesitant to accept the practice of radionics, for it has been likened to quackery even though very strong evidence of the effectiveness of the treatment can be validated. Many people have been cured by treatment with radionics in Europe, but when broken bones of racehorses are healed so that those same horses can go on to run faster and win more races, concrete evidence exists to show that radionics treatments work. That kind of evidence refutes any claims that the cures are related to naïve acceptance or the power of positive thinking.

The principles of radionics were first discovered by an American. Dr. Albert Abrams, a physician and leading specialist in diseases of the nervous system, made a chance discovery during the examination of a patient that led him to explore and originate a completely new method of diagnosis. He found that he could identify the unique energy patterns of different diseases. Later on, he designed instruments to correct those energy patterns and thereby heal the diseases. Dr. Abrams's basic diagnostic techniques were given credence after an investigation by the Royal Society of Medicine in England. Much valuable research was carried out at Oxford in the 1940s, and a new mathematical precision was added to the process in the identification and treatment of disease. Dr. Abrams's work was carried on by another American, Dr. Ruth Drown, a chiropractor, who added a further dimension to radionics. She discovered that it is possible to treat a patient at a distance by using a blood sample as a link between patient and instrument.

Radionics treatment involves using a small particle of the body to determine the rate of vibration of that person. The frequencies are determined by use of a radionics machine, sometimes called "the little black box." It incorporates a cup to hold the specimen and a series of dials fueled by electricity. The operator puts the specimen (hair, fingernail, or blood sample) in the cup and begins the process of finding the frequency of the individual by placing his finger on a rubber pad connected to the machine. He turns each dial, one by one, until he feels a response in his fingertip. With that subtle-body response he sets all the dials so that the combination of frequencies matches that of the individual to be healed. After finding the frequency of the person's energy and diagnosing the imbalance within the system, the operator of the radionics machine can transmit back to the patient specific frequencies that are needed to effect a healing.

Radionics, as a science, is concerned with the energy patterns emitted by all forms of matter. When radionics is used as a diagnostic tool, as well as a healing device, the distortions in these patterns can be identified and measured so that the trained practitioner builds up a holistic blueprint of the patient for future treatment. (The holographic principle that every particle contains the whole can be related to the cellular structure of the body. Radionics works on that principle by finding the rate of vibrational frequency from hair, blood, or a fingernail rather than the DNA molecular structure.)

The holographic principle indicates that every particle of an object contains the essence of the whole. Holographic photography is a method that allows an object to be photographed so that it can be seen in three dimensions. The amazing part of the process is that if a piece of this photograph is cut away and examined under laser light, a smaller but intact photograph of the original object is revealed, proving the principle in a dramatic way. Since every part of the body carries the rate of vibration of the whole system, the only thing that is needed to find this frequency is a specimen such as a piece of hair or a sample of blood. Just as a piece of an apple contains the ingredients of the whole, the particle of blood or hair contains the energetic structure of the entire organism. By virtue of an affinity between the healing force fields in the Universe, the practitioner sends out frequencies through the air waves which match that of his patient and the cure is effected without any human contact between the practitioner and the patient. The radionics machine works on the same principle as radio waves. Just as each radio station has a broadcasting frequency, which can be received by tuning the dial to that particular band, the radionics machine utilizes the frequency of an individual to tune into the body.

A recent scientific breakthrough concerning the DNA molecular structure confirms that this procedure can be accurate. It has been discovered that a different DNA makeup exists within each human being. That specific DNA pattern can be detected from any part of the body, even if, as is useful in the case of a criminal investigation, the sample—blood, let's say—is very old. This process is now being used by law-enforcement agencies and detectives to enable them to identify criminals through the DNA molecular structure. A particle of a fingernail can also reveal this all-important information. The conclusive proof offered by this new investigative technique may protect many innocent people from being convicted of a crime based on circumstantial evidence.

Specific illnesses and specific organs also have their special rates of frequency. When a particle of the body reveals the vibratory rate, that frequency might match the frequency of arthritis, heart problems, or diabetes, for instance, and a diagnosis can be made of the illness or affliction of the individual without ever examining the patient. The diagnosis will go to the root of the problem of the imbalance, even if symptoms suggest something else. Homeopathic remedies, as an example, also have a vibrational rate. Instead of prescribing a specific homeopathic remedy to be ingested, the radionics practitioner can simply program the remedy rate into the radionics machine and healing is effected altogether on the etheric level.

Crystals and Bach flower remedies also have their specific rates of frequency and can be used with the radionics machine. The effectiveness of long-distance treatment with radionics supports the metaphysical theory that illness originates on the etheric level and therefore must be cured on that level as well.

Perhaps even more important than the potential of curing physical illness and disabilities is the ability to effect cures on a psychological level. Mental illness, anxieties, and hypersensitivity are often aggravated by stress. Wherever tension exists in the body, the natural health-giving life energies cease to flow and illness can occur, sometimes months or years later. Since radionics allows the practitioner to deal with the whole patient, not just the outward evidence of symptoms, relief can occur on all levels: physical, mental, and emotional. And since radionics treats the whole system, an astrological chart can indicate the need for treatment in general if any planet that rules the ascendant or the sixth house is in difficult aspect to any other planet. Therefore, radionics can be used to cure any physical weakness, tiredness or serious disability as well as any specific illness that is indicated in the astrological chart.

Psychic healers automatically work on this higher, Plutonian level by attuning their energy to universal etheric energy and naturally projecting that vibrational frequency to the patient. That quality of healing energy is not broken down into specific frequencies, but works on an overall level, much as rest is a cure-all for fatigue, whether the fatigue comes from overwork, lack of sleep, or stress. However, the ultimate success of treatment with radionics seems to relate to the level of consciousness and sensitivity of the operator of the little black box. The practitioner must also be a pure instrument with the motivation of working on a higher cosmic level (Pluto).

So the practitioner may utilize Bach flower remedies, crystals, homeopathic remedies, or color, as he sees fit. Since radionics treatment might be capable of affecting karma, it is important to determine whether such assistance falls within the karmic context of the patient. This is where the ultimate cosmic sense of responsibility and motivation (Pluto) on the part of the practitioner enters in. To treat someone against his will is to "rescue" and invite disastrous results. The patient must not only want to be treated, but also to get well, or it would be considered unethical to give treatment at all.

My introduction to radionics came at the first new-age health conference I held in Ibiza, Spain. One of my guests was a lovely English lady, Sybil Baillie, who wore a neat tweed suit and looked as if she had just arrived from her country home to have tea at Brown's in London. Her conservative image was put to rest when she rose from the audience to discuss her work with radionics. She described how she healed people, on a regular basis, by sitting at home and sending out vibrations by way of a little black box. Sybil's discussion of the cures affected by the use of radionics could not be doubted. Her entire persona bespoke a serious commitment and dedication to her work. However, it can be hard to ignore the possibility of the power of suggestion with such cures.

One of the stories she told made an indelible impression. Sybil began her healing work by using homeopathic medicines, treating only her family and some close friends. After her children were grown and with time on her hands, she studied radionics and eventually began to practice on a more serious basis. Her enlarged clientele was sufficient to keep her quite busy.

One day the family dog was missing. When Sybil went looking for him, she discovered that he had been outside in the rain for a whole night. She found him lying limply by a fence, unable to walk into the house. Since he was sixteen years old and looked quite the worse for the wear, she expected that this adventure might be his last. She felt quite sad, but decided the least she could do would be to give him a radionics treatment. She didn't expect any result except that she might help him die in a less painful way. To her great surprise, a few hours after the treatment the dog got to his feet, shook himself with the vigor of a puppy, and went outside to continue the adventure that was cut short by the rain and his momentary illness. The dog lived another five years. Since the dog wasn't affected by the power of suggestion and he had obvious symptoms of pneumonia, it would be safe to say that his cure was the result of the treatment.

Sometime later I accompanied Sybil to a radionics conference in London and was spellbound by another animal story. An elegant white-haired lady confessed that her practice had become so large, she'd decided to confine herself to treating horses. After a short time she was so busy, she was even more overworked. When top trainers realized that she could save their prize horses even after a leg had been broken, she was swamped with work. She's treated racehorses from England to Australia. Generally, if a Thoroughbred breaks a leg, he is destroyed as an act of mercy. If he can be saved, his breeding value may remain intact, but his glory days are past. After being treated through radionics, however, these exquisite patients not only continued to race, they piled up even more wins than before. It appeared that they possessed a renewed level of energy as well as knitted bones. The lady's statistics were quite impressive. Treatment and cure was effected at a distance of hundreds and even thousands of miles.

Research has been in progress for some time into the use of radionics in connection with agriculture and horticulture. These investigations can be very important to counteract the present-day use of chemical fertilizers, weed killers, and pesticides. Since the overall concept of radionics is one of restoring harmony and equilibrium, working with the forces of nature through radionics may be one way of healing our planet.

Since individual health is very dependent on the restoration of balance on earth, especially for future generations, the healing of Mother Earth is one of the most important current issues in our society. It is essential that each individual focus his attention to that end. The wholehearted acceptance and use of theories and methods of healing that have proven to work on a natural level can be an all-important first step toward better life on earth.

Dream Analysis

he higher self has many ways of trying to get information down into the level of concrete consciousness, and dreaming is one of them. Neptune is the planet that describes the dream state. It also describes fantasies and concepts of the waking state. We may not clearly understand how and why ideas and concepts are suddenly born, but we do know that fantasies play a large part in the creative potential of an individual. So if we can learn how to activate the right hemisphere of the brain more fully and trust our dreams and concepts, we can allow more creative potential to enter our lives.

One of the best ways of revealing information of a higher nature to ourselves is through dreams. Many therapists use only dream analysis in their work with their patients. Of course, Sigmund Freud was the first and most famous therapist to adopt the theory that dreams consistently reveal information to the individual from the subconscious mind. Carl Jung then took matters a step farther and coined the term *collective unconscious*. His belief was that we not only have a subconscious mind of our own, but that mankind has a higher connection to each other through the collective unconscious, and that information is accessed and passed on from that level, as well as from the subconscious mind. This theory seems to be borne out through the *hundredth monkey theory*. That term was adopted because of the amazing behavior of monkeys in South Pacific islands. The monkeys had always eaten their potatoes unwashed. One day, a monkey walked to the water's edge and began to wash his potato before he consumed it. Soon all the monkeys were washing their potatoes. But the amazing part of the theory is that monkeys on other islands suddenly began washing their potatoes, too. The monkeys on the first island didn't seem to have any method of revealing the new procedure to their cousins far away, but somehow the other group of monkeys got the message.

Jung developed a specific method of interpretation of the symbols that come through dreams. Many therapists have added to what both Freud and Jung developed in connection with dream interpretation and have devised their own systems. The famous psychic Edgar Cayce made an important observation about dreams when he pointed out that all dreams about vehicles represent the human body. A house can also represent the body. If, for instance, a person has a dream about faulty plumbing in his house, it doesn't take a great deal of scientific training to make the connection that the broken plumbing system in the house might indicate that the plumbing system in the body of the dreamer may need some attention.

Not all dreams are that simple or clear, however. The gestalt method of interpreting dreams is one that reveals many profound yet obscure truths through the language of dreams. Interpreting a dream in the gestalt manner is done by creating a dialogue between two factors in the dream. This facilitates a clear analysis of the dream. In order to act out the conversation between these two opposing voices, it is helpful to place two chairs so that they face each other. Each chair represents one person or a voice selected from the dream. The first step is to become one part of a dream. That part of the dream, either a person or an object from the dream, occupies one chair. To occupy the second chair, it is necessary to choose to be another part of the dream. That part may also be a person or an object from the dream. The two parts of the dream then begin to have a conversation.

When this is done in a therapeutic situation, the person analyzing his own dream moves from chair to chair as he takes on each part of the dream. When you are doing this for yourself, you may ask a friend to direct you to move from one chair to another, or you may use your imagination to visualize each part of the dream and each part of the conversation. It is a little more difficult when you do this on your own, but it can be done with patience and trust in yourself. As you continue the dialogue, which is necessarily contradictory, a message begins to emerge.

A correlation can be made between aspects in an astrological chart and dreams. In my book *Astrological Aspects, Your Inner Dialogues*, I propounded the theory that difficult or hard aspects between planets represent the difficult and contradictory messages that are continually stimulated in a person's life. Whether an individual can understand the message from the comprehension of his astrological chart alone, or whether dreams must come forth to make those messages clear, is unimportant. The important part of what dreams and astrological symbolism are trying to reveal is the necessity of reconciling those conflicting dialogues.

Let's use a dream I had many years ago as an example. In my dream, I was waiting for my friend Alex, a very popular and handsome actor, to meet me and other friends of his in a pretty little coffee shop. Alex's two male friends were discussing a plan to kill him. They seemed unconcerned that I might overhear them and didn't seem to notice the look of horror on my face. I simply couldn't believe my ears. These two men were Alex's best friends. When Alex arrived, he took a seat near me, and I began to warn him of what was to take place. I told him, as quietly as possible, what I had overheard and how I planned to thwart their attempt to do away with him. His response was to completely disavow what I was telling him. He said, "Jeannie, don't be ridiculous." I continued to stress that I was telling him the truth and there was good cause to be worried. I told him that his friends were going to capture him and take him away in an open Jeep, but that I had a plan. I would sit in the middle of the backseat, between one friend and Alex, and when the Jeep turned a corner, I would give a good push and shove him out of the Jeep so that he could get away. He continued to ignore my warning and tell me he wouldn't even listen to me. I began to feel frustrated and foolish. I decided that I better save myself since I couldn't seem to convince him of the danger. As we climbed into the Jeep, he sat in the middle and I found myself on the left side of the backseat. As the Jeep turned a corner, I jumped out and ran down an alley to my apartment. No one was chasing me, but nevertheless, I was happy and safe when I climbed the steep winding stairs to the top of what looked like a water tower that seemed to be my apartment.

When I awakened from that dream, I hadn't a clue what it could mean. I selected one part of the dream to analyze. I became me and figuratively sat in one chair. Then I became my friend Alex and mentally sat in the other chair. We began a dialogue. I said, as me, "How can you be so carefree and appear never to worry about anything at all?" Then from the point of view of my friend Alex, I said to myself, "Jeannie, life is too short to worry." As me, "But you seem so unconcerned about everything except what brings you pleasure." As Alex, "Jeannie, you know I work very hard, but I take life as it comes. If you cannot enjoy things, life is not worth living." The conversation continued in that vein, until I finally understood what my dream was trying to reveal.

I have Pluto right on the ascendant, but I have Saturn in the sixth house in exact opposition to Pluto and therefore opposite my ascendant. Saturn acts like a restraint that might come in the form of health problems or pressures that would prevent me from living the life of a totally indulgent child. One part of me, especially when I was younger, wanted to be like a willful child, whose message is "I want what I want when I want it." Some part of me longed to be a carefree, playful child, indulged by a loving daddy, with the same kind of seemingly carefree life led by Alex. But another part of me was overly concerned with serious matters. I became a workaholic and was very stoic about responsibilities. Having never had an indulgent father, I had whipped into the parent ego state (represented by Saturn) as a tiny child and adopted the idea that I must take the weight of the world on my own shoulders. The resulting tension in the body naturally affected my abundant health and vitality (represented by Pluto). The necessary struggle that would reconcile the conflicting parts of myself was revealed through the dream.

What my dream was telling me was that each part of my dream is a part of me and that it was time to balance these parts (oppositions in the astrological chart) before it was too late. I represented Saturn in the chart, whereas Alex represented Pluto. The fact that I chose the Saturnian facet as myself made clear which aspect of me was winning at that time. Alex appeared to be a carefree international traveler and playboy without a worry in the world. My life, at that time, was so pressured that I hardly had time to leave my apartment to take care of necessities other than my work. The water tower even accurately described my apartment, which was located on a high floor at the back of a very interesting building in New York. But the apartment was somewhat isolated from the rest of the building.

Since it was clear that it was time to incorporate some fun and relaxation into my life, I decided to travel somewhere at least once every two months. Eventually this culminated in living my life in two places. I spent part of the time in Ibiza, Spain, where no one comprehends my desire to work, and the rest of the time in New York, a very high-pressured city of ambitious people. Ibiza is a Scorpio island, called the Island of Love, but there is a very high spiritual side as well. I did manage to write two books there, even though everyone commented that no one can ever get any serious work done on the island. But I also helped start a theater group and took part in the production of *Oliver!*, which was the first in a series of annual, extravaganza musical productions each Christmas that utilized the extraordinary talents found on that island. So that allowed me to express the Plutonian Scorpio side of myself. New York is a Cancer city. (I am a Scorpio with Cancer on the ascendant.)

That dream has become even more meaningful with time. I can give myself permission to combine two life-styles and know that is the way I can achieve balance in my life.

You can also use the aspects in your astrological chart as a way of getting in touch with inner conflicting dialogues. Select an aspect in your chart that you do not understand. For instance, if you have a planet in opposition to your ascendant, or to a planet located in the first house, choose those two planets as the two dialogues you want to reconcile (just as the two I chose in my dream). Pick a phrase for each planet as a start. If Venus is one of the planets involved, a Venusian message says, "I just want everything to be peaceful. I really need harmony. I don't want to make waves.

Peace at any price." Let's say the Moon is opposite Venus in your chart. The messages of the Moon are, "I'm easily hurt and very vulnerable, so please don't hurt my feelings. I feel abandoned. Since I didn't get nurtured in life, I don't expect to be understood and nurtured now." If these two planets begin to talk to each other and establish a dialogue, as in my example, you will understand very quickly what the conflicting messages are saying in your chart. In this case, with Venus and the Moon in opposition, it would be difficult for you to ask for what you want because of your vulnerability and fear of more abandonment. Therefore, instead of allowing pleasure, peace, and love into your life, you might take the easy way out and neglect to ask for what you crave. Other people (represented by the Moon) may never understand that the nicer you are, the less you get your own needs met. You then continue in a pattern where lack of pleasure, or too much adaptability on your part, keeps you vulnerable and hurt.

PHRASES FOR
EACH PLANET

SUN—I must be the boss and have my own way. Please tell me I'm wonderful. I need to be acknowledged.

MOON—Please don't hurt my feelings. I'm very vulnerable.

MERCURY—Stick to the facts, please. I need concrete proof in order to make my decision.

VENUS—Just be nice. Good manners go a long way toward resolving conflicts.

MARS—A good argument clears the air. How boring life would be if everyone agreed about everything.

JUPITER—I need to be optimistic about everything, so don't rain on my parade.

SATURN—Life is not just a bowl of cherries. A meaningful existence sometimes means hardship, but responsibility pays off.

URANUS—Don't fence me in. I can't stand to follow the rules someone else has set.

NEPTUNE—Life is beautiful and people are just wonderful. If you don't have trust, you're nowhere.

PLUTO—I want what I want when I want it, the way I want it. So don't get in my way.

If you do not have a copy of your astrological chart, refer to the Appendix for information about ordering one.

Meditation

*B*esides their music, one of the most important contributions the Beatles made to Western civilization was the introduction of meditation to masses of people. As a result of their trips to India in the sixties and their investigation into the practice of meditation, they inadvertently gave permission to millions of people in the West to follow their lead. Their guru, the Maharishi Mahesh Yogi, became a guru to many people, and transcendental meditation turned into a million-dollar business as a result. It is quite likely that people who never would have been tempted to try meditation became interested in that discipline because it was the fashionable thing to do. Whatever the individual motivation, it became a popular sport rather than an exclusive activity of holy men in the East.

The Beatles' trip to India resulted in the Maharishi's second visit to the United States. He had gained a small following on his first trip to America in the late fifties and had taken a group back to India with him. After the Beatles' approbation, he was received with great fanfare and acclaim in this country. Within a short time, his organization was reaping fantastic earthly benefits by charging $75.00 for a personal mantra. (That fee would be worth about

$475.00 by today's monetary standards, if a standard .08% rate of inflation per year were considered.) Many teachers, such as the young Maha-ji and Bagwhan, followed the Maharishi's pilgrimage to the seat of financial security. Soon everyone who could afford it had a guru. Certainly there were many devoted and highly· evolved teachers, but there were just as many charlatans who emerged to take advantage of a hot trend. Along with the ashrams of Indian spiritual leaders came groups devoted to the Jim Joneses of the times. Many tragedies have occurred in the name of spiritual enlightenment, the latest being the sexual indiscretions and financial scandals that have come to light in connection with television evangelists.

When new trends begin to reveal signs of tarnish, it is fairly common to throw the baby out with the bathwater. As a result, occult practices became somewhat suspect, and the practice of meditation is not as widely discussed as it was in the days of the flower children. Truly devoted seekers of the truth continue to practice meditation quietly on their own, without outer signs that broadcast their practice to others.

Many people operate on a humanitarian and spiritually elevated level without daily meditation, but meditation enables a person to consciously and deliberately go into an alpha state (described by Pluto), which builds the quality and strength of the aura (Neptune). Consequently, this higher level of energy feeds the brain with supercharged fuel. (See Chapter 16.) Creatively active people must be able to tap a source of inspiration (Uranus), whether conscious or unconscious, that enables them to express a greater degree of creative results. Actors and musicians, as an example, study their craft for years to learn how to develop techniques they can fall back on if they are not "up" for a performance.

In spite of his heavy drinking, Richard Burton depended on some mystical inner process that enabled him to achieve greatness on the stage and in films. He couldn't explain what happened or how it came about, even to himself. An actor, dancer, or musician must give a performance that transcends his personal feelings, even if he is sick or emotionally devastated. For example, many dancers have given truly great performances when they are in great pain from injured muscles or ligaments. Artists have painted their greatest masterpieces when they were in true agony of the soul. Mozart composed soul-soaring music when he was terribly ill.

Sandy Meisner, a superb acting teacher, created an exercise for his students that helped to develop a higher level of interaction between two actors. He used the term *independent activity* to direct his students' attention onto a transcendent level and away from acting a part. One student was to concentrate on an activity that was enormously compelling, such as carving a sonnet on the head of a pin. The other student was to focus on getting the attention of the first actor away from his activity so that a creative friction could exist. When the two actors are completely involved in their independent activities, it is as if the left hemisphere of their brain (Mercury) is so completely occupied that the right hemisphere (Neptune) is free to soar to new levels of inspiration. (This is the kind of concentration that is developed with meditation so that loftier thoughts and energy become part of the individual system.) When a second actor entered the scene in progress, it had to be done in such a way that it would automatically pull the first actor's attention away from that activity. Otherwise the first actor would continue concentrating on his activity. When the true interaction took place, something special happened. Higher energy was released, sparks were generated, and electricity (Uranus) was in the air.

Great singers such as Joan Sutherland can produce almost otherworldly sounds that seem to emerge from the ethers by concentrating on techniques that free the vocal cords from any strain. These techniques enable a pure sound to emerge that seems to reverberate outside of the singer's aura. This quality of attention and concentration is, in itself, a form of meditation. All great singers, dancers, and actors use their bodies as vehicles and learn how to allow a quality of energy and activity to pour forth that is distinctly beyond the norm. This is meditation in action, for the meditation process must be accompanied by creative work or it is purely mystical. That in itself is not futile, but it is passive rather than active, and thus only the first step.

If a person has chosen to walk the path of enlightenment and to tap a universality within himself, daily meditation is the single most important activity he can engage in. It is only through this concentrated practice that a firm connection is made between the spiritual nature and the physical, mental, and emotional vehicles. There are no shortcuts.

The deliberate attempt to bring higher energy into all daily activities stabilizes that mystical process of creativity, and meditation then becomes the platform of the greatest security in life. Daily meditation eventually brings profound changes into the external events in one's life. Motivation (Pluto) to use this higher energy for the well-being of mankind is the match that lights the cosmic fire which must, then, boomerang in a positive way. Most importantly, meditation enables each person to touch the people around him on a higher level of consciousness. The supercharged energy produces a magnetic force which enables others to tap their own level of soul consciousness. And energy that is sent out must return in kind, magnified many times. Therefore, inadvertently, when the underlying motivation is for the well-being of all of mankind, a higher energy is released in one's own life. This concept of motivation is the true key to unlocking the mysteries of Plutonian energy.

Pluto describes the cosmic playground. It is on that level of existence that all doors are opened. The deliberate and conscious choice to transmute the little will (I want what I want when I want it) onto the higher level (I want only what is right for all concerned) brings a release from the burden of making the wrong choice. The higher self has a chance to bring in what is truly productive and positive for one's life. There may be some blocks, however, to easy access of such existence if there are karmic guilts to be resolved from other times. But even if the automobile has already been damaged from careless driving, either in the present life or from a past-life situation, the desire to take responsibility to repair the damage lifts the consciousness to a new level.

The Akashic Records store all thoughts, deeds, and actions of anyone who has ever lived on earth. In the days before computers, it seemed impossible to have so much information housed in the ethereal space, but now that we understand how microchips store data, it doesn't seem so farfetched anymore. Each person can access and read his own records by lifting his consciousness to the cosmic, Plutonian level, and when an individual is ready to face the truth about his past deeds and make restitution, he is able to read his own records quite easily. He needs no props, such as hypnosis, to be able to read, confront, and deliberately set about rewriting those records. In fact, it is important to go to those records cold turkey, and to do so willingly, so that the conscious mind becomes part of the process. For it is the coordination of tapping higher consciousness (Pluto) and integrating the concrete mind (Mercury) which allows man to walk with his feet on the ground and his head in the skies. Meditation facilitates this kind of coordination and puts the power of the mind into proper perspective.

Although prayer is an important religious activity, its function is quite different from that of meditation. Prayer (Mercury) is basically a function of asking, whereas meditation opens avenues for listening (Uranus). Visualization (Neptune) is similar to prayer in that it creates an avenue for the manifestation of higher spiritual concepts (Pluto) to materialize on the earth plane (Saturn). Meditation makes the results of visualization easier, as the mind becomes more in control of the thoughts, rather than the other way around.

There are many methods of meditation and many misconceptions about its practice. Meditation is more than just a way of establishing a peaceful inner feeling. It serves a very practical purpose in the everyday process of living, of raising the vibrational and health level within the human system. More importantly, daily meditation creates the actual bridge, called the Antahkarana, of subtle etheric structure that serves as a conduit, allowing free passage of energy from the higher etheric level (Pluto) down through the denser bodies. Conversely, it allows the spiritual part of man (Uranus), trapped in his dense physical vehicle (Saturn), to bring forth a higher level of energy to light up the heavy physical body. Each man has his own specific atomic point in the ethers. Through meditation, each person can find his own point in the heavens and actually come into contact with his soul. The yearning for the soul connection is the basis of all longings in life. For with the awareness of that higher point, man can tap an eternal wellspring of abundant joy.

Perhaps the greatest misconception about meditation is that it is a passive activity. Certain kinds of music serve an important inspirational function, for example, creating an external ambiance that can penetrate the very pores and cells of all the systems of the body, but listening to music is a passive experience rather than an active one. Meditation must incorporate active concentration to bring about the desired results. Many individuals are concerned about an inability to control the mind and thoughts during meditation. Some may try to create a mental void. This focus on deficiency and failure disappears with the true method of meditation, which is active. Meditation is a profoundly engrossing process of concentration, but that concentration must be on something rather than on nothing. The end result is a dynamic ability to build more creative thought forms.

By the very nature of man's descent into the earth plane, the focus of his existence is brought down into density. One of the physical laws ruling existence on the earth plane is the law of gravity (Saturn). And it is important for man to be grounded in order to exist on the physical level. It is difficult to function efficiently if one is flying above the earth like Peter Pan. Before entering the physical plane, each individual builds a heavy framework in the form of a bony skeleton (Saturn) to protect the fragile spiritual nature from the force of the elements, like choosing an automobile that will make travel safer and easier. In imagination we could color gravity, and the physical body, in dark tones. But meditation is the science of light, and its practice develops the ability to work with the substance of light energy. With meditation, the physical vehicle becomes illuminated with the light of the spirit, which shines through darkness on the physical plane. The difference in the quality of life before and after the practice of meditation is the difference between walking on a road on a very dark night without a flashlight, and walking on the same road on a night brilliantly illuminated by the full moon. Meditation turns on an inner lamp and fans a brighter inner flame.

The spiritual nature of man is the true driver of his vehicle. If the driver of a car is tired, asleep, or is not properly positioned in the driver's seat, the automobile may take an erratic or even dangerous course on the roads. When the spiritual part of man enters the body before birth, during birth, or shortly thereafter, it is not uncommon to feel reluctant about taking another trip on the highway of life. A person may consciously or unconsciously avoid taking full control of the operation of his own automobile. He may try to drive with half of his spiritual body hanging out of the window or slumped down so that he can't really see the road ahead. Meditation enables the spiritual body to sit upright, fasten the seat belt, and take conscious, efficient, and effective control. At an even higher level, meditation allows the spiritual self to attune to a protective automatic pilot that is clearly more sophisticated and always aware of the road conditions ahead.

The ideal meditative state is to live each moment in touch with one's own specific atomic point in the ethers. Then every activity is a form of meditation. Joseph Campbell stated that underlining sentences in books was his form of meditation. No matter what method one chooses, it is the daily exercise of controlling the thoughts formed by the mind so that those thoughts are born on a higher level of consciousness that is important, for the mind is the builder. When one can focus attention and concentration at will, thoughts are directed from an inner state of clarity rather than from reactions to outer circumstances. At that point, a person is on the way to greater liberation and freedom. Fear, anxieties, and worries have no room to grow roots when the calm inner light is bright. The condition of the physical body may or may not always reflect that inner state of being, but there is one window into the inner being, and that is through the eyes. If one has ever looked into the eyes of a master, the brilliance of the light is unmistakable.

Meditation can be used to heal oneself and to heal others. A healer must first develop alignment of all his own vehicles in order to emit a frequency of healing energy through his system. A true healer works with the magnetic force and radiation of soul energy. It is through his own daily meditation that he is able to tap his own soul consciousness (finding his own atom) and then understand how to radiate the soul will to the soul level of the person who is to be healed (finding the specific atom of the other person). The radiation of the healer's energy illuminates the person to be healed. The radiation from the healer must also be high enough in frequency to impose a vibratory rate that will charge the splenic center of the other person. (We have noted that etheric energy enters the body through the spleen and therefore through the center between the shoulder blades and into all the chakras.) The patient is either completely healed or is enabled to live more peacefully if he is handicapped by the karmic limitations that manifest in the physical body.

Dr. Andrijah Puharich, the physicist who sponsored Uri Geller's visits to the United States, found a way to measure the energy from the hands of healers by having them charge a glass of water. He discovered that the measurable electrical content of the water was the same for all the specialized healers he tested. They were able to charge water to a level of eight megahertz. Through meditation, each individual begins a process of raising his own vibratory rate to a higher level, first through the alignment of the vehicles. With the additional motivation of developing healing ability and being of service to mankind, a person begins to polarize himself onto the level of soul will rather than that of personal will.

There are several ways to meditate. It is possible to meditate on symbols, colors, sound, the chakras, on mantras, invocations, and on seed thoughts. It is advantageous to pick one type of meditation that seems most comfortable and stick with that method. After the practice of meditation becomes second nature, it is possible to choose a different type of meditation for a specific purpose or to practice more than one method on a daily basis.

First, it is important to sit in a comfortable position, but with a straight back. This way the energy can flow straight down through the crown chakra into the system. If it is possible to sit in a yoga position, with ankles placed on top of opposite thighs, do so. A half yoga position will do nicely, however, if you cannot achieve the full position. (Half position is achieved by sitting erect on a flat surface with the left leg bent and the left heel pulled tightly into the groin. The right leg is bent and the right heel is placed on top of the left thigh. If you simply cannot lift the right leg on top of the left, the closest approximation is still beneficial.) Open hands and legs allow energy to dissipate outside of the body; the yoga positions close off the electrical circuits of the body, allowing the energy and vibrations to cycle through the body, thereby facilitating the continual buildup of vibrations within. You may continue to close off the circuits by placing each thumb and forefinger together and then placing the hands on the knees. Tibetan lamas teach another method of rechanneling energy throughout the system: loosely place slightly curved hands in front of the body, with thumbs together, at the solar plexus. The elbows are slightly extended at the side of the body.

In the Indian technique, the eyes are closed. The Tibetans, however, meditate with downcast eyes that are slightly open. The gaze is directed at a point on the floor in front of you, a comfortable distance away. This open-eye method accomplishes two things: it inhibits any tendency to fall asleep, and it facilitates a constant state of meditation, even when one is walking around. If you can meditate with your eyes slightly open, you can meditate anytime, anywhere. If you are meditating on symbols or the chakras, however, you may find it easier to close your eyes.

A mantra is a word or a phrase that carries high vibratory energy through its meaning. It can be a seed thought that invokes a noble purpose or feeling, for instance. The sound, repeated over and over again, focuses attention on its esoteric meaning. One mantra that is universal and extremely powerful is "ohm mani padme hum" (Ohm mah'ne pahd'me hoom). This is the short form of a longer mantra that invokes a feeling of compassion for mankind in general, and each sentient being in particular. This mantra works on the heart center to develop a feeling of universal love. It is a beautiful phrase to repeat over and over again, opening the heart chakra to new energy. It is particularly important to say when the heart feels constricted.

The period of time just before the full Moon is noticeably very high in energy. Universal energy begins to build with the new Moon phase, reaching its fullness with the full Moon, only to slack off in the Moon's waning phase. If a person can attune himself to the same rhythm in his scheduled activities, he operates on the same cycle as nature and can achieve greater harmony within his system. It is a good idea to start new activities with the advent of the new Moon and allow them to develop until the full Moon. It is possible to invoke and breathe in greater physical energy from new Moon to full Moon. Meditation, especially the night just before the full Moon, is especially potent at this time. It is necessary to consciously open the system to take in a new level of energy, however. Otherwise, the energy bounces around throughout the unbalanced system, causing havoc with emotional reactions. There are groups that meet just prior to the full Moon for the purpose of invoking energy, which can then be dispensed individually toward all sentient beings in the following waning period. It is not uncommon to hear snoring from many people in these groups, as people often fall into deep sleep when surrounded by very high energy. If the system cannot handle the level of vibration that is generated, the protective device of sleep shuts them away from excess electrical energy they may not be able to take in. For information about full Moon meditations, contact Lucis Trust, 113 University Place, New York, NY (212-982-8770); London, England; or Zurich, Switzerland for information.

Another very powerful meditation is called the Great Invocation. The Great Invocation was given to Alice Bailey, who wrote many books for the master D. K. Although these books are quite esoteric, they reveal many truths for students who are ready and bring about a level of inspiration that is almost a meditation in itself.

The Great Invocation

From the point of Light within the mind of God
Let light stream forth into the minds of men.
Let light descend on earth.

From the point of Love within the heart of God
Let Love stream forth into the hearts of men.
May Christ return to Earth.

From the center where the will of God is known
Let purpose guide the little wills of men.
The purpose which the Masters know and serve.

And from the center which we call the race of men
Let the Plan of Love and Light work out
And may it seal the door where evil dwells.

Let Light and Love and Power restore the Plan on earth.

It is very beneficial to repeat this mantra at least once or twice a day in combination with other methods of meditation you might choose.

Another powerful mantra is the Twenty-third Psalm from the Old Testament in the Bible. Each phrase of this psalm actually stimulates a specific chakra as it is repeated. The benefits from the stimulation of the chakras can be increased by mentally focusing on the correct chakra with each phrase.

The Lord is my shepherd; I shall not want (root chakra). He maketh me to lie down in green pastures (sacral): he leadeth me beside the still waters. He restoreth my soul (solar plexus): he leadeth me in the paths of righteousness for his name's sake (heart chakra). Yea, though I walk in the valley of the shadow of death, I will fear no evil: for thou art with me; thy rod and thy staff they comfort me (throat chakra). Thou preparest a table before me in the presence of mine enemies (crown chakra): thou anointest my head with oil; my cup runneth over (brow chakra). Surely goodness and mercy shall follow me all the days of my life: and I will dwell in the house of the Lord forever.

Notice that the attention goes from throat chakra straight up to the crown chakra, bypassing the ajna or brow chakra until the last. This directs energy throughout the entire chakra system and then sends forth energy to mankind through the center between the eyes.

Meditation on symbols representing the physical, mental, and emotional bodies helps to align the three major vehicles through which we operate on the earth plane. First visualize a circle and mentally place a dot inside (this relates to the physical level of being). See the circle moving clockwise and then place a dot inside, each time the circle rotates. Continue to see the circle moving clockwise with a dot in the middle. Do this for five minutes. Next visualize an equal-sided cross (this represents the emotional level of being). Do this for five minutes. Finally, see an equilateral triangle for five minutes (this relates to the combination of physical, emotional, and mental levels of being). You may have difficulty making one or more of these symbols clear in your mind. Be patient and continue trying to see them clearly. You can see white symbols on a dark background or black symbols on a white background. Either way is effective. If one or more of the symbols presents some difficulty, you can be sure that symbol represents one of the vehicles that needs balancing the most. Keep on focusing your attention on all three symbols. Eventually, you will find a greater synchronization between all three vehicles, and you will feel new energy as a result of alignment and balance.

To facilitate new energy moving throughout the system, some

motion can be useful, as can sound and the visualization of color. Tibetan monks sway slightly during meditation. That helps to free the body mechanism, allowing energy to pour through all the vehicles. You can aid this process by imagining the spirit finding its perfect balance within the physical vehicle. Chanting utilizes sound, vibration, and the breath to lift the level of consciousness.

It is possible to augment the natural color of the aura through a form of meditation and visualization of color, for color in the system is important for a vital constitution. (See Chapter 21.) Sound is also very important for maintenance of high energy. Playing spiritual music, such as the Gregorian chants, or listening to temple bells during meditation is a way of raising the vibrational level in the surrounding atmosphere, as well as allowing the resounding vibrations to hit chords within the body. (See Chapter 21.)

Lastly, a focus of attention on the third eye, or brow chakra, helps to balance the right and left halves of the brain. It is through this chakra center that energy is sent forth into the world. The visualization of a cross of light pouring down through the crown chakra and released outwardly through the brow represents the symbolic release from the cross of the material and the uplifting onto the level of soul awareness. This is the way to cleanse all the vehicles of impurities, whether they have their origin in past lives, in present circumstances, or on a physical, mental, or spiritual level. New inpouring of etheric energy purifies and balances the system, allowing new vitality and health to become part of life.

The important thing in meditation is to focus on a seed thought that will facilitate new motivation in life. This focuses the mind onto one intention that is repeated and repeated until it becomes an automatic part of the consciousness. That seed thought might be one connected to service toward mankind, for example. A simple thought such as "Send me, use me" can be all powerful in changing mental attitudes from a self-serving approach toward principles that begin to uplift consciousness and attention onto higher levels.

That uplifting is the greatest challenge for every living being on earth. Meditation is the way in which the struggle between the little will and the higher will can take place. That struggle, which cannot be avoided, can be likened to Moses struggling with the angel on the mountaintop. It is the struggle to turn oneself over to the will of the spirit or the higher self. The little self may have difficulty letting go of the games he has cleverly devised, but eventually this struggle leads to higher initiation and enlightenment, for the transference of energy onto the soul level allows each individual to live without fear and in greater joy.

Most important of all, be sure you are ready to change your level of consciousness, and therefore your life, before you begin to practice daily meditation. Once begun, you will never be the same again.

It is my sincere desire that each person will be able to find his own atomic point, make contact with his higher self and his motivation for the highest, greatest good for all, and shed his own particular quality of brilliant light into the darkness on earth. The earth plane is entering a phase of transformation of its own. As we come into the true Aquarian Age the boundaries of hatred, prejudice, and separation will have no place in man's heart and mind. We will learn to see our own light in the eyes of everyone with whom we come in contact. It is an ideal way to see only the beauty that is reflected in the eyes of others. Then each and every man will be truly healthy and free.

A P P E N D I X   I

Tables of the Ascendant

here are twelve houses in the zodiac wheel, but twenty-four hours in a day. So the ascendant changes every two hours, as a general rule, starting at sunrise. For instance, if you were born between 6 A.M. and 8 A.M., your rising sign would be the same as your Sun sign, since the Sun comes up over the horizon at approximately 6 A.M. Therefore an Aries born at 6 A.M. would also have Aries on the ascendant, or rising. If the Aries was born between 8 and 10 A.M., the second sign of the zodiac, Taurus, would be on the ascendant. If that Aries person were born between 10 A.M. and 12 noon, he would have Gemini (the next sign on the zodiac wheel) on the rise. Born between approximately 10 A.M. and 12 noon, the Taurus's ascendant would be Cancer, the sign that follows Gemini. A Gemini born at 6 AM. would have Gemini rising, and so forth.

To help clarify this principle, I've prepared the following tables that give a general timing. If you were born between the first and the fifteenth of the month, look at the closest list or interpolate between the two dates. If the birthlace is considered in the erection of a horoscope prepared especially for an individual, the exact degree of the ascendant may modify this general rule, simply because longitudes and latitudes will indicate the precise degree and minute of the sign on the ascendant. In this way you can approximate your rising sign.

In some instances, the ascendant can fall on the cusp between two signs and only the exact erection of a chart will clarify which sign actually rules the ascendant. Latitudes far to the north or far to the south can change this rule considerably.

If you want a more precise calculation, you can order a printout of your astrological chart. The printout you receive will not provide an interpretation of your personal chart, but it will tell you the exact position of the houses and planets at the time of your birth. Send birth date, time, and place to Jupiter Pluto Communications, 204 E. 77th Street, New York, N.Y. 10021, plus $15.00 to cover costs.

The following tables will give you an approximation of your ascendant (or rising sign).

January 1		January 15	
12:25 A.M.	Libra	2:00 A.M.	Scorpio
3:00 A.M.	Scorpio	4:30 A.M.	Sagittarius
5:30 A.M.	Sagittarius	6:45 A.M.	Capricorn
7:40 A.M.	Capricorn	8:15 A.M.	Aquarius
9:20 A.M.	Aquarius	9:40 A.M.	Pisces
10:40 A.M.	Pisces	10:35 A.M.	Aries
11:50 A.M.	Aries	12:05 P.M.	Taurus
1:05 P.M.	Taurus	1:45 P.M.	Gemini
2:40 P.M.	Gemini	3:55 P.M.	Cancer
5:00 P.M.	Cancer	6:25 P.M.	Leo
7:25 P.M.	Leo	9:00 P.M.	Virgo
10:00 P.M.	Virgo	11:25 P.M.	Libra

February 1		February 15	
1:00 A.M.	Scorpio	12:10 A.M.	Scorpio
3:30 A.M.	Sagittarius	2:30 A.M.	Sagittarius
5:45 A.M.	Capricorn	4:45 A.M.	Capricorn
7:15 A.M.	Aquarius	6:20 A.M.	Aquarius
8:40 A.M.	Pisces	7:40 A.M.	Pisces
9:50 A.M.	Aries	8:50 A.M.	Aries
11:05 A.M.	Taurus	10:05 A.M.	Taurus

12:45 P.M.	Gemini		1:40 A.M.	Gemini
3:00 P.M.	Cancer		2:00 P.M.	Cancer
5:20 P.M.	Leo		4:25 P.M.	Leo
8:00 P.M.	Virgo		7:00 P.M.	Virgo
10:25 P.M.	Libra		9:45 P.M.	Libra

March 1			*March 15*	
1:25 A.M.	Sagittarius		12:30 A.M.	Sagittarius
3:45 A.M.	Capricorn		2:45 A.M.	Capricorn
5:20 A.M.	Aquarius		4:20 A.M.	Aquarius
6:40 A.M.	Pisces		5:40 A.M.	Pisces
7:50 A.M.	Aries		6:50 A.M.	Aries
9:25 A.M.	Taurus		8:05 A.M.	Taurus
10:45 A.M.	Gemini		9:35 A.M.	Gemini
12:55 P.M.	Cancer		11:55 A.M.	Cancer
3:25 P.M.	Leo		2:55 P.M.	Leo
6:00 P.M.	Virgo		4:55 P.M.	Virgo
8:25 P.M.	Libra		7:25 P.M.	Libra
10:55 P.M.	Scorpio		9:55 P.M.	Scorpio

April 1			*April 15*	
1:45 A.M.	Capricorn		12:25 A.M.	Capricorn
3:20 A.M.	Aquarius		2:55 A.M.	Aquarius
4:40 A.M.	Pisces		3:40 A.M.	Pisces
5:55 A.M.	Aries		4:50 A.M.	Aries
7:10 A.M.	Taurus		6:05 A.M.	Taurus
8:50 A.M.	Gemini		7:50 A.M.	Gemini
10:55 A.M.	Cancer		10:00 A.M.	Cancer
1:20 P.M.	Leo		12:25 P.M.	Leo
4:05 P.M.	Virgo		3:10 P.M.	Virgo
6:20 P.M.	Libra		5:25 P.M.	Libra
9:05 P.M.	Scorpio		8:05 P.M.	Scorpio
11:30 P.M.	Sagitarius		10:45 P.M.	Sagittarius

May 1			*May 16*	
1:20 A.M.	Aquarius		12:20 A.M.	Aquarius
2:40 A.M.	Pisces		1:40 A.M.	Pisces
3:55 A.M.	Aries		2:45 A.M.	Aries
5:05 A.M.	Taurus		4:05 A.M.	Taurus

6:45 A.M.	Gemini	5:40 A.M.	Gemini
9:00 A.M.	Cancer	8:00 A.M.	Cancer
11:25 A.M.	Leo	10:20 A.M.	Leo
2:00 P.M.	Virgo	1:00 P.M.	Virgo
4:25 P.M.	Libra	3:25 P.M.	Libra
7:05 P.M.	Scorpio	6:00 P.M.	Scorpio
9:30 P.M.	Sagittarius	8:25 P.M.	Sagittarius
11:45 P.M.	Capricorn	10:45 P.M.	Capricorn

June 1		*June 16*	
12:40 A.M.	Pisces	2:50 A.M.	Aries
1:50 A.M.	Aries	2:05 A.M.	Taurus
3:05 A.M.	Taurus	3:50 A.M.	Gemini
4:50 A.M.	Gemini	6:00 A.M.	Cancer
7:00 A.M.	Cancer	8:25 A.M.	Leo
9:25 A.M.	Leo	11:00 A.M.	Virgo
11:55 A.M.	Virgo	1:25 P.M.	Libra
2:25 P.M.	Libra	4:00 P.M.	Scorpio
4:55 P.M.	Scorpio	6:25 P.M.	Sagittarius
7:25 P.M.	Sagittarius	8:45 P.M.	Capricorn
9:45 P.M.	Capricorn	10:15 P.M.	Aquarius
11:20 P.M.	Aquarius	11:35 P.M.	Pisces

July 1		*July 16*	
1:05 A.M.	Taurus	12:00 A.M.	Taurus
2:45 A.M.	Gemini	1:35 A.M.	Gemini
5:10 A.M.	Cancer	4:00 A.M.	Cancer
7:25 A.M.	Leo	6:25 A.M.	Leo
10:00 A.M.	Virgo	9:00 A.M.	Virgo
12:25 P.M.	Libra	11:25 A.M.	Libra
3:05 P.M.	Scorpio	2:00 P.M.	Scorpio
5:30 P.M.	Sagittarius	4:25 P.M.	Sagittarius
7:45 P.M.	Capricorn	6:45 P.M.	Capricorn
9:20 P.M.	Aquarius	8:20 P.M.	Aquarius
10:40 P.M.	Pisces	9:40 P.M.	Pisces
11:50 P.M.	Aries	10:50 P.M.	Aries

August 1

12:45 A.M.	Gemini
3:00 A.M.	Cancer
5:25 A.M.	Leo
8:00 A.M.	Virgo
10:25 A.M.	Libra
12:55 P.M.	Scorpio
3:40 P.M.	Sagittarius
5:45 P.M.	Capricorn
7:20 P.M.	Aquarius
8:40 P.M.	Pisces
9:55 P.M.	Aries
11:05 P.M.	Taurus

August 16

2:00 A.M.	Cancer
4:25 A.M.	Leo
7:00 A.M.	Virgo
9:25 A.M.	Libra
12:00 P.M.	Scorpio
2:30 P.M.	Sagittarius
4:45 P.M.	Capricorn
6:15 P.M.	Aquarius
7:40 P.M.	Pisces
8:50 P.M.	Aries
10:05 P.M.	Taurus
11:40 P.M.	Gemini

September 1

1:10 A.M.	Cancer
3:25 A.M.	Leo
5:55 A.M.	Virgo
8:25 A.M.	Libra
11:05 A.M.	Scorpio
1:30 P.M.	Sagittarius
3:45 P.M.	Capricorn
5:15 P.M.	Aquarius
6:40 P.M.	Pisces
7:50 P.M.	Aries
9:00 P.M.	Taurus
10:55 P.M.	Gemini

September 16

12:00 A.M.	Cancer
2:30 A.M.	Leo
4:55 A.M.	Virgo
7:20 A.M.	Libra
10:00 A.M.	Scorpio
12:25 P.M.	Sagittarius
2:45 P.M.	Capricorn
4:20 P.M.	Aquarius
5:40 P.M.	Pisces
6:50 P.M.	Aries
8:05 P.M.	Taurus
9:55 P.M.	Gemini

October 1

1:20 A.M.	Leo
4:10 A.M.	Virgo
6:25 A.M.	Libra
8:55 A.M.	Scorpio
11:30 A.M.	Sagittarius
1:45 P.M.	Capricorn
3:20 P.M.	Aquarius
4:40 P.M.	Pisces
5:50 P.M.	Aries
7:05 P.M.	Taurus

October 16

12:25 A.M.	Leo
2:55 A.M.	Virgo
5:20 A.M.	Libra
7:55 A.M.	Scorpio
10:30 A.M.	Sagittarius
12:35 P.M.	Capricorn
2:15 P.M.	Aquarius
3:40 P.M.	Pisces
4:55 P.M.	Aries
6:05 P.M.	Taurus

| 8:55 P.M. | Gemini | 7:40 P.M. | Gemini |
| 10:55 P.M. | Cancer | 10:15 P.M. | Cancer |

November 1		*November 16*	
1:55 A.M.	Virgo	12:55 A.M.	Virgo
4:20 A.M.	Libra	3:25 A.M.	Libra
6:55 A.M.	Scorpio	5:55 A.M.	Scorpio
9:35 A.M.	Sagittarius	8:25 A.M.	Sagittarius
11:40 A.M.	Capricorn	10:45 A.M.	Capricorn
1:20 P.M.	Aquarius	12:15 P.M.	Aquarius
2:35 P.M.	Pisces	1:40 P.M.	Pisces
3:40 P.M.	Aries	2:50 P.M.	Aries
5:15 P.M.	Taurus	4:05 P.M.	Taurus
6:45 P.M.	Gemini	5:40 P.M.	Gemini
9:10 P.M.	Cancer	8:10 P.M.	Cancer
11:25 P.M.	Leo	10:25 P.M.	Leo

December 1		*December 16*	
12:00 A.M.	Virgo	1:25 A.M.	Libra
2:25 A.M.	Libra	3:55 A.M.	Scorpio
4:55 A.M.	Scorpio	6:25 A.M.	Sagittarius
7:30 A.M.	Sagittarius	8:45 A.M.	Capricorn
9:45 A.M.	Capricorn	10:15 A.M.	Aquarius
11:20 A.M.	Aquarius	11:40 A.M.	Pisces
12:35 P.M.	Pisces	12:45 P.M.	Aries
1:45 P.M.	Aries	2:05 P.M.	Taurus
3:00 P.M.	Taurus	3:55 P.M.	Gemini
4:40 P.M.	Gemini	5:55 P.M.	Cancer
6:55 P.M.	Cancer	8:35 P.M.	Leo
9:35 P.M.	Leo	11:10 P.M.	Virgo

Doctors and Health-care Practitioners and Products

Association for Research and
    Enlightenment
Box 595
Virginia Beach, VA 23451
(804) 428-3588

Dr. Edward Bach Centre
Mount Vernon
Sotwell, Wallingford
Oxon, England 0X10 0PZ

Mr. John Beaulieu
10 Leonard Street
New York, NY 10013
(212) 431-6223

Mr. Sigmund Bereday
Hudson House
Ardsley-on-Hudson, NY 10503
(914) 591-8837

Dr. Richard Blasband
c/o American College of
    Orgonomy
Box 490
Princeton, NJ 08542
(201) 821-1144

Dr. Ilan Bohm
240 E. 79th Street
New York, NY 10021
(212) 517-7773

Dr. Virgil Chrane
2880 L.B.J. Highway,
    Suite 100
Dallas, TX 75234
(214) 241-5050

Dr. Elizabeth Dane
45 University Place
New York, NY 10017
(212) 986-1685
          or
1538 North Martel Avenue
     #414
Los Angeles, CA 90046
(213) 850-7468

Dr. Mark H. Friedman, DDS
     (practice limited to TMJ
     and facial pain)
660 Gramaton Avenue
Mt. Vernon, NY 10552
(914) 668-3454

The Hoxsey Clinic
Tijuana, Mexico

Dr. Ken Kobayashi
Natural Remedies Center
143 E. 35th Street
New York, NY 10016
(212) 685-4325

Carl Stough Institute
54 E. 16th Street
New York, NY 10016
(212) 861-9000

Sunrider Herbs
Jupiter Pluto Communications
204 E. 77th Street
New York, NY 10021

Mrs. Eva Tamminga (Aloe
     Vera and Bee Propolis)
1818 Lake Shore Drive, Unit
     21
Austin, TX 78701
(512) 442-0326

Vita Florum Products
Box 85, Station A
Toronto, M5W 1A2 Canada
(416) 964-1126

Ms. Marion Weisberg,
     (T.A. therapist)
315 Central Park West
New York, NY 10025
(212) 496-7503

Index

Dear Friends,

In order to share information that comes my way with my friends and clients, I publish a monthly newsletter that relates to new techniques and advances emerging around the globe. Reports from light centers springing up around the world enable you to participate and share from a distance, and tell how to find these centers when you wish to visit them in person.

Perhaps most important of all, discussion of current cycles described by astrology can help you understand the significance of trends in your own life. We will look at the financial picture, for instance, and the situation connected to land and real estate, to be alert for changes in the coming times. Periodically, we will include articles by experts in the variety of fields connected to the healing profession: psychologists, psychiatrists, nutritionists, body therapists as well as financial analysts. Each issue will be packed with pertinent information.

Subscription price is $49.95 for one year. (You will receive two free issues if you subscribe for two years in advance.) Please send check or money order payable to Jupiter Pluto Communications, 204 E. 77th Street, New York, N.Y. 10021.

It will be my joy to be in touch with you on a continuing basis.

Yours truly,
Jeanne Avery

— —

Detach and return this portion with payment.

Please send check or money order in the amount of $49.95 for a ☐ one year ☐ two year subscription to Kaleidoscope, New Age Newsletter, payable to: Jupiter Pluto Communications, 204 E. 77th Street, New York, N.Y. 10021.

Name _____

Address _____

City _____ State _____ Zip _____

Birth date _____ Time _____ Place _____

☐ Please send gift subscription in my name.
☐ Please send price list of services.

For information about workshops and classes held in Ancramdale, NY, on a beautiful twenty-one-acre estate, please write to me at 88 Friar Tuck Lane, Ancramdale, NY 12503.

Books

Crystal Enlightment
    by Katrina Raphael